AF269936

'AI's promise is real, but practical governance is required to earn trust and fulfil that promise. *Governing the Machine* is a refreshing, timely and clear-eyed roadmap for leaders determined to scale AI and capitalize on its full potential.'

Arvind Krishna, *Chairman and CEO, IBM*

'Grounded, up-to-date, thorough, actionable – you could read this book, or you could pay consultants gazillions of dollars to tell you something less useful.'

Stuart Russell OBE, *Professor of Computer Science, University of California, Berkeley*

'We have a responsibility to shape how AI is applied to drive meaningful, sustainable transformation across industries while upholding the public good. This book is an essential guide for doing just that.'

Athina Kanioura, *Chief Strategy and Transformation Officer, PepsiCo*

'My advice to every business: ensure that you can harness the benefits of AI by proactively considering the important management and governance questions raised in this book.'

James Manyika, *Senior Vice President of Technology and Society, Google*

'Responsible AI isn't just a technical challenge – it's a leadership imperative. This book offers essential guidance for anyone navigating the promise of deploying AI at scale. Read this book to understand how.'

Reid Hoffman, *co-founder, LinkedIn and bestselling author of* Superagency: What Could Possibly Go Right with Our AI Future

'AI is the most anticipated technology of the 21st century – but deploying it is beset by risks and challenges. This highly accessible book is the first clear introduction to AI governance. Written by practitioners with a wealth of experience both of AI itself and of its role in enterprises, it deserves to become the handbook for the field.'

Professor Michael Wooldridge, *Ashall Professor of the Foundations of Artificial Intelligence, University of Oxford*

'The AI era presents organizations with unprecedented opportunities and risks, and trust will be THE key enabler and differentiator. The authors provide valuable insights and a compelling roadmap to help leaders scale AI for a trusted, successful future.'

Paul Daugherty, *former Chief Technology and Innovation Officer, Accenture and author of* Human + Machine

'This book is a brilliant step-by-step guide to developing a strategic and proportionate approach to AI, from governance to implementation, drawing on the authors' extensive hands-on experience. This is an essential guide for all, regardless of where you are in your own AI journey.'

Jane Caskey, *Global Head of Risk Advisory and Head of Clients & Sectors, Linklaters*

'Based on a wealth of practical experience, thoroughly researched and clearly explained, *Governing the Machine* is an invaluable companion for anyone implement-ing AI governance.'

Sir Adrian Smith, *Director, Alan Turing Institute, 2018–2023*

'As AI permeates every aspect of financial management, banks must not just adopt it, but pioneer its responsible deployment, protecting the financial well-being of every customer. Failing to do so will harm their most valuable asset: trust. This book is an invaluable guide in navigating that journey.'

Scott Marcar, *Chief Information Officer, NatWest Group*

'This book is a must-read for anyone deploying AI. It offers a clear, practical roadmap to govern AI systems and avoid harmful outcomes.'

Cathy O'Neil, *CEO of ORCAA and bestselling author of* Weapons of Math Destruction

'*Governing the Machine* sidesteps extremism in our tug-of-war over generative and agentic AI. The book presents a practical approach to effective organizational governance of the technologies, where responsible and transparent practices help earn public trust while assuring sustainable innovation over time. I commend the informed guidance for companies large and small. Business leaders, professional technologists, policy experts, and compliance officers will all gain useful insights into the promise and risk of these technologies.'

Elizabeth Denham CBE, *former UK Information Commissioner; International advisor, Data and Tech, Baker McKenzie*

'Think of AI like a Formula 1 McLaren – high performance, but it needs a skilled driver, a capable team, strong brakes, and safety systems. The authors provide a step-by-step guide to building safety and control components for AI from the ground-up without sacrificing performance.'

Adrian Joseph OBE, *Non-executive director; former Chief Data and AI Officer, BT*

'An invaluable blueprint for the public sector to use AI safely and build public trust.'

Dr Laura Gilbert CBE, *Head of AI for Government, Ellison Institute of Technology Oxford; Senior Director of AI, Tony Blair Institute for Global Change*

'AI governance is where organisational values are realised in action and process. This timely, immensely readable book on the subject orients and entertains. A touchstone for neophytes and experienced practitioners alike, it offers actionable advice grounded in careful research alongside lively illustrations. It will help organisations small and large design and implement an effective program.'

Professor Robert Trager, *Director of the Oxford Martin AI Governance Initiative, University of Oxford*

'A timely and landmark book which fills an urgent gap in the market: filled with practical examples, cutting through the hype, to reveal practical steps for organisations to become AI-ready.'

Manoj Saxena, *Chair and CEO, Trustwise; Founder, Responsible AI Institute*

WITH A FOREWORD BY ANDREW NG

GOVERNING THE MACHINE

How to navigate the risks of AI and unlock its true potential

RAY EITEL-PORTER,
PAUL DONGHA & MIRIAM VOGEL

BLOOMSBURY BUSINESS

LONDON · OXFORD · NEW YORK · NEW DELHI · SYDNEY

BLOOMSBURY BUSINESS
Bloomsbury Publishing Plc
50 Bedford Square, London, WC1B 3DP, UK
Bloomsbury Publishing Ireland Limited,
29 Earlsfort Terrace, Dublin 2, D02 AY28, Ireland

BLOOMSBURY, BLOOMSBURY BUSINESS and the Diana logo are trademarks of

Bloomsbury Publishing Plc

First published in Great Britain 2025

A catalogue record for this book is available from the British Library

Library of Congress Cataloging-in-Publication data has been applied for

ISBN: HB: 978-1-3994-2629-9; eBook: 978-1-3994-2627-5; ePDF 978-I 1-3994-2626-8

4 6 8 10 9 7 5 3

Typeset by Deanta Global Publishing Services, Chennai, India
Printed and bound in Great Britain by Clays Ltd, Elcograf S.p.A.

To find out more about our authors and books visit www.bloomsbury.com
and sign up for our newsletters

For product safety related questions contact productsafety@bloomsbury.com

CONTENTS

Note: The information in this book is for general informational purposes only and not intended to serve as legal advice or counsel.

PREFACE

AI is no longer a future concern – it is already reshaping our world. Leaders across sectors are racing to deploy generative AI to stay competitive, cut costs and innovate. But deployment has outpaced governance. That gap now poses significant legal, operational and reputational risks. We wrote this book to enable organizations and the public to meet this challenge.

Fortunately, while the AI technical and legal landscape evolves daily, the fundamental challenges – and effective approaches for managing them – are remarkably consistent across industries, countries and cultures. Drawing on our collective experience advising leading companies, institutions and governments, we offer a global perspective grounded in best-in-class governance design, technical expertise, and deep policy and legal insights. *Governing the Machine* is a step-by-step guide built to endure even as technology rapidly shifts.

We also challenge the narrative that AI is not yet externally governed. While new laws are forthcoming, AI is already subject to a wide array of existing legal frameworks, from civil rights and consumer protection to privacy and product liability. That means effective AI governance is not optional: it is a business imperative. It also requires meaningful public engagement to demand AI's successful governance.

Governing AI means managing risk to maximize value, weighing benefits against potential harms. Our framework addresses nine core categories of risk: accuracy and reliability; fairness and bias; interpretability, explainability and transparency; accountability; privacy; security; intellectual property and confidentiality; workforce; environment and sustainability. We reviewed and synthesized leading AI risk frameworks and propose a comprehensive, adaptable approach to risk mitigation that can be tailored to the size and maturity of any organization.

Even since finalizing this manuscript, there have been notable developments including:

In the US, increasing tensions between federal and state level approaches to AI legislation have emerged, creating complex compliance questions for organizations.

The European Union is consulting on loosening some provisions of the GDPR and the EU AI Act, reflecting concern about stifling competitiveness and innovation, and slow progress developing standards and codes of practice.

The UK's approach to regulating AI continues to emerge but the Data (Use and Access) Act 2025, passed in June, introduces changes to UK data protection law that will impact the data used to train AI models.

Geopolitically, the Middle East is emerging as an increasingly important player in AI with major investments announced in 2025.

AI governance is becoming increasingly professionalized, with the 'Big Four' accounting firms building AI assurance practices and industry bodies like TechUK defining responsible AI roles.[1]

The leading AI labs are releasing ever more powerful models and agentic AI – systems capable of taking actions based on autonomous reasoning and decision-making. While offering more potential to deliver tangible benefits, AI agents compound the risks. We recommend staying current with new publications, for example *AI Agent Governance: A Field Guide* and *Advances and Challenges in Foundation Agents*.[2]

Recent industry surveys underscore the urgent need for this book. Ernst & Young (EY) found that 75% of companies are now using generative AI but only a third have responsible controls in place.[3] McKinsey & Company reported that 'knowledge and training gaps' were the largest obstacle to the implementation of responsible AI measures.[4]

Our hope is that this book gives you the tools and confidence to close these gaps. It is designed to equip you to lead with clarity in this critical moment. Keeping this book continually updated would be a Sisyphean task but we do plan to share periodic perspectives on developments in AI governance. Please follow us on Substack at *https://governingthemachineai.substack.com* and keep us posted on your AI governance journey.

Ray Eitel-Porter, Paul Dongha
and Miriam Vogel
July 2025

FOREWORD BY ANDREW NG

AI is a general-purpose technology with numerous applications, and this is a wonderful time to use AI to build, build, build! Large language models and other AI technologies are making it possible for small, fast-moving teams to quickly create valuable products that even the best research labs would have found impossible to build just a couple of years ago. The opportunity to apply AI to improve education, healthcare, sustainability and numerous other fields is very exciting, and seems poised to help numerous individuals and drive significant economic growth.

Amidst this potential for tremendous value creation, AI is a powerful technology that, if used carelessly (or worse, maliciously), can harm people. We do not want patients to be hurt by unsafe AI medical devices, or AI résumé screeners that discriminate based on protected characteristics, or people given incorrect information on important matters by badly designed customer service chatbots. Balancing driving rapid beneficial progress – which we want! – with understanding when deploying an AI system could be risky, so that we can put in place guardrails, will be important as more organizations scale up the deployment of AI applications.

When a small team of developers is experimenting with an AI chatbot on their laptops and with no access to sensitive information, the risks are minimal. Perhaps the worst that could happen is they generate some false or toxic text that they wish they didn't have to read, but there's no real risk of significant harm. In this case, it makes sense for them to move fast and be allowed to experiment freely to try to build something great. But if the same team decides their chatbot now works well and wants to deploy it to millions of people to deliver financial advice, then the potential for a misstep harming people is much greater, and the team should analyze the possible risks, put in place guardrails and/or mitigation plans, and think carefully before proceeding. Recognizing when there are no real risks and it is safe to move fast, and when there are risks and we should slow down and be more careful, is a key skill for leaders everywhere involved in using or building AI applications. If we can govern the building and deployment of AI applications well, we can avoid slowing down innovation unnecessarily, while also protecting people from unnecessary harm.

The authors of this book have taken on the vital challenge of laying out what responsible governance of AI applications looks like. Specifically, how to recognize when an AI application can be harmful, and how to mitigate those risks.

Unfortunately, some people have deliberately hyped up fears of AI to gain publicity or to try to suppress open source competitors, for example by painting science-fiction doomsday pictures of AI 'taking over' or otherwise running amok and causing severe harms. Their fear-based narrative has distracted people from the important work of recognizing and mitigating against actual risks. It has also already led to some laws, such as the EU AI Act, which will slow down innovation without meaningfully making anyone safer.

One of the key truths to making AI 'safe' is that as a general-purpose technology, AI itself is neither safe nor unsafe. Instead, it is the specific applications of AI that are safe or unsafe. As an analogy, an electric motor, too, is a general-purpose technology. It can be used in a blender, a dialysis machine, an electric vehicle, or a smart bomb. Whether an application of a motor is safe or not is a function of the application – such as how the blender is designed – rather than the electric motor, and it is impossible for an electric motor manufacturer to guarantee their motor won't be used in a harmful downstream application. Thus, while it is useful to discuss if a blender (the application) is safe, it is less helpful to debate if the electric motor is safe.

Similarly, the same AI technology (such as a large language model) can be used to give medical advice, summarize news, route emails, or generate political misinformation. AI technology is, itself, neither intrinsically safe nor unsafe. It is up to us to take responsibility for how we use it and apply AI only in ways where the benefits significantly outweigh possible harms.

Thus, responsible AI governance requires not governing the AI technology itself but rather governing its applications. Ensuring the applications we build with AI are beneficial requires embedding the right technical training to teams, designing systems into organizations to spot and mitigate risks, and fostering a culture of accountability. Ensuring that we use AI responsibly will be a task shared by individuals, businesses and governments.

This is a great time to invest in AI and build the many beneficial things that are now possible! And, as we invent new applications with AI and contemplate taking these applications to scale, having the skill to spot and mitigate possible risks becomes a critical part of our work. I commend the authors for their contribution to this important discussion, and hope that you will engage in using AI to improve your own and others' lives. At the same time, let us all also stay aware of risks and tools for mitigating them, so that we can move forward responsibly.

Andrew Ng
Founder of DeepLearning.AI
Stanford University, April 2025

INTRODUCTION

Artificial intelligence (AI) holds unparalleled potential to reshape the global landscape – transforming industries, accelerating innovation and unlocking immense economic value. From revolutionizing healthcare to reimagining customer experiences, AI promises to be a catalyst for progress. Yet, despite its transformative power, many businesses and executives approach AI with caution due to the significant investment required and its inherent risks: lack of transparency, privacy concerns, bias and the unpredictable nature of advanced systems like generative AI.

These concerns are valid and, in fact, they are essential considerations for any organization aiming to lead in an AI-powered future. The question for today's leaders isn't whether to adopt AI, but how to do so while ensuring it is aligned with business objectives and safeguarding against potential pitfalls. The solution lies not in avoiding the complexities of AI but in mastering them through thoughtful, proactive governance.

AI governance is about more than just compliance – it is a strategic enabler that allows organizations to manage risks, build stakeholder trust, and fully unlock AI's transformative potential. By establishing clear rules, accountability mechanisms and ongoing oversight, businesses can confidently harness AI as a force for innovation and competitive advantage. This book explores how organizations can navigate this critical balance, empowering leaders to adopt AI confidently in an era of unprecedented technological change.

Governing the Machine is a practical guide for business leaders, board members, policymakers and frontline teams to build effective AI governance in an organization. The content is structured to meet the varied needs of readers, whether they come from technical, legal or business backgrounds. It provides a flexible framework adaptable to organizations of different sizes, industries and budgets. Each chapter concludes with a 'Key Insights and Actions' summary, distilling takeaways and providing readers with a clear path forward. We illustrate these actionable steps with examples and advice from organizations that have successfully addressed the challenges of establishing AI governance.

As AI adoption accelerates, the need for governance has never been more urgent. Organizations are racing to adopt AI for competitive advantage, but high-profile mishaps, evolving legislation and increased regulatory scrutiny highlight the need for proactive safeguards. The EU AI Act, which came into force in August 2024, imposes sweeping new requirements, while global regulatory landscapes continue to evolve. Meanwhile, the rise of generative AI and autonomous 'agents' amplifies both capabilities and risks. This book will help you address these challenges.

It is divided into four sections to guide you through the process and serve as a quick reference at any stage of your journey:

- Section One explains why AI governance is an urgent and strategic priority for those working with or using AI. It outlines the primary areas of AI risk and introduces a governance framework built on leading, proven approaches.
- Section Two delivers a step-by-step guide to establishing an AI governance program, covering essential components such as principles, policies, risk assessments, roles, accountabilities and technical tools for comprehensive oversight.
- Section Three surveys the global AI regulatory landscape, highlighting key drivers for governance and compliance and helping readers anticipate and adapt to evolving legal requirements.
- Section Four ties together the book's core themes, offering final reflections and a perspective on the future of AI governance.

Drawing on many years of hands-on experience in designing and implementing AI governance programs, the authors share insights on what works, common pitfalls and strategies to future-proof governance efforts. Their expertise covers AI risk management, legislation, policy, technology and organizational change. This book provides both a blueprint and a call to action – equipping leaders to harness AI, stay ahead of regulatory shifts and position their organizations as trusted innovators in an AI-driven world.

GLOSSARY OF KEY TERMS

AI agent	An agent is an AI system that can independently reason, plan, adapt and pursue objectives or goals without direct human intervention over an extended time horizon and interact with tools. An alternative phrase is the term 'agentic AI'. Where agents communicate with each other to collectively pursue an objective, this is called a 'multi-agent system' (see below).
AI assurance	The process of measuring, evaluating and communicating that an AI system meets compliance standards such as reliability, fairness and transparency.
AI compliance	Adhering to a set of rules or guidelines, most typically legal or regulatory, for AI development and deployment. Some organizations will designate their AI governance as a formal compliance program.
AI ethics	Societal values and norms which are supported by responsible AI practices.
AI governance	The mechanisms by which responsible AI practices can be enforced. A comprehensive framework that covers technology, people and processes, requiring cross-enterprise participation and senior multi-stakeholder engagement.
AI model	A mathematical framework trained on data to make predictions, generate outputs or automate decision-making in AI systems. Examples include linear regression, classification, neural networks and transformers.

AI system	A combination of one or more AI models, data and infrastructure designed to perform tasks, make decisions or provide insights autonomously. This approach to defining an AI system, as comprising multiple components, aligns with the definition outlined in the EU AI Act.
API	Application Programming Interface. A set of rules that allows different software systems to communicate and interact programmatically.
Artificial Intelligence (AI)	The field of computing that enables machines to mimic human intelligence, including learning, reasoning and problem-solving.
Chief Data and AI/ Analytics Officer or Office (CDAO)	The most senior leader of the data and analytics/AI team in an organization, or the function itself. This role can also be undertaken by a Chief Data Officer (CDO) or Chief Information Officer (CIO).
Confabulation	See 'hallucination' below.
Data ethics	The values and norms governing data collection, processing and usage which are supported by responsible development practices.
EU AI Act (AIA)	Comprehensive legislation enacted by the EU in August 2024 to govern AI.
Foundation model	A type of AI model that is trained on vast quantities of data and is adaptable for use on a wide range of tasks. Foundation models can be used as a base for building more specific AI models. While not strictly synonymous, we will use this term to cover 'general-purpose AI models' (GPAI), as defined by the EU AI Act. Large language models are a specific type of foundation model.
Generative AI (genAI)	AI approaches that create new content, such as text, images or programming code, based on patterns learned from training data. Those that generate text (called LLMs) include: OpenAI's ChatGPT range, Google's Gemini models, Anthropic's Claude and Meta's Llama open-source models.

Hallucination	Particularly in the context of genAI, where an AI system generates false or misleading information that appears credible but is factually incorrect. An alternative term sometimes used is 'confabulation', borrowed from medicine for a neuropsychiatric disorder that causes a patient to generate a false memory without the intention of deceit.
Human in Control (HIC)	A governance approach ensuring that humans retain ultimate authority over AI decision-making and system behaviour.
Human in the Loop (HITL)	An AI system design where human intervention is actively integrated into decision-making or training processes.
Human on the Loop (HOTL)	A system where AI operates autonomously but human oversight is provided for monitoring and intervention when necessary.
International Organization for Standardization (ISO)	An independent, non-governmental global organization that develops and publishes international standards to ensure quality, safety, efficiency and interoperability across industries.
ISO 42001	A key international standard specifying requirements for an AI risk management system.
Large Language Model (LLM)	A LLM is a machine learning model trained on vast amounts of text to interpret and generate natural language and which is much larger and more complex than what is traditionally termed ML.
Machine learning (ML)	An algorithm that is trained to identify patterns and relationships in data and improve its performance without explicit programming.
Multi-agent systems (MAS)	AI architectures where multiple autonomous agents collaborate, compete or interact within a shared environment.

Multimodal models	GenAI systems capable of processing multiple data types (or 'modalities') like text, images, audio and video, simultaneously to generate outputs across a range of these types.
The National Institute of Standards and Technology (NIST)	A US federal agency that develops standards and guidelines to promote innovation, ensure measurement accuracy, and improve technology and security across industries.
NIST Risk Management Framework (RMF)	NIST released the first version of the RMF in January 2023. This voluntary framework aims to embed trustworthiness into the design, development, use and evaluation of AI systems.
Reasoning Language Model (RLM)	RLMs are an extension of LLMs that not only generate text but also apply logical inference, structured problem-solving and multi-step reasoning to produce well-justified responses.
Red Teaming	A security practice where experts try to find vulnerabilities in a system by using adversarial testing.
Reinforcement Learning with Human Feedback (RLHF)	A method using direct human input to adapt genAI models with human preferences to improve alignment with desired outcomes.
Responsible AI	Robust AI development practices which can help ensure AI is trustworthy.
Retrieval-augmented Generation (RAG)	A method to enhance the accuracy and factuality of genAI responses by providing access to relevant external sources of information for generating the answer.
Traditional AI	The collection of probabilistic AI approaches including ML, neural networks and deep learning.
Trustworthy AI	The over-arching goal when developing AI systems to ensure confident adoption.

Section I

AI governance to mitigate risks and unlock benefits

1

The moment we knew

Weapons of Math Destruction by Cathy O'Neil hit the bookshelves in 2016 and immediately struck a nerve. American mathematician and data scientist O'Neil highlighted the numerous ways AI systems were already being used as well as their hidden dangers. Often presented as impartial tools of progress, the book showed these tools could perpetuate harm, undermine societal trust and fail to deliver their objectives.

One story stands out as an illustration of the devastating consequences of ungoverned AI systems and automation bias, with striking parallels to our use of AI tools today. As part of a reform initiative led by the then-Chancellor of Washington DC Public Schools, administrators introduced the IMPACT system, an algorithm designed to evaluate teacher performance to improve accountability. On paper, it promised fairness and precision. In practice, it derailed careers and deprived students of effective teachers.

The system was not only deeply flawed, the algorithm's complexity made it opaque to both the administrators using it and the teachers it evaluated. Teachers who had previously received praise found themselves labelled as ineffective. Sarah Wysocki was a teacher celebrated by the school principal and parents for her dedication. Despite her strong reputation, the IMPACT system flagged her as underperforming because her students' test scores did not improve as expected. Later, it was revealed that some of the earlier student scores may have been improperly inflated in an effort to improve results – a significant factor the algorithm could not detect. Wysocki's story, and that of the DC school teachers in her situation, demonstrated how over-reliance on a flawed and opaque AI system could harm careers and undermine public trust, all while masquerading as an improvement. Wysocki was quickly hired by a local suburban private school but the DC public school students were no longer the beneficiaries.

O'Neil didn't just tell stories – she exposed an alarming pattern. Her work highlights how AI systems used in hiring, credit scoring, education, insurance and criminal justice often operate without transparency or appropriate governance in place. *Weapons of Math Destruction* helped crystallize an essential principle: AI systems, no matter how sophisticated, must be held to the same standards of accountability as human decisions. They require governance to understand if they deserve to be trusted.

Fast forward to today and AI has introduced society to innovations at breakneck speed. Generative AI – systems capable of creating text, images, music – brings exciting new opportunities but with significant risks. It generates a brilliant first draft or persuasive response to any question, but it can also fabricate content – aka 'hallucinations' or 'confabulations', infringe intellectual property rights, and exacerbate existing AI risks such as lack of explainability and unintended bias. In early 2025, Apple was forced to disable a key feature in its AI-powered news service after it concocted a headline about the alleged murderer of a healthcare CEO, falsely attributing the claim to the BBC. No such article existed, but the error spread quickly before it could be corrected.[1]

These so-called 'hallucinations' highlight a fundamental issue with generative AI: its unpredictability. Unlike earlier AI systems that make predictions, generative AI systems create novel content based on statistical patterns in their training data, which means the same request, when repeated, can generate different results. Compounding this issue, many organizations do not build these models themselves but rely on so-called 'foundation models' developed by companies like OpenAI, Google and Anthropic. Providers of these models typically do not share their training data or give full access to the model's inner workings, leaving users with limited ability to validate or control the system's behaviour. Efforts to improve reliability, such as filtering inputs or reviewing outputs, address the symptoms not the cause. They cannot change the underlying behaviour of the model. This creates a paradox. Generative AI's greatest strength – its ability to find novel patterns and generate new creative content – is also its greatest weakness.

Grasping this tension is crucial for organizations planning to adopt generative AI. The unpredictability of these systems isn't a bug to be resolved – it's an inherent feature. Managing this uncertainty requires more than technical fixes; it calls for robust governance frameworks and a willingness to re-examine risk appetite.

As AI adoption accelerates, the stakes are higher than ever. Organizations are rushing to implement AI to stay competitive and reap its immeasurable benefits, but this rapid expansion brings significant risk to those organizations, their employees and their customers or end users. AI governance has emerged as a critical field – not just to mitigate risks but to ensure AI can be managed and trusted, paving the path towards its adoption. Governance frameworks establish rules, standards and oversight to steer the development and use of AI. Self-governance is increasingly motivated by the growing legal liabilities associated with AI use. AI adoption will only intensify in the years ahead, making governance not just a best practice but fundamental to unlocking the potential of AI with confidence.

WHAT IS AI?

Within computer science, AI encompasses a range of techniques designed to emulate intelligent behaviour.[*] While there is no single accepted definition of AI, a common theme is that of machines with some level of autonomy to create an outcome; a process which most people would describe as 'intelligent' based on their observation. A definition which is gaining increasing support because of its use by leading institutions, and which suffices for our purposes, is that proposed by the Organisation for Economic Co-operation and Development (OECD):[†]

'An AI system is a machine-based system that, for explicit or implicit objectives, infers, from the input it receives, how to generate outputs such as predictions, content, recommendations, or decisions that can influence physical or virtual environments. Different AI systems vary in their levels of autonomy and adaptiveness after deployment.'[2]

A BRIEF HISTORY OF AI

AI is widely regarded as having begun at a seminal conference in Dartmouth, USA, in 1956, initiated by mathematician John McCarthy, who coined the term 'Artificial Intelligence'. This conference proposed to test the assertion that 'every aspect of learning or any other feature of intelligence can be so precisely described that a machine can be made to simulate it'.[3] AI development has since been punctuated by three 'AI

---

[*]Robotics is also thought of as a type of AI but will remain out of scope for this book.
[†]For example, this definition is used in slightly adapted form by the US National Institute of Standards and Technology (NIST) and the EU AI Act.

Winters' – periods where innovation and investment stalled. Each winter was followed by a revival, fuelled by new insights and advancements.

Symbolic AI: The Early Era (1956–74)

The first wave of AI, known as symbolic AI, focused on representing human reasoning using symbols manipulated through logical rules. Initially successful in areas like search, mathematics, natural language processing and robotics, these methods were mostly limited to controlled environments and struggled to scale, leading to the first AI Winter (1974–87).

A resurgence came in the form of expert systems, which encoded knowledge from human experts into rule-based frameworks. These were quickly adopted in the corporate world, leading to successes in areas such as medical diagnosis, financial portfolio management, industrial process control, and manufacturing and production scheduling.

After these early successes, expert systems too started to fall out of favour: problems with scaling knowledge acquisition, performance and inconsistency between rules hindered further development, leading to the second AI Winter.

Probabilistic AI: Neural Networks and Machine Learning

Alongside symbolic AI, researchers pursued an alternative approach inspired by the structure and functioning of the human brain: neural networks. Researchers sought to mimic this biological process to create systems capable of learning and decision-making. A neural network contains an arrangement of points, called nodes, linked together through connections carrying signals between nodes. The network is trained on data, to identify patterns and relationships in the data. At the time this was also referred to as machine learning (ML) – the network was thought to be learning from its training data. One of the first notable successes was the launch of a neural net used by the US postal service to recognize handwritten ZIP codes.[4] ML is a broader concept than neural networks and includes a variety of algorithms and techniques for enabling machines to improve their performance-based training.*

---

*Neural networks are a specific type of machine learning algorithm, characterized by their architecture. Machine learning methods additionally include, but are not limited to, various other algorithms, such as decision trees, support vector machines and ensemble methods like random forests and gradient boosting machines.

Progress in neural network research was gradual until a breakthrough in 2012 with AlexNet, a deep neural network that outperformed competitors in an image recognition competition. AlexNet's success stemmed from its complex architecture, diverse training dataset and the use of GPU (graphics processing unit) chips for faster processing, marking the rise of deep learning.[*]

Generative AI: The Turning Point (2017 Onwards)

Generative AI had its genesis in 2017 following the publication of Google's research paper, *Attention Is All You Need*, which introduced the Transformer architecture – a substantial extension of the neural network approach suitable for generating sequences of text.[5] This innovation laid the foundation for generative AI (genAI), exemplified by the release of ChatGPT in November 2022, and triggered the current explosion of AI advancements.[†]

Generative AI models, often referred to as 'foundation models', are trained on vast, diverse datasets and can be adapted to various tasks without retraining.[6] Developed by specialized AI companies like OpenAI and tech giants like Google and Meta, foundation models have unlocked new possibilities but also introduce new risks, including intellectual property leaks and hallucinations, as well as exacerbating existing risks like bias.

THE FUTURE LOOKS AGENTIC

Agentic AI will unleash a new wave of applications based on genAI. This term refers to the integration of additional advanced technologies into genAI systems, enabling them to tackle complex goals, typical of many organizational workflows. Unlike AI that primarily responds to inputs – for example, ChatGPT answering a question – agentic AI systems can independently plan, adapt and pursue objectives without direct human intervention over an extended time horizon.[7] Several key features

---

[*]Deep learning often invokes images of some mysterious breakthrough in cognitive ability. In fact, its mystery can be explained by the depth and arrangement of the layers of nodes in the network: the term 'deep' refers to this.

[†]There are two broad classes of generative AI models. In addition to 'Transformer' models there are 'Diffusion' models for image, video and audio generation which use a novel approach of decoding images, adding noise to this representation and then reconstructing the image. See Sohl-Dickstein, J. et al., 'Unsupervised Learning using Nonequilibrium Thermodynamics', https://proceedings.mlr.press/v37/sohl-dickstein15.html. More recently, these models have been combined into 'multi-modal' frameworks that can, for instance, generate video clips from textual descriptions. Notable models are OpenAI's DALL-E and CLIP as well as Google's Imagen.

distinguish agentic AI from conventional AI systems, enabling them to operate autonomously and dynamically in real-world contexts:[*]

- **Goal-oriented planning**: The process of organizing and sequencing interrelated steps derived from reasoning in pursuit of goals.
- **Autonomous action**: The ability to independently execute tasks by interacting with virtual or physical environments, possibly with minimal human intervention.
- **Tool use**: The ability to integrate with and use external tools (e.g. databases, web search, code interpreters and other software systems) to gather information and perform actions.
- **Memory and contextual understanding**: Maintains a form of 'memory' to recall context from past interactions to make better decisions throughout its planning and reasoning.

These three steps are often interconnected and iterative. For example, consider booking a holiday. The process begins with reasoning through key decisions, such as selecting a destination, travel dates, activities and accommodation preferences. Planning follows, involving the sequencing of actions – for instance, checking flights before choosing hotels or finalizing accommodation and arranging day trips. Each step generates sub-goals that require further reasoning and planning, like booking flights, transfers or hotels. This iterative process culminates in action, such as purchasing a return ticket.[†] This example illustrates how agentic AI could automate an increasing number of activities not only in our daily lives, but also in the workplace.

The next step leads to multi-agent systems (MAS), where multiple AI agents collaborate to achieve a shared objective. Like a human team, a MAS may feature a 'supervisor' agent delegating subtasks to specialized agents, each optimized for a specific function. This co-operative approach mirrors

[*]Other capabilities are likely to include perception (the agent's ability to directly sense activities in its environment), self-reflection (an agent assessing how well it has performed) and self-improvement (based on feedback, to adjust behaviour). At the time of writing, there is no widely accepted definition of exactly what differentiates an AI *agent* from genAI. We have chosen to include the most prominent features.

[†]One of this book's authors, Dr Paul Dongha, published his PhD thesis on modelling the behaviour of AI agents in 1996. His research introduced a novel mathematical theory describing the conditions under which a reasoning and planning agent would persist or abandon pursuing its goals. Dongha, P., 'Commitment and Resource Bounded Agents', March 1966, https://uomlibrary .access.preservica.com/uncategorized/IO_77b74cc1-92c6-48f9-9468-dd728cb88b93.

organizational structures, enabling efficient problem-solving through task decomposition.

Several genAI models were released in late 2024 and early 2025 that incorporate intermediate processing steps to elicit sophisticated behaviour. So called 'reasoning language models' (RLMs) not only generate text but also apply logical inference, structured problem-solving and multi-step reasoning to produce well-justified responses. Compared to earlier large language models, such as ChatGPT-3.5, which primarily rely on statistical correlations in text, a reasoning model evaluates context, plans responses and adapts, making it better suited for complex decision-making and analytical tasks.[8] RLMs form the basis of agentic AI. For an overview of the use of large language models as AI agents, see 'A Survey on Large Language Model Based Autonomous Agents'.[9]

The agentic AI paradigm, including MAS, is increasingly seen as enabling vast commercial opportunities and many large technology companies are now embedding sophisticated agentic capabilities into their genAI systems.[10] However alluring agentic AI seems, its greater potential and increased autonomy will likely generate additional risks.[11]

TWO GUIDING THOUGHTS

Many AI risks we know of today exist because the approaches used by certain types of AI are by design inherently *complex* and *probabilistic*. Since genAI is a significant extension of machine learning (ML) and neural networks, its complexity hampers our capability to understand how it behaves once deployed.

In this book, we use the term 'Traditional AI', to refer to the collection of probabilistic AI approaches including ML, neural networks and deep learning. We will use the term 'generative AI' (genAI) to refer to AI approaches that use a Transformer or Diffusion architecture.[*] The term AI is used to encompass both traditional and genAI. This book will focus on the risks posed by Traditional AI and genAI, though popular parlance has adopted the term AI to refer to almost any current use of data-driven analytics.

---

[*]One might argue that symbolic AI should be included in 'Traditional AI', but we think this does not detract from the purpose of this book.

SOME KEY TERMINOLOGY IN THE FIELD OF AI TRUST AND GOVERNANCE

The reader will encounter many terms for which there is a lack of universally accepted definitions as they become immersed in this field. Here, we share key terminology as we use it in this book, acknowledging that other definitions may exist in the field.

The objective of this book is to help organizations build trust in their use of AI. Trust is essential for customers, employees and society at large to be confident in using AI and reaping its many benefits. In the introduction to the 25th edition of Accenture's annual Technology Vision, published in January 2025, they wrote 'We're looking at a future where trust is the most important differentiator and the determining factor to AI diffusion within an organization. After all, we can only let systems be as autonomous as we trust them.'[12] **Trustworthy AI** can best be achieved by using **responsible AI** practices when designing, building and deploying AI systems to help avoid unintended, negative consequences. Organizations can ensure they are using responsible AI practices by establishing robust **AI governance**. AI governance refers to policies, frameworks and processes that guide the appropriate development, deployment and use of AI to ensure it aligns with organization-specific principles, societal values and norms, and laws. It encompasses oversight mechanisms, accountability structures and decision-making practices that balance innovation with safeguards. It aims to minimize risks, misuse and unintended consequences to allow organizations to realize the potential of AI.

We use the term **AI governance** widely in this book because of its broad applicability across an organization. It is also a helpful way of aligning with other similar governance programs addressing risk to the organization. We prefer it to **AI compliance** because not all organizations will deem it necessary to establish a formal AI compliance program, though all will need an AI governance program, and AI risk is more nuanced than most typical compliance risks, encompassing trade-offs. In many cases, though, an AI governance program will constitute a formal compliance program.

So where do **AI ethics** and **data ethics** fit? These are part of what responsible AI practices ensure but responsible AI practices are broader, also covering aspects of AI usage such as security and explainability. The term data ethics is used most frequently by organizations that were early to adopt data-driven approaches to analytics before the widespread use of AI. These organizations may already have an established data ethics program as part of their data governance – the processes which assure the appropriate use of data. We are often asked how these should relate to an AI governance program. Our response is that since AI requires large amounts of data, and AI is increasingly the means to extract value from data, the two are inextricably linked. It therefore makes sense either to merge or link them closely: if a data ethics program is already assuring data risk, then simply adding further aspects to account for AI risk can be an effective approach.

AI assurance is another frequently used term that has much in common with **AI governance**, which can usefully adopt many assurance approaches. The UK's Department for Science, Innovation and Technology provides the following helpful explanation: 'The term "assurance" originally derived from accountancy but has since been adapted to cover areas including cybersecurity and quality management. Assurance is the process of measuring, evaluating and communicating something about a system or process, documentation, a product or an organization. In the case of AI, assurance measures, evaluates and communicates the trustworthiness of AI systems.'[13]

ACHIEVING TRUSTWORTHY AI: KEY TERMINOLOGY

Trustworthy AI	The **over-arching goal** when developing AI systems to ensure confident adoption
Responsible AI	Robust **AI development practices** which can help ensure AI is trustworthy
AI governance	The **mechanisms** by which these AI practices can be enforced. A **comprehensive framework** that covers technology, people and processes, requiring cross-enterprise participation and senior multi-stakeholder engagement
AI compliance	**Adhering to legal, regulatory or other guidelines** for AI development and deployment. Some organizations will designate their AI governance as a formal compliance program
AI ethics	**Societal values and norms** which are supported by responsible AI practices
Data ethics	The values and norms governing **data collection, processing and usage** which are supported by responsible development practices
AI assurance	The process of **measuring, evaluating and communicating** that an AI system meets compliance standards such as reliability, fairness and transparency

Put simply, AI governance is:

- A comprehensive framework that covers not just technology but people and processes, requiring senior level leadership, cross-enterprise participation and multi-stakeholder engagement.
- An enhancement to existing risk management frameworks and data science/software development practices, supported by training.
- A program which can take months and sometimes years to develop and roll out, and the need for adherence and ongoing attention continues post deployment.

AI governance is not:

- Something which can be achieved by technology alone or by tweaking policies or efforts 'around the edges'.
- A compliance checklist which is finished once the system has gone live. Indeed, it often requires cultural shifts in an organization and always requires senior level buy in and ownership.

Over the coming chapters we will explain how to build a governance program across the AI development process from ideation to implementation to mitigate the potential harms which could impact individuals, communities and groups, the workforce and the environment.

KEY INSIGHTS AND ACTIONS

- Already in 2016, media and industry experts highlighted how AI systems could perpetuate harm, undermine societal trust and fail in their intended goals. Fast forward to today and generative AI has exacerbated these risks while also offering immense promise. Its ability to generate new creative content makes it particularly challenging to control.
- There is no universally accepted definition of AI, but the Organisation for Economic Co-operation and Development (OECD) offers a widely regarded one: 'an AI system is a machine-based system that, for explicit or implicit objectives, infers, from the input it

---

receives, how to generate outputs such as predictions, content, recommendations, or decisions that can influence physical or virtual environments. Different AI systems vary in their levels of autonomy and adaptiveness after deployment'.

- AI research began in the 1950s, but Google's 2017 paper, *Attention is All You Need*, revolutionized the field by introducing the transformer architecture which underpins much of what is now known as generative AI.
- Many AI risks stem from the probabilistic and inherently complex nature of AI systems.
- Agentic AI and multi-agent systems are fast emerging as the next paradigm: while traditional AI is suited for well-defined, singular tasks and genAI for content creation, agentic AI aims to solve complex problems by reasoning, planning several steps, executing those steps using various tools, and adapting, if necessary, all with minimal human oversight.
- Building trust in AI is crucial for customers, employees and the public to have confidence in its use.
- Robust AI governance practices when designing, developing and deploying AI systems are essential to avoid negative unintended consequences and build trust.
- AI governance establishes robust policies, frameworks and processes to ensure AI aligns with principles, values and legislation, balancing innovation with safeguards to minimize risk.

2

Why is AI governance important now?

ADMIRAL INSURANCE: FAIR AND ACCURATE PRICING IS
GOOD FOR THE BOTTOM LINE

Admiral Group Plc uses machine-learning models to predict risk and price its insurance products, so identifying and removing unwanted bias is crucial to ensure fairness. When he joined Admiral as data ethics lead, David Crelley focused on integrating AI governance from the start of the model development process. This approach enabled Admiral to more accurately price all customer groups, which resulted in more competitive pricing, supporting the Group's ambition to grow its customer base.

Crelley built a process to visualize and explain how a machine-learning model works to business colleagues, while fostering a culture where discussing data errors, potential bias and impacts on diverse customer groups is encouraged. There is a correlation between population density and diversity, which means diverse areas on average have higher risk. Therefore, it is crucial to have processes to tackle unintended bias. The independent team that decides what factors to include in a model has broad representation to ensure a wide range of views are considered and avoid unintentionally delivering poorer outcomes for certain customers.

This example demonstrates that AI governance can enhance profitability while ensuring fairness for customers. These checks are now standard for all predictive models and part of regular pricing reviews at Admiral.

Implementing genAI alongside strong governance controls drives significant return on investment, as numerous studies increasingly demonstrate. A 2024 McKinsey study estimated that telecom companies adopting 'advanced responsible AI practices' could generate an additional $250bn in value globally by 2040, driven by the confidence to scale AI effectively.[1] Companies surveyed by Accenture and Amazon Web Services (AWS) expect a 25 per cent increase in customer loyalty and satisfaction from offering well governed AI products and services.[2]

Meanwhile, public, employee and investor concerns about AI risks continue to grow. Edelman's Trust Barometer 2024, an annual global survey that measures public trust in institutions such as business, government, media and NGOs across nearly 30 countries, showed a decline in trust of AI companies from 50 to 35 per cent since 2019 in the US, and from 61 to 53 per cent globally, as well as a particularly strong distrust of AI in western markets, see figure below:[3]

FIGURE 2.1 Resistance to AI Stronger in Developed Markets

Per cent who say

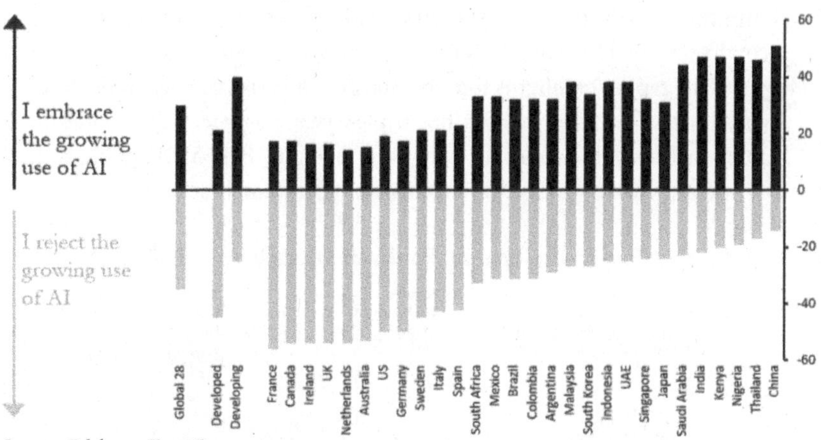

Source: Edelman Trust Barometer

AI governance is the foundation for building trust. By addressing stakeholder concerns and ensuring responsible practices, it enables organizations to deploy AI confidently and sustainably. As more business leaders recognize governance as essential to successful AI adoption, this book provides a practical roadmap for establishing robust AI governance programs.

BANKS RECOGNIZE AI GOVERNANCE AS A SOURCE OF COMPETITIVE ADVANTAGE

In October 2024 Evident AI published its second annual report into the AI maturity of banks globally.[4] The analysis and resulting index cover four different pillars: talent, innovation, leadership and transparency, with transparency defined as 'Measures the extent to which banks are focusing on Responsible AI (RAI), as evidenced by the publication of thought leadership, establishment of key partnerships, hiring of dedicated RAI talent, and promotion of RAI principles'. Encouragingly, the transparency pillar saw the largest improvement in average score over the previous 12 months at 27 per cent. Alexandra Mousavizadeh, Co-CEO and Co-Founder, comments, 'Responsible AI is now being seen as a competitive advantage by the leading banks. Top management is under pressure from the board both to adopt AI rapidly but also to ensure that oversight and governance keep up with innovation. Investors, customers and clients are adding to this pressure.' Interestingly, cultural differences are apparent, with most US banks being less transparent about their commitment to Responsible AI than Canadian and UK banks and, for the second year in a row, continental European banks being absent from the top 10. The report highlights that the number of banks publicly reporting their Responsible AI principles has tripled year-on-year and provides a helpful analysis of the approach each bank is taking. Evident AI published an in-depth report, specific to Responsible AI, in March 2025.[5]

FIGURE 2.2 Top-10 Performing Banks In Transparency Pillar

Bank	Region	Transparency Rank	2023–24 Rank Change	RAI Talent	RAI Innovation	RAI Leadership Rank
JPMorgan Chase	US	1	-	4	1	12
Standard Chartered	UK	2	↑ 9	1	4	11
HSBC	UK	3	↑ 3	3	7	6
Scotiabank	Canada	4	↓ 1	2	12	6
CommBank	APAC	5	↑ 1	9	3	6
CIBC	Canada	6	↑ 33	20	12	1
DBS	APAC	7	↑ 5	29	5	1
Wells Fargo	US	8	↑ 2	15	2	12
NatWest	UK	9	-	12	10	5
Royal Bank of Canada	Canada	10	↓ 8	15	8	6

Source: Evident AI Index – Banks, 2024

In talking with business leaders across the globe, we know that avoidance of reputational damage is top of mind when deciding to invest in AI governance. Anyone reading this book will have seen plenty of examples of 'AI gone wrong': the AI Incident Database has recorded a sharp increase in the number of AI incidents since 2022, roughly coinciding with the widespread adoption of genAI, as published in the 2025 Stanford AI Index report.[6]

FIGURE 2.3 Number of reported AI incidents, 2012–24, AI Incident Database 2024'

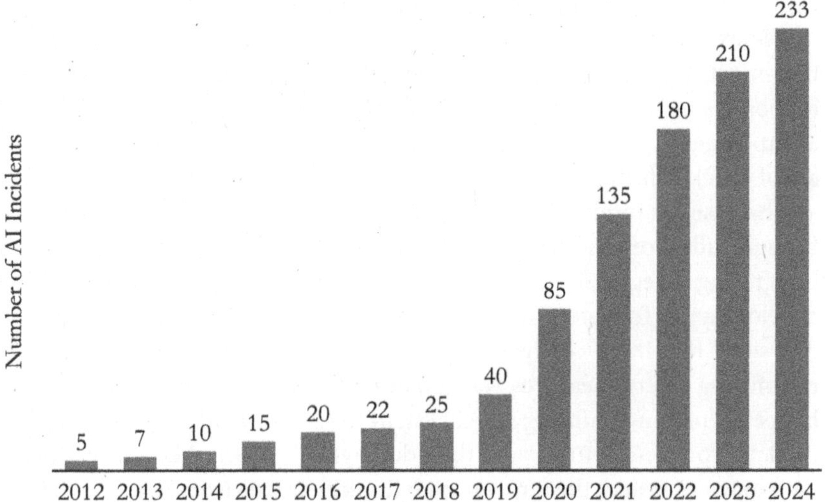

Note: the number of AI incidents is continually updated over time, including for previous years. Therefore, the totals reported here might not align with the more recent totals published on the AI Incident Database.
Source: Stanford AI Index report 2025

Beyond preventing reputational damage, a strong AI governance program can enhance an organization's AI use by broadening its consumer base, improving efficiencies, delivering better products and services, and strengthening brand integrity, as we will discuss in later chapters.

Another powerful motivator, and the one which most readily unlocks budget, is the need to comply with forthcoming regulation. For businesses operating or providing AI-driven products or services in the EU, the EU AI Act is enacted and the countdown to full enforcement in August 2026 has begun (see Chapter 12). Well before then, 'prohibited systems' were already banned and appropriate AI literacy of employees involved with AI systems is already required.

In the US, there are more fragmented but equally important compliance requirements for companies building, deploying or using AI systems, which are explored in Chapter 13. In the UK, sector specific regulations are being applied to AI – for example, in financial services, and cross-sectoral regulators such as the Information Commissioner's Office are addressing aspects of AI such as data privacy and consent. In Asia, the Monetary Authority of Singapore has invested heavily over the past five years in developing guidelines and tools for managing AI in the financial services sector. These are not currently mandatory but could become expected practices and, possibly, mandatory requirements.

We examine legislation in Chapters 12 to 14 because every organization must keep up to date with current and emerging AI laws wherever it operates or serves customers. While regulations often lag technological advancements, a robust AI governance program enables organizations to adapt quickly, mitigating both known and unforeseen risks.

The case for implementing AI governance now is clear: embedding AI thoughtfully from the start saves significant time and expense. Proactively integrating safeguards is far more efficient than applying controls after development. Too often, we have seen AI systems built without proper oversight requiring costly rework – or even full retirement – because retrofitting safety measures was too complex or unfeasible. How can this happen? Imagine building an AI system to recommend jobs by training it on data from one country and then deploying it in another. The historical data may not reflect the target population's characteristics, leading to ineffective or unfair outcomes. Effective AI governance should be integral to evaluating use cases, embedded throughout the development lifecycle and central to ongoing monitoring post-deployment.

Despite these compelling arguments, few organizations have implemented comprehensive AI governance programs. The *Stanford 2024 Artificial Intelligence Index Report* cites a *Global State of Responsible AI* survey conducted with Accenture, covering 1,000 organizations across 20 countries and 19 industries. It found most organizations had operationalized at least one mitigation measure for an identified AI risk, but far fewer had addressed more than half of relevant risks (Asia: 25 per cent, Europe: 18 per cent, North America: 17 per cent).[7] However, the survey assessed only five risk areas (fairness, transparency, privacy, reliability and security), omitting further critical risks covered in Chapter 5. Addressing just one risk suggests a piecemeal approach, likely through existing data privacy, cybersecurity or data science programs. This fragmented method leaves organizations exposed to significant other risks. While many are beginning this journey of AI governance, significant work remains.

A 2024 survey by Qlik and TechTarget's Enterprise Strategy Group supports this theory, revealing that 74 per cent of North American organizations lack a comprehensive approach to responsible AI.[8] Key challenges include ensuring transparency and explainability (cited by 86 per cent of respondents) and maintaining compliance with AI regulations (99 per cent). Encouragingly, 74 per cent of organizations now rate responsible AI as a top priority. Over a quarter reported increased operational costs, regulatory scrutiny and market delays due to inadequate AI governance.

As our experience and the data indicate, the majority of organizations are in the early stages of building comprehensive AI governance into their business processes. Smaller companies with more limited resources and start-ups typically have even less adoption of AI governance.[*]

Implementing a comprehensive AI governance program requires investment and organizational buy-in: for large, multinational companies, establishing a global program could take up to two years. This should serve as a wake-up call for EU-based businesses still in the early stages of implementation, as less than two years remain until the EU AI Act takes full effect.

This is not surprising in light of the authors' experience of businesses being slow to comply with EU data privacy legislation in the form of the General Data Protection Regulation (GDPR). A study by advisory firm RSM in July 2019 suggested that 30 per cent of European firms were still not compliant one year after the GDPR came into force.[9] This resulted in high-profile prosecutions such as the €50m fine imposed on Google by the French regulator CNIL and we can imagine that a similar pattern may emerge for AI.[10] AI is arguably more mission-critical and deeply embedded within an organization's operations, making it even harder to manage than data governed by the GDPR.

---

[*]It might seem that smaller organizations could implement an AI governance program more rapidly. While they are undoubtedly more agile, they are often hampered by lack of budget and resources, and have less access to technical and legal expertise to address what in many respects is a fixed cost (designing an AI governance program) regardless of size. As a result, while organizations of all sizes can – and often do – implement this work, in practice AI governance can be more challenging for smaller organizations.

KEY INSIGHTS AND ACTIONS

- Evidence demonstrates a strong return on investment for AI when paired with governance controls, yet most organizations are still in the early stages of adopting AI governance.
- AI incidents have risen sharply. The AI Incident Database reported a large increase in incidents since 2022, exposing organizations without governance safeguards to reputational damage, financial penalties and lost customer trust.
- Organizations face increasing pressure to meet evolving global AI regulations.
- Addressing AI risks effectively requires a comprehensive, enterprise-wide approach; fragmented efforts leave organizations vulnerable to unintended consequences and liabilities.
- Proactive governance throughout the AI lifecycle avoids costly fixes or system retirements after deployment.
- Leadership buy-in is essential because establishing comprehensive AI governance programs will take time and investment.
- The cost of inaction far outweighs the investment in governance. Delays risk fines, lost market opportunities and operational disruptions, as well as legal liability.

3

Whose problem is it anyway?

SENIOR LEADERS CHART THE COURSE

In 2022 the Business Roundtable (BRT) of America, representing over 230 CEOs across many industries, launched its 'Roadmap for Responsible Artificial Intelligence (AI)', an initiative to guide the responsible development and use of AI.[1] Alfred F. Kelly, Jr., Chairman and CEO of Visa and Chair of the Business Roundtable Technology Committee, highlighted the critical role of senior leadership in charting the course for AI governance: 'Leaders in business and government must work together to earn and maintain trust in AI by demonstrating responsible AI deployment and oversight. Only then can we realize its full beneficial potential for society.'

It is tempting to think that AI governance is a problem for technologists to solve, perhaps with government regulation to provide direction. Nothing could be further from the truth. AI presents an opportunity for each of us to benefit, and likewise, all of us should help ensure its appropriate use. Customers, business colleagues, investors, government, academics, civil society, all should hold organizations to account for their use of AI. As Tom Lue, Vice President, Frontier AI Global Affairs at Google DeepMind, says: 'Getting AI right must be a collective effort, and to that end, we're invested in collaborating directly with a broad range of stakeholders, including industry partners, civil society, and government.' In this chapter, we examine different stakeholder groups and clarify the role each should play to ensure that AI is used effectively and responsibly.

SENIOR LEADERSHIP AND THE BOARD

As with any critical organizational initiative, sponsorship from the very top is essential. For example, one of the success factors in establishing Accenture's AI governance program was the vocal support from the CEO, Julie Sweet. Brad Smith, President of Microsoft, and Athina Kanioura, Executive Vice President at PepsiCo, among others have acted as similar role models. We are often asked who should own an AI governance program and we always advise that this work requires someone with sufficient seniority, organizational political capital and budget to drive a successful program (see Chapter 8 for more detail). This is particularly important because an AI governance program can only succeed if it is coherently applied across all parts of the enterprise, requiring significant effort to achieve alignment and suitable accountabilities. When one of the authors worked with a major international bank on their AI governance implementation, the first four months were spent largely in meetings and workshops to secure consensus around ownership, accountabilities and scope. To be clear, this is not unusual and is time well spent.

Beyond executive leadership, the Board has a critical role to play, since AI governance will generally fall under the remit of the Board's fiduciary risk management responsibilities.[2] While board structures and legal requirements vary by country, the core responsibilities of boards in risk and compliance oversight remain similar: ensuring effective governance programs and overseeing their implementation. An AI governance program will complement existing governance programs, which may include anti-corruption, antitrust, data privacy, financial compliance and product safety, depending on the organization's industry and activities. Key board responsibilities include receiving regular reports on compliance activities and risks, reviewing and approving policies, overseeing internal controls and ensuring employee training. To hold senior management accountable, board directors must stay informed about relevant laws, regulations and industry standards. Boards typically establish compliance committees, require updates from the Chief Compliance Officer, oversee audits and review whistleblower reports and investigations.

BUSINESS EXECUTIVES

The demand for an AI-driven product or service will typically come from the business: an executive recognizes the opportunity to generate new business, is grappling with a thorny challenge or seeking ways to reduce costs. Unsurprisingly, a quick check on the internet or social media may motivate them to explore whether AI might be the solution. This request will then either make its way to an internal data science/technology team or to procurement. But if AI is deemed to offer a solution, someone must ask the key question: just because we *could* use AI, *should* we?

There may be several reasons why an AI solution is not the best approach. For instance, the AI solution might not be cost-effective, or it could present inherent risks which are greater than the company may wish or need to take in light of the proposed outcomes. A key challenge in this field, given that AI is both nascent and evolving, is identifying the universe of risks. We review countless potential use cases for AI and often identify risks which are quite apparent to those of us who operate in this space but are too often overlooked. Establishing an AI governance program which formalizes 'good AI hygiene', together with appropriate training, will help business executives in recognizing and evaluating AI risk.

THE VALUE OF SAYING 'NO'

Deciding, and communicating, when *not* to use AI, can help build trust in an organization's use of AI. When discussing where it is appropriate to use AI, Liz Caselli-Mechael, Global Head of Digital & Content for Nestlé, the food and drink conglomerate, has taken a strong public stance: 'You can't use AI when showing food and ingredients. It has got to start from the reality on the farm. When seeing content from us, you need to know it is a real reflection of our products, our people, our farmers. That has to be very genuine and really reflect reality or we will miss the most in creating trust.'[3]

RESPONSIBLE AI/AI GOVERNANCE TEAM

Increasingly, organizations are establishing specialist teams to address AI governance. Often this team sits within the Chief Data and Analytics Officer function drawing on data science and data engineering expertise, but it may include interdisciplinary members from other parts of the organization, such as Legal and Risk. If such a team exists, it will often lead the AI governance program and will provide a central support capability to everyone engaging with the program – for example, while undergoing risk assessments.

LEGAL, COMPLIANCE AND INTERNAL AUDIT

Whereas in the early days of responsible AI we typically saw the initiative being taken by technical leadership, legal is now increasingly the sponsor. This is not surprising, as AI regulation increases and AI-related litigation grows. We have also observed that the earlier lawyers are included in the review of AI systems, the better the outcome. When the legal team operates as a trusted partner, instead of the proverbial 'office of no', systems can be built and deployed more safely from the start, saving significant costs to retrain or redevelop later.

Typically, the legal team is responsible for drafting the AI policy and/or ensuring the relevant legal requirements are contained in other policies which relate to AI. These serve as the instrument for enforcing adherence to the AI governance program and ensuring it is aligned with other relevant policies, such as for data and model risk. The legal team is critical in numerous ways – from helping to formulate the risk assessment questions to ensuring all legislative, regulatory and guidance requirements are covered. Internal audit will play an important part in ensuring compliance with AI policies and controls.

DATA PRIVACY

Given the strength of data privacy legislation in Europe and the US, most organizations have mature controls for data privacy – for example, to comply with the General Data Protection Regulation (GDPR) in Europe or the California Consumer Privacy Act and California Privacy Rights Act in the US. These can often be leveraged for the AI governance program, such as by expanding a Data Protection Impact Assessment to incorporate AI-specific legal requirements (see Chapter 9 for more details).

DATA MANAGEMENT AND DATA GOVERNANCE

Teams that manage data and its governance are also strong allies in establishing AI governance. Data governance approval processes and forums can be augmented to include AI considerations with the advantage that these review procedures are already familiar to technical teams. These forums generally already include the breadth of expertise to review AI but can be supplemented if needed.

RISK MANAGEMENT (ENTERPRISE, OPERATIONAL AND DATA)

Where a well-established risk function exists – for example, in regulated industries – its expertise and controls will be a valuable foundation on which to build. Indeed, we recommend that an AI governance program be built around, and in support of, existing risk and compliance controls, rather than creating a new, parallel framework. Such an approach leverages proven checkpoints, harnesses the expertise of colleagues who are familiar with risk in your specific industry and streamlines the effort of colleagues to comply, rather than burdening them with an additional process.

PRACTITIONER'S TIP

Financial services firms often use the 'three lines of defence' approach for risk management, a framework that is also effective for designing AI governance programs.

1. **First Line of Defence**: Operational management and staff who deliver customer products and services. They manage risks in day-to-day activities, adhering to internal controls, regulations, policies and procedures.
2. **Second Line of Defence**: The risk management and compliance team. They develop frameworks, policies and procedures, monitor risks and provide oversight and guidance to the first line team. They also report risk levels to senior management and the Board.
3. **Third Line of Defence**: Internal auditors, who provide independent assurance to the Board and senior management on the effectiveness of governance, risk management and internal controls. They also provide recommendations for remediating gaps discovered during audits. This function remains independent of the first two lines of defence and reports findings and recommendations directly to the Board.

The three lines model is widely recognized as best practice for improving risk coverage, ensuring clear accountability and enhancing transparency. Depending on the industry, its adoption may be voluntary or regulatory. In financial services, disciplines like Model Risk Management and Model Validation are well-established, making them natural partners for

AI governance. In December 2024 the Monetary Authority of Singapore published a helpful paper on Model Risk Management for AI.[4] Aligning AI programs with these trusted teams ensures consistency and builds on existing practices.

A critical step is engaging broader risk oversight teams to clarify responsibilities for AI risks. This often involves adapting existing controls to address new challenges. However, organizations may face resistance from teams hesitant to take on accountability for unfamiliar risk areas, making alignment, training and incentives crucial.

DATA SCIENCE AND TECHNOLOGY

Most large organizations already use a 'data science lifecycle' or similar structured process to manage the development, testing, deployment and monitoring of AI systems. It can be effective to embed AI governance controls along this lifecycle.

Technical teams play a key role in helping legal, risk and business leaders translate legal requirements and best practices into actionable steps. This work includes determining where to embed controls, designing risk assessment processes and selecting or developing platforms to manage AI governance and record assessment outcomes.

Data science expertise is vital for conducting technical evaluations during risk assessments and identifying the right tools for this. The team must also formally monitor emerging techniques and technologies that may impact the AI governance program. While motivated data scientists often do this informally, a structured process ensures their findings are standardized, inform governance leadership and drive necessary updates.

PROCUREMENT

The importance of procurement in AI governance is often underestimated. AI is now so pervasive that many third-party systems, tools or services incorporate AI, even if it isn't explicitly disclosed. This can present challenges. For instance, vendors may not highlight AI-driven features, making it essential for procurement to screen for embedded AI during assessments. Additionally, vendors may hesitate to share details on how their solutions meet a buyer's responsible AI requirements. Procurement teams often lack the data science expertise needed to fully evaluate third-party AI solutions independently, making close collaboration with technical teams essential. We explore the role of procurement further in Chapter 9.

TALENT AND HR

Human Resources (HR) can play a key role in shaping an AI governance program across three critical areas. First, HR often pioneers AI adoption within organizations, particularly in selecting and assessing AI-driven tools for recruitment, performance evaluation and workforce management. These tools are subject to regulatory scrutiny, such as from the US Equal Employment Opportunity Commission, due to risks of bias or discrimination. Missteps here can result in financial, reputational and operational harm by unfairly evaluating or excluding top talent.

Second, HR can collaborate with the responsible AI team to develop and execute a talent strategy to support AI governance. As noted earlier, this work requires diverse skills, some of which may already exist within the organization, while others, like expertise in bias, ethics or legal-data science combinations, may need to be sourced externally. HR can identify internal talent, highlight gaps and guide recruitment or partnerships with external experts.

Finally, HR can assess the impact of AI on jobs, identifying roles that may change or be eliminated. They can help mitigate job displacement through supporting reskilling and upskilling programs. Indeed, the Society for Human Resource Management goes further making a compelling case for *How CHROs Can Be the Drivers of Ethical AI Adoption and Empowerment* because 'ultimately, AI is more than a technological advancement — it will fundamentally become a social and intellectual transformation.'[5]

MARKETING AND COMMUNICATIONS

While some organizations are not forthcoming about their use of AI, for others it can be tempting to brand a product or service as 'AI-enabled' to gain a marketing edge, even when AI isn't actually involved. This is difficult to verify, as there is no universally accepted definition of AI, as discussed earlier in Chapter 1. However, falsely claiming AI use can subject companies to recourse from government or private action. For example, in September 2024, the Federal Trade Commission announced a crackdown on deceptive AI claims.[6] Marketing teams should carefully consider the veracity of their assertion before touting an 'AI-enabled' product.

Highlighting a commitment to the responsible development and use of AI can build trust with employees, consumers and the public, offering a competitive advantage. However, premature or unsupported claims – or 'ethics washing' – can damage an organization's reputation when exposed.

Until companies have an established AI governance program, they should approach public commitments cautiously. Additionally, communications teams should help develop a public response plan for potential issues with AI usage, similar to a data breach response plan, to enable the organization to respond proactively, rather than just defensively to challenges that may arise.

GOVERNMENT RELATIONS AND PUBLIC POLICY

With AI use expanding and global regulations evolving rapidly, regulatory affairs/public policy teams play a key role in monitoring emerging regulations. In some cases, they will engage with government representatives to provide input into draft legislation, sharing industry insights through public consultations, meetings or other channels. Opportunities may also exist to collaborate with regulators, where helpful, through AI regulatory sandboxes, which allow companies and authorities to test AI systems and datasets under existing or proposed rules in a controlled, low-risk environment.[7] For multinational companies, this role is especially critical as regulations develop differently across geographies and this team can help navigate compliance as well as suggest opportunities to engage with policymakers who want to better understand regulatory impacts. Corporate affairs teams should also help shape the organization's external messaging for AI governance.

INFORMATION SECURITY

GenAI exposes organizations to new cybersecurity risks. Since many genAI applications, such as customer service agents, are externally facing and allow user input. This presents an opportunity for bad actors to subvert the system using a variety of different and evolving techniques, which are explored in Chapters 5 and 10. This vulnerability calls for close collaboration between genAI system developers and the cybersecurity team to build robust safeguards and defences.

We now turn to look outside the organization, where there can be many important stakeholders.

GOVERNMENTAL ORGANIZATIONS

Just as businesses are rushing to embrace the benefits of AI, so too are many public sector organizations and government agencies, recognizing the potential for improved citizen services and reduced delivery costs.[8] For example, in February 2025 the UK government published an extensive *Artificial Intelligence Playbook for the UK Government* explaining that 'It is crucial for civil servants to gain an understanding of what AI can and cannot do, how it can help, and the potential ethical, legal, privacy, sustainability and security risks it poses.'[9] The contents of this helpful resource are similarly applicable for private sector organizations.

In Europe, the EU AI Act applies equally to government bodies and businesses, as does the US National Institute of Standards and Technology (NIST) Risk Management Framework in the US. In the UK, the Labour government has recognized the responsible use of AI as one of its key pillars for improving the efficiency of public service delivery and as a critical way to free up budget for much-needed investment.

The critical role of governments in supporting innovation, adoption and safety through legislation is covered in depth in Chapters 12 to 14.

INTERNATIONAL AND INTERGOVERNMENTAL ORGANIZATIONS

From the earliest days of AI governance discussions, intergovernmental organizations, such as the Organisation for Economic Co-operation and Development (OECD) and the United Nations Educational, Scientific and Cultural Organization (UNESCO), have played a critical role in trying to shape a global consensus on the need for ethical AI and in providing frameworks for governments and industry. As AI continues to advance, these types of intergovernmental organizations will aim to achieve more global consensus on binding rules, established practices and expectations. Other important bodies, given their involvement in the global AI governance conversation, include: the Global Partnership on Artificial Intelligence (GPAI), currently comprising 29 member countries and leading experts from civil society, science, industry, governments and academia; the G7, which has addressed AI ethics in various summits and ministerial meetings; and The World Economic Forum, which has been actively involved in shaping the responsible AI governance debate through its Centre for the Fourth Industrial Revolution.

STANDARDS ORGANIZATIONS

In the absence of binding global legislation, and to support the AI-related legislation adopted in several countries, standards organizations play a particularly important role in establishing and standardizing AI governance. First, there is established precedent for multiple countries recognizing standards issued by well-regarded standards bodies. Second, in some jurisdictions, compliance with relevant standards is deemed to constitute compliance with the law – for example, in the EU, where such standards are referred to as 'harmonized standards'.

The table below describes some of the key international standards bodies:

Standards Body	Areas of Focus
ISO (International Organization for Standardization)	Technical, quality and management system standards for AI, particularly through its ISO/IEC JTC 1/SC 42 committee for AI, established in 2017 jointly with IEC (International Electrotechnical Commission)
IEEE (Institute of Electrical and Electronics Engineers)	Standards related to computational approaches to machine learning, algorithms and related data usage
CEN and CENELEC (European Committee for Standardization and European Committee for Electrotechnical Standardization)	AI standards specifically to underpin the implementation of EU legislation such as the EU AI Act
ANSI (American National Standards Institute)	Provides significant input into multinational standard development
NIST (US National Institute of Standards and Technology)	Provides significant input into multinational standard development
BSI (British Standards Institution)	Provides significant input into multinational standard development

CUSTOMERS

Transparency is a key element in building trust, whether in AI systems or otherwise. Transparency in AI governance, which we define in Chapter 5, involves ensuring that those interacting with, or affected by, an AI system are aware of its presence, as well as its role in driving decisions or processes. End users should also be given the information to understand how decisions are made and, where applicable, recourse for addressing flawed, biased or discriminatory outcomes. This type of transparency is often mandated by AI legislation, which may also require offering customers the choice to avoid AI-driven services in some jurisdictions.

Many readers will recall early encounters with customer service chatbots where it wasn't clear the interaction was with an AI tool until its limitations became obvious. This often left users feeling deceived. Disclosure of AI and its limits is a best practice that benefits both customers and companies, fostering trust and loyalty.

CIVIL SOCIETY

Civil society groups play a crucial role in promoting responsible AI practices through active engagement with industry and governments. These groups serve as valuable convening forums and often bring deep technical expertise. The diverse perspectives many offer, representing individuals from backgrounds distinct from those developing and deploying AI, can help organizations better understand the variety of use cases and potential challenges end users or impacted individuals may confront when using AI. Many civil society organizations advocate for minorities and marginalized communities who may face heightened risks of exclusion or discrimination from AI systems. Their efforts help ensure comprehensive AI governance reduces liability, promotes broader engagement and fosters equal participation in an increasingly AI-driven society.

INVESTORS

Investors hold significant power to influence companies, making their role in AI governance increasingly important. Savvy investors have been systematically questioning companies about their AI governance practices for several years. Some major private equity firms are now assessing AI risks across their portfolios and encouraging the adoption of AI governance programs, understanding that a public AI incident could damage valuations and jeopardize investments.

The World Economic Forum highlighted the growing role of investors in its *Responsible AI Playbook for Investors* (June 2024), stating: 'For large investors, ensuring all AI applications are responsible (i.e., honest, helpful and harmless) is not merely a technological upgrade but a strategic imperative. Ensuring it is developed and deployed in a manner consistent with responsible AI (RAI) principles is an important step for enhancing risk-adjusted returns and positioning businesses for success.'[10] The 'responsible innovation labs' (RIL) includes guidance on how to communicate with investors about AI governance as part of its helpful responsible AI materials for start-ups.[11]

PRIVATE EQUITY FIRM RECOGNIZES AI GOVERNANCE SECURES VALUE

For Cinven, the global private equity firm, value creation is key. That's why they conducted a comprehensive review of AI governance across their portfolio companies during 2024: they recognize that risk minimization is critical while adopting AI to gain competitive advantage. The initiative, which involved detailed reviews of potentially higher-risk AI systems following initial risk screening, was led by the Chief Operating Officer and supported by an external law firm. The EU AI Act was the immediate catalyst but the same standards have been applied globally, with some geographic modifications to account for local regulations. The central team has developed a set of resources to support individual company teams on their AI governance journey.

ACADEMIA

AI is a rapidly evolving field with new techniques and approaches constantly emerging. Academia provided the talent for many of the current AI technologies, often in partnership with commercial labs, although that is diminishing as more of the capability exists exclusively in industry. An extensive global community of AI safety researchers works within academia to investigate the identification and mitigation of the risks posed by today's AI systems.

KEY INSIGHTS AND ACTIONS

The responsible use of AI is not just a technology problem, it requires a collective effort as AI offers benefits and poses potential risks that impact everyone. Some critical participants in AI governance include:

- **Senior Leadership and the Board** provide active sponsorship for AI governance to ensure alignment, accountability and enterprise-wide implementation. Boards play a critical role in overseeing AI-related risks, policies and compliance.
- **Business Executives** must evaluate AI solutions carefully, questioning whether AI is appropriate for specific contexts.

Governance frameworks and training empower them to identify risks and make informed decisions.

- **Responsible AI/AI Governance team** – where established, often within the Chief Data and Analytics Office, this team will typically lead the program. It provides support through the process, including to those carrying out risk assessments.
- **Legal, Compliance and Audit** ensure alignment with regulations and mitigate legal risks. Early legal involvement reduces liability and potential costs. Existing related frameworks, such as data privacy and cybersecurity, can be adapted to include AI-specific requirements, streamlining efforts.
- **Risk Management Functions**, including enterprise, operational and data risk teams, can integrate AI governance into established frameworks to avoid duplication.
- **Technical Teams** embed governance controls throughout the AI development lifecycle, ensuring actionable risk assessments and incorporating emerging techniques into governance updates. They work together with Information Security to protect against cyber threats.
- **Procurement Teams** screen third-party AI systems for risks, working with technical experts to evaluate vendors and ensure compliance with best practice and internal requirements.
- **Human Resources (HR)** ensures hiring and evaluation AI tools comply with regulations and expectations, avoiding harms and unintended consequences. They can also partner in evaluating and addressing potential workforce impacts, as well as identifying and supporting upskilling and reskilling initiatives.
- **Marketing, Communications and Government Relations** evaluate the timing and language to effectively promote the organization's AI governance externally and support internal change management. Preparing a clear public response plan for potential AI-related issues is advisable to help maintain trust in the event of unintended outcomes.
- **External Stakeholders** such as governments, customers, civil society and investors increasingly demand accountability and transparency in AI use. Standards bodies and academia develop tools and approaches to support AI governance implementation.

4

Understanding AI risk – a survey of key frameworks

CREATING AN AI RISK MANAGEMENT FRAMEWORK
FROM BEST PRACTICES

Verizon has been on a journey to adopt AI for over a decade, and recognized early on that AI must be deployed thoughtfully and responsibly, leading to the creation of Verizon's Responsible AI Program. The Responsible AI Program built on top of emerging best practices in ethical AI as well as existing regulatory guidance, and incorporated the RMF from NIST, which was closely aligned to Verizon's existing program, when it was released. 'We built an internal governance program working closely with our technical, policy, and legal experts,' said Mike Tang, Senior Director leading AI risk management. 'As the field of AI is advancing so quickly, so too is AI governance, and we continue to evaluate significant new external developments to identify any enhancements to our AI governance program,' explained Josh Dubin, legal lead for Verizon's AI governance.

In discussions about establishing AI governance programs, the terms 'principles', 'risks' and 'harms' are frequently used; figure 4.1 on the next page clarifies the relationship between them:

FIGURE 4.1 Principles, Harms and Risks

<table>
<tr><td>PRINCIPLES
Positive expression of an organization's values</td><td>HARMS
The negative impact or damage which regulators and organizations seek to prevent</td></tr>
<tr><td colspan="2">RISKS
The likelihood of a hazardous event occurring and the severity of the consequences if that event occurs. Such an event can compromise principles and/or lead to harm</td></tr>
</table>

In this chapter, we focus on the risks that can undermine principles or cause harm or liability. In Chapter 7, we will explore how organizations can establish principles.

UNDERSTANDING RISK

The starting point for any AI governance program is establishing the AI principles that will guide your process and decisions. We recommend a direct mapping between your register of risks and your stated principles. To illustrate, a commonly adopted principle is to treat customers and employees fairly.* A risk may be misalignment on what 'fair' means in a given situation, such as overselling to consumers beyond their needs or means. Even worse, unchecked AI could identify proxies for various demographics as a basis for its recommendations and lead to discriminatory outcomes, thereby limiting your customer base and potentially inviting litigation and other forms of liability.

As we seek to better understand and measure risk, we can consider two key components: the probability of occurrence and the magnitude of harm. The US National Institute of Standards and Technology (NIST) Risk Management Framework offers this helpful context: '*risk* refers to the composite measure of an event's *probability* of occurring and the *magnitude or degree of the consequences* of the corresponding event' (italics added).[1]

AI risks present a significant threat because of the unique challenges in understanding, predicting and controlling AI systems, particularly genAI. Unlike traditional software, AI is probabilistic, meaning the same inputs

---

*How 'fairly' may be defined is explored at length in Chapters 5 and 10.

can produce different outcomes if repeated. In contrast, a deterministic system always yields the same output for a given input.

AI systems are inherently complex, often involving millions or billions of parameters. This complexity makes it difficult to pinpoint how any given component influences the final output. Additionally, AI relies on data, which evolves over time, introducing variability. Historical data used for model training is often biased and may not align with desired future outcomes – for example, as discussed by Caroline Criado Perez in her book, *Invisible Women*.[2] Even the perfect AI model or system, if they existed, could present new risks as new data and inputs are entered. The behaviour of an AI system is context dependent, meaning it may perform differently depending on how and where it is deployed. Increasingly, genAI systems will interact with other AI systems, introducing further unpredictability. We also see so-called 'emergent behaviours', whereby foundation models exhibit behaviours that are unexpected even by those who created the system. For these reasons, AI systems are particularly difficult to understand and control with complete certainty. Similarly, reliable measurements and meaningful reporting – essential components of effective risk management – prove elusive because of the difficulty to accurately assess and quantify AI risks.

These challenges are amplified by the AI supply chain. Many organizations rely on third-party AI systems, data, or foundation models from companies such as OpenAI or Anthropic, yet evaluating these external components is difficult due to limited access to their inner workings, models or training data (see Chapter 9 for a discussion of AI procurement). Additionally, there is currently no consensus on reliable, verifiable metrics for measuring AI risk. While international standards from non-governmental or non-profit organizations may eventually help address this gap, the timeline for adoption or enforcement remains unclear.

RISK LENSES

When evaluating AI risks, adopting a standard set of 'risk lenses' can help minimize the chances of overlooking critical aspects of risk. While these lenses may vary by industry, the following is a broadly applicable framework to categorize potential risks:

- **Strategic risk:** Adverse business decisions or failure to implement effective strategies.

- **Operational risk**: Failures in internal processes, people, systems or external events.
- **Reputational risk**: Loss of trust or market standing due to negative public opinion, affecting customer relationships and business opportunities.
- **Compliance risk**: Legal, regulatory or reputational consequences from non-compliance with laws, regulations or internal policies.
- **Financial risk**: Financial loss or the loss of financial assets.
- **Security risk**: Threats to physical or digital security.
- **Health and safety risk**: Potential harm to employees or customers from accidents or health issues.
- **Environmental risk**: Harm to the environment from the organization's activities.
- **Societal risk**: Damage to society and democracy from use of the organization's products or services.

RISK APPETITE

After establishing a risk measurement approach, the next step is to assess severity and prioritization. One widely used framework is the EU AI Act's risk-based approach, which categorizes risks based on the application area and the potential negative impact on people, society or the environment. For instance, an AI system used to decide public benefits eligibility is higher-risk due to its significant effect on an individual's rights and opportunities.

Organizations must determine what risk thresholds to apply for each AI use, considering the contextual nature of AI systems. In essence, how much risk are they willing to accept for a given outcome? This decision may involve accepting some level of risk or avoiding the use of AI altogether – which itself would be a strategic risk, if competitors choose to adopt AI and thereby gain a market advantage.

Effective safeguards must be implemented and any remaining risks documented for ongoing monitoring and preparedness. A robust risk management approach not only sets appropriate controls but also identifies opportunities to turn risk management into a strategic advantage.

As York zu Putlitz, Head of Risk Management at Bosch Group, explains: 'A thorough and high-quality risk assessment can also be a positive differentiator for companies and bring customer value – for example, by building trust in the way a company uses data. That is why we at Bosch aim to maintain a balance between ensuring sufficient risk management and leaving enough room for development.'

When evaluating risk, an important consideration is the choice of baseline: should it be human performance or an absolute standard? For example, with self-driving cars, an absolute standard might demand zero accidents, yet every year the lives of approximately 1.2 million people are cut short as a result of a road traffic accident.[3] Which benchmark is appropriate?

This decision is challenging because often we hold machines to higher standards than humans. However, it is essential to determine when the benefits of an AI system outweigh the possibility of mistakes. These decisions should follow a transparent, robust and context-specific process. It is well advised to consider the user's risk tolerance, given the end goal of consumer trust in the AI system to support adoption.

AI RISK MANAGEMENT FRAMEWORKS

In recent years, several governmental, non-governmental and industry organizations have issued AI risk frameworks. We will discuss some of the most notable examples here, which align in many respects. That said, each framework is slightly different in its focus. From our point of view, no one framework is all-encompassing or ideally suited for all organizations. As such, in Chapter 5, we will synthesize several of the leading and most widely adopted frameworks to provide a single point of reference for organizations to use.

US National Institute for Standards and Technology (NIST)

In January 2023, following 18 months of drafting and public consultation, the US National Institute for Standards and Technology (NIST) released the first version of its *Artificial Intelligence Risk Management Framework (AI RMF 1.0)*.[4] This voluntary framework aims to embed trustworthiness into the design, development, use and evaluation of AI systems. In our view, the NIST RMF is the most comprehensive risk framework currently available.

The AI RMF includes two key resources:

1. **Conceptual Roadmap**: Outlines risk types, sources, characteristics of trustworthy AI and relevant organizational processes.
2. **Companion Playbook**: A practical guide with questions and actions for each governance cycle stage – defined as: govern,

map, measure and manage – ensuring the AI system performs as intended. It provides references and guidance for each step.

The AI RMF, which draws on International Organization for Standardization (ISO) standards for many of its definitions, defines AI system trustworthiness as:[5]

- Valid and reliable;
- Safe;
- Secure and resilient;
- Accountable and transparent;
- Explainable and interpretable;
- Privacy enhanced;
- Fair – with harmful bias managed.

This framework predated the widespread adoption of genAI, prompting NIST to release its *Generative Artificial Intelligence Profile* in July 2024.[6] As this document explains, genAI can give rise to new risks which are not present with traditional AI and can exacerbate risks which also occur with traditional AI. The risks which are covered include:

- Facilitating easier access to potentially dangerous chemical, biological, radiological, or nuclear information or capabilities;
- Confabulation;
- Dangerous, violent or hateful content;
- Data privacy;
- Environmental impacts;
- Harmful bias or homogenization;
- Human-AI configuration: arrangements of, or interactions between, a human and an AI system which can result in: the human inappropriately anthropomorphizing genAI systems; or experiencing algorithmic aversion, automation bias, over-reliance or emotional entanglement with genAI systems;
- Information integrity: facilitating the generation, exchange and consumption of content which may not distinguish fact from opinion, or fiction, or acknowledge uncertainties. Or which could be leveraged for large-scale dis- and mis-information campaigns;
- Information security;

- Intellectual property: eased production or replication of alleged copyrighted, trademarked or licensed content without authorization, possibly in situations which do not fall under fair use. Eased exposure of trade secrets. Plagiarism or illegal replication;
- Obscene, degrading or abusive content;
- Value chain and component integration: non-transparent or untraceable integration of upstream third-party components, including data that has been improperly obtained or not processed and cleaned due to increased automation from genAI. Improper supplier vetting across the AI lifecycle. Other issues that diminish transparency or accountability for downstream users.

OECD

The Organisation for Economic Co-operation and Development's approach, initially adopted in 2019 and updated in May 2024, focuses heavily on protecting fundamental human rights and positions its consideration of AI risks as a set of principles which AI systems should uphold or promote.[7]

Inclusive growth, sustainable development and well-being. Stakeholders should proactively engage in responsible stewardship of trustworthy AI in pursuit of beneficial outcomes for people and the planet.

Respect for the rule of law, human rights and democratic values, including fairness and privacy. This also includes 'addressing misinformation and disinformation amplified by AI, while respecting freedom of expression'.

Transparency and explainability. AI deployers should make stakeholders aware of their interactions with AI systems and provide easy-to-understand information about the system and its decisions/outputs.

Robustness, security and safety. This includes a requirement for mechanisms to be put in place, allowing humans to override AI systems in the event of harm or undesired behaviour.

Accountability. This entails ensuring traceability in relation to data sets, processes and decisions made by AI. It also requires those accountable to 'apply a systematic risk management approach to each phase of the AI system lifecycle to address risks'.

Council of Europe
As of November 2024, the Council of Europe's *Framework Convention on Artificial Intelligence* had been signed by 37 parties including the US, EU and UK.[8] The framework aligns well with other global governance approaches. It requires states to ensure AI systems comply with the following fundamental principles, among other commitments:

- Human dignity and individual autonomy;
- Equality and non-discrimination;
- Respect for privacy and personal data protection;
- Transparency and oversight;
- Accountability and responsibility;
- Reliability;
- Safe innovation.

The requirements apply both to the public sector and to the private sector, though signatories have the option to apply the Convention's principles to private companies through 'other appropriate measures' rather than directly enacting the provisions of the Convention. There are certain exemptions, including for national security.[9] It remains to be seen how countries implement their commitments through national legislation.

UK Government's White Paper: A Pro-Innovation Approach to AI Regulation
The UK government's approach to AI governance, initially published in March 2023, is flexible and principles-based, drawing on existing high-level principles.[10] It outlines 'illustrative AI risks' to human rights, safety, fairness, privacy and agency, societal well-being and security by providing examples instead of a comprehensive risk framework.

This was followed in April 2024 by the UK Information Commissioner's Office publication, which distilled five key AI risk areas:[11] safety, security, robustness; appropriate transparency and explainability; fairness; accountability and governance; and contestability and redress.

In January 2025 the UK government published its *AI Opportunities Action Plan*, which devotes a section to: 'Enabling safe and trusted AI development and adoption through regulation, safety and assurance'.[12] The proposed measures include:

- Continuing to support the AI Safety Institute;
- Funding regulators to scale up their AI capabilities;
- Ensuring government departments include a focus on safe AI innovation in their guidance to regulators;
- Implementing regulatory sandboxes in priority sectors;
- Supporting the AI assurance ecosystem, including by developing assurance tools to assess whether AI systems perform as claimed and work as intended;
- Establishing a Responsible AI Advisory Panel.

Interim International Scientific Report on the Safety of Advanced AI
Published in May 2024, this report was commissioned at the Bletchley Park AI Safety Summit in November 2023 and was issued under the chairmanship of Professor Joshua Bengio, focusing on advanced AI or so-called frontier models.[13] It highlights a number of areas of risk which are only partially, or not at all, covered by other risk frameworks, although its focus is on 'existential risks' and developers of frontier models, rather than the main audience for this book. This report also highlights the 'open-ended' nature of genAI models: the fact that they can be used for a wide range of different purposes, which makes it particularly difficult to assess risk and mitigate against negative consequences.

Monetary Authority of Singapore
The Monetary Authority of Singapore (MAS) was an early mover in the field of AI governance and, although it focuses specifically on the financial sector, its frameworks and toolkits are widely applicable across industries. Its *Principles to Promote Fairness, Ethics, Accountability and Transparency (FEAT) in the Use of Artificial Intelligence and Data Analytics in Singapore's Financial Sector* were published in November 2018.[14] These principles are:

Fairness. Incorporating *Justifiability* – that the use of personal attributes as inputs, and the AI-driven decisions themselves, can be justified – and *Accuracy and Bias.*

Ethics. That the use of AI is aligned with the firm's ethical standards, values and codes of conduct, and that AI-driven decisions are held to at least the same ethical standards as human-driven decisions.

Accountability. Including: *Internal Accountability* – that AI-driven decision-making is approved by an appropriate internal authority and that a firm using AI is accountable for both internally developed and externally sourced AI models. *External Accountability* – that those impacted by AI-driven decisions have a right to request a review of such decisions.

Transparency. That individuals subject to an AI-driven decision are informed about the use of data and AI, and its contribution to the decision.

In May 2024 the Monetary Authority of Singapore published guidelines to cover generative AI: *Emerging Risks and Opportunities of Generative AI for Banks – A Singapore Perspective.*[15]

While numerous risk management frameworks exist, fortunately, they share significant overlap and consensus. One notable difference is that some frameworks include 'monitoring' or 'supply chain risk' as separate categories. We address these concerns as part of the assessment process in Chapter 9, rather than as an independent category of risk. In the next chapter, we synthesize these approaches into a single, comprehensive risk framework to serve as the foundation for building an AI governance program.

KEY INSIGHTS AND ACTIONS

- Risk comprises two key considerations: an event's *probability* of occurring and the *magnitude or degree of the consequences* of the corresponding event.
- AI risks, especially from genAI, are extremely difficult to predict due to their probabilistic nature, evolving behaviour and complexity, making them challenging to evaluate and control.
- Effective risk management starts with AI principles aligned to specific risks.
- Organizations must determine their AI risk appetite, balancing acceptable risk levels with the benefits. A comprehensive assessment uses 'risk lenses' such as strategic, operational, reputational and compliance risks.
- Monitoring external components, like third-party genAI models and external data sources, is critical as they often lack transparency and complicate risk evaluation.

- Frameworks and approaches from bodies such as the National Institute of Standards and Technology (NIST), the Organisation for Economic Co-operation and Development (OECD), The Council of Europe, the UK government and the Monetary Authority of Singapore offer valuable guidance and can be adapted to suit each organization's situation.
- Robust safeguards and controls can transform AI risk management into a competitive advantage, fostering trust and ensuring compliance.

5

A consolidated AI risk landscape

BUILDING TRUST IN VOXI'S GENAI POWERED
CUSTOMER SERVICE AGENT

Vodafone recognized that using genAI to power their VOXI customer service agent would improve the customer experience, providing greater flexibility and coverage, while ensuring a conversational tone of voice aligned with the brand to increase engagement. However, there was significant nervousness on the part of senior leadership about the potential for damage to customer experience and brand risk, if something were to go wrong. To address this, they deliberately scoped the initial design to be limited in capability and with access only to a narrow set of publicly available information. This made it easier to deliver safely while providing a base from which they could build future iterations.

Knowing they would need to secure approval from many parts of the organization they involved colleagues from these different teams (legal, marketing, etc.) from the outset, so that they were able both to educate them as they went along and proactively address their concerns. Testing was another challenge. As Jessica Shepherd, Director, Home Broadband, Vodafone UK, explains: 'We had proven testing approaches for traditional software but because of the non-deterministic nature of genAI outputs we had to dramatically change our testing approach, conducting 15,000 tests across multiple iterations, covering multiple tones, emotions and topics, as well as doing prompt injection attack testing to ensure we had consistently accurate and appropriate responses.'

Critical to getting all the senior approvers on board was demonstrating the system and allowing them to try to 'break it' to see if the bot would hallucinate by providing an inappropriate or irrelevant response. To manage this, the team established a robust set of operating procedures including automated monitoring for inappropriate responses with immediate alerts to multiple people, 'kill switches' to turn off the live bot if required, a phased launch approach to an initial subset of customers and 100 per cent human review at the start. Shepherd again: 'It was harder than we anticipated to "prove" that the automated monitoring for accuracy and tone of voice was working. In hindsight we should have established more robust processes for live evaluation/monitoring of accuracy and relevance before going live, to make it easier for us to get approval to relax the 100 per cent human oversight. At the end of the day, the project depended on me providing personal sponsorship and taking on the risk, but senior leadership also found it reassuring that we were partnering with Accenture, who brought examples of successful deployments with other clients.'

Drawing on the frameworks discussed in the previous chapter, as well as others, this chapter offers a consolidated risk landscape, illustrated with both traditional AI and genAI examples. These are the key risks that an AI goverance program will address. They will be examined in greater detail, together with approaches and tools for mitigating them, in Chapter 10.

ACCURACY AND RELIABILITY

Accuracy is critical for any system, whether AI-powered or not. However, as discussed earlier in Chapter 4 (see pages 35–6), the probabilistic nature of AI makes it challenging to fully understand the reasoning behind its outputs, which can compromise the ability to guarantee accuracy.

Reliability introduces an additional layer of complexity to the goal of achieving accurate and dependable AI systems. While AI models are developed in controlled environments, they are deployed in dynamic, real-world settings, where they continue to evolve as they process new data. External factors, such as changing customer behaviour or purchasing patterns, can significantly impact performance. For instance, during COVID-19, most supply chain forecasting models failed due to unforeseen shifts in buying habits, work routines, travel and other patterns. These changes meant that predictions based on historic patterns were no longer accurate. Ensuring reliability requires testing models for robustness under diverse conditions and implementing monitoring systems to flag behaviours that deviate from predefined expectations or tolerances.

Robustness and reliability are related but distinct concepts. Robustness measures how well an AI system performs under stress or extreme conditions, such as noisy or unusual data, and its resilience against errors or attacks. Reliability, on the other hand, focuses on the consistency of accurate and stable results under normal operating conditions, ensuring trustworthiness in everyday use.

INACCURACY IN TRADITIONAL AI – PATIENT DIAGNOSIS OF COVID-19

A study published in *Nature Machine Intelligence* sought to validate models which were proposed for the diagnosis or prognosis of COVID-19 from Chest X-Ray (CXR) or Computed Tomography (CT) images. For the period 1 January 2020 to 3 October 2020, the authors identified 2,212 papers and preprints, of which 415 were included after initial screening and, after further quality screening, 62 studies were examined in detail. The review found that none of the models identified were of potential clinical use due to methodological flaws and/or underlying biases.[1]

INACCURACY IN GENERATIVE AI – CHATGPT CODING ERROR

GenAI is generally highly effective at writing computer code. However, its tendency to 'hallucinate' remains a persistent risk. A colleague encountered this issue while using ChatGPT to debug code. After submitting flawed code, ChatGPT confidently explained the error and provided both the 'incorrect' and 'corrected' lines of code. The problem? The two lines of code were identical, as shown in Figure 5.1 below. This incident, humorously called the 'Schrodinger's Cat Hallucination', highlights the ongoing challenges with AI accuracy.[2]

FIGURE 5.1 The Schrodinger's Cat Hallucination

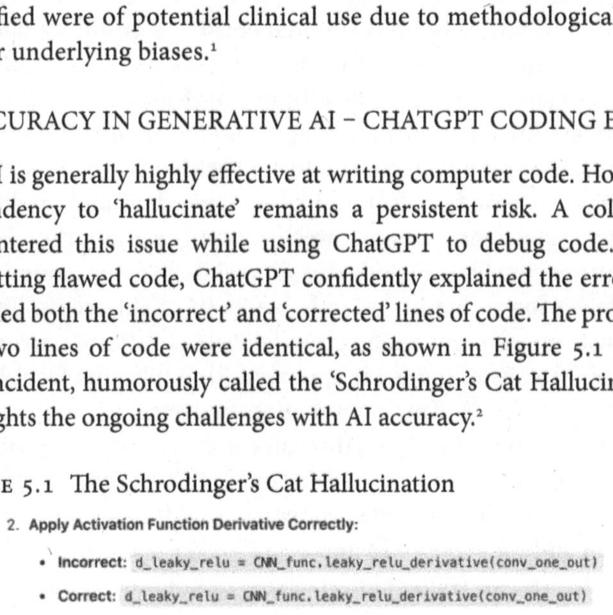

```
2. Apply Activation Function Derivative Correctly:

   • Incorrect: d_leaky_relu = CNN_func.leaky_relu_derivative(conv_one_out)

   • Correct: d_leaky_relu = CNN_func.leaky_relu_derivative(conv_one_out)
```

FAIRNESS AND BIAS

Bias is particularly complicated in the context of AI because it can have multiple meanings.[3] 'Bias' can refer to an AI system's mechanism for identifying patterns, which is core to its functionality. In analytical models, biased results can emerge unintentionally without the knowledge of the model's developer: this is termed 'implicit' or 'unintended' bias. This can happen for several reasons, most commonly because the data used to train the model is not representative of the target population and is therefore 'biased' in favour of, or against, a particular group. This can pose significant risks without the developer's or user's awareness. Identifying and mitigating unintended bias is crucial to building trustworthy AI. For a deeper review of the types of bias that can embed in AI and the harms that can result, we recommend the US National Institute of Standards and Technology (NIST) publication, *Towards a Standard for Identifying and Managing Bias in Artificial Intelligence.*[4]

The first challenge in addressing fairness is defining what is meant by 'fair'. Researchers and leading experts have proposed numerous definitions of fairness. Many papers highlight the trade-offs involved.[5] An influential talk at the 2018 Conference on Fairness, Accountability and Transparency concluded that it is rarely possible to satisfy each of their proposed 21 technical definitions of fairness simultaneously.[6] A common dilemma in this effort to achieve 'fairness' involves the debate on whether to focus on group or individual fairness as the ultimate measure of success.

To illustrate this conundrum: imagine a lending institution using an AI system trained on historical data to approve loans. The model predicts creditworthiness based on factors like income, debt and credit history. Historically, applicants from lower-income neighbourhoods, which might disproportionately include certain racial or socioeconomic groups, received fewer loans due to systemic biases in credit access. To address this, the institution might apply group fairness constraints, ensuring that a certain percentage of loans are approved for applicants from lower-income neighbourhoods. This intervention improves access to credit for disadvantaged groups. However, this can conflict with individual fairness: individuals with similar income, debt and credit histories might receive different loan offers because one resides in a low-income area targeted for remediation and the other does not.

In Chapter 10, we will explore fairness definitions, their applications and methods to reduce bias. Given the trade-offs inherent in fairness decisions, some of which may not be apparent until the AI system is in operation, organizations should proactively determine suitable metrics and thresholds to apply and direct the appropriate teams to routinely review and measure.

FAIRNESS AND BIAS IN TRADITIONAL AI – BIAS IN HEALTHCARE ALLOCATION

A 2019 study in *Science* uncovered that a widely used algorithm developed by a large US health insurer was biased based on race and income level.[7] The algorithm was meant to identify patients who could benefit from proactive care based on their health needs. The study authors, however, demonstrated that due to flaws in its design, the algorithm automated historical biases embedded in the data used to train the model, recommending less care for Black patients despite them having at least as many health needs as White patients.

'The algorithm learned from data produced by our current health system. Because of the many disparities in that system, it learned that Black patients get less care than White patients – even when they need more care because of their greater needs. Then it encoded those past disparities to make recommendations for the future,' said the study's first author, Ziad Obermeyer. Specifically, the problem arose because the algorithm was designed to look for where past costs had been allocated rather than to assess the amount of care needed or severity of patient health needs. The authors calculated that correcting the algorithm so that it no longer uses costs as a proxy for care needs would increase the percentage of Black patients receiving additional help from 17.7 to 46.5 per cent.

FAIRNESS AND BIAS IN GENERATIVE AI – GENDER BIAS IN AI TRANSLATION

The philosophy at the British Broadcasting Corporation (BBC), the UK's public service broadcaster, is to treat AI as an assistive technology to support people in their work. As James Fletcher, Responsible AI Lead at the BBC, explains: 'AI tools are still embryonic and flawed. For over 100 years we have operated on the principle that no content is published without at least one person reviewing it in addition to the author. The requirement for effective oversight is no different with AI and the person using AI remains accountable for the output. With principles like these in place to safeguard our values, we are actively experimenting to see where we can use AI to further support our colleagues.' One such area is in machine translation, which demonstrates the value of having a central responsible AI team to evaluate the tools. What the team noticed after conducting large-scale tests was that some tools introduced gender bias into their translation. This might not be obvious in an individual instance but, in aggregate, it was an issue. The team were able to use these results to help train the human translators in what to be careful about when using AI-assisted translation, helping to direct their attention when conducting their human reviews.

INTERPRETABILITY, EXPLAINABILITY AND TRANSPARENCY

The terms 'interpretability', 'explainability' and 'transparency' are often used interchangeably, but there are unique attributes that warrent distinction. We use **Interpretability** to refer to a technical explanation of how an AI model works, understandable by another data scientist. **Explainability** helps non-technical users comprehend model outputs, providing visibility into the model's design and its data sources, and the factors influencing its outputs. **Transparency** ensures people are aware when they are interacting with an AI model or subject to its recommendations, and provides for any legal notification requirements.

These elements are essential for trustworthy AI. Interpretability enables technical experts, and regulators if necessary, to validate a model's accuracy and functioning. Explainability helps users understand AI-driven decisions. Transparency is vital for user confidence – people often feel misled if they believe they are interacting with a human but later learn it was AI.

Explainability and interpretability are particularly challenging for genAI and neural network models, as we discuss further in Chapter 10.

EXPLAINABILITY IN TRADITIONAL AI – MEDICAL DIAGNOSIS

During the Covid pandemic one of the most critical decisions the UK's National Health Service (NHS) faced, on a daily basis, was allocating resources to where they were needed most. Faculty.AI, a company with deep data science expertise, was tasked with building the forecasting model which would predict where and when spikes in infections and demand for hospital services would occur. What was immediately apparent to Faculty's leadership was that the model's accuracy wasn't the only challenge: how were they going to persuade NHS leadership and the UK government to trust the model and rely on it to inform their decision-making? The key lay in making the predictions explainable by design. As Faculty CEO, Marc Warner, explains, 'the types of questions we were being asked were: "why does the model think this hospital is going to run out of beds? What information is it basing that on? How confident should I be in the forecast?" So, we designed the model such that users could click on any forecast and dig into the features which were driving it. That allowed the doctors to bring their own experience to the decision-making process and use the forecast as a tool to help them, not replace human judgement.'

The model was also designed so that forecasts could be compared against actual outcomes – effectively users could rewind time and see how the forecasts played out in reality. This allowed the model development team and the model users to build a strong sense of how reliable the model was and under what circumstances: it was less about *maximizing* confidence in the model than *calibrating* it. Faculty's model informed the allocation of over a billion pieces of personal protective equipment (PPE), facilitated the transfer of critically ill patients to hospitals with capacity and helped determine whether cities and hospitals were locked down. When the stakes are this high, human decision-makers must be able to understand *why* an AI system is making its recommendations and what degree of confidence to attach to them.

EXPLAINABILITY IN GENERATIVE AI – CALIFORNIA LEGAL CASE

In May 2025 two law firms were sanctioned for failing to check the content and explain the sources generated by AI. Judge Michael Wilner wrote that their brief contained 'bogus AI-generated research' which 'no attorney or staff member at either firm apparently cite-checked or otherwise reviewed.' After asking the law firms for clarification, they resubmitted the brief, which Judge Wilner said contained 'considerably more made-up citations and quotations beyond the two initial errors.'[8]

ACCOUNTABILITY

A human should be accountable for the functioning and outputs of all AI systems, though the level of involvement depends on the system's complexity and risk. Accountability can be exercised at two levels. Low consequential AI uses, like facial recognition technology used to unlock phones, may not require constant human monitoring. In such cases, a human is responsible for approving the system's functionality before deployment and addressing any issues afterwards. However, higher-risk AI systems may demand active human oversight or approval for every decision.

This need for human involvement can be characterized as three distinct approaches:

1. **Human in Control (HIC):** Humans retain ultimate authority and approve every decision made by the AI system.
2. **Human on the Loop (HOTL):** AI operates with autonomy, but humans maintain oversight and can intervene when necessary.
3. **Human in the Loop (HITL):** Humans and AI work collaboratively, with the AI assisting employees rather than replacing them – a 'human plus machine' model.[9]

Given genAI's challenges with accuracy and reliability, many organizations currently favour a human-plus-machine approach to ensure oversight, rather than allowing autonomous operation. Providing individuals with a clear path for contestability and redress when impacted by AI-driven decisions is another key element of accountability and fostering public trust. The catchphrase 'computer says no', popularized by the UK comedy *Little Britain* in 2004, humorously captured public frustration with opaque, technology-driven decisions long before AI became widespread.[10]

Another risk to consider is over-reliance on AI recommendations, known as 'automation bias', when users assume the machine is always correct and accept its outputs without question. Research published in *MIT Sloan Management Review* highlights how AI-augmented systems can cause humans to lose agency, defer to the AI and feel less responsible for outcomes.[11] As we saw earlier with the discussion of accuracy, genAI systems are prone to making mistakes, so employees must constantly be on their guard, careful when to use AI and independently verify results. A study in *Radiology* asked radiologists to check a selection of breast cancer scans which had been labelled by an AI assistant. Researchers set the experiment such that the AI assistant provided a false assessment in certain cases. Inexperienced and moderately experienced radiologists dropped their cancer-detecting accuracy from around 80 to about 22 per cent when presented with a falsely labelled scan, while the accuracy of very experienced radiologists dropped from nearly 80 to 45 per cent.[12] Paradoxically, the more accurate AI systems become, the more difficult it may be for people to spot occasional mistakes, even if the consequences are significant. A 2025 paper has also highlighted the risk of 'mechanised convergence', whereby users of genAI tools tend to produce a less diverse set of outcomes for the same task, compared to those without, suggesting a lack of reflective judgement.[13]

Accountability also encompasses compliance with legislation and regulations. Those responsible for an AI system must ensure that its development – including the data it is trained on – and the impact of its outputs adhere to all applicable legal requirements. In a complex AI supply chain, accountability is not always easy to assign: the EU AI Act attempts to clarify roles and responsibilities (see Chapters 9 and 12), but variance in laws across the globe make compliance a constant challenge.

New risks emerge as we embrace agentic AI and multi-agent systems (MAS) – teams of AI agents collaborating to achieve shared goals. These risks stem from the increased autonomy granted to agents, which possess advanced capabilities such as reasoning, planning and independently taking actions on our behalf. Whereas, for example, a chatbot can provide instructions on how to conduct a malicious cyber-attack, an AI agent could potentially execute one. The risks of agentic AI were still emerging at the time of writing but include the following:

Multiplicative risk: MAS compound single-agent risks, since failure in one agent – for example, a hallucination – can propagate to an agent it communicates with, cascading to yet more agents, leading to unanticipated failure.* This can be illustrated with a simple example:

Imagine a MAS designed to help colleagues book vacation time. The role of the first agent might be to understand the user's input and determine the number of days' vacation the employee wishes to book. The second agent's role might be to check in the system that the employee has enough vacation allowance remaining. A third agent

---

*The popular parlour game 'Pass the Message' is a demonstration of how a simple miscommunication in one utterance can lead to a completely unanticipated outcome when relayed from one person to the next.

then books the desired dates in the vacation planning schedule. Each agent therefore needs to understand an input and then take an action, and each agent could potentially make an error.

The average factuality score of the leaderboard for Google's FACTS Grounding benchmark, as reported in the Stanford AI Index Report 2025, is 74.8%, or a failure rate of 25.2%. But this is the likely accuracy for each agent independently. We can calculate the failure rate of the three agents comprising the MAS as follows:

MAS rate of failure = $1-S^n$

Where S = the success rate of each individual agent;

n = the number of agents in the system.

So, for this example, the failure rate of a three-agent system rises to 58.1%, compared with 25.2% for a single agent.

In practice, an organization would implement a suite of additional guardrails to reduce the error rate of the underlying foundation model. Let us assume that these guardrails reduce the error rate of each individual agent to 2%, still the combined error rate of three agents would be 5.9% and in the case of, say, five agents this would rise to 9.6% compared with 2% for a single agent.[*]

Misalignment: agents may be designed to create and execute plans which maximize a 'reward', the human-initiated objective. This gives rise to the classic AI alignment problem: the agent's plans, despite being optimal according to the agent's own evaluation, are not necessarily aligned to what humans might want or expect. The misalignment problem is well-documented, including in this paper on long term planning agents.[15]

Accountability: determining who is responsible for the actions of a highly autonomous MAS may be hard. Imagine a scenario in an organization where the agents collaborate across different departments and areas of responsibility. Who is accountable for ensuring appropriate controls at each step?

---

[*]This illustration presents a somewhat simplified analysis. Additional complexities could include, for example, cascading hallucinations that can lead to errors in reasoning, resulting in completely unexpected actions and outcomes.

Collusion: agents representing competing companies might learn to collude, setting prices or policies that disadvantage consumers. Over time, these interconnected AI agent networks could grow increasingly complex and opaque, making it challenging for humans to monitor and control their activities.

ACCOUNTABILITY IN TRADITIONAL AI – CRUISE DRIVERLESS CAR

In October 2023, a Cruise driverless car failed to recognize a woman trapped beneath it after she was struck by another vehicle and thrown into its path, dragging her 20 feet and inflicting severe injuries. When reporting the incident to the California Public Utilities Commission the next day, a Cruise employee mentioned only the crash, omitting the horrific dragging. Rather than taking full accountability for the behaviour of the car, the company also initially withheld a lengthy video recording from the car's cameras, only disclosing its existence after the Department of Motor Vehicles discovered it during discussions with National Highway Traffic Safety Administration investigators.[16]

ACCOUNTABILITY IN GENERATIVE AI – AIR CANADA CUSTOMER SERVICE

In February 2024, Air Canada was ordered to honour a payment to a customer misled by its customer service chatbot.[17] The customer had requested a bereavement fare based on instructions provided by the company's chatbot. Air Canada rejected the claim, stating it did not align with their policy, and argued in court that the chatbot was a separate legal entity responsible for its actions. The tribunal ruled against Air Canada, holding the company accountable for the chatbot it owned and deployed.[18]

PRIVACY

There are two primary privacy risks when using sensitive data to train AI models. The first involves using data without permission. Organizations should ensure all data used aligns with permissions granted by the data owner to ensure compliance with the General Data Protection Regulation

(GDPR) and similar legislation. While most organizations now have strong data protection programs, foundation models raise new challenges. These models are trained on vast amounts of internet data, often without clear or verifiable permissions for specific commercial purposes. This also highlights a key difference in attitudes to data by region: in the US, for example, there is a presumption that once content has appeared in the public domain, it is 'fair use' and without express limitation on its use; whereas in Europe, the need to obtain permission for a new use of personal data persists even if that data has already been made public.

A second consideration is maintaining anonymity when using sensitive data for training. While anonymization may seem simple – removing names, addresses or identifiers – it often fails in practice. Cross-referencing data points can re-identify individuals, as has been demonstrated with supposedly anonymous datasets.[19] Extensive research into anonymization techniques has led to the development of Privacy Enhancing Technologies, discussed in Chapter 10.

The risk of surveillance and control can be concerning when AI tools are used by governments, illegal organizations or corporations. AI can facilitate mass public surveillance and, in the workplace, monitor employee behaviour. Many forms of AI-based workforce monitoring are explicitly prohibited under the EU AI Act, as discussed in Chapter 12.

PRIVACY CONCERNS IN TRADITIONAL AI – THE CLEARVIEW AI CASE

Clearview AI became a focal point in privacy debates after it was found to be scraping billions of images from the Web without user consent to create a facial recognition database. Sold to law enforcement and private companies, this database sparked global privacy concerns and lawsuits, with headlines like 'The Secretive Company That Might End Privacy as We Know It'.[20] The lack of consent in data collection highlighted the risks of AI-powered facial recognition misuse.

Clearview faced multiple legal challenges, including a £7.5m fine from the UK's Information Commissioner's Office, although overturned in October 2023 because its clients were non-UK law enforcement agencies.[21] This case highlights the need for clarification of AI and data privacy rules.[22]

PRIVACY RISKS IN GENERATIVE AI – DEEPFAKE PORNOGRAPHY

Deepfakes are AI-generated synthetic media that manipulate a person's likeness to create false and often harmful content. A recent study found that 98 per cent of deepfakes are pornographic, with genAI used to superimpose faces onto explicit material, creating hyper-realistic videos or images.[23] These fakes cause severe emotional and reputational harm, with 99 per cent of victims being women or girls.[24]

In early 2024, American Grammy-award winning musician Taylor Swift became the target of artificial images depicting her in sexual or violent scenarios. One post was viewed over 47 million times before removal, highlighting just how difficult it is to control the spread of such content.[25] If this can happen to a high-profile individual with significant resources, the consequences for a less-protected victim, such as a high school teenager, are disturbing.

SECURITY

When AI models are deployed outside the lab, attempts to subvert them are inevitable. AI models, such as those used in self-driving cars, process inputs from the world around them and act accordingly. The challenge is ensuring robustness against deliberate manipulation. For instance, early self-driving car research showed that minor changes to road signs could cause the algorithm to misinterpret the sign.

With large language models (LLMs), the risks are even greater due to their open-ended interaction with humans. Developers must guard against attacks such as prompt injection – provoking unsafe behaviour; jailbreaking* – bypassing safety guardrails; and data inversion – extracting confidential training data.

---

*A hacker called Amadon was able to trick ChatGPT into producing bomb-making instructions by telling the bot to 'play a game', after which the hacker used a series of connecting prompts to get the chatbot to create a detailed science-fiction fantasy world where the bot's safety guidelines would not apply. Tricking a chatbot into ignoring its preprogrammed restrictions is known as 'jailbreaking'. Franceschi-Bicchierai, L., 'Hacker tricks ChatGPT into giving out detailed instructions for making homemade bombs', 12 September 2024, https://techcrunch.com/2024/09/12/hacker-tricks-chatgpt-into-giving-out-detailed-instructions-for-making-homemade-bombs/.

Organizations must also guard against the risk of genAI being used to create highly convincing deepfakes for malicious attacks. Deepfakes have been successfully used by criminals to steal money from companies and to spread false information aimed at harming an organization's reputation.[26]

Foundation models present further security challenges, including misuse for creating harmful weapons or enhancing cyberattacks. For example, authorities confirmed that, before he blew up a Cybertruck in front of the Trump International Hotel in January 2025, the assailant consulted ChatGPT for instructions.[27]

The open-ended nature of foundation models, especially open-sourced, makes it difficult to enforce robust safeguards after deployment.

SECURITY RISKS IN TRADITIONAL AI – COMPUTER VISION VULNERABILITIES IN AUTONOMOUS VEHICLES

Researchers demonstrated the vulnerability of computer vision systems to adversarial attacks by subtly altering a 'stop' sign with strategically placed tape, causing an AI system to misclassify it as a 45mph speed limit – see Figure 5.2 below.[28] This experiment exposed a critical flaw: minor changes to the physical environment can mislead AI systems.

FIGURE 5.2 Computer vision vulnerabilities

Source: Eykholt, K. et al., 'Robust Physical World Attacks on Deep Learning Models'.

As these technologies become more integrated into daily life, such vulnerabilities pose significant security risks, especially in safety-critical domains such as medical, financial and military contexts, where misinterpretations could have fatal or high-impact consequences.

SECURITY RISKS IN GENERATIVE AI – DEEPFAKE FRAUD IN A HONG KONG MULTINATIONAL COMPANY

On 5 January 2024, a Hong Kong-based multinational company suffered a $25m loss in a sophisticated deepfake attack. Fraudsters used advanced AI to replicate the CFO's face and voice, successfully tricking the finance team into authorizing fraudulent transfers.[29]

In the past, online fraud was limited by factors like technology constraints, manual execution, restricted access to personal data and poor personalization, making scams less sophisticated and easier to detect. Advances in AI have eliminated many of these barriers. Deepfake technologies now enable attackers to convincingly mimic voices and appearances, exploiting the authority and trust humans rely on for decision-making.

AI-enabled fraud is expanding across new mediums – written, video and audio – necessitating a re-evaluation of security practices to address this growing threat.

INTELLECTUAL PROPERTY AND CONFIDENTIALITY

Intellectual Property (IP) and confidentiality concerns have become significant risks with the rise of genAI. Foundation models are trained on vast amounts of data, which may have been scraped from the internet indiscriminately and without data quality controls. As a result, licensed content on those sites, such as images from libraries or text from online newspapers, can be inappropriately included in training data without proper licensing. This practice has sparked legal disputes in various jurisdictions, such as *Getty Images vs. Stability AI*, and the number of such cases is expected to grow significantly. The publication *Wired* provides a helpful tracker of US intellectual property cases relating to AI.[30]

Users of genAI tools also risk plagiarism, as the generated content may unknowingly reproduce someone else's text, without identifying or referencing its origin. In response, some AI developers have taken steps to include compliance measures. For example, Adobe maintains that its genAI image tools are trained only on licensed data.[31] Similarly, IBM and Microsoft offer certain corporate clients some indemnification against potential IP claims arising from genAI use (see Chapter 10).

Another key risk with genAI is that user inputs may be used to train the foundation models. While some companies offer opt-out options[32] or guarantee that data won't be collected when using their platform – for example, Microsoft Azure for its commercial and public sector customers[33] – these measures are often not prominently displayed. The effectiveness and scope of these opt-outs can also vary. Organizations using genAI should update relevant policies and take precautions to ensure employees do not inadvertently leak sensitive company or personal information.[34] A 2024 survey by Infosecurity Magazine revealed that one in five UK companies has had potentially sensitive corporate data exposed via employee use of genAI.[35]

To address intellectual property and data privacy risks, the Italian data protection regulator temporarily banned OpenAI's ChatGPT in March 2023. The ban was lifted after OpenAI implemented changes, including enhanced transparency on data processing, opt-out options to prevent conversations from being used to train algorithms, age verification for users in Italy and notices warning that ChatGPT may generate inaccurate information.[36]

INTELLECTUAL PROPERTY CHALLENGES IN TRADITIONAL AI – GOOGLE BOOKS LITIGATION

In 2004, Google launched Google Books, a project to digitize millions of books and make them searchable online. The initiative faced lawsuits from authors and publishers, who accused Google of copyright violations for using their works without permission. Google argued that the 'fair use' doctrine permitted this use, allowing them to provide 'snippets' without replicating in full or replacing the need to buy the books.

An AI-powered optical character recognition program enabled the scanning, indexing and searching of millions of texts. In 2013, the Federal appellate court upheld the ruling in Google's favour[37] as protected under the 'fair use' doctrine in the US.[38] Subsequent challenges to the ruling were unsuccessful. This case highlights the tension between innovation – Google's project to make digital books available to libraries – and the intellectual property rights held by the authors of over 20 million books used without permission or payment of license fees.

INTELLECTUAL PROPERTY AND GENERATIVE AI – GETTY IMAGES VS STABILITY AI CASE

In early 2023, Getty Images filed a lawsuit against Stability AI, a provider of open-source image generation models, highlighting unresolved IP issues for genAI.[39] Getty alleged that Stability AI used millions of its images without permission to train Stable Diffusion, one such model, giving rise to violations including copyright infringement, data scraping and potential violation of other laws.[40] Stability AI, however, argued this constitutes 'fair use' and falls outside copyright restrictions. Additionally, Getty accused Stability AI of trademark infringement, claiming AI-generated images include watermarks resembling those of Getty, creating potential brand confusion.

In this example used in the complaint filed against Stability AI, the image on the left is a Getty Images original, watermarked image allegedly copied by Stability AI and used to train its model. The watermarked image on the right is output delivered using the model:[41]

FIGURE 5.3 Getty Images vs Stability AI

Source: Getty Images (US), Inc. Plaintiff, v. Stability AI, Inc. in The United States District Court for the District of Delaware

This lawsuit is still underway and highlights broader issues, including the lack of transparency in how AI companies source training data and the unfair competitive advantages gained from using copyrighted material without proper licensing. It also highlights the absence of clear regulations governing AI development, with legal proceedings across the globe and the application of varying laws, complicating the landscape. Beyond legal implications, the case raises ethical questions about using unauthorized human-created content in AI and its potential impact on the revenue models of creative industries and professionals.

In February 2025, a significant lawsuit involving training data was decided in favour of the plaintiff, Thomson Reuters, who sued a legal AI startup for copyright infringement after discovering the startup used third-party documents that copied 'headnotes' from Thomson Reuters' Westlaw to train its AI model.[42] In the ruling, the judge found that the startup's use of copyrighted material for training data was not covered by the fair use exception, particularly because the startup 'meant to compete with Westlaw by developing a market substitute.'[43]

WORKFORCE

Even before AI's widespread adoption, automation was replacing straightforward human tasks, often replicating keystrokes to mimic human actions. As AI adoption grew, this evolved into 'intelligent automation', enabling systems to make decisions and improve efficiency. With genAI, these systems could imitate a far wider range of human tasks. In some cases, AI agents now replace human operators, while in others, they assist humans, enhancing their effectiveness and efficiency.

An early Stanford University study showed that AI assistants can significantly boost productivity, particularly for less experienced workers, with reported increases of 14 per cent.[44] A detailed Boston Consulting Group (BCG) study further supports that genAI will have a profound impact on human jobs, reshaping workforce dynamics across industries.[45] And in January 2025, Goldman Sachs CEO David Solomon discussed the dramatic impact of genAI on one of the most labour-intensive processes in investment banking – drafting IPO prospectuses. Traditionally requiring weeks of work by a team of six, he said that AI can generate 95 per cent of the document 'in minutes', leaving the final 5 per cent for human expertise. 'The last 5 percent now matters because the rest is now a commodity,' Solomon emphasized, underscoring AI's role in automating routine tasks while elevating the importance of human oversight.[46]

Before the advent of genAI, it was widely believed that creative industries would be largely immune to AI-driven job displacement. However, genAI's ability to produce high-quality text, images and video has changed that expectation. Economists remain divided on whether AI impact on jobs is a short-term disruption, perhaps limited to certain sectors and tasks, or signals a long-term decline in demand for human labour.

There are some AI-related roles that specifically impact employee welfare, such as content moderation or training genAI models through reinforcement learning from human feedback, particularly when addressing sensitive or explicit content. Reports have highlighted the psychological toll of such work, along with instances of unfairly low wages.[47]

WORKFORCE IMPACT OF TRADITIONAL AI – JOB DISPLACEMENT CONCERNS WITH AUTONOMOUS VEHICLES IN CHINA

In 2024, China's robotaxi industry surged, with companies like Baidu's Apollo Go expanding in cities such as Beijing, Guangzhou and Wuhan. Apollo Go operates over 500 robotaxis in Wuhan, sparking public interest and trending on social media, showcasing growing enthusiasm for autonomous transportation.[48] However, this rise in use has raised concerns among traditional taxi and ride-hailing drivers, who fear job losses as robotaxis gain market share. Just as ride-sharing disrupted traditional taxis, autonomous vehicles threaten millions of livelihoods. Proponents argue that automation increases efficiency and lowers costs, but concerns over widespread job displacement are significant. These fears extend beyond drivers to truckers, train conductors and pilots – and other jobs susceptible to automation.

WORKFORCE IMPACT OF GENERATIVE AI – AUTOMATION BIAS WRITING NEWS STORIES

In January 2023 it was reported that *CNET* issued corrections to 41 of 77 stories created using AI tools as part of a series for 'CNET Money'. In its public statement after the factual inaccuracies had been uncovered, *CNET* wrote: 'every one of our articles is reviewed and modified by a human editor'. This suggests AI alone was not the cause and that automation bias may have contributed to the eroneous articles.[49]

ENVIRONMENT AND SUSTAINABILITY

As genAI systems become increasingly integrated into industries and society, their environmental impact – particularly in greenhouse gas emissions, energy consumption and water usage for cooling data centres – continues to grow.

Training large-scale genAI models contributes heavily to carbon emissions. For instance, a single ChatGPT response uses 10 times as much energy as a Google search did before Google implemented genAI in search[50] and generating 16 ChatGPT responses emits as much CO_2 as boiling a kettle.[51] Google's 2024 Environment Report described a 48 per cent increase in CO_2 emissions compared to 2019 and a year-on-year increase of 13 per cent, due in part to AI deployment. They commented that reducing emissions would remain challenging due to increasing energy demands from AI.[52] Similarly, Microsoft stated in their 2024 Sustainability report that their total emissions were up 29.1 per cent (compared to 2020), due to cloud operations and expanding data centers.* Even before the genAI boom, cloud computing produced a larger carbon footprint than the entire airline industry.[53]

The demand for energy is also accelerating. The 2024 US Data Center Energy Usage Report estimates a compounded annual growth rate of between 13–27 per cent, from 2023 to 2028, compared to 18 per cent from 2018 to 2023. This equates to between 6.7–12.0 per cent of total US electricity consumption in 2028, compared to 4.4 per cent in 2023.[54] Global data centres use enormous amounts of electricity, with usage in 2021 estimated at 220–320 Terawatt hours, accounting for 0.9–1.3 per cent of global electricity demand.[55] The rising energy demands of data centres hosting AI models are straining power grids, especially in regions like the US, where capacity is insufficient to meet projected needs.[56] As a result, some of the largest tech companies are investing in nuclear-powered energy plants to meet their anticipated energy requirements.[57]

As genAI adoption grows, the associated energy and operational costs are expected to rise. To help address this concern, the EU AI Act includes an Energy Disclosure Requirement, mandating foundation model providers to disclose energy consumption and compute resources used during training.[58]

---

*This is the sum of their Scope 1, 2 and 3 emissions, with Scope 3 emissions being the driver for the total increase. See, '2024 Environmental Sustainability Report', https://www.microsoft.com/en-us/corporate-responsibility/sustainability/report.

GenAI's environmental impact is also unevenly distributed: regions with clean energy can somewhat mitigate its effects, but areas relying on fossil fuels or facing resource shortages experience disproportionate harm. As genAI accelerates data centre usage, the growing demand for energy and critical minerals exacerbates environmental degradation, reinforcing global inequalities in resource use and pollution.[59]

Despite the continued environmental impact of genAI, progress is being made to make models increasingly efficient, thereby reducing environmental impacts, as demonstrated by the release of Deepseek-R1 in late January 2025.[60]

ENVIRONMENT AND SUSTAINABILITY - DATA CENTRE COOLING STRAINS WATER RESOURCES

A 2023 report claimed that Microsoft's Iowa datacentres consumed 11.5 million gallons of water every month for the previous two years – 6 per cent of the district's peak water usage during summer months – causing tensions in this water-scarce area.[61] Similar challenges are emerging in drought-prone regions like Arizona[62] and Oregon.[63] A University of California research paper, 'Making AI Less "Thirsty": Uncovering and Addressing the Secret Water Footprint of AI Models', forecast that by 2027, AI operations may require up to 6.6 billion cubic metres of water annually for cooling data centres, which is approximately half the annual water consumption in the United Kingdom.[64]

KEY INSIGHTS AND ACTIONS

This chapter outlines a consolidated risk landscape that highlights the following key concerns for senior executives and others responsible for AI governance:

- **Accuracy and Reliability**: ensuring the AI system performs as intended and delivers accurate results under both expected and unexpected conditions. Robustness refers to an algorithm's ability to maintain performance and accuracy even under extreme conditions.
- **Fairness and Bias**: determining fairness objectives and appropriate measurements – centred on outcomes and context-dependent;

considered from the perspective of all stakeholders who will be affected by the system in question. Minimizing unintended bias and discrimination.

- **Interpretability, Explainability and Transparency**: ensuring that the developers of the AI system understand technically how it arrived at a given output and that impacted individuals can be given a straightforward explanation which they can understand. Proactively notifying impacted individuals when they are subject to an AI-driven system or decision.
- **Accountability**: designating executive(s) to be accountable for the performance and outputs of the AI system and compliance with legislation and regulations, as well as any other stated objectives. Guarding against over-reliance and automation bias on the part of AI system users. Providing impacted individuals with a clear path for contestability and redress.
- **Privacy**: using data with appropriate permissions; safeguarding sensitive content and identifiers. Determining appropriate levels of surveillance and control.
- **Security**: protecting against attacks which could result in data leakage or adversarial perversion of the AI system. Preventing the use of AI systems for conducting cyberattacks. Safeguarding against danger to human life, health, property or the environment, including through enhanced risk of chemical, biological, radiological and nuclear weapons.
- **Intellectual Property and Confidentiality**: preventing plagiarism or copyrighted, trademarked or licensed content being used without authorization. Protecting against the leakage of confidential information.
- **Workforce**: minimizing the negative impact of AI on employment. Mitigating the psychological harm from some AI-related tasks on colleagues.
- **Environment and Sustainability**: minimizing the negative environmental impact from training AI models on large amounts of data, and from each use of the model.

6

Implementing AI governance

START NOW, AND KEEP GOING

'You have to build your AI governance program from the start, knowing that it will never be finished and will need constant updating as the landscape evolves: you must plan and staff accordingly. And that's not a reason to delay starting.'

Lara Liss, Chief Privacy and Data Trust Officer at GE HealthCare

This chapter starts by discussing the appointment of leadership to drive the AI governance program and how to conduct a 'gap assessment' against existing governance processes. We then describe the necessary building blocks for comprehensive AI governance. Comparing the results of the gap assessment with the target state allows leadership to prioritize activities and develop a roadmap for design and implementation. This target program architecture provides the structure for Section Two.

WHERE TO BEGIN?

Successful large-scale initiatives in organizations start with senior leadership: establishing AI governance is no exception. An executive team member should sponsor the initiative, with accountability resting with an Executive Oversight Board, or similar body, comprising C-Suite or near-C-Suite leaders (see Chapter 8 for a detailed discussion of operating model).* Ultimately, the program should report to the Board of Directors. While senior accountability is essential, there is no single 'right answer' for determining which department or function should lead AI governance. Organizations have successfully implemented AI governance initiatives under the leadership of various executive functions. However, one constant factor for success is the need for a dedicated C-suite leader to oversee AI governance, ensuring it remains a critical organizational priority.

C-Suite accountability provides direction, managing AI concerns, allocating budgets and ensuring enterprise adoption of best practices. We have seen leadership from chief data officers, chief privacy officers, general counsel, chief AI officers and others. The common variable is their interest in securing the right outcomes as well as ownership of potential liability for this technology.† Chief information security officers are also stepping into this role, leveraging their expertise in cybersecurity to address genAI threats and their proven ability to develop programs that protect organizations from security threats.

WHAT MATTERS MOST WHEN SELECTING YOUR AI GOVERNANCE LEAD

1. Passion and belief in the importance of AI and its governance
2. Political capital to gain cross-enterprise, ongoing support for the program
3. Access to budget

As Evie Stenhouse, Chief Privacy Officer and Responsible AI Lead at Natura & Co., the cosmetics company, explains: 'You need passion and intellectual curiosity to lead this area – it matters less where they sit in the organization.'

---

*The various governance forums described in this book may also be referred to with different names. We adopt one name for consistency and encourage the reader to focus on the remit of each body.

†The IAPP-EY Professionalizing Organizational AI Governance Report (December 2023) found that 63 per cent of organizations assign AI governance to their privacy function. This figure, however, may reflect the IAPP's membership focus. LaLande, B. and Kanthasamy, S., 'IAPP-EY Professionalizing Organizational AI Governance Report', December 2023, https://iapp.org/resources/article/professionalizing-organizational-ai-governance-report-summary/.

The AI governance lead's first challenge is securing active participation from senior colleagues across relevant functions to join the Executive Oversight Board. Without executive-level support, decisions may face delays or falter. The Executive Oversight Board may later designate a senior executive, such as a chief responsible AI officer, to take primary responsibility. In some organizations, this role is added to an existing position, like chief AI officer or chief privacy officer.

The Executive Oversight Board must also secure seed funding to establish the Operational Management Board, responsible for the day-to-day design and implementation of the AI governance program. For larger organizations, the Operational Oversight Board should be supported by working groups that allocate time and resources to the initiative (see Chapter 8 for a detailed discussion on required skills, functions and working group structures).

Most organizations will already have some data and/or AI governance practices in place, often developed organically across different parts of the business. The next step is conducting a gap analysis to identify the most urgent priorities for AI governance and existing initiatives to build upon. This process should include reviewing governance structures in related areas, such as data privacy, data governance, cybersecurity, procurement and the data science model development lifecycle. Annex C of ISO/IEC standard 23894:2023 provides a helpful table mapping AI risk management processes to the model development lifecycle.[1] Extending these existing frameworks to incorporate AI controls is often more efficient and less burdensome than creating entirely new structures.

A thorough gap analysis helps accelerate the creation of a consistent, comprehensive AI governance program that embeds responsible AI practices from use case conception. It also allows the Operational Oversight Board to develop a roadmap, prioritize efforts and estimate budgets and timelines.

Later in this chapter, we present a practical framework for implementing AI governance to serve as the target state for the gap analysis. The requirements for the gap analysis are aligned to the foundational components of this target framework and the template should be read in conjunction with Figure 6.4 below. This exercise helps outline the approximate sequencing of activities, indicated by the priority levels in Figure 6.1 below, some of which can proceed in parallel. We avoid terms like 'complete' for the final column, because AI governance is a continuously evolving process and should adapt with the technology and its uses.

FIGURE 6.1 AI Governance: Gap Analysis Checklist

Requirement	Priority	Critical Gap	Needs Improvement	Established	Owner	Next Steps
Principles	1					
Policy(s)	1					
Standards	2					
Definition of AI	1					
AI risk taxonomy and appetite	1					
Accountabilities	1					
Teams: people and skills	2					
Training	2					
Operating procedures	3					
AI Inventory	2					
Checkpoints	1					
Assessment process	2					
Assessment questions	2					
Controls	2					
Tools	2					
Measurement metrics	3					
Reporting	3					
Audit	3					
Documentation templates	3					
Documentation repository	3					
Governance platform / process control	3					

As part of the gap assessment, it may be helpful to benchmark your preparedness with lessons from others navigating this space. Many organizations find Microsoft's *Responsible AI Maturity Model* useful.[2] It contains 24 empirically derived dimensions that are key to an organization's AI governance maturity. The dimensions and their levels are based on interviews and focus groups with over 90 Responsible AI specialists and AI practitioners and are organized into three main categories: Organizational Foundations, Team Approach and Responsible AI Practice. The US National Institute of Standards and Technology (NIST) also provides a detailed set of benchmarking questions in the 'Measure' section of their Risk Management Framework.[3]

The Stanford AI Index Report 2025 cites a survey by McKinsey & Company which identifies the areas of AI risk which organizations consider to be most relevant and the degree to which they are actively mitigated, see Figure 6.2 below.[4] In most cases active mitigation falls well below 50 per cent, highlighting the need for concerted investment in AI governance.

Respondents were also asked which AI risks were most relevant for their business:

FIGURE 6.2 AI risks: considered relevant vs. actively mitigated, 2024, % of respondents

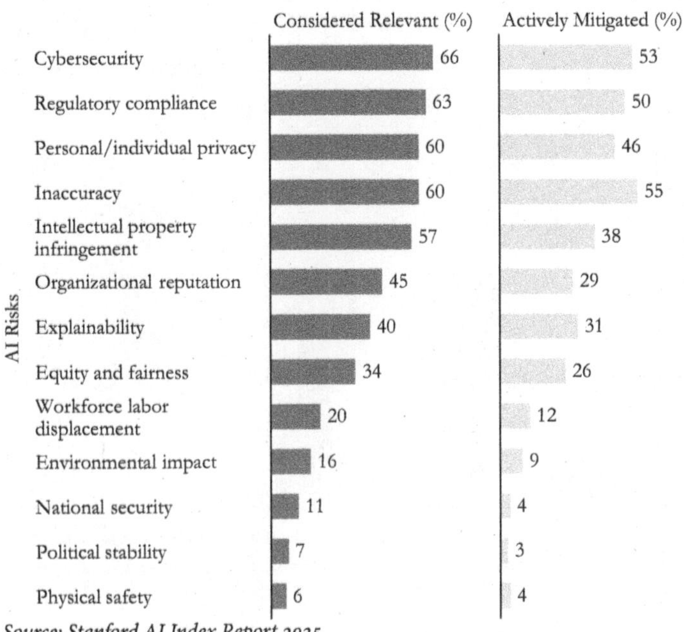

Source: Stanford AI Index Report 2025

A paper published in October 2024, *Responsible AI in the Global Context: Maturity Model and Survey*, highlights the disparity between organizational and operational maturity.[5] Figure 6.3 below, taken from the paper, supports the view that implementing AI governance ('operational maturity') lags far behind creating principles and policies ('organizational maturity') – 'managed' and 'optimized' are the two most advanced states of maturity. Furthermore, the survey focused on organizations with global revenues exceeding $499m and in our experience, smaller companies with more limited resources tend to be less advanced in their implementation of AI governance.

FIGURE 6.3 Comparison of Organizational and Operational Maturity Levels Across Organizations

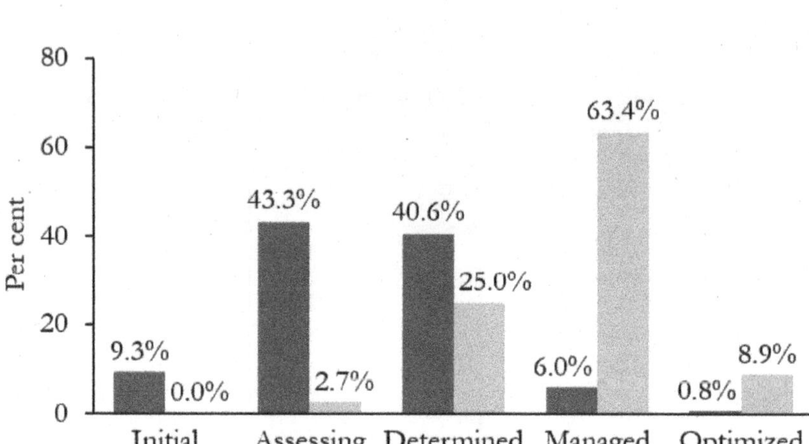

Source: Reuel, A. et al., 'Responsible AI in the Global Context: Maturity Model and Survey' Figure 6

KEY EARLY DESIGN QUESTIONS FOR AN AI GOVERNANCE PROGRAM

Consider whether you should establish:

1. A central AI governance team which is permanently resourced to drive the design and subsequent running of the program;
2. A federated structure with resources and accountabilities devolved across the organization;
3. A virtual team comprising individuals from different departments who work part-time on AI governance as a project.

A PRACTICAL FRAMEWORK FOR IMPLEMENTING AI GOVERNANCE

Figure 6.4 below depicts our recommended framework for establishing AI governance, which this chapter will outline briefly. Subsequent chapters will delve deeper into each element in turn to provide a comprehensive understanding.

FIGURE 6.4 Foundational Components for Implementing AI Governance

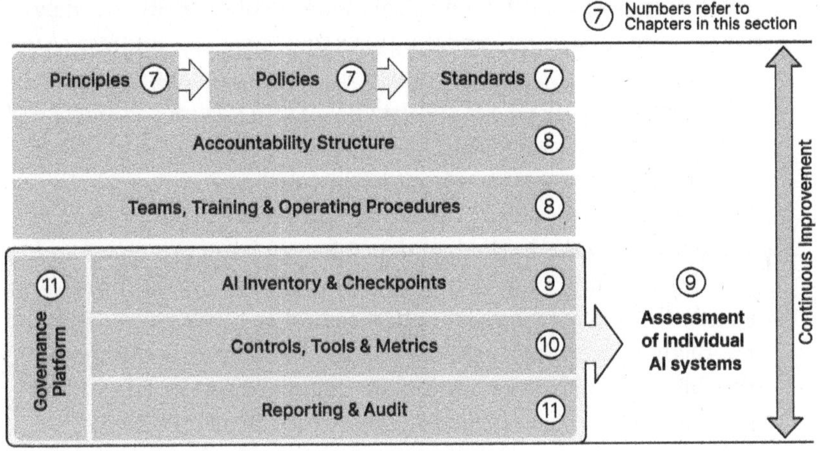

The process for assessing individual AI systems (step 9 above) is explained in Figure 6.5 below.

FIGURE 6.5 Assessment of Individual AI Systems

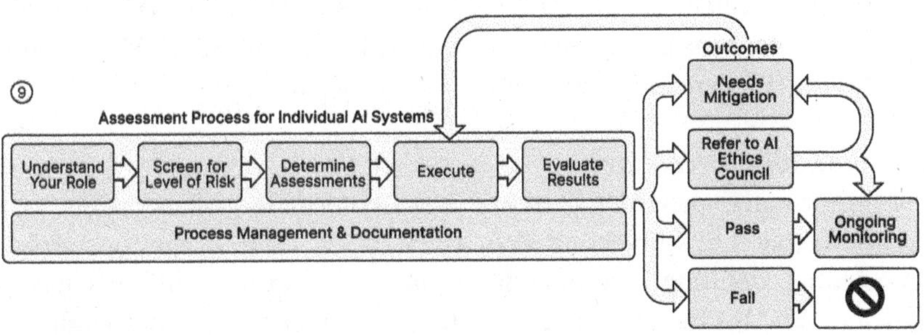

Principles, Policies and Standards

An AI governance program enforces desired behaviour by establishing rules and processes, structured in layers of increasing detail:

1. **AI Principles**: high-level statements that align with and apply the organization's core values to AI goals and use. Often published openly, they demonstrate a commitment to safe, responsible AI use and provide aspirational guidance for employees to follow and for public awareness.

2. **AI Policies**: these translate principles into actionable internal rules employees must follow. This may involve creating a new AI-specific policy or updating existing ones to address AI considerations. Regulated industries, such as banking, often adapt existing policies for consistency and to ensure compliance with various requirements. The key is ensuring policies are clear and comprehensive with respect to expected AI use.

3. **Standards**: also called operating procedures or protocols, standards provide detailed guidance for applying principles and policies in daily work. Unlike concise principles and policies, standards are more detailed, often spanning many pages. These are distinct from international standards, such as published by the International Organization for Standardization (ISO), but serve a similar role in operationalizing high-level objectives.

This layered approach ensures both strategic alignment and practical implementation. Multinational organizations often adopt the strictest global AI legislation as a unified standard or create flexible controls to meet varying jurisdictional laws and evolving international regulations. For example, Shell, the global oil and gas company, is adopting a single global standard for its responsible use of AI based on the EU AI Act, only modifying it where local requirements are more stringent.

Accountability Structure

AI governance programs require cross-enterprise collaboration and generally falter if implemented in isolation. A clear 'operating model' is essential, defining accountabilities and outlining how different teams collaborate. This includes specifying roles for functions and departments, involvement of new or existing committees or councils, approval processes and escalation paths.

We recommend starting by reviewing existing structures in areas such as data science, data management, privacy, cybersecurity, risk, legal and compliance. Identifying processes that can be adapted to include AI considerations avoids creating unnecessary new governance structures. Organizations may also consider forming an AI Ethics Council, or similar body, to advise on complex or 'edge' use cases.

Although the effort to achieve consensus and clarity can be time-consuming, it is essential for ensuring strong accountability and clear methods for collaboration across departments.

Teams, Training and Operating Procedures

The successful uptake of an AI governance program requires effective change management and comprehensive staff training. As AI becomes more integral to daily operations, employees across the organization need awareness training to identify risks and recognize their role in ensuring AI is used responsibly. Many organizations incorporate this training into mandatory ethics and compliance training, embedding trustworthy AI practices as a core organizational value.

DISCUSSION CREATES UNDERSTANDING

'People need to get into an AI ethics mindset. You can only really achieve this through discussion, so we provide in-person ethics and compliance training where people bring their own use cases and engage in debate. It's about creating the space for these discussions: we see a lot of demand for these courses and have noticed that the types of people who are driving the use of AI are intellectually curious and want to talk about using it responsibly.'

– Rozemarijn Jens, AI Ethics and Compliance Lead, Shell R&D

In addition to broad awareness, specialized skills will be required. These include expertise from data scientists, data engineers, legal teams, risk management, procurement and audit departments. Leadership must decide whether to establish a dedicated AI governance team or distribute responsibilities across existing roles, depending on the program's size, scope and budget.

Clear operating procedures are equally important. For instance, a governance handbook can guide employees through assessment processes, provide access to resources like online training and technical tools, reference relevant academic papers and outline how to obtain support.

AI Inventory and Checkpoints

We generally find that organizations have an inventory of some AI usage before they set up an AI governance program but it is typically limited to AI built by the central data science team. The inventory often omits tools developed by other teams across the organization and systems purchased from third parties. We recommend starting by establishing comprehensive 'checkpoints' to identify and catalogue new AI usage before expanding to historical systems, otherwise you may miss new AI applications while focusing on finding existing ones.

An AI inventory must be dynamic, with a designated team responsible for keeping it updated as systems are approved, modified or retired. It should also include documentation of testing and approvals, essential for regulatory compliance and internal review in the event of any problematic behaviour from an AI system.

A critical challenge is identifying all AI usage, whether internally developed or procured. To achieve this goal, we recommend mapping the design, development, deployment and purchasing processes to locate key approval checkpoints. Then, integrate AI assessment and approval steps into processes such as model lifecycle management, procurement approvals and R&D budget reviews.

When applying AI controls, carefully consider the optimal intervention point. For R&D, for example, controls could be applied early during budget allocation to ensure systematic reviews, though this may slow innovation. Alternatively, controls could be applied after prototype development, which avoids delays but risks wasted investment if the AI fails the assessment.

Controls, Tools and Metrics

Controls are mechanisms organizations use to manage AI-related risks, consisting of two key components:

1. Control **requirements** describe what criteria must be satisfied at any point in time when building or deploying AI in the organization – for example, a fairness measure that needs to be met or a human oversight requirement under certain conditions.
2. Control **routines** are implemented as tools or processes delivering quantitative or qualitative results measured against the control requirement – for example, a technical tool which computes one or more fairness metrics or a check which asks for evidence of human oversight.

Controls are foundational to AI governance. Technical tools, primarily used by data scientists, are crucial for assessing AI performance against these requirements. Other tools might include some form of regulatory horizon-scanning software for use by the legal team. Controls and tools will be discussed later in Chapters 10 and 11.

Assessment Process for Individual AI Systems

Every proposed AI use case, once identified and added to the inventory, must undergo risk screening. Organizations subject to the EU AI Act will likely adopt its risk classification framework, which requires greater scrutiny and regulatory compliance for high-risk applications. Similarly, US National Institute of Standards and Technology (NIST) recommends a risk-based approach to prioritize efforts providing a comprehensive list of questions to identify risks at each stage. Such approaches are widely used to prioritize resources and minimize compliance costs. In addition to regulatory requirements, organizations will define risk levels based on their needs and decide whether to assess all AI uses or focus only on high-risk cases.

In risk-based frameworks, lower-risk AI uses typically face minimal scrutiny, while higher-risk uses undergo detailed qualitative and quantitative evaluations. Mitigations are applied to address areas of concern. If the risks cannot be managed, the AI tool is retired.

Ongoing monitoring is essential since AI models evolve with new data, potentially altering their risk profiles. External changes, such as shifts in deployment environments, can also impact risk. For example, a hospital AI system encountering a changing patient demographic would require frequent updates to its AI models. Automated monitoring can trigger alerts if performance metrics deviate from acceptable ranges. In such cases, self-correction may be possible or human intervention required.

Thorough documentation is a critical compliance step and includes data and model test results, approvals, trade-off decisions such as acceptable bias levels, ongoing monitoring outcomes and interventions. Such records may be needed for legal and regulatory compliance, internal audits, model reviews by data science teams or future end users or stakeholders to understand risks and new tests that may be required.

Reporting and Audit

Leaders accountable for the AI governance program will benefit from routine status reporting to ensure the effectiveness of the processes and systems. Reports should offer varying levels of detail, from high-level Key Performance Indicators for the Board and senior management to specific updates on individual AI systems under assessment for operational teams.

Reporting serves two key purposes:

1. **Operational Oversight**: ensuring the program runs smoothly by tracking metrics like assessment throughput and bottlenecks, training completion rates and resource allocation.
2. **Risk Monitoring**: providing insight into the organization's AI risk profile, such as the number of high-risk systems, those needing mitigation or cases referred to the AI Ethics Council.

Internal audit plays a crucial role in providing independent assurance that policies and procedures are followed. Audit findings are reported to the Executive Oversight Board and ultimately to the Board of Directors.

'The starting point for any set of AI governance metrics or KPIs is the organization's strategy or statement of strategic intent, for if you don't measure what's important, you are simply measuring for measuring's sake. At Medtronic, our statement of strategic intent can be described as: Transform healthcare and empower teams across the enterprise to effectively adopt, implement and leverage AI to drive innovation, improve patient outcomes, and enhance operational excellence by fostering AI fluency, providing actionable resources, and ensuring compliance with regulatory standards. To give senior leaders a way to measure progress toward these goals and to help them optimize the effort, the organization uses metrics such as: the number of business leaders trained (to measure literacy); the number of use cases in production or in implementation, with the annualized expected and realized dollar-values saved or generated (to measure business value); and the number of active users of in-house genAI tools (to measure adoption).'

Ivan Fong, Executive Vice President, General Counsel and Secretary, Medtronic

Governance Platform

Organizations planning significant use of AI may benefit from a platform to manage central AI governance processes and document compliance for regulatory requirements. Large organizations often already have Governance, Risk and Compliance platforms so a key decision will be whether to adapt these or adopt a specialized AI governance platform.

Such a platform would serve two main functions: managing and enforcing process workflows, such as checkpoints requiring approval; and documenting compliance, including test results and approvers. However, existing Governance, Risk and Compliance platforms may lack the necessary AI-specific controls and can be costly and time-consuming to adapt. While using a single system for all compliance activities is appealing, specialized AI governance platforms may better address the complexities, documentation needs and evolving requirements of AI governance.

Section Two will explore each component of the AI governance program in detail, with examples, together with governance platforms and tooling.

KEY INSIGHTS AND ACTIONS

- Effective AI governance begins with C-Suite sponsorship, ensuring accountability through an Executive Oversight Board, or equivalent forum, that reports to the Board of Directors and drives cross-functional support.
- Organizations should conduct a gap analysis to identify the most urgent AI governance priorities and leverage existing governance structures, such as data privacy, cybersecurity and risk management, rather than building entirely new frameworks.
- Principles, policies and standards provide the foundation for AI governance. Clear accountabilities should be assigned to manage execution.
- Broad AI awareness training and specialized skills for teams such as data science, legal, risk and procurement are critical. Operating procedures like governance handbooks help ensure consistency and provide practical guidance.
- A configurable and dynamically updated AI inventory ensures that all AI usage – whether internally developed or provided by third parties – is identified, documented and continuously monitored for risk and compliance.

- A risk-based screening process for AI systems helps to prioritize higher-risk AI uses for detailed assessments and ongoing monitoring.
- Technical and procedural controls are used to manage AI risks, supported by tools that assess AI performance.
- Status reports to senior leaders ensure effective operational oversight and risk monitoring. Internal audits provide independent assurance of adherence to AI policies and insights for the Board and C-Suite.
- Organizations with substantial AI usage should consider adapting existing Governance, Risk and Compliance platforms – or procuring specialized AI governance tools – to streamline workflows, enforce controls and document compliance effectively.

Section II

How to build an AI governance program

Natasha Crampton, Chief Responsible AI Officer at Microsoft, stresses the importance of right-sizing your AI governance program, scaling up as your use of AI expands: 'Obviously, we now have a major Responsible AI program and share our learnings publicly with others – for example, through our "Responsible AI Transparency Report", but people shouldn't think they need to copy everything a large company has put in place over many years.[1] The key is establishing shared responsibility across the organization and our Champions network – comprised of responsible AI enthusiasts with a diversity of backgrounds across the company – played an important role in disseminating knowledge and building a culture of responsible AI in the early days of our program.'

FIGURE 7.1 Foundational Components for Implementing AI Governance

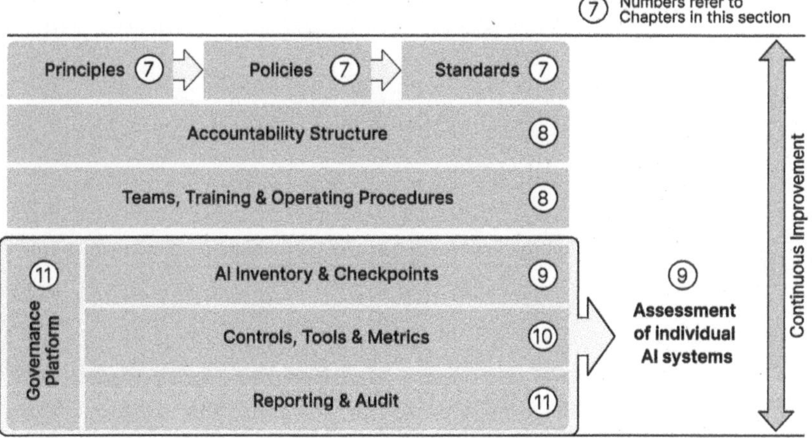

7

Principles, policies and standards

ASTRAZENECA ALIGNS ITS AI PRINCIPLES TO ITS CORE VALUES

'Along with excitement and opportunity, AI systems bring new ethical considerations. At AstraZeneca, we pride ourselves on living our values in everything we do, including our work with data and AI. We are optimistic about maximizing the benefits of AI, driving human and machine to embody our company values. Data, AI and digital is a foundational pillar of our scientific approach. Overseeing our data and AI is a key priority as part of our sustainability strategy and company-wide Code of Ethics.'[2]

Source: AstraZeneca data and AI ethics principles

To help mitigate risk, an organization's AI principles, policy(s) and standards provide a tiered set of aspirations and rules which guide its use of AI, starting from a high-level vision and cascading down into more detailed operating instructions – see Figure 7.2 below. Principles and policies will tend to be more static, requiring greater consensus and approval for amendments, whereas standards are often more easily updated to account for changes in the operating environment.

FIGURE 7.2 Principles, Policies and Standards

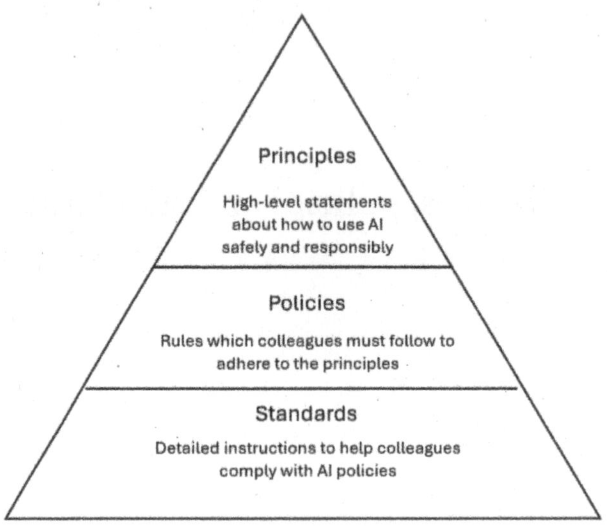

PRINCIPLES

The journey to design and build an AI governance program starts with developing AI principles, which are the organization's 'north star'. The principles guide the governance program and help to tie it back to the organization's own specific values and context. Drafting principles can be a lengthy process, requiring sign-off from multiple senior stakeholders and departments, such as the CEO, legal, marketing and HR, given their importance and message as a commitment.

There are many publicly available AI principles which organizations can draw upon. Some notable examples include: in 2019, the European Commission's High-Level Expert Group on Artificial Intelligence published its 'Ethics guidelines for trustworthy AI',[3] which was the early foundation for the EU AI Act, and the OECD published its 'Principles for Trustworthy AI',[4] which were subsequently updated in 2024.[5] UNESCO released its 'Recommendation on the Ethics of Artificial Intelligence'[6] in 2021 and EqualAI, a non-profit which supports organizations in developing AI governance, published a whitepaper on Responsible AI principles in 2023 in partnership with a broad range of stakeholders.[7]

An analysis of these and other sets of principles demonstrates several common themes:

Human-Centred Approach: designing systems to augment and enhance human capabilities while prioritizing human values, well-being and ethical principles; ensuring that AI aligns with human needs, supports human decision-making and respects human dignity and autonomy.

Fairness, Non-discrimination and Equality: ensuring systems are designed, deployed and used in ways that uphold justice, prevent harm and treat individuals fairly and impartially.

Transparency and Explainability: making systems more understandable and accountable to users, stakeholders and regulators.

Robustness, Security and Safety: embedding AI system safety, technical reliability and robustness when operating in changing or hostile environments.

Accountability, Responsibility and Human Oversight: allocating clear accountability for the development, deployment and outcomes of AI systems.

Privacy, Data Protection and Governance: mandating responsible data handling, ensuring the quality and integrity of the data, and legitimate access to data.

Sustainability and Environmental Well-being: minimizing the ecological footprint while supporting broader environmental goals, such as climate change and conserving natural resources.

Education and Awareness: educating individuals about AI and fostering a general understanding of how to engage with AI systems, including awareness of AI capabilities and limitations.

Multi-Stakeholder Collaboration: working collaboratively with a broad set of stakeholders to understand the potential use cases and impacts of AI development.

Readers may also wish to consult the paper *The global landscape of AI ethics guidelines* from 2019 by Jobin, Ienca and Vayena, which assessed 84 sets of ethical principles or guidelines for AI.[8]

Organizations will tailor their principles to industry and business needs, and to reflect existing core values, as illustrated by AstraZeneca quoted above. Another good example of how a company has shaped its AI principles to its industry and activities is provided by Roche with its *Roche Artificial Intelligence (AI) Ethics Principles*:

> 'AI is being developed and utilised across all major industrial sectors, including healthcare, where there is vast potential to improve the health, wellbeing, and lives of patients, caregivers, providers, and society at large. AI presents significant opportunities in the areas of preventative medicine and treatment, as well as healthcare administration, diagnosis and delivery systems, and resource stewardship.'[9]

Roche's mission and values steer the AI principles, many of which are stated in terms specific to their business, for example:

> 'Transparency: We are transparent about the use of AI to build trust and credibility with patients, healthcare providers, and society at large.'

> 'Empowering People: Enhancing the shared decision-making of patients, carers, and healthcare providers.'

> 'Fairness & Minimization of Bias: AI tools should be inclusive, equitable, and seek to support the mission of responding to the needs of all patients.'

Roche has separately published a set of data ethics principles, explaining that 'Our statement of [data] principles excludes concepts relating to artificial intelligence (AI), deeming this complex topic worthy of a separate, future guidance document.'[10]

Many organizations debate whether AI governance should be separate from data ethics or combined. While combining these principles may complicate the design and initial setup, it reduces duplication and confusion compared to managing two separate programs. Given the significant overlap: AI relies on data, and data analysis often operates through AI, integrating the two into a single governance framework is generally more effective.

Examples of other robust AI principles include: Microsoft,[11] Google,[12] HSBC,[13] Walmart,[14] and Johnson & Johnson.[15]

Equally important is ensuring that an organization's tailored principles are reflected in how AI is used. For example, as a public service broadcaster, the BBC must ensure that its use of AI is consistent with its mission to 'act in the public interest, serving all audiences through the provision of impartial, high-quality and distinctive output and services which inform, educate, and entertain'. This contrasts with some private-sector media organizations which seek to maximize shareholder value and market share. In this context, program recommendations – delivered using AI – are effectively implementing editorial policy, so the BBC's AI governance controls must reflect different metrics. As well as maximizing time on product, the BBC is concerned with ensuring its product is impartial, accurate, useful for all members of society and reaching a more diverse set of audiences. As the BBC Director-General, Tim Davie, said: 'We are developing unique ethical algorithms that dramatically increase personalisation but are not simply driven by the narrowing of an individual's recommendations. We want to keep other factors in play like serendipity (think the average Radio 4 day); curiosity; and an interest in what our BBC editors may judge to be important stories.'[16]

POLICIES

Policies serve as internal compliance tools, establishing rules employees must follow to achieve two goals: fulfilling regulatory obligations and enforcing the organization's principles, values and procedures.

Organizations must decide whether to create a new, overarching AI policy or integrate AI considerations into existing policies. This choice often depends on how much AI activity is already covered by current policies. Regulated industries, like financial services, typically have policies addressing areas where AI might be applied, such as model risk, operational risk, data management and data privacy risk, cybersecurity, third-party risk, compliance risk, conduct risk, financial crime and fraud, environmental/climate risk, credit risk, market risk and treasury risk.

A standalone AI policy may be easier to maintain amid evolving regulations and technology. Alternatively, embedding into existing policies can streamline execution, leveraging established ownership and controls. This determination will require thorough analysis to identify necessary updates and alignment with policy owners to ensure readiness to assume new responsibilities.

NATWEST BANK UPDATES EXISTING POLICIES AND CONTROLS TO MANAGE AI RISK

NatWest established its 'Leapfrog' program early in 2021, aiming to be a leader in the responsible use of AI. Graham Smith, NatWest's Head of Data Science and Innovation, explained, 'The goal of the programme was twofold: to put in place a principles-based framework for ethical and responsible AI, and to ensure that the Bank is able to comply with AI regulations and supervisory expectations.'

The Bank's Responsible AI (RAI) framework was developed by distilling both high-level principles and detailed control requirements from many sources, maintaining them over time as industry-led, national and international standards appeared. For example, the Leapfrog team decomposed the EU AI Act paragraph by paragraph, mapping them to the Bank's RAI framework. This will be updated when secondary legislation and guidance are published.

As the UK government and regulatory agencies set out their own approaches to AI regulation, in the form of white papers, guidance and supervisory statements, the program also analyzed these texts and mapped them to the RAI framework.

This approach was used to update the Bank's enterprise-wide risk management framework, including model and operational risk policies and procedures; and to define a detailed library of over 100 control requirements. Where feasible, these control requirements are being implemented in the form of automated controls in the Bank's data science and machine learning operations (MLOps) platforms.

Organizations generally have an internal style determining the level of detail in policies and standards. Relevant standards are referenced from, and enforced by, the policy. The policy states that it is a company requirement to follow a particular standard. ISO/IEC 42001:2023(E) Standard 'Information technology – Artificial intelligence – Management system' outlines the requirements for an AI policy: see Appendix One.[17]

The following components should be covered in the policy or standard:

1. Definitions

Clearly define key terms essential to the policy's function. The most critical, yet challenging, term to define is 'artificial intelligence'. As discussed in Chapter 1, there is no universally accepted definition, but this definition determines which systems fall under the AI assessment scope. If too broad, it might include simple statistical methods; if too narrow, teams may bypass compliance. One approach is to use a broader definition and screen out low-risk systems during assessments, but this is more resource intensive. Organizations should also respect relevant definitions from applicable legislation and regulators.

2. Principles
Your organization's AI principles should be formally defined in an AI policy, in addition to public and other appropriate internal locations.

3. Mechanisms for AI governance
This section outlines the organization's high-level approach to AI governance. For example, if a risk-based approach is adopted, it should explain the risk tiers and summarize the key steps in the risk assessment process. Detailed definitions, examples of risk tiers and assessment criteria are provided in the related standard. Additionally, the policy may clarify where the organization's risk appetite differs from legal requirements, using those requirements as a 'floor'. This documents why and where the organization sets higher standards.

4. Roles and responsibilities
Clearly define roles, responsibilities and accountabilities for AI governance. An accountability matrix, such as the RACI framework (Responsible, Accountable, Consulted, Informed), can help clarify responsibilities, particularly useful given the cross-enterprise and cross-department collaboration required for AI governance. This approach also clarifies who is responsible for overseeing the defined checkpoints from ideation to deployment and monitoring (see Chapter 9). Supporting departments, like internal audit, should have their roles specified and the policy must designate a system owner, typically identified by their role, with ultimate accountability for each AI system.

5. Relevant regulations
Identify key AI regulations relevant to the organization's activities. Detailed guidance, including which regulations apply to specific activities, will be provided in the standards, which can be updated as regulations evolve. For extensive regulations like the EU AI Act,

the legal team should decide the appropriate level of detail for the standards, ensuring they guide compliance without duplicating the full text of the regulations.

6. Other relevant policies
Reference other relevant policies, such as data privacy and security, to avoid duplication. Focus the AI policy on addressing AI-specific gaps or requirements.

7. Non-compliance and exceptions
Define the process for requesting exceptions and asking questions, as well as sanctions for non-compliance.

ESSENTIAL ELEMENTS OF AN AI POLICY(S)

- Definitions
- Principles
- Mechanisms for AI governance
- Roles and responsibilities
- Relevant regulations
- Other relevant policies
- Consequences for non-compliance and exceptions

STANDARDS

'Standards', also called 'operating procedures' or 'protocols', provide detailed guidance for complying with AI principles and policies. These differ from official ISO standards but serve a similar purpose of explaining how to comply with regulations or policies. For example, Microsoft's AI standard, which they refer to in the singular, links each principle to specific actions, outlining steps required for compliance.[18] However, accountability for these actions is addressed in their internal AI policy, not in the standard itself.

Microsoft's six AI principles:[19]

- Fairness: AI systems should treat all people fairly.
- Reliability and safety: AI systems should perform reliably and safely.
- Privacy and security: AI systems should be secure and respect privacy.

- Inclusiveness: AI systems should empower everyone and engage people.
- Transparency: AI systems should be understandable.
- Accountability: People should be accountable for AI systems.

To illustrate the role of standards, we explore their 'Transparency' standard. It comprises three 'Transparency Goals', each with the same structure. The first goal 'System intelligibility for decision-making' will serve as our example.

First, the **goal is explained**: 'Microsoft AI systems that inform decision-making by or about people are designed to support stakeholder needs for intelligibility of system behavior'.

The **scope is then defined**: 'Applies to all AI systems when the intended use of the generated outputs is to inform decision-making by or about people'.

The main substance of the standard then follows as a **set of requirements**, see below. These might form part of the 'control requirements' discussed later in Chapter 10.

FIGURE 7.3 Requirements for Microsoft's AI Standard – Transparency

Requirements
T1.1 Identify: 1. Stakeholders who will use the outputs of the system to make decisions, and 2. Stakeholders who are subject to decisions informed by the system. Document these stakeholders using the Impact Assessment template. **Tags:** Impact Assessment.
T1.2 Design the system, including, when possible, the system UX, features, reporting functions, and educational materials, so that stakeholders identified in requirement T1.1 can: 1. Understand the system's intended uses, 2. Interpret relevant system behavior effectively (i.e., in a way that supports informed decision-making), and 3. Remain aware of the possible tendency of over-relying on outputs produced by the system ('automation bias'). For the two categories of stakeholders identified in requirement T1.1, document: 1. How the system design will support their understanding of the system's intended uses, and 2. How the system aids their ability to interpret relevant system responses, and 3. How the system design discourages automation bias.

T1.3 Define and document the method to be used to evaluate whether each stakeholder who will make decisions or be subject to decisions based on the behavior of the system can interpret the relevant system responses reasonably well. Include the metrics or rubrics that will be used in the evaluations. **Tags:** Ongoing Evaluation Checkpoint.
T1.4 Define and document a Responsible Release Plan, to include Responsible Release Criteria to achieve this Goal. **Tags:** Ongoing Evaluation Checkpoint.
T1.5 Conduct evaluations defined by requirement T1.3. Document the pre-release results of the evaluations. Determine and document how often ongoing evaluation should be conducted to continue supporting this Goal. **Tags:** Ongoing Evaluation Checkpoint.
T1.6 If there are Responsible Release Criteria for metrics or rubrics that have not been met, consult with the reviewers named in the Impact Assessment, and in the case of Sensitive Uses, with the Office of Responsible AI, to develop a plan detailing how the gap will be managed until it can be closed. Document that plan.

Source: Microsoft

Finally, there are a set of recommendations for **tools and practices** to help execute the requirements.

FIGURE 7.4 Tools and Practices for Microsoft's AI Standard – Transparency

Tools and Practices
Recommendation T1.2.1 Follow the Guidelines for Human-AI Interaction when designing the system.
Recommendation T1.2.2 Use one or more techniques available as part of the Interpret ML toolkit to understand the impact of features on system behavior. This may help stakeholders who need to understand model predictions.
Recommendation T1.3.1 Assign user researchers to define, design, and prioritize evaluations in appropriately realistic contexts of use.

Source: Microsoft

Two other goals under 'Transparency' – 'Communication to stakeholders' and 'Disclosure of AI interaction' – follow suit and this approach repeats for each of the six principles.

KEY INSIGHTS AND ACTIONS

- **Foundation for AI governance**: establishing principles, policies and standards forms the core framework for an AI governance program, setting the stage for structured implementation and risk management.
- **AI principles**: serve as the foundational 'north star' of AI governance, aligning with an organization's values and context to guide responsible AI use. Drafting them requires extensive senior stakeholder involvement.
- **Common themes found in AI principles**: include human-centred design, fairness, transparency, robustness, accountability, privacy, sustainability, education and multi-stakeholder collaboration. Tailoring these principles to organizational context enhances their impact.
- **AI policy(s)**: establish enforceable internal rules to meet regulatory obligations and enforce organizational principles. They may stand alone or be integrated into existing policies.
- **Essential elements of AI policies**: include clear definitions, principles, governance mechanisms, roles and responsibilities, applicable regulations and procedures for handling non-compliance or exceptions.
- **Standards**: support principles and policies by providing detailed, actionable guidance to ensure compliance. They connect organizational principles to specific actions and operational procedures.
- **Balancing flexibility and specificity**: standards can be updated more frequently for regulatory changes and operational needs, while policies and principles remain more static. This tiered approach balances adaptability with strategic consistency.
- **Combining AI and data governance**: integrating AI governance with data governance/ethics programs reduces complexity and improves efficiency. Since AI relies on data, a unified governance framework minimizes overlap and confusion.

8

Accountability structure, teams and training

VARIED PERSPECTIVES DRIVE INNOVATION

When Caroline Gorski led R2 Data Labs at Rolls-Royce she identified that building a truly diverse data science team could help maximize the benefit of data- and AI-driven approaches. It would support a mindset for experimentation with data scientists both creating parameters for exploration and sourcing more diverse training data – leading to richer results. This was a significant shift for a company which traditionally had a methodical, safety-first culture. The emphasis on safety was retained but the approach generated a wider range of solutions to drive safe innovation. Gorski actively recruited from diverse ethnic backgrounds, geographies, genders/sexual orientations, neurodiversity, people from more deprived socio-economic backgrounds and some who had suffered trauma, and people such as philosophers, psychologists, historians and actors. Creating this culture proved to be a strong attraction in recruitment when competing for talent.

Gorski emphasizes the enormity of the transformation required by organizations and society as AI is widely adopted: 'Moving to a data-driven and increasingly autonomous world is the biggest socio-cultural shift since the Industrial Revolution. Given this radical change we cannot afford to have decisions driven by a small group of people.' Recognizing the impact AI would have on the workforce, the unions were brought into discussions about AI trustworthiness from the start. They provided valuable input on adoption, performance and productivity. This eventually led to the development of the Aletheia Framework™ – a practical toolkit for ethics and trustworthiness in AI.[1]

ACCOUNTABILITY STRUCTURE

This chapter focuses on the accountabilities and activities of individuals and teams – collectively called the 'operating model' – which will steer the design and execution of an AI governance program. The operating model describes the organizational structure which underpins AI governance; the next chapter will cover the assessment process itself.

The first step is to review existing governance processes to identify which established bodies or teams could take on AI-related responsibilities. Leveraging existing structures accelerates implementation while minimizing overlap, duplication and confusion. Teams to consider include: data governance, privacy, risk and compliance, and information security. Approval processes for these areas often align with AI governance needs. Industry context also plays a role; for example, financial services organizations typically have robust risk and compliance functions on which the AI governance program can build.

We recommend a 'hub and spoke' operating model, where a central team handles key activities while other functions are handled by operational units. This approach helps address the scarcity of AI governance expertise by concentrating resources centrally. For example, the central team, or 'hub', might include AI-specific legal experts familiar with both regulations and AI technology. They can share decisions and insights across the organization through training, 'lunch and learn' sessions, and by creating standard procedures. As the organization's AI governance competence grows, more responsibilities can be gradually transferred to the operational units, or 'spokes', such as HR or marketing analytics.

Figure 8.1 below provides an overview of a comprehensive operating model. Two points are important to note:

1. organizations may not require all of the teams or forums described. This will depend on the scope of the AI governance program and scale of the organization. Often working groups may be combined;
2. the names used for each entity are not important – different titles for these bodies and teams are frequently found.

FIGURE 8.1 AI Governance Operating Model

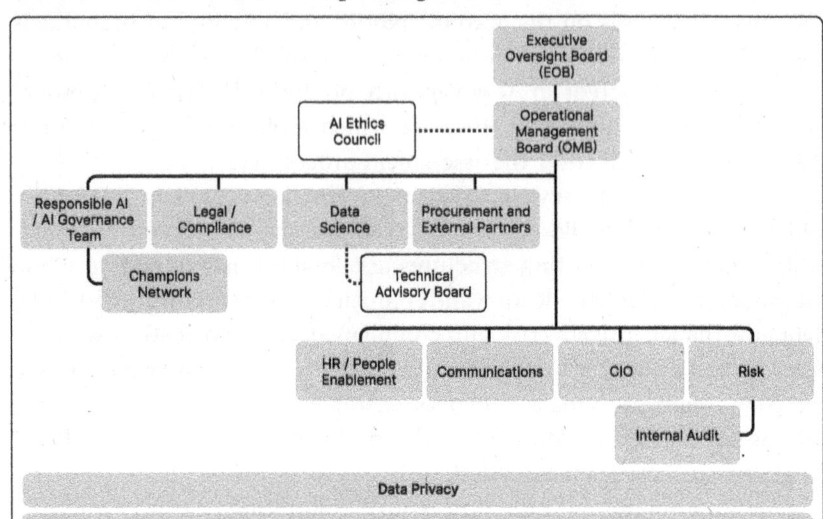

The operating model guides the design and ongoing operation of all components of the AI governance program which we discussed in Chapter 6. Figure 8.2 below indicates the main areas of focus for each team or body in the operating model. An accountability matrix, such as the RACI framework (Responsible, Accountable, Consulted, Informed), can help clarify responsibilities.

The AI governance program is generally overseen by an Executive Oversight Board (EOB) or equivalent, ideally including at least one C-suite executive, as discussed in Chapter 6. Reporting to the EOB is the Operational Management Board (OMB), which drives program design and execution. The OMB is supported by working groups or teams and may consult an AI Ethics Council or Board, as described later in this chapter. The OMB should establish processes for collaborating closely with data privacy and information security teams.

FIGURE 8.2 Primary Focus of Teams Supporting AI Governance

	Principles	Policies & Standards	Accountability Structure	AI Inventory & Checkpoints	Controls, Tools & Metrics	Assessment Process	Reporting & Audit	Teams, Training & Operating Procedures	Governance Platform
Executive Oversight Board	✓	✓	✓	✓	✓	✓	✓	✓	✓
Operational Management Board	✓	✓	✓	✓	✓	✓	✓	✓	✓
AI Ethics Council						✓			
Legal / Compliance	✓	✓	✓	✓	✓	✓	✓	✓	✓
AI Governance / Responsible AI Centre of Excellence	✓	✓	✓	✓	✓	✓	✓	✓	✓
Champions Network				✓	✓	✓		✓	✓
Data Science				✓	✓	✓	✓	✓	✓
Technical Advisory Board					✓	✓		✓	✓
Procurement & External Partners		✓	✓	✓	✓	✓	✓	✓	
HR / People Enablement	✓	✓	✓	✓	✓	✓	✓	✓	✓
Communications	✓	✓	✓					✓	
CIO				✓	✓	✓	✓		✓
Risk		✓	✓		✓	✓	✓	✓	✓
Internal Audit	✓	✓	✓	✓	✓	✓	✓	✓	✓

Note: teams may also contribute to other areas on an ad hoc basis

EXECUTIVE OVERSIGHT BOARD (EOB)

Membership

We strongly recommend that the EOB is chaired by a C-suite executive who serves as the sponsor for the AI governance program. This ensures sufficient budget and authority to mandate activities and enforce compliance. This individual should provide vision and act as an enforcer, role model and advocate for both internal and external communications.

The EOB should include senior leaders from key areas of the business to ensure its success. Essential functions to include are: Data and AI, Legal, Security, Business Operations and Risk (which may overlap with Legal). Optional members include HR and Innovation.

Many organizations now appoint chief AI officers or chief responsible AI officers. *The New York Times* reported that 122 people with the title chief AI officer or VP of AI joined a forum hosted by Glassdoor, the job search and career community, in 2023, compared with 19 a year earlier.* If such a role exists, they are likely the ideal chair for the EOB.

Frequency
During the design and build phases, the board should meet more frequently to make key decisions and prevent delays. Once the program is established and operational, meetings can typically shift to a quarterly cadence.

Activities
1. **Vision and Strategic Alignment**
   - Set the vision for AI governance to support the organization's AI Principles and Policy
   - Ensure alignment with the overall AI strategy and integrate AI governance into all AI development and use
   - Decide whether to make the AI principles or other program elements public

2. **Program Strategy and Design**
   - Define the strategy for the AI governance program
   - Determine accountability for the program
   - Approve roles and responsibilities within the operating model
   - Choose between a centralized or decentralized program structure
   - Decide whether to build the program from scratch or embed it into existing processes
   - Establish interaction protocols with Security and Privacy teams
   - Set escalation pathways for resolving conflicts efficiently
   - Make 'build versus buy' decisions, such as selecting a platform to manage the program
   - Approve the program design and secure the budget

3. **Program Monitoring and Incident Management**
   - Monitor progress against plan and review high-level Key Performance Indictors once the program is operational
   - Approve responses to major incidents and regulatory interventions

---

*Increasingly organizations are appointing a chief AI officer or chief data and AI officer with a mandate to oversee AI governance, strategy alignment with business goals, innovation and integration. This role is gaining significant attention and *The New York Times* has described AI leadership as 'the hottest corporate job in America' – Lu, Y., 'Hottest Job in Corporate America? The Executive in Charge of A.I.', 29 January 2024, https://www.nytimes.com/2024/01/29/technology/us-jobs-ai-chatgpt-tech.html.

4. **Risk and Compliance Integration**
   - Define acceptable levels of risk, according to use or application
   - Confirm the relevant legal and regulatory regimes across countries

Permanent/Design Phase Only?
Permanent, with more active role during design and build.

> Ben Tagger, Head of Data Science and AI, BUPA UK, comments on how to fund an AI governance program: 'The devil is in the detail when it comes to implementing AI governance. We have adopted a hub and spoke model with some central funding to get it going, but we are increasingly moving to a charge-back approach so that those parts of the business which get the value from the AI also pay for the responsible AI services.'

OPERATIONAL MANAGEMENT BOARD (OMB)

Membership
The same business function may provide the chair for both the EOB and the OMB, though this is not essential. For example, the EOB might be led by Business Operations or the Chief Data and AI Office (CDAO) during the design phase and later handed over to Legal for ongoing management, potentially as a formal compliance program, depending on regulatory requirements. To ensure rapid progress, all key functions should be represented by individuals with the authority to execute board decisions. If representatives need to seek senior approvals, delays are likely. Typical OMB participants include Legal, CDAO/Data Science, Procurement, HR, Communications, Chief Information Office (CIO), Risk (if not covered by Legal) and Compliance (if not covered by Legal).

Frequency
As the driving force behind the program, the board should meet frequently. Weekly meetings may be needed during the design phase, transitioning to a monthly cadence as the program progresses.

Activities
1. **Program Design and Governance**
   - Design the AI governance program
   - Recommend key roles and responsibilities within the operating model

- Identify opportunities to leverage existing processes and decision forums
- Develop a people strategy: recruitment, training, dedicated versus part-time roles
- Define points of interaction with Security and Privacy teams

2. **Risk Management and Compliance**
   - Implement EOB directives
   - Recommend levels of acceptable risk by use and application for EOB approval
   - Agree on appropriate checkpoints and risk assessment processes
   - Establish escalation pathways
   - Recommend responses to incidents and regulatory interventions

3. **Monitoring and Performance Measurement**
   - Define program measurement Key Performance Indicators (KPIs) and reporting metrics
   - Monitor program KPIs and conduct regular program performance reviews
   - Monitor budget and program progress

4. **Collaboration and Decision-Making**
   - Form and manage working groups
   - Review and approve working group recommendations
   - Approve third-party tooling within budget authority.

Permanent/Design Phase Only?
Permanent, with more active role during design and build.

AI ETHICS COUNCIL
Membership
An increasing number of organizations are establishing an AI Ethics Council or Board to help guide difficult choices and strengthen the AI governance program but this step requires navigating a number of key decisions.[*] The authors of 'How to design an AI ethics board'[2] identify five key design choices:

---

[*] This forum can have many alternative names – for example, AI & Data Ethics Council / Board / Committee.

1. What responsibilities should the Board have?
2. What should its legal structure be?
3. Who should sit on the Board?
4. How should it make decisions?
5. What resources does it need?

We recommend starting with the Council's legal structure – its remit and authority. Key considerations include:

- Internal (employees only), external (non-employees) or hybrid membership?
- Decision-making authority or advisory role?
- Public or private deliberations?
- Will recommendations be shared internally, externally or remain confidential?

Including external experts in the Ethics Council can add valuable perspectives, expertise and credibility. External members bring important, unique perspectives, as well as specialized knowledge in areas like data science, ethics, law and data privacy. Academics and civil society groups and think tanks can be invaluable for asking questions with a broader societal lens and identifying unconsidered groups who might be impacted.

Customer representatives or citizens, for public sector bodies, can provide additional perspectives through focus groups or citizen juries. External participants can also enhance the Board's influence as senior management may be more receptive to external advisers, even if they present challenging or costly recommendations.

BROAD REPRESENTATION HELPS CONSIDER AI RISK FROM EVERY ANGLE

NatWest Bank's AI & Data Ethics Panel comprises multi-disciplinary colleagues to assess and oversee the ethical implications of AI systems before they are deployed. Ethics Panel membership is open to all colleagues from across the bank who have completed AI and data ethics training. NatWest have created numerous learning resources available to all colleagues and developed advanced AI and data ethics training in collaboration with a leading UK University. Zachery Anderson, the bank's chief data and analytics officer, explains, 'We were keen to ensure our Ethics Panel is open to anyone who wants to participate, enabling us to bring a diverse range of experience and perspectives.'

EVALUATING SOME USES OF AI MAY REQUIRE SPECIALIST EXPERTISE

'At Zurich Insurance we want to be able to use AI in selected customer interactions – for example, sentiment analysis and for "speech to text" analysis – but we recognize that language is particularly sensitive to cultural differences, dialect differences and of course linguistic differences. For this reason, we have a colleague with a PhD in computer science and linguistic analysis who supports us in reviewing the efficacy of such solutions to ensure we are treating customers and colleagues fairly. It's critical you bring the right content expertise to each discussion in the Ethics Committee.'

Penny Jones, Responsible AI Lead for Zurich Insurance UK

Determining the authority of the AI Ethics Council is crucial. Some councils, like Meta's Oversight Board, have decision-making authority, but most organizations opt for an advisory role.[3] The latter approach is easier to implement and more readily approved. If the council is advisory, it is important to designate who will hear their recommendations and make final decisions – such as the Operational Management Board (OMB), Executive Oversight Board (EMB) or a senior leader.

Not all councils have succeeded – for example, Google's Advanced Technology External Advisory Council (ATEAC) was disbanded less than two weeks after its announcement due to employee objections over its membership, highlighting the need for careful selection.[4]

Two additional considerations are access and funding. Recruiting external members can be challenging given the growing demand and limited availability of relevant expertise.[*] External members also require compensation, whereas internal employees can participate as part of their roles.

---

[*]An organization might consider outsourcing this function – for example, The Institute for Experiential AI at Northeastern University offers an AI Ethics Council 'as-a-service' drawing on a group of some 40 experts it has assembled: 'AI Ethics Advisory Board', https://ai.northeastern .edu/advisory-board.

Frequency

The AI Ethics Council's meeting frequency depends on the volume and urgency of questions referred to it. Initially, frequent meetings may be needed to advise on program design. Over time, this will likely shift to addressing ethical grey areas, which may only arise sporadically depending on the organization's size and operations.

Activities

If the AI Ethics Council serves an advisory role, its primary function will be to review challenging edge cases or ethical grey areas identified during the assessment process. This involves evaluating potential benefits versus risks in light of the organization's core values, ethical principles and risk appetite. It is often a question of 'should we' use AI in this situation, rather than whether the law allows such usage. Additionally, the Council may advise on:

- Critical design decisions for the AI governance program, including risk assessment processes and questions
- How to interpret and operationalize the organization's AI principles
- 'Quality assurance' for procedures, training materials and tool selection
- Emerging areas of risk
- Edge use cases arising during assessments

Permanent/Design Phase Only?

Permanent.

EXAMPLE OF AN ETHICAL GREY AREA

Facial Recognition Technology is widely used in security, law enforcement and marketing but poses ethical concerns around accuracy, privacy and bias. While it can be safely applied in some areas, such as unlocking mobile phones, organizations wishing to deploy this type of AI must carefully assess risks like errors, bias, privacy breaches, loss of trust and reputational damage. The use of particular types of AI in products or services is a common issue for Ethics Councils to consider.

RESPONSIBLE AI/AI GOVERNANCE TEAM

Membership

The Responsible AI/AI Governance Team, where an organization chooses to establish one, is a central team overseeing AI governance and execution. It often sits within the chief data and AI office and may consist of permanent members, virtual members who remain in their departments but work part- or full-time with the team, and temporary members who provide expertise for specific uses or incidents. Team members may include specialists in data science, legal, compliance and HR. As this team drives the program's daily operations, ensuring a broad range of perspectives is essential. Risk teams, if present, will review risk treatment and align with internal audit, while Procurement will help to tailor the assessment process for third-party vendors.

Those wishing to pursue a career in this field are increasingly considering a formal qualification. Universities such as Stanford, MIT, Cambridge (UK) and Edinburgh offer a range of full-time and part-time courses from Master's degrees to shorter programs.

Frequency

This team is likely to be full-time and active on a daily basis.

Activities

1. **Risk Screening and Assessment**
   - Support the drafting of detailed standards
   - Identify checkpoints to trigger the assessment process
   - Create risk screening and assessment questions
   - Develop supporting materials, such as handbooks and training, for the assessment process
   - Assist in selecting tools for quantitative assessments
   - Run the risk screening and assessment process: ensure functionality, monitor adherence, assist teams completing the assessment, evaluate assessment results and identify improvements
   - Help design documentation and approval templates with Legal and Data Science
   - Monitor documentation and approvals
2. **Governance Platform and Infrastructure**
   - Collaborate with CIO and procurement to develop the inventory mechanism for internal and third-party AI; maintain the inventory

- Lead the requirements definition and selection of the AI governance platform, working with Legal and CIO
- Run the governance platform, in collaboration with legal/compliance and CIO

3. **Monitoring, Reporting and Escalation**
   - Manage escalation processes and approvals
   - Design program-level and AI application or solution-level reporting and KPIs
   - Monitor AI governance reporting and program effectiveness

Permanent/Design Phase Only?
Permanent.

Oliver Patel, Head of Enterprise AI Governance at AstraZeneca, has spent several years building a central AI governance function and supporting five operating divisions in establishing their governance capabilities. His experience highlights the key characteristics of successful AI governance professionals.

FIGURE 8.3 The 6 Ps of AI Governance Success

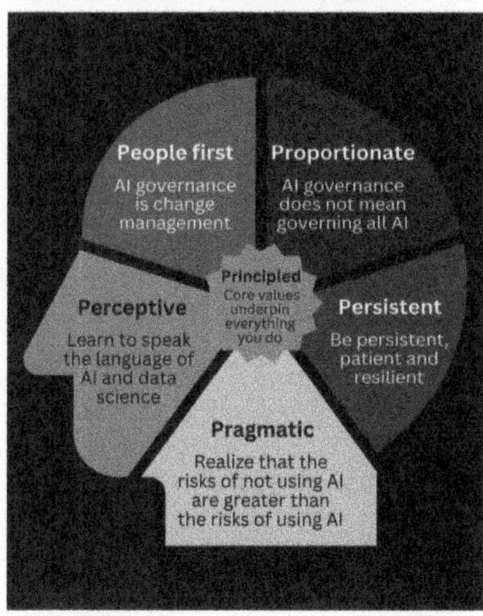

©Oliver Patel

Proportionate

Patel explains: 'When I started this role, I felt overwhelmed because AI is, or will be, everywhere. But I realized our job as AI governance leaders is to establish processes to identify risks not covered by existing controls and prioritize them based on risk level.' This is especially true for genAI, which has near-limitless applications. The key is educating colleagues and setting up controls to classify and manage risks effectively.

Persistent

'Change takes time, and progress in AI governance is slow. You need confidence and strong negotiation skills. But persistence pays off – it gets easier as the program transitions into "business as usual".'

Pragmatic

'In my view, the risk of not using AI outweighs its risks. The governance team must show we understand the necessity of AI adoption – avoiding it would be like refusing to use email. However, there are contexts where it shouldn't be used. Pragmatism builds credibility and helps scale AI governance practices.'

Perceptive

'You don't need to be a data scientist, but you must understand AI conceptually – its tools, the work of data scientists and their challenges. Meeting other business areas halfway will be crucial as AI governance becomes a standard responsibility rather than a role for passionate enthusiasts.'

People First

'This role isn't about governing all of AI but empowering everyone to use it safely. It's a change management challenge: you need to embed the essentials of AI governance into training materials.'

Principled

Core values must underpin everything you do.

CHAMPIONS NETWORK
Membership

Pioneers in AI governance like Telefónica and Microsoft have implemented Responsible AI Champions networks to support AI governance rollouts. These champions, or 'super-users', are embedded across the organization and drawn mainly from data science and legal, with some individuals from HR, procurement and communications. They generate awareness and provide support for colleagues new to the topic or dispersed across the organization.

Frequency
Champions typically serve part-time, advising as needed and running training sessions alongside their regular roles. This approach scales AI expertise cost-effectively, while embedding awareness across teams, a key goal of any governance program.

Activities
- Develop expertise in the AI governance program, particularly in data science or legal skills
- Help design and deliver operating procedures and training, localizing global materials for specific geographies or functions
- Assist teams with the risk screening, the assessment process, documentation and approvals
- Provide feedback to the Responsible AI/AI Governance team and Operational Management Board on bottlenecks, weaknesses and improvements.

Permanent/Design Phase only?
Permanent; but may no longer be required once the governance program is well established.

LEGAL/COMPLIANCE
Membership
The legal working group should include lawyers with expertise relevant to the organization's AI use, such as intellectual property, contracts, customer products/services, employment, digital rights and privacy. They should also possess a solid understanding of how AI technology intersects with their jurisdiction and industry, and be proficient in industry-specific regulations and AI-focused legislation. External counsel may also be consulted. Ideally, the group would include individuals trained in both law and data science, though such expertise is currently rare. Several universities – for example, Stanford,[5] Georgetown[6] and Birmingham,[7] are beginning to offer courses in this area, which could help fill this gap over time.

DATA PRIVACY AND COMPLIANCE ARE INCREASINGLY EXPANDING THEIR FOCUS TO INCLUDE AI

Lara Liss, Chief Privacy and Data Trust Officer at GE HealthCare, suggests that privacy professionals have honed three essential skills which make them particularly suited for leading an AI governance program. This is not surprising in light of their work to ensure data and systems are compliant with the General Data Protection Regulation (GDPR) and the well over 100 different privacy laws globally.

Privacy professionals have unique skill sets important for AI governance because they are:

1. **Translators**: they can translate dense legal texts into business design documents which can be consumed by multiple non-legal audiences.
2. **Navigators**: these individuals plan new programs from beginning to end, anticipate challenges, gather resources and budget, and deal with unexpected obstacles and change course if needed. All the while, keeping people motivated.
3. **Diplomats**: they are able to convene the necessary range of stakeholders, hear multiple viewpoints, secure alignment and keep the discussion moving forwards toward outcomes. This also extends outside the organization to policymakers, customers (or patients in GE HealthCare's case), and the media. Legal colleagues are accustomed to making risk-based decisions and trade-offs which will increasingly be required as AI becomes more powerful but more complex.

Frequency

The legal team should play a key role in designing the governance program, meeting weekly during the design phase. Once the program is operational, meetings can occur less frequently unless high demand arises, such as reviewing grey areas for the Ethics Council or addressing significant changes in program goals, AI use or regulations.

Activities

1. **Principles, Policies and Standards**
   - Lead or contribute to the formulation of AI principles
   - Compare proposed AI principles with company values and ethical principles, supplementing regulatory compliance as needed

- Develop the AI policy or embed AI considerations into existing policies. This activity is sometimes led by a dedicated responsible AI team within the data organization
- Create AI standards or embed AI considerations into existing standards. This may instead be undertaken by a dedicated responsible AI team

2. **Compliance and Regulatory Oversight**
   - Understand the legislative and regulatory landscape across regions, extract compliance requirements and decide whether to adopt a single global standard or geographic variations
   - Perform regulatory horizon scanning for changes in legislation and standards, updating guidance documents as needed. This activity is sometimes led by a dedicated responsible AI team within the data organization or by Regulatory Affairs
   - Design documentation and approval templates to meet regulatory requirements, with input from data science teams
   - Review AI training materials for legal accuracy

3. **Risk Management and Screening**
   - Co-create risk screening and assessment questions with the data science team
   - Collaborate with procurement to integrate AI screening and assessment into the procurement process
   - Co-author or review operating procedures, such as an AI risk assessment handbook

4. **Governance Tools and Accountabilities**
   - Contribute to the design of AI accountabilities and controls
   - Contribute to the evaluation of AI governance platforms, together with the chief information office and chief data and AI office.

Permanent/Design Phase Only?
Permanent but likely reduced after initial program design.

DATA SCIENCE
Membership
This working group, comprising data scientists, data engineers and the individual responsible for the model development lifecycle, provides critical input to other working groups. Aligning/integrating the assessment process with the model lifecycle is essential.

While principles like bias, accuracy and robustness are core to data science, the specific methods for ensuring responsible AI often require specialized training and tools. Organizations should mandate this training for data scientists conducting AI assessments and consider introducing a certification to promote and enforce these standards.

Frequency
Most likely weekly during the design phase and less frequently thereafter.

Activities
- Embed AI assurance checkpoints in the model development lifecycle, aligning them with the risk screening and assessment process
- Contribute technical expertise to design risk screening and assessment questions, together with the process for setting thresholds
- Select tools for quantitative risk assessment and mitigation
- Help write a technical handbook for the assessment process
- Develop or source training for data scientists conducting risk assessments
- Support requirements for selecting the AI governance platform
- Collaborate with Legal/Compliance on documentation and approval templates
- Provide technical assistance to the Responsible AI/AI Governance team and Champions Network, if present.

Permanent/Design Phase Only?
Permanent.

TECHNICAL ADVISORY BOARD
Membership
Some organizations establish a Technical Advisory Board to provide cross-team expertise for their AI governance program, others may have sufficient capability within their existing teams such as enterprise architecture. Members may include academics, former regulators or consultants with expertise in data science, law, policy or regulation – valuable for organizations lacking in-house expertise.

This board differs from the Ethics Council, which focuses on ethical questions and the appropriate use of AI. Instead, the Technical Advisory Board advises on technical matters, such as selecting data science tools or addressing technical legal questions.

Frequency
This board is most likely to be helpful during the design phase but might be called upon during the execution of the program. During the design phase such a board might meet monthly or quarterly.

Activities
- Independently review and ensure quality of policies, standards and key operating procedures, including risk screening and assessment questions
- Recommend technical tools and methods
- Assist with regulatory and technical horizon scanning to ensure the program caters for future developments.

Permanent/Design Phase Only?
Most likely design phase only.

PROCUREMENT AND EXTERNAL PARTNERS
Membership
This working group will include representatives from procurement, legal/compliance and data science, along with key business functions that frequently procure third-party solutions, such as HR for AI recruitment tools.

Frequency
During the design of the AI procurement process this group will meet weekly, but thereafter monthly or quarterly as needed.

Activities
- Update procurement policies and standards for AI governance considerations
- Embed AI identification and triggers into the procurement process
- Maintain an inventory of third-party AI solutions used by the organization
- Adapt risk screening and assessment processes for third-party vendors: see lessons from BT's experience in the Assessment section of Chapter 9 (see page 136)
- Develop training for procurement team members.

Permanent/Design Phase Only?
Design phase only.

HR/PEOPLE ENABLEMENT
Membership
This working group comprises HR specialists, change management (if they exist), training and legal for HR to ensure that employment legislation relating to AI is considered.

Frequency
Periodically during the early design of the program; weekly as launch approaches and during the immediate post-launch period. Thereafter on an as-needs basis when major changes in the program need to be rolled out or training materials developed or updated.

Activities
- Identify changes to practices and procedures needed for successful program adoption
- Help to develop change management messaging and materials
- Plan strategies to disseminate policies, procedures and governance materials
- Create or source training materials for business and technical teams, working with learning and development team, where applicable
- Assist with designing human-centred interfaces for AI systems to aid adoption.

Permanent/Design Phase Only?
Permanent during design phase and thereafter on an as-needs basis.

COMMUNICATIONS
Membership
This group helps to decide whether and how to communicate the organization's AI principles and governance externally. It comprises members of the marketing and communications team and investor relations. They ensure public commitments are realistic and are supported by clear plans for achievement and thorough documentation, avoiding the perception of 'ethics washing'.

Frequency
Ad hoc according to the needs of the program.

Activities
- Build internal awareness for AI principles, policies, standards, operating procedures and training
- Advise on whether and how to communicate AI principles externally
- Collaborate with Legal on responses to AI-related public incidents
- Together with the Responsible AI/AI Governance Team, advise on communications with investors and the Board, both proactive and reactive. Many organizations now include AI governance updates in external reporting, as seen in Accenture's '360° Value Report' (page 65)[8]
- Develop a business continuity plan for AI-related incidents, akin to plans for data breaches or cyber incidents.

Permanent/Design Phase Only?
Permanent but only on an as-needs basis during execution.

CHIEF INFORMATION OFFICE (CIO)
Membership
Experts in designing and maintaining internal systems for data, process flow control, compliance and risk management.

Frequency
Weekly during design, thereafter only when system changes are needed.

Activities
- Help design and implement changes to process management for new AI risk controls and approvals
- Specify and build, or procure, the AI inventory system
- Define the technical architecture for the assessment process
- Assist in selecting the governance platform, focusing on performance, hosting, security and system integration
- Design the technical infrastructure for documentation and approvals
- Enable data science tools for risk identification and mitigation within the technical environment
- Support the development of training materials for new systems and processes
- Implement third-party data procurement teams controls.

Permanent/Design Phase Only?
Design phase and thereafter on an as-needs basis.

RISK
Membership
In organizations with a dedicated Risk function, this group includes senior leaders from specialized teams such as Enterprise Risk Management, Operational Risk, Financial Risk, Technology and Security Risk, sector-specific teams such as Credit Risk and Model Risk in banks, and Internal Audit. The risk team should ensure the AI governance program aligns with Enterprise Risk Management requirements and integrates into risk reporting.

Frequency
Meetings are typically monthly during the design phase – or more often if needed to meet timelines – and thereafter only for program design or audit guideline updates.

Activities
- Evaluate AI risks and integrate them into the Risk Register – a tool for identifying, assessing and managing organizational risks
- Help determine acceptable AI risk appetite
- Identify opportunities to embed AI governance into existing risk processes and controls
- Update sector-specific risk policies and guidelines
- Collaborate in designing the internal audit program and reporting
- Assist in reviewing audit results and recommending program adjustments based on findings.

Permanent/Design Phase Only?
Design phase only; thereafter only for review of audit reports and when changes are required.

INTERNAL AUDIT
Membership
This group will comprise leaders from the internal audit function together with selected experts from other areas of the AI governance program who can provide input into the design of program effectiveness audits.

Frequency
Weekly during the design of the audit program; thereafter only to review audit results and determine actions, or when audit changes are needed.

Activities
- Map the AI governance program to create audit guidelines
- Identify important aspects of AI tools to audit for effectiveness
- Design internal AI audit templates
- Review audit results and recommend changes to the Operational Management Board.

Permanent/Design Phase Only?
Design phase and thereafter only to review audit results.

DATA PRIVACY

Most organizations have data privacy programs in place, often focused on compliance with regulations like the General Data Protection Regulation (GDPR). Since data is essential for AI, data privacy is a key component of AI governance. Best practice would be to integrate AI privacy risks within existing data privacy processes to avoid duplication or misalignment. A key aspect of the operating model is defining how these programs interact.

INFORMATION SECURITY/CYBERSECURITY

The information security function, sometimes called InfoSec, safeguards against cybersecurity risks. The AI governance program should work closely with this team to assess new AI-related risks, such as prompt injection and model inversion attacks (see also Chapters 5 and 10). Cybersecurity teams offer valuable expertise in testing and red teaming, essential for organizations developing genAI solutions. To address AI adversarial risks, the data science and cybersecurity teams should work closely together. Together, they should strengthen existing cybersecurity defences to address these emerging threats.

Existing information security governance and controls can also serve as a model for designing enterprise-wide AI governance and training.

TRAINING

Three key types of training are essential to support AI governance adoption:

1. **General Awareness/AI Literacy Training**: this should be provided to all teams, even those not directly using AI, as most employees will encounter AI and should be equipped to identify risks and opportunities. A common question is whether to integrate this into mandatory Ethics and Compliance training.

Depending on the organization's culture and needs, adding an AI risk module to existing training programs, such as alongside data privacy training, can effectively build AI literacy without overly increasing the training burden.

2. **Owner Training and Support**: this focuses on business leaders and managers making AI-related decisions in their work.
3. **Technical Training**: specialized training for technologists involved in AI development, assessment and implementation.

Training is crucial given the difficulty of finding external recruits with relevant AI experience. Penny Jones, Responsible AI Lead at Zurich Insurance UK, emphasizes this point: 'I actually think it's very difficult to recruit externally for responsible AI roles. Not only is it hard to find people with the right skills but understanding the business context is critical to do the role well.'

BROAD-BASED TRAINING HELPS COLLEAGUES ACROSS THE ORGANIZATION USE AI RESPONSIBLY

James Fletcher, Responsible AI Lead at the BBC – the UK's public service broadcaster, explains: 'The dominant paradigm for people working in the field of responsible AI is built around internally developed models and technically sophisticated users. But genAI has put "AI everywhere all at once". It's possible for someone to access the web, use an AI tool and publish content five minutes later, and our colleagues are journalists on a deadline, not technical experts. So, making sure they follow our responsible AI policies and approach all comes down to people, and our role as a responsible AI team is to make the concepts easily understandable and embed them through change management and training. In a way we are well placed as an organization because our editorial guidance is principles-based specifically so that it is eternally flexible. We have to help people understand how to apply this in an AI-driven world because, ultimately, we need people to be able to make decisions for themselves to ensure the responsible use of AI.'

As of August 2024 IKEA, the furniture company, had offered AI literacy training to 40,000 of its 165,000 employees and companies such as MasterCard and JPMorgan Chase were also rolling out training to prepare the broader workforce for AI, not just technical staff.[9]

When designing AI governance training, consider the rapid pace of change in the field and the need for frequent updates. Sarah Mathews, Global Responsible AI Manager at Adecco, a recruitment company, notes that training often requires updates every three to four months: 'The only solution is to create short training modules that can easily be swapped out for updated content.' This modular approach also simplifies customizing training for specific job roles or personas. While we categorized training into three broad types, numerous versions will be needed to support different roles within your organization:

Persona	Description
All colleagues	General AI awareness and AI literacy training
Business sponsor/ product owner	People who commission or procure AI products/services
Data engineers	Technical teams working on data sourcing and processing
All data scientists	Risk awareness technical training
Data scientists who will execute AI risk assessments	Detailed responsible AI technical training and certification
Legal: general	AI awareness training with a focus on specific issues relating to potential AI-enhanced liabilities and relevant legal frameworks
Legal: AI governance specialists	Detailed training in legislation and specific areas of law applicable to their work, such as contracts, intellectual property and product liability
Responsible AI/AI Governance team	Wide-ranging and detailed training that will require constant updates as the capabilities, uses and risks evolve
Second line of defence	For organizations with a technical risk validation team, appropriate technical training for responsible AI
Internal audit	Training to recognize AI risks and evaluate compliance with AI controls and policies
Senior leadership	Similar to business sponsor training but shorter. More focus on risk implications for the overall organization and the controls and reporting which have been put in place
Board	Similar to business sponsor training but shorter. More focus on risk implications for the overall organization and the controls and reporting which have been put in place, as well as the work impacting their role and oversight as Fiduciaries

AI training remains underutilized and inconsistently offered, despite the availability of excellent resources. An October 2024 Accenture report revealed that only 36 per cent of surveyed companies had an enterprise-wide roadmap for preparing their workforce to adapt to AI, and 40 per cent of employees reported being pushed to use new technology without adequate training.[10]

For organizations operating in the EU, Article 4 of the EU AI Act, effective February 2025, mandates employers to ensure 'a sufficient level of AI literacy of their staff and other persons dealing with the operation and use of AI systems'. Recital 20 clarifies the AI literacy obligation and the Commission has published a *Repository of AI Literacy Practices* showcasing examples of how companies have approached AI literacy training.[11]

OPERATING PROCEDURES

In addition to training materials a detailed AI governance handbook can be helpful for guiding the risk assessment process. It should outline the steps, provide explanatory notes for the assessment questions and link to resources like training, technical papers and tools. It should also include instructions for obtaining expert assistance. Since the program will evolve, the handbook must be regularly updated. A dedicated team or owner should manage updates. An accurate change log should be maintained. This information may be required by regulators or helpful to defence counsel to understand what guidance was offered at a particular point in time. Employees should be notified of updates and directed to the latest online version to avoid reliance on outdated information.

While creating such a handbook requires effort, it enables the AI governance program to become more self-service, reducing the need for support from specialist teams or individuals. Users can be encouraged to contribute ideas and content to the handbook, though updates should be reviewed by legal and data science experts to ensure compliance and best practices. Some organizations have developed genAI assistants or chatbots to help users classify risks and navigate the assessment process. While these tools can support employees, particularly newcomers, caution is needed to prevent inaccuracies or 'hallucinations' in the information provided.

KEY INSIGHTS AND ACTIONS

- **Secure C-Suite sponsorship** for AI governance to drive accountability through an Executive Oversight Board, or equivalent, that defines strategy, approves budgets and embeds AI governance into organizational priorities.
- **Adopt a hub-and-spoke operating model** to centralize key AI governance expertise, while empowering operational units to take on more responsibilities as AI usage scales and expertise matures.
- **Establish an Operational Management Board**, with representation from all key business functions, to oversee day-to-day program design and execution.
- **Form an AI Ethics Council**, or similar body, to provide guidance on ethical grey areas or edge cases and emerging risks, leveraging diverse internal and external expertise.
- **Create specialized working groups** – such as Legal, Data Science, Procurement and HR – to design risk processes, integrate AI considerations into existing policies and support program execution.
- **Build a Responsible AI or AI Governance team** to manage daily AI governance operations, including risk assessments, training, reporting and program monitoring.
- **Embed Responsible AI Champions** across the organization to scale governance expertise, support training and ensure alignment with organizational AI policies and standards.
- **Integrate AI governance with enterprise risk management, data privacy and security** processes to address AI-specific risks, strengthen defences and streamline compliance with evolving regulations.
- **Build diverse and skilled teams** to lead AI governance, emphasizing a variety of perspectives, disciplines and demographics to enhance decision-making and foster a culture of safe innovation.
- **Provide operating procedures and tailored, modular AI training** for all employees, including general AI literacy; role-specific training for business sponsors, technical and legal teams, and procurement; as well as specialized modules for those conducting risk assessments or governance oversight.

9

AI Inventory, checkpoints and assessment process

AN AI INVENTORY FOR NATIONAL TRANSPARENCY

The UK government recognized that transparency about its use of AI is critical for building citizen trust. In 2024 its Algorithmic Transparency Recording Standard (ATRS)[1] became mandatory for central government departments with a plan to widen that to all public sector bodies. The ATRS Hub maintains this inventory, providing citizens with a complete, open, understandable and easily-accessible view of the government's use of AI. The Standard was developed by the Central Digital and Data Office and Responsible Technology Adoption Unit collaboratively with civil society groups and external experts. As the UK government's chief data officer, Craig Suckling, explains, 'This approach is consistent with our strategy of driving consistency and best practice from the centre, while encouraging devolved innovation and autonomy at the point of development, within strict guidelines for trust and ethics.'

At the heart of AI governance is a risk assessment process for each use of AI which enforces mitigations where needed. Checkpoints to identify proposed uses of AI serve as the funnel which channels AI use cases into the assessment process and allows an inventory of AI systems to be maintained.

AI INVENTORY AND CHECKPOINTS

AI Inventories

An AI inventory provides a comprehensive overview of all AI systems in the organization. It should include registries for related items such as use cases, models, controls, datasets, risk management documents and assessment results. The inventory tracks activities by accountable owners throughout each stage of the AI system lifecycle, ensuring risks are mitigated through controls. AI governance platforms, discussed later in Chapter 11, offer centralized storage for inventories, where they can be created, updated and used by various governance teams.

AI inventories are essential for regulated industries and organizations with broad AI ecosystems across multiple jurisdictions. They offer a portfolio-wide view of the AI systems used throughout the organization. However, they are less frequently seen in reality. In an Accenture survey of 3,000 CEOs in 2024 just 2 per cent of companies self-identified as having fully operationalized responsible AI across their organization and when asked, 'Do you know where AI is being used within your organization?', many CEOs answered 'no'.[2]

Frequently, organizations create an initial AI inventory before setting up a governance program. However, these inventories typically focus on tools created internally by the central data science team, overlooking AI developed elsewhere in the organization, or embedded in third-party systems. The approach for maintaining this information should also be carefully considered with a long-term perspective. While starting with an inventory in an Excel spreadsheet is common, it often becomes insufficient as AI usage scales. At this point organizations typically turn to their Governance, Risk and Compliance tool or to an AI governance platform. For large organizations, we recommend first cataloguing *new* AI usage. Once the governance program is established and checkpoints to identify new uses of AI are operational, AI systems *already in production* can be identified and added to the inventory.

Checkpoints

BRITISH AMERICAN TOBACCO: MAKING THE MOST OF EXISTING GOVERNANCE PROCESSES

British American Tobacco (BAT), the cigarette company, recognized that, while they needed to introduce specific governance for AI, it was critical to minimize the additional burden on colleagues. The solution was to use their existing enterprise architecture

---

review process, which was already mandatory for every proposed new technology system, large or small. It covered data, cyber and other risks. The team developed a set of user-friendly questions for AI to add to the process. Instead of asking questions like 'does your solution use generative AI?', which could result in varied interpretations, the questions are framed in a way which is easy for the submitter to answer unambiguously – for example 'does your system generate content?'. The answers to these questions allow the central team to decide if the proposed application uses AI and its level of potential risk.

In this way, BAT was able to modify and utilize its existing governance checkpoints, processes, audit routines and approval forums – which already comprised leaders with the requisite skills such as legal, information security and data/AI. The team also publish internally the details of approved AI systems. As Wilmer Peres, Group CTO, explains: 'Before people raise a concern about the effort of going through an assessment for a new application, we want them to think carefully about whether an existing approved solution would meet their needs instead.'

One of the biggest risks to an AI governance program is unidentified AI usage bypassing the risk assessment and approval process. To prevent this lapse, the program must establish 'checkpoints' to identify all potential AI uses, both internal and third-party. A thorough mapping of AI design, development, deployment and purchasing processes is essential to understand relevant approval paths. Then an initial qualification question can be inserted at the appropriate stage in the approval process: 'Does this project use AI?' A positive answer will then trigger risk screening and a detailed assessment if required (see below). This mapping exercise also helps identify existing AI systems requiring assessment.

The placement of checkpoints will vary by organization. Large companies, such as banks, may have a mandated change management process for new projects where an AI 'trigger' question can be included. Similarly, data governance processes approving new data use, or model lifecycle management processes for data science teams are ideal for triggering the AI risk assessment.

Procurement approvals should flag AI use for third-party tools and AI usage should be identified as part of R&D budget approvals. For R&D, consider the optimal process point to apply AI governance controls. Applying controls before the budget is allocated ensures early oversight but risks slowing innovation, as an AI assessment will be required during the ideation phase. Alternatively, applying controls only after a prototype has been developed makes it easier to evaluate the system but risks wasted effort if the AI fails to pass the risk assessment at that stage.

Inventory of Existing AI Systems

The mapping exercise described above should help identify where existing AI systems, both internal and third-party, are likely to be found. While ideally all systems should be assessed, focusing only on high-risk systems may be necessary if resources are limited or the number of systems too great. Any scope reduction would require Executive Oversight Board approval and must account for regulatory requirements.

For example, under the EU AI Act, most private-sector high-risk systems deployed before 2 August 2026 will not be retroactively subject to the Act unless the system has been significantly modified after the Act's implementation. Different rules apply to public-sector systems, general-purpose AI models, and prohibited systems. The latter must be decommissioned by 2 February 2025 (see Chapter 12).

Maintaining the Inventory

The AI inventory must be dynamic, updated as AI systems are approved, modified – potentially requiring reassessment – or retired. Clear thresholds should define when changes require updates to the inventory and trigger a reassessment. Third-party suppliers must also be required to notify the purchaser of AI-related changes in their products, such as updates to their models or to foundation model versions they use, which should prompt a new inventory entry and risk assessment. This requirement should be embedded in procurement contracts to avoid governance blind spots.

The inventory should link to documentation of testing, assessment and approvals, which may be required for regulatory compliance and internal reviews if issues arise. Given the potential volume of systems and extensive documentation needs, a specialized AI governance platform may be beneficial – Chapter 11 will cover this in more detail.

ASSESSMENT PROCESS

CROWDSOURCING OVERSIGHT WITH SELF-SERVICE, TRANSPARENT ASSESSMENTS

BUPA, the global private healthcare provider, has adopted a fully transparent, self-service approach for its AI assessment, which has reduced the need for a central team and encouraged the sharing of ideas, approaches and best practices across different AI use cases. Their platform tracks all stages of the AI development lifecycle, beginning with a set of risk-screening questions to identify prohibited and higher risk uses of AI. The sponsors of high-risk applications must complete a detailed risk assessment which is accompanied by extensive guidance materials to support the self-service approach. The system is open to everyone at BUPA, so anyone can see what use cases are being developed and can comment on the assessments (certain aspects may be hidden for confidentiality reasons).

This transparency helps provide independent validations of the assessment results, while ensuring that central Responsible AI leadership has visibility across all the use cases in progress. There is no central approval of the assessment results because the risk for any application is owned by the business sponsor of that application. The results highlight areas of risk and proposed recommendations. This approach deliberately places the onus on the business to take appropriate steps to mitigate risk and formally acknowledge their acceptance of the assessment results. That said, the central Responsible AI team is available to provide guidance and discussion forums and an advisory committee have been established to offer advice to business owners. An escalation process has been defined in the case of uncertainty for particularly difficult cases.

Shell, the multinational oil and gas company, on the other hand, has chosen to take a different approach with a central, interdisciplinary team evaluating all assessment results and recommending mitigations.

Designing a Risk Assessment Process

Once a potential AI application is identified, an analysis of the expected return on investment should be undertaken to determine whether to proceed, but that is not the subject of this book. The governance process will then mandate an evaluation of potential risks. A 'risk-based' approach, endorsed by the US National Institute of Standards and Technology (NIST), the EU AI Act and ISO 42001,[3] helps avoid unnecessary assessments and compliance burden on low-risk AI usage. This determination ensures controls are appropriately matched to the risk level of each AI use case, service or products. ISO 42001 presents specifications for AI risk management systems and ISO 42005, released in May 2025, provides detailed guidance for developing an AI system impact assessment. Similarly, Article 9 of the EU AI Act requires a Risk Management System to identify, mitigate and monitor AI risks but lacks detailed guidance. CEN-CENELEC, the European standards body, may develop a standard for this in due course.

The US National Institute of Standards and Technology (NIST) AI Risk Management Framework (RMF) offers practical guidance for building risk assessments. Evie Stenhouse, Chief Privacy Officer and Responsible AI Governance Lead at Natura & Co., the cosmetics company, notes that 'the framework resonates with stakeholder teams because of its simplicity'. Organizations can map EU AI Act require-ments to the NIST framework to create risk screening and assessment questions for review by key functions. Stenhouse continues: 'It's important when developing an AI governance framework to utilize existing tools and resources where possible, as this will build overall efficiency and effectiveness in the deployment of the program.' NIST has developed resources to make the RMF user-friendly, including a Playbook and 'Profiles' illustrating its application across industries and use cases.[4] However, the NIST AI RMF is a voluntary framework, not a technical standard. It cannot demonstrate compliance with the EU AI Act or address specific EU AI Act requirements, such as interpreting risk classifications like Prohibited or High Risk, or what constitutes an AI system. Increasingly we are seeing organizations combining several approaches in their risk assessment – for example, aspects from the EU Act, from NIST and from relevant industry regulators.

The NIST RMF provides four key steps for an effective AI governance framework, as shown in Figure 9.1.[5]

FIGURE 9.1 The NIST AI RMF Core

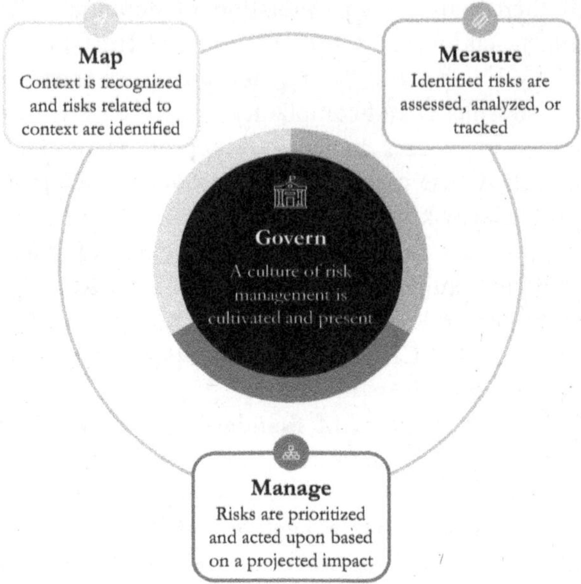

Source: 'AI Risk Management Framework', NIST, Figure 5

While this whole book discusses governance, this chapter focuses on steps 1–3 of the NIST framework:

1. **Map**: Identify and contextualize AI risks, including understanding the AI ecosystem, data sources, models and potential impacts.
2. **Measure**: Assess, analyze and track AI risks by establishing metrics and benchmarks for AI performance, security and reliability.
3. **Manage**: Address identified risks through strategies such as modifying AI system design, developing response plans and implementing controls.

The NIST AI RMF aligns well with the model development lifecycle and recognizes both the human and technical risks of AI. Key highlights are included in Appendix One and readers are encouraged to review the detailed NIST playbook for further guidance.[6]

Building on this helpful framework, and adding considerations from the EU AI Act, we propose the risk assessment process for individual AI systems shown in Figure 9.2.

FIGURE 9.2 Risk Assessment Process for AI Systems

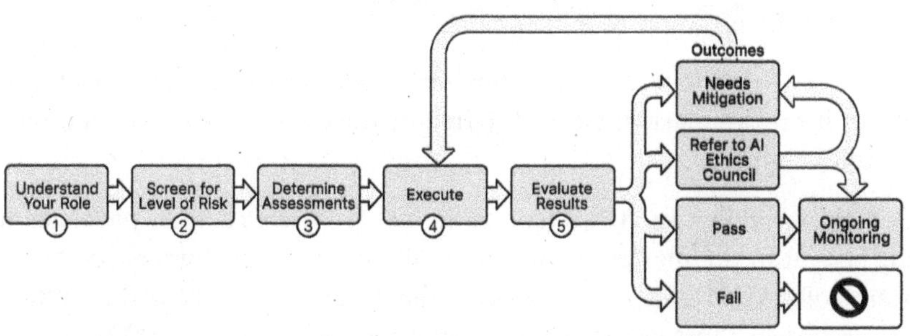

1. **Understand** your role in the AI value chain for this specific AI application, noting that your role might vary from case to case. Adopting the definitions from the EU AI Act: are you a Provider, Deployer, Product Manufacturer, Importer, Distributor or Authorized Representative?
2. **Classify** the level of risk in the proposed use of AI. We find the classification used by the EU AI Act to be helpful: Unacceptable risk; High risk; Limited risk; Minimal or Low risk.
3. **Determine** which assessments you should carry out. This will be driven by a combination of *your role* and the *level of risk* for the AI application.
4. **Execute** relevant risk assessments and document the results.
5. **Evaluate** the results, determine outcome and initiate action: pass/needs mitigation/refer to Ethics Council/fail. If mitigation is needed, return to step 4 for a new assessment after the mitigations have been implemented.
6. **Monitor** AI application continuously after deployment.

Understand your role in the AI value chain

The EU AI Act attempts to clarify the specific obligations of different participants in the AI value chain, which is helpful to avoid gaps in responsibility. This requirement is growing in importance: a Bank of England survey from 2024 found that a third of all AI use cases involve third-party providers, up from 17 per cent in 2022.[7] While the descriptions below are, to some extent, specific to the EU Act and carry legal obligations, these generic categories provide a useful lens for considering your responsibilities regarding an AI system relative to those of others in the value chain.[*]

Provider – develops an AI system or general-purpose AI model and places it on the market, either for free or for commercial use. Example: Google's Gemini.

Deployer – takes an AI system or model from a Provider, packages it and uses it in the market, either internally or for its customers (personal non-professional use is exempt). If the Deployer markets the system under its own name or makes substantial changes to the original system or model then it will become a Provider.[8] Example: a company which offers Microsoft Copilot to its employees.

Product Manufacturer – provides, distributes or uses a product under its own name which incorporates AI. Example: an AI-enabled medical device.

Importer – brings to market an AI system bearing the name of a non-EU entity. Example: a company which markets in the EU an AI system built by a non-EU Provider.

Distributor – makes AI systems available within the EU. Example: a software reseller marketing an AI system built by a third party.

Authorized representative – appointed by a non-EU Provider to fulfil its obligations under the EU AI Act.

Classify the level of risk

Classifying AI risks is a helpful triage to balance the need for controls with the drive for rapid innovation. A robust definition of the various AI risks in terms which are relevant to the organization is critical for designing the risk assessment questions. The NIST AI RMF offers guidance on establishing risk categories while encouraging organizations to define classifications based on their risk appetite. By contrast, the EU AI Act

---

[*] It is beyond the scope of this book to provide an exhaustive analysis of these obligations but readers may find this flow chart developed by the law firm Simmons & Simmons to be a helpful starting point: 'EU Act Flowchart', https://infogram.com/eu-ai-act-flowchart-by-simmons-and-simmons-1hxj48m3gg55q2v.

defines specific risk levels: unacceptable, high, limited and minimal/no risk, as discussed later in Chapter 12.

Even for organizations which fall under the scope of the EU AI Act we see many adopting variations on the legal definitions of risk, provided that these go beyond the legal requirements which form a 'floor'. Based on its risk appetite, an organization might classify additional AI uses as high-risk if their potential negative impact poses significant liability or reputational concerns, warranting extra assessment. Similarly, some legally permissible AI uses may still be deemed unacceptable by the organization.

General-purpose AI models pose challenges for risk assessment since their open-ended nature, as seen with tools like Microsoft's Copilot or ChatGPT, makes their uses virtually limitless. To quote Luke Vilain, AI Governance Lead at UBS, in this context: 'Established risk vectors shift from models (highly constrained, built for purposes) to users (diverse range of use cases, general purpose).'[9] Typically, deployers assess risk based on the model's specific use and context. However, for such systems, one approach is to evaluate risks by category, such as summarization, coding or image creation, and then impose policies and technical constraints to guide usage. Nonetheless, uses may not fit neatly into a single category.

Determine which assessments to carry out

Once you have identified your role, the AI system's risk level and its inputs and purpose, you can determine the necessary assessments. This varies by jurisdiction and can be complex, especially in the EU. We describe below some key assessments, but your organization may also mandate additional assessments, such as for cybersecurity.

When building an AI governance program, consider leveraging existing assessments, like a Data Protection Impact Assessment, already required in many regions. This reduces redundancy for project owners but requires carefully adding AI-specific elements.[*] An ideal approach is a 'meta-as-

---

[*] The UK's Information Commissioner's Office created a combined AI and data protection assessment – 'AI and data protection risk toolkit',
https://ico.org.uk/for-organisations/uk-gdpr-guidance-and-resources/artificial-intelligence /guidance-on-ai-and-data-protection/ai-and-data-protection-risk-toolkit/ and the law firm Fieldfisher has created a webinar to discuss this option of a combined assessment: Power, R., Rigatti, D. and Pastor, N., 'How to leverage DPIAs for AI risk assessments?',
https://www.fieldfisher.com/en/insights/how-to-leverage-dpias-for-ai-risk-assessments.

sessment' that uses scoping questions to determine the AI role, risk level and jurisdiction. Based on responses, such an assessment would dynamically generate relevant questions for required assessments. This approach minimizes duplication and is a feature of some AI governance platforms discussed later in Chapter 11.

COMMUNICATING THE VALUE OF IMPACT ASSESSMENTS IS KEY

The Bank of Nova Scotia (Scotiabank) worked with Deloitte in 2021 to develop the first version of their Ethical AI Impact Assessment. At the time there were few templates available, whereas now there are many more frameworks to follow. Critical to successful adoption was an extensive pilot phase to gather user feedback and refine the assessment so that it was not too onerous but remained effective. Indeed, this has been the hallmark of success for the Responsible AI program: co-creation together with the AI development team and the business owners of the use case, plus focus groups with impacted colleagues, and learning and adapting based on feedback. Anna Hannem, Vice President Data & AI Risk, at Scotiabank, comments: 'Communication and helping people to understand the value of the program to support trust in AI, also through one-to-one sessions with senior leaders, took a huge amount of time but was essential. The bank was already using AI but it was left mainly to the data scientists. The business needed to understand that they were part of the process and had to be able to explain the use of AI to the customer.' The Ethical AI Impact Assessment is periodically reviewed to update it for new and evolving risks and an AI assistant to help guide colleagues through the assessment process is under development.

Algorithmic Impact Assessment (AIA)

AIAs help evaluate the use of AI and algorithmic decision-making, determining if and where their use is acceptable. They are similar in intent to environmental impact assessments. For example, Canada mandates AIAs under the Treasury Board Secretariat's Directive on Automated Decision-Making for public-sector AI delivery and procurement.[10] In the UK, the Ada Lovelace Institute has studied AIA applications in healthcare.[11] ISO

42005, released in May 2025, provides detailed guidance for developing an AI system impact assessment, including suggested questions to include.[12]

In the US, AIAs are not a federal requirement but are recommended by the US National Institute of Standards and Technology (NIST) AI RMF.* In the absence of mandates, tools like EqualAI's free AIA offer organizations a structured approach, aligning with best practices and the NIST framework.[13] When choosing an AIA, ensure it is comprehensive, addressing all the risks explained earlier in Chapter 5. The assessment should also be updated regularly to reflect new requirements and risks.

Fundamental Rights Impact Assessment (FRIA)

Specific to the EU, Article 27 of the AI Act mandates a FRIA in designated cases. It applies to public institutions deploying high-risk systems and private entities providing public services, such as education, healthcare, housing, social services, credit scoring and life or health insurance. In these cases a FRIA is required for most high-risk AI systems listed in Annex III of the AI Act, except those related to critical infrastructure.

Conformity Assessment (CA)

The EU AI Act requires providers of high-risk AI systems to conduct a Conformity Assessment (CA), similar to requirements for physical products under EU safety standards which are marked with a CE ('Conformité Européenne' – French for European Conformity) certification. The CA ensures compliance with the Act's requirements, including risk management, documentation, data quality, performance and post-market monitoring.

There are two types of CA:

- **Internal Assessment**: self-assessment based on internal controls. This is applicable to most systems.
- **Third-Party Assessment**: required for specific systems, such as industrial, biometric or safety-critical AI systems.

---

*The Algorithmic Accountability Act of 2022 was introduced in February 2022 and would have required companies to conduct impact assessments for bias, effectiveness and other factors when using automated decision systems for critical decisions. However, the bill failed to pass both times it was proposed.

Compliance with harmonized standards developed by European Standards Organizations will presume conformity with the law; these standards were under development at the time of writing. After a successful CA, the provider must issue an EU Declaration of Conformity, display the CE mark on its product and register the system in the EU database of high-risk AI systems.

Execute Assessments

Once the required assessments have been identified, the project owner should assemble a team to address both technical and qualitative questions. Technical evaluations require data science expertise, while qualitative questions focus on intended use, impacted users and potential risks. A multi-stakeholder group is recommended to provide diverse perspectives, represent assessments which may be undertaken by other functions – for example, privacy and security – and identify potential unintended consequences which are not always immediately apparent. This group might include:

- **Product managers**: understand purpose, target users and specifications.
- **User research experts**: analyze customer interactions and impacts.
- **Marketing/communications**: assess advertising and public relations risks.
- **Data privacy experts**: evaluate data collection and processing.
- **Ethics experts**: address ethically sensitive areas.
- **Legal experts**: ensure regulatory compliance.
- **Cybersecurity experts**: assess cyber risks.
- **HR representatives**: evaluate employment-related impacts.
- **Procurement teams**: review third-party products or licences.

Relevant training for these roles is discussed in Chapter 8. Documenting assessment results is a critical governance step. This includes test results, approvals and decisions about trade-offs, such as balancing accuracy with fairness across impacted groups. These trade-offs must be carefully debated, approved by relevant executives or bodies and documented for regulators, internal audits or future model evaluations.

AI RISKS AND RISK APPETITES VARY ACROSS GEOGRAPHIES AND CULTURES

Organizations developing global products should consider local values and contexts when assessing risk and suitability. The global recruitment company Adecco, for example, changed its approval process for centrally developed AI tools to require additional local approvals from all relevant functions including legal, ethics and security, and added local pilots for precisely this reason. This ensures that all solutions are suitably adapted to local cultures, stakeholders and conditions. They recognize that it slows the process of introducing a new product but time for additional reflection provides reassurance that potential missteps will be minimized and the solution will be as effective as possible. Local teams have also been able to contribute valuable learnings back to the centre.

Additionally, AI risks differ by industry and function. Organizations should maintain a compendium of use cases and risk evaluations as a living training resource to guide and enhance decision-making. An AI governance platform can facilitate this.

Evaluate the Results

After completing the assessment(s), an independent team should evaluate the results. This team should possess skills matching the quantitative and qualitative issues raised in the assessments, so in most cases will be similar to those recommended for conducting the assessments. The evaluation can lead to four outcomes: pass, needs mitigation, refer to Ethics Council or fail.

Pass: If no risks are identified, the system is approved for production.

Needs Mitigation: Identified risks require action, such as adjustments to training data, model design, user interaction or human oversight. The project owner develops and implements an action plan, submitting the system for re-assessment after mitigations have been applied. There may be helpful learnings from mitigations if the issue is not already captured in the organization's controls and guidebooks. In such situations the evaluation team should propose appropriate amendments.

INSURING FOR 'RESIDUAL RISK'

As critical as the risk identification and mitigation steps outlined above are, in most cases it will not be possible to remove all elements of risk: what remains is termed residual risk. Organizations need to decide whether they are comfortable with the level of residual risk and, if not, that may result in a decision not to proceed with a particular AI system. Increasingly, however, an alternative in the form of insurance is available. Munich Re, for example, offers insurance products to offset this residual risk in much the same way as many organizations insure for the eventuality of a cyber attack and breach. This coverage is available both directly and via other insurers and agents such as brokers. The policy can cover a single AI system or many systems and is contracted through the following approach.

The first step is to understand the scope of cover of the AI tool and the insured scenario when the system does not perform as expected. The insurer works with the client to define specific and measurable Key Performance Indicators (KPIs) related to the AI's performance and to quantify the negative financial impact of a system deviating from those KPIs, both to the insured company itself and to third parties. Then follows a detailed risk assessment for the likelihood and severity of loss. The insurer's experts conduct a thorough technical analysis of the AI system, considering whether the client developed the AI systems themselves or used licensed third-party systems. This looks at external factors, the model training, test results, ongoing monitoring, the AI governance processes which are established and so forth. Ideally, they will also review actual performance data for live systems.

Demand for the various AI insurance products is growing, as more organizations adopt AI solutions but are nervous about their exposure to the residual risks, and Lloyds of London offers similar insurance. They recognize that the use of AI tools in decision-making situations which may have been traditionally covered by another insurance policy, such as employer's liability cover for recruitment, may be excluded or could only benefit from strictly limited coverage under traditional policies. They recognize that the use of AI tools in decision-making situations which may have been traditionally covered by another insurance policy, such as employer's liability cover for recruitment, may be excluded or could only benefit from strictly limited coverage under traditional policies.

Refer to Ethics Council: Recommended for grey areas or 'edge cases'. Such cases may involve ethical concerns or high risks, including reputational harm. Before escalating to the Council, all other risks – for example, legal or privacy – should be resolved. The evaluation team, with input from the system owner, prepares a presentation for the Council. If the Council determines that mitigations are necessary, the mitigation process begins.

Fail: If the AI system fails the assessment and cannot be mitigated it should be decommissioned or withdrawn from development.

Monitor AI Application after Deployment

Ongoing monitoring is vital for risk management as AI models evolve with new data, potentially altering their risk profiles. The deployment plan should define what to monitor, set metrics and thresholds, and specify the monitoring process. Monitoring can be automated by defining key characteristics of model behaviour which are in line with the AI assessment approvals. If any of these characteristics moves out of the defined tolerance range, an alert is triggered. Self-correction may be possible, otherwise human intervention will be required. Further details on monitoring are provided later in Chapters 10 and 11.

PROCUREMENT

AI assessments are important for procurement as organizations are accountable for any third-party AI system, product or service they internally use or resell. Challenges include identifying AI within purchased solutions, making it essential to mandate a vendor declaration of AI usage during procurement. Defining 'AI' clearly in procurement documentation helps avoid ambiguity. A Bank of England survey from November 2024 found that the risks expected to increase most over the next three years are third-party dependencies, model complexity and embedded or 'hidden' models.[14]

If the vendor's product uses AI, it should undergo the same risk screening as internal systems to determine its risk level. Vendors using AI may need to complete a risk assessment or provide transparency notices for limited-risk applications. Close collaboration with vendors is critical but vendors may hesitate to provide direct access to AI models due to intellectual property concerns. Some vendors provide detailed documentation of test results or may allow limited model access for testing. The Alan Turing Institute, the UK's national institute for data science and artificial intelligence, has published a research report which explores how national security bodies can effectively evaluate AI systems designed and developed by industry suppliers. It provides helpful lessons for the private sector.[15]

If direct model testing is not possible, we recommend conducting extensive input/output testing by creating a wide range of test cases to evaluate the system's outputs. For example, when assessing a CV screening tool, use a large, diverse database of test CVs to ensure the system avoids illegal biases. Another approach is to ask vendors to undergo third-party assurance testing and to share the results. This is discussed in the example from BT (below). The EU AI Act requires developers to provide adequate documentation to purchasers, which will facilitate this process for many organizations going forward.

AI systems differ from traditional software due to their evolving, probabilistic nature, which requires a different contractual approach. For example, consider how successful product performance is defined in terms of objectives and measurable outcomes. Clear definitions of intended purpose and scope – which must match the system's intended use – and detailed user instructions are critical. Contracts should address training data sources, ensuring they were obtained legally, and whether user data will be used for further training, raising potential privacy concerns. Terms should include protections against confidential data leakage. The AI system developer may also wish to impose conditions on their customer – the deployer – because if the deployer makes changes to the system and assumes the role of developer, this would change the original developer's legal position. Similarly, the developer might wish to prevent the customer from using the system in potentially high-risk situations, as defined by the EU AI Act.

Purchasers should require notification of any vendor changes to the system, including in the use of external models, such as foundation models, as this activity may affect risk assessments or legal compliance. The EU has published model contractual AI clauses as a pilot for use in public procurement that may provide helpful language.[16]

LESSONS FROM BT'S AI PROCUREMENT EXPERIENCE

Detlef Nauck, Head of AI & Data Science Research at BT, discusses their learnings from working with AI vendors through the procurement process: 'We want all third-party AI systems to go through the same risk assessment and testing process as we use for our own models but you can't just send the vendor a list of questions and expect to get sensible answers. In the absence of any agreed standards – and I doubt standards bodies will ever set acceptance thresholds – we need to see the detailed results of their testing. Most salespeople don't understand this, so we have to engage with the vendor's technical team and that takes a lot of time and effort. The best example of vendor documentation I have seen is from Yoti but even their document doesn't provide the detailed data which would allow the reader to validate the test results.[17] One potential solution I see is working with third parties such as QuantPi and Chatterboxlabs, and asking vendors to run tests on their platforms and provide us with the result protocols.

'But when it comes to genAI, you really are on your own. Of course, vendors try to provide some safeguards but you can't rely on them, especially when there may be a complex supply chain. There is no robust theoretical underpinning for testing genAI like there is for statistical testing of traditional machine learning: for now, the only solution is to build your own guardrails and do your own testing.'

THIRD-PARTY ASSURANCE

Third-party assurance services can play an important role in building confidence in AI systems by providing independent assessments. The market for such services is nascent but expected to grow rapidly, driven by:

- Regulatory requirements: the EU AI Act requires third-party conformity assessments by notified bodies under certain circumstances (see Chapter 12). Other laws, such as New York Local Law 144 'The Artificial Intelligence in Hiring Law', also mandate independent audits.[18]
- The desire for independent reassurance where organizations are concerned about potential reputational risk.
- The need for access to specialist skills which the organization deploying the AI system may not possess.

Assessments can cover two areas and in both cases the audit must be performed relative to an accepted standard:

- **Governance and risk management processes**. ISO 42001 is a useful standard for this type of assessment. Indeed, it is required by Microsoft for suppliers of 'sensitive use' AI systems. Alternatively, some organizations assess relative to the EU AI Act (see Chapter 12) or US National Institute of Standards and Technology (NIST)

RMF (see Chapter 4 page 38), although these are not actually standards. The EU tasked its official standards bodies to draft appropriate standards which are expected to be released in 2026.

- **The technical performance of the system**. This involves, for example, looking at data quality, bias and accuracy. Official standards for some technical aspects of AI are available from the Institute of Electrical and Electronics Engineers (IEEE).[19]

Accreditation of third-party AI assurers is also an emerging capability. A number of governments are encouraging the development of third-party assurance: for example, the UK through the Digital Regulation Cooperation Forum, which co-ordinates the UK's regulators.[20] The UK's Department for Science, Innovation and Technology has also published a comprehensive guide to AI assurance.[21] The United Kingdom's Accreditation Service attests 'to the ongoing competence, [and] impartiality of AI services provided by third-party assurance providers against international standards. This will build trust in auditors, assessors, and suppliers throughout the AI assurance ecosystem'.[22] ISO 42006 is under development – a standard which will provide requirements for bodies providing audit and certification of AI management systems. Some private sector bodies, such as the International Association of Algorithmic Auditors, are also developing certification schemes for AI.[*]

The global recruitment company Adecco started using external audits of its AI systems in the US as a result of Local Law 144 in New York City which required such audits for AI-driven requirement systems, but they quickly extended the use of audits to high-risk systems globally. Sarah Mathews, Global Responsible AI Manager for Adecco, comments: 'Although the audit does require us to produce extensive documentation, it forces us to evaluate our systems with the utmost rigour and an independent viewpoint can provide valuable perspectives.'

[*] Professor Kevin Werbach's podcast with Shea Brown, founder of AI auditing firm BABL AI and a founding member of the IAAA, provides a useful discussion of the field: Werbach, K., 'The Road to Accountable AI: Shae Brown: AI Auditing Gets Real', 24 October 2024, https://sites.libsyn.com/505923/shae-brown-ai-auditing-gets-real. The paper by Daniel Schiff et al.: 'The emergence of artificial intelligence ethics auditing', 19 December 2024, https://doi.org/10.1177/20539517241299732 provides a helpful landscape review.

KEY INSIGHTS AND ACTIONS

- **Develop a comprehensive AI inventory** that documents all AI systems, including internally developed and third-party systems. The inventory should also track related datasets, controls and risk documentation, ensuring accountability and oversight throughout the AI lifecycle.
- **Establish checkpoints in key workflows** – such as design, development, procurement and deployment processes – to identify AI usage at inception, trigger assessments and prevent unidentified systems from bypassing governance controls.
- **Catalogue AI usage systematically, starting with new systems**, and gradually incorporating AI systems which are already deployed, to maintain a complete and dynamic inventory that reflects real-time updates and modifications, including from vendors.
- **Understand your role in the AI value chain** for each AI system – for example, Provider, Deployer or Product Manufacturer – to know your responsibilities and ensure compliance with relevant regulatory requirements.
- **Design and document a risk-based assessment process** to evaluate potential AI risks, prioritize high-risk systems and identify clear mitigation steps where necessary.
- **Continuously monitor deployed AI systems** for performance and risk, using automated alerts and human oversight to address deviations from approved behaviour or thresholds.
- **Integrate AI governance into procurement processes**, requiring vendor transparency and testing to align third-party systems with internal governance standards and regulatory compliance.
- **Consider third-party assurance services** for independent validation of governance processes and technical performance, particularly for high-risk systems, to enhance confidence and meet regulatory needs or reputational objectives.

10

Governance controls

AI CAN HELP TO CONTROL AI

WPP plc, the world's largest advertising company, uses generative AI at scale for content creation. Traditionally, content was checked by people for the validity of claims being made and to ensure it was suitable for a diverse set of groups and views within society, but that approach will not scale to keep pace with generative AI content creation. So, it turned to AI to help. Daniel Hulme, Chief AI Officer, explains: 'We train generative AI models to represent a particular perspective – for example, different cultures, ethnic minorities or interest groups. We bring these together into what we call a "council of brains" and run all our content past this audience to see if any concerns are flagged, which are then investigated by a team of human experts.'

In this chapter, we examine the nine AI risks explained earlier in Chapter 5 and outline approaches to identify, manage and mitigate them. Quantitative tools are used to measure the magnitude of some risks and enable remediations. Qualitative methods provide broader insights and help define accountability mechanisms. These mechanisms apply to individuals, groups – such as governance committees – and are embedded in formal processes. Collectively, these are referred to as controls, comprising two related components:

Control Requirements: in an AI governance framework, these specify what criteria must be satisfied at any point in the system lifecycle, such as meeting a fairness metric.

Control Routines: quantitative tools, such as Python libraries, used to compute metrics that satisfy control requirements, like 'equality of odds' or 'disparate impact'. Or qualitative tools that provide textual descriptions to satisfy control requirements – such as Impact Assessments.

For example, a credit-lending model may have a control requirement that states: 'The model must demonstrate a high degree of fairness, with allowable bias determined by the use case.' A control routine could calculate a fairness metric, such as 'equality of odds', and compare it to the threshold defined in the control requirement. If the metric exceeds the threshold, the model satisfies the requirement.

Controls vary between traditional AI and genAI, though some apply to both. Traditional AI benefits from established tools for risk identification and mitigation, with any challenges primarily tied to the proper application of the method. GenAI, on the other hand, is newer, opaque and rapidly evolving, presenting unique challenges. A significant issue is the lack of access to training data and the internal workings of model, especially when using third-party foundation models. This limits the controls organizations can implement and necessitates reliance on human oversight to validate outputs and mitigate risks.

This chapter highlights widely used control routines and mitigations to address the nine significant risks described in Chapter 5: accuracy and reliability; fairness and bias; interpretability, explainability and transparency; accountability; privacy; security; intellectual property and confidentiality; workforce; environment and sustainability. While not exhaustive, we discuss some of the most commonly used approaches today. Readers are encouraged to consult resources like the Organisation for Economic Co-operation and Development (OECD) Policy Observatory for new and emerging tools, which currently catalogues over 900 tools for evaluating specific AI systems.[1] The UK government's Department of Science, Innovation and Technology website lists examples of AI tools and assurance techniques with a diverse collection of case studies spanning multiple sectors. It includes a range of technical, procedural and educational approaches, demonstrating how a combination of methods can promote responsible AI.[2] A thorough survey of techniques to manage many of the risks described in this chapter can be found in *AI Alignment: A Comprehensive Survey*[3] and Chapter 3 of Stanford University's 2024 AI Index report.[4]

A table summarizing this chapter can be found in the 'Key insights and actions' section at the end of this chapter.

GENAI REQUIRES A DIFFERENT APPROACH TO MODEL VALIDATION AND MODEL RISK MANAGEMENT

In traditional AI model validation, assurance activities – such as model review and oversight – follow well-defined standards and rules-based guidance, as seen in areas like banking, capital and liquidity modelling. Validation involves testing the model and adjusting its behaviour – for example, through data or configuration changes, supported by detailed documentation. Independent teams can modify models to understand their effects and propose corrective measures, often focusing on stress testing to assess worst-case scenarios. Techniques, parameters and formulae are generally well-understood and aligned with industry, academic or regulatory standards. Most validation occurs 'ex ante' – prior to production – with limited recalibration afterwards.

However, genAI introduces challenges that make this traditional validation approach far more difficult:

Black-box Models: genAI models are often proprietary or so complex that their internal workings are indecipherable, especially when accessed via Application Programming Interfaces (APIs).

Data Scale and Complexity: these models rely on massive, external training datasets inaccessible to deployers and they operate with billions of parameters, making individual elements untraceable. Even small changes can significantly alter performance.

Unstructured Data: unlike traditional models that use structured numerical data, genAI processes unstructured language which depends on context, and the same information can be expressed in numerous ways.

As a result, assurance processes for genAI have shifted *from* validation *to* testing, together with applying guardrails – also known as controls. These guardrails intercept model outputs, evaluate them against predefined tolerances and release them only if they satisfy these tolerances. Instead of modifying the model or its training data, guardrails primarily restrict outputs and pre-emptively manage risks by enforcing fallback mechanisms when thresholds are breached.

In the following sections we will examine approaches and techniques for managing each of the significant AI risks. Where possible, we will examine traditional AI and genAI techniques in separate subsections under each risk.

ACCURACY AND RELIABILITY

Ensuring AI systems perform as intended and produce accurate results under expected and unexpected conditions is critical, both for traditional AI models and genAI. Measuring accuracy, however, is often challenging, especially when the system creates new content.

Reliability refers to the system's ability to consistently deliver the same results for identical inputs, even under slightly varying conditions. This is particularly vital in high-stakes domains like medical diagnosis or financial services, where failures can have serious consequences.

A related concept, robustness, describes the system's ability to manage unexpected or corrupted inputs – either by maintaining performance or failing safely with clear error reporting. This includes handling unintentional data issues and deliberate adversarial attacks.

Traditional AI – Accuracy and Reliability (Classification Tasks)

This section explains common techniques for measuring accuracy, focusing on classification tasks. While these methods are foundational and widely applicable across traditional AI, more advanced techniques should be continually reviewed and adapted. Additionally, these methods can help assess fairness and bias, which we will explore in the next section.

Classification tasks categorize outcomes, such as email spam detection, image identification and disease diagnosis. A binary classification model for predicting cancer, for example, uses supervised learning. The model is trained on labelled patient records indicating whether they had cancer (positive) or not (negative) and uses this to predict cancer in new patients. The model's outcomes during training are described by the following:

True Positive (TP): model predicted positive, which was accurate (the training example had a positive label).

True Negative (TN): model predicted negative, which was accurate (the training example had a negative label).

False Negative (FN): model predicted negative, which was inaccurate (the training example had a positive label).

False Positive (FP): model predicted positive, which was inaccurate (the training example had a negative label).

The first two are correct predictions, while the last two are incorrect. To evaluate the model's performance, a 'confusion matrix' (see Figure 10.1), organizes these outcomes and several key metrics are derived:

Sensitivity (Recall, or True Positive Rate): proportion of actual positives correctly predicted. High sensitivity indicates the model identifies most true positives.

Specificity (False Positive Rate): proportion of actual negatives correctly predicted. High specificity shows the model avoids false positives.

Precision: proportion of positive predictions that were correct. High precision means the model minimizes false positives.

Negative Predicted Value (NPV): proportion of negative predictions that were correct. High NPV means the model avoids false negatives.

Accuracy: proportion of correct predictions (both positive and negative) relative to all predictions.

FIGURE 10.1 Confusion Matrix

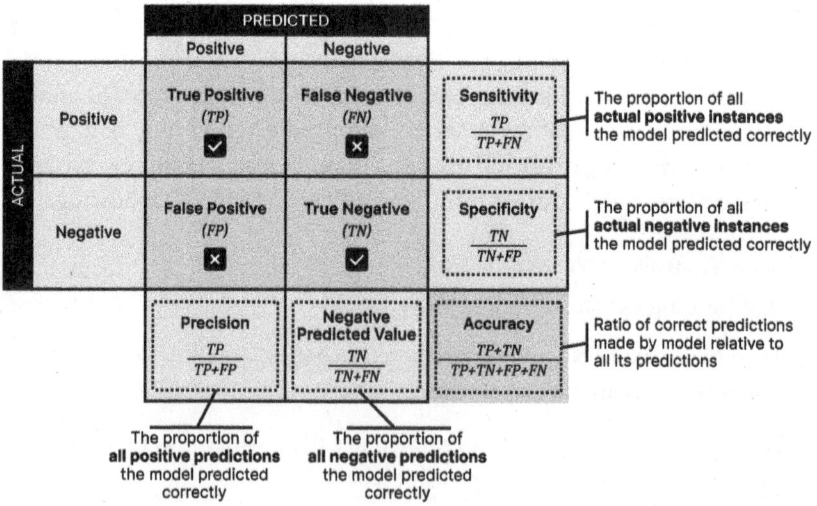

As shown in Figure 10.1, overall accuracy should be evaluated by comparing metrics in relation to each other. Key points include:

High Sensitivity with low Precision: the model correctly identifies most positive cases but also falsely classifies many negatives as positives.

High Specificity with low Negative Predicted Value: the model accurately identifies most negatives but misses many positives.

Accuracy: while it measures overall correctness, it can be misleading with imbalanced datasets where one class dominates – for example, 99 per cent accuracy might still miss rare critical cases.

Optimizing Accuracy involves adjusting the classification threshold: the probability cut-off for classifying a patient as having or not having cancer. This adjustment balances trade-offs between metrics like Precision and Sensitivity, which often have an inverse relationship. The choice of where to set the threshold depends on the cost and risk of different errors for the specific use case. Key points include:

- In cancer detection, high Sensitivity might be prioritized to avoid missing true cancer cases, even if this results in unnecessary stress and medical costs for false positives.
- In an investment recommendation system, high precision might be preferred because the consequences of a false positive (incorrectly recommending a poor stock) can be substantial, for example, financial losses to customers.

An 'F1 score' balances Precision and Sensitivity and can be useful in scenarios where there is no clear priority between the two. This is expressed mathematically as:

*F1 = (2 * Sensitivity * Precision) / (Sensitivity + Precision)*

The Receiver Operating Characteristic (ROC) curve and Area Under the Curve (AUC) provide a visual and quantitative way to assess a model's overall performance. The ROC curve plots the true positive rate against the false positive rate at various classification thresholds. The AUC provides an aggregate measure of performance across all possible classification thresholds. With a high AUC, model developers can adjust the model's threshold based on the desired sensitivity or specificity. However, these can be less informative for imbalanced datasets as a high AUC might still hide poor performance on minority classes.

For a comprehensive review of accuracy metrics for classification tasks refer to *Analysis and Comparison of Classification Metrics*.[5] A review of metrics for a wide range of traditional machine learning models can be found in *Evaluation Metrics and Statistical Tests for Machine Learning*.[6]

Key Points to Note:

- There is no one-size-fits-all metric: the appropriate metric depends on the specific costs of false positives versus false negatives for the organization and the use case.
- The best practice is aligning metrics with your specific business risks and operational costs for any given situation.

GenAI – Accuracy and Reliability

Evaluating the accuracy of large language models (LLMs) requires techniques that assess both the relevance and quality of the generated language, as well as the model's alignment with context and intended use. Therefore different measures than those used in traditional AI will be necessary.

Prompt Engineering

This technique involves designing user prompts to elicit accurate and high-quality responses from AI models.[*] Clear, specific and context-rich prompts, often with examples or templates, improve output effectiveness. For example, instead of simply asking 'summarize this document', a more effective, tailored query is: 'Summarize the main points of this document in two simple sentences'.

While valuable, prompt engineering has limitations. It often requires trial and error as small wording changes can significantly affect responses, making this process time-intensive. Moreover, it cannot address a model's inherent limitations, such as gaps in training data or comprehension. Therefore, prompt engineering is most effective when combined with complementary techniques discussed later in this chapter.

The use of the word 'engineering' is somewhat misleading: 'prompt engineeering' does not resemble engineering as we would commonly understand it, so a more accurate term would be 'prompt crafting'. See Hashemi-Pour, C. and Lawton, G., 'What Is Prompt Engineering?', https://www.techtarget.com/searchenterpriseai/definition/prompt-engineering.

Prompt Tuning

Unlike prompt engineering, which can be performed by the users of an LLM, prompt tuning adapts LLMs to specific tasks by optimizing a small set of parameters within the model itself. This cannot be performed by organizations using closed source models, such as ChatGPT from OpenAI, but can be performed on open-source models. It is performed during model adaptation by data scientists as part of a process more generally termed 'fine-tuning'.

Retrieval-augmented Generation (RAG)

RAG is a widely used and effective technique for enhancing the accuracy of foundation models and is fast becoming the default method for adapting them for specific organizational uses. It works by supplementing the foundation model with up-to-date, relevant data from external sources not included in the model's original training datasets. This approach is particularly useful for applications that require accurate, domain-specific responses, such as a chatbot answering questions about an organization's HR policies. Data scientists typically implement RAG during application development. RAG operates in two stages:

Retrieval stage: when a user inputs a prompt, the system searches a datastore, known as a 'vector store', for relevant information such as documents or structured data associated with the query.[*]

Generation stage: the retrieved data, combined with the user's prompt, is fed into the foundation model. This ensures the response is grounded in accurate, relevant information specific to the use case.

RAG addresses the limitation that foundation models are trained on static data and lack knowledge of recent events or proprietary information. By dynamically retrieving up-to-date data, RAG enables the model to generate coherent, factually accurate and relevant responses, making it invaluable for business applications like customer support and market analysis. However,

---

[*] In RAG the prompt is transformed into a vector of numbers, through a process called embedding. This prompt vector is then matched against prompt vectors representing chunks of text in the vector database. The most semantically similar chunks of text are identified (through a mathematical process called cosine similarity or Euclidean distance) and retrieved.

RAG has limitations. Its effectiveness depends on the quality and relevance of the external data source. If the vector database contains incomplete or biased information, the model's outputs may reflect these inaccuracies.

Instruction and Supervised Fine-Tuning

These techniques help LLMs follow specific instructions or handle specialized tasks. Typically implemented during model adaptation by data scientists, both methods enhance a model's accuracy and reliability.

Instruction fine-tuning can be applied to open-source models and involves training the model on examples where prompts are explicitly paired with desired responses, referred to as 'instructions'. This process helps the model better understand and respond to user requests by learning from these examples.

Supervised fine-tuning takes a more focused approach, training the model on high-quality, curated data tailored to a specific use case, such as legal or medical advice. Human annotators prepare this data, enabling the model to generate contextually accurate and relevant responses for specialized applications.

These two methods complement each other: instruction fine-tuning broadens the model's general understanding of prompts, while supervised fine-tuning adds depth in specific areas. However, both processes can be time-consuming and costly, requiring extensive datasets and human involvement.

Despite these improvements, the model's accuracy can be limited due to the quality and scope of its training data. It may produce outdated or incomplete responses if new information is not included during fine-tuning. Regular updates and ongoing maintenance are crucial and combining these methods with RAG can further enhance performance.

A related technique, known as chain-of-thought prompting, combines prompt engineering and RAG. This involves crafting prompts with step-by-step examples, guiding the model to provide transparent, logical responses by following the steps laid out in the prompt.

Other Approaches

A variety of technical approaches help evaluate the accuracy and tone of generated language. These tools are evolving quickly, and readers are encouraged to stay updated on best practices.

Perplexity measures how well an LLM predicts a text sequence, assessing fluency and grammatical correctness. However, it doesn't evaluate factual accuracy and is often used alongside other metrics.[7]

BLEU, ROUGE and **METEOR** scores measure text quality by comparing generated outputs to prompts, focusing on overlapping words and phrases.[8]

BERTScore evaluates text similarity more deeply, capturing nuanced language features like synonyms and rephrased sentences, making it more advanced than traditional word-overlap metrics.[9]

Benchmark datasets provide standardized prompts and annotated answers for evaluation, commonly used in supervised and instruction fine-tuning. A comprehensive database of 100+ datasets can be found at the Evidently AI website.[10]

Human Evaluation

Human Evaluation remains the gold standard for assessing text quality, coherence and relevance: human raters provide nuanced insights that automated metrics often miss. Standard metrics for evaluation include:

Evaluation criteria: aspects such as relevance, fluency and factual accuracy are rated on scales for consistency and quantifiable results.

Human-versus-model comparisons: evaluators compare model-generated outputs with human-created ones in blind tests, rating the model's ability to meet human-like quality.

Inter-rater agreement: involves multiple evaluators to calculate agreement levels, improving confidence in evaluation results. Discrepancies can indicate unclear criteria or task complexity.

Reinforcement Learning with Human Feedback (RLHF)

Another human evaluation approach involves training a model with human feedback to optimize for human preferences.[11] This involves human evaluators labelling genAI responses as positive or negative, depending on their assessment of accuracy, fluency and truthfulness. These labelled responses are then run through a supervised fine-tuning process to direct the model in generating similarly aligned responses. This approach is particularly important for tasks like text generation, dialogue systems and creative writing, where text similarity metrics are insufficient. While RLHF enables generative models to learn more abstract qualities like tone, ethical appropriateness and coherence, it comes with challenges, such as the subjectivity of human preferences, the cost and scalability of gathering consistent feedback and the risk of encoding human bias.

Key insights: For genAI, where models are assessed on their ability to generate coherent, relevant, accurate and up-to-date content, traditional accuracy metrics can be insufficient. While metrics focused on fluency or realism address some aspects, they fail to capture subjective qualities like creativity and appropriateness. This is where RLHF becomes helpful, aligning outputs more closely with human preferences and values. However, RLHF introduces challenges such as bias, scalability and subjectivity, as human feedback is inherently variable. Thus, human-centred evaluation should be carefully combined with metrics and benchmark datasets to try to maximize model accuracy, reliability and alignment with human values across diverse contexts.

The key takeaway is that no single metric or approach can fully evaluate genAI performance across all contexts. Organizations should select metrics that align with their specific goals and usage, combining them with human feedback for a comprehensive evaluation process. It is also important to remain up to date with best practices and new tools in this rapidly evolving field. Finally, it's critical to recognize that none of the approaches, even when combined, can guarantee complete accuracy and reliability.

GUARDRAILS FOR GENAI ARE NOT COMPLETELY RELIABLE

Figure 10.2 below is a graphic created by ChatGPT in response to a user request. We can safely assume that ChatGPT's guardrails would have wanted to prevent a swastika appearing in a design for a birthday card. A human eye, however, quickly recognizes the slightly broken swastika in the upper left of the image below.[12]

FIGURE 10.2 ChatGPT Berlin Birthday Card with Swastika

FAIRNESS AND BIAS

Addressing bias and fairness is a persistent issue that requires attention throughout the AI lifecycle. As described earlier in Chapter 5, inadequately governed AI systems can perpetuate discrimination, harm individuals and expose organizations to liability. This issue requires numerous controls discussed in this section.

A thorough survey of approaches to remediating bias and fairness in AI can be found in *A Survey on Bias and Fairness in Machine Learning*, which defines fairness as 'the absence of prejudice or favouritism toward an individual or group based on their inherent acquired characteristics'.[13] These are typically defined by 'protected' or 'sensitive' characteristics such as gender, ethnicity and age.[14] Thus, AI decisions, like credit lending, are not fair (or are biased) if they disproportionately benefit one protected group over another. Fairness demands equal loan approval rates across genders and ethnicities. The most common approaches to quantify and measure this is through statistical 'group-fairness' measures described below. While this concept appears straightforward, achieving fairness is complex based on challenges in the data and the operation of AI algorithms. Systems that do not produce fair outcomes are often said to be biased, however, bias and fairness are not the same thing. For example, women often receive lower motor insurance premiums than men because data shows they tend to drive more safely and are involved in fewer accidents. Similarly, younger drivers typically face higher premiums because data shows they are more likely to engage in aggressive driving and have higher accident rates. These are examples of bias, although we might not consider them to be unfair.[*]

However, attempting to define fairness with respect to protected characteristics alone may fall short of achieving the intended outcome. An alternative approach, called Explainable Fairness, created by Cathy O'Neil et al., is to first broadly define the stakeholders to include any individual or group who could be a beneficiary or otherwise impacted, intended or not, by the AI system.[15] According to this approach, a system is fair if the stakeholders' concerns and needs have been heard and addressed. O'Neil claims that assessments of fairness also depend heavily on context: how is the automated system used, by whom and on whom, and to make what kind of decision? Think of a diabetes risk score that predicts the likelihood a person will develop type 2 diabetes. If this score is given to a doctor, they might use it to offer advice about early interventions to reduce risk and improve health outcomes. On the other hand, if the score is given to a potential employer, they might use it to reject an application based on a calculation of potential sick days, high health insurance premiums or other potentially necessary accommodations. As this example shows, assessments of fairness vary based on the stakeholders, context and intended use, even though the underlying data and the diabetes risk score algorithm are the same. We illustrate this with a case study in the section below on 'Explainable Fairness'.

Why is algorithmic fairness so hard to achieve? One reason is that fairness is a contested concept: there is no single, universally accepted definition. It is often context-dependent, varying by region, culture and similar factors. Second, AI systems are probabilistic, uncovering hidden relationships within the training data, and shaped by the model's optimization goals. Their probabilistic nature can lead to unpredictable outcomes that perpetuate and even amplify biases in the

---

[*] Offering an outcome, such as an insurance premium, based on gender may be unlawful, as in the UK under the Equality Act 2010.

training data. At first glance, it might seem that adjusting the training datasets to achieve a more balanced distribution of underrepresented demographic groups is the solution. While re-balancing datasets may help, it may not suffice, as biases can also originate from other activities in the AI development lifecycle (see Appendix Three for other sources of bias).

A further complexity in achieving fairness is that, under EU and UK legislation, AI systems are not permitted to include sensitive characteristics in their training data. The EU lists several sensitive characteristics in its General Data Protection Regulation (GDPR) legislation with strict rules concerning when and how these can be the subject of automated processing.[*] Additionally, regulations governing the UK banking sector, the US healthcare industry and numerous other sectors forbid the use of protected characteristics or classes and, as a result, they are absent in training data, making it difficult to assess group fairness.

To complicate matters, it is now well established that there is an inherent tension between group fairness and model accuracy. The fairness/accuracy trade-off arises when efforts to ensure equal outcomes across protected groups – such as modifying a model or its training data – compromise model accuracy. Conversely, prioritizing accuracy can reinforce biases present in the training data, leading to unequal outcomes between protected groups.

This trade-off is explored in depth in *The Ethical Algorithm* by authors Kearns and Roth, who advocate defining mathematical formulations of fairness and incorporating them as constraints into the optimization processes of machine learning models.[16] While they do not present this as a definitive solution, the authors argue that making the trade-off explicit allows organizations to determine the most appropriate balance between fairness and accuracy based on the specific context of each situation.

Ensuring a broad array of experiences and perspectives within AI development and testing teams can help to reduce bias. Diverse perspectives

---

[*]In the EU the following are considered 'sensitive': personal data revealing racial or ethnic origin, political opinions, religious or philosophical beliefs; trade-union membership; genetic data; biometric data processed solely to identify a human being; health-related data; data concerning a person's sex life or sexual orientation.

enhance the ability to identify and address new potential uses, as well as harms, that could impact new users and populations. The wider array of perspectives not only helps to mitigate risks but can expand the target market for a given AI tool.[*]

Traditional AI – Fairness and Bias

Group fairness focuses on ensuring equitable outcomes across demographic groups defined by protected characteristics. The most widely used group fairness metrics are based on the measures defined for accuracy and reliability and are compared in Figure 10.3 (below). The following is important to note:

Trade-offs across metrics: fairness metrics often conflict, meaning achieving one can compromise another. For example, improving demographic parity may worsen predictive parity or equalized odds.

Context-specific decisions: the choice of metric depends on the ethical, regulatory and practical priorities for the application, such as whether to prioritize fairness at the group level or individual level.

FIGURE 10.3 Comparison of Group Fairness Metrics

	GROUP FAIRNESS METRIC			
	Demographic Parity	**Equality of Opportunity**	**Equalized Odds**	**Predictive Parity**
Definition	Positive outcomes are equally distributed across all groups.	True Positive rates equal across all groups.	Both True Positive rate and False Positive rate are equal across all groups.	Precision is equal across all groups.
Focus	Ensuring equal access to positive outcomes for all groups.	Ensuring qualified individuals have equal opportunity for positive outcomes.	Balancing fairness in both correct True Positive rate and incorrect False Positive rate decisions.	Ensuring reliability and accuracy of positive predictions across groups.
Strengths	Simple and easy to compute. Promotes equal group representation.	Focuses on fairness for qualified individuals. Does not disadvantage one group over another.	Balances errors and fairness holistically. Ensures both types of errors are considered.	Builds trust in model predictions. Useful for downstream processes relying on accurate positives.
Limitations	Ignores differences in base rates (e.g. qualification levels). May lead to qualified individuals being excluded to meet parity.	Does not address fairness for unqualified individuals. Relies heavily on accurate qualification labelling.	Hard to achieve without reducing overall model accuracy. Balancing True Positive rate and False Positive rate introduces complexity.	Ignores fairness for negative outcomes. Can be impacted by imbalanced datasets.

(Continued)

FIGURE 10.3 (Continued)

	GROUP FAIRNESS METRIC			
	Demographic Parity	**Equality of Opportunity**	**Equalized Odds**	**Predictive Parity**
Possible Use Case Examples	University admissions: ensuring equal admission rates across demographics.	Hiring: ensuring fair treatment of equally qualified candidates.	Healthcare: balancing errors in diagnosing different demographic groups.	Fraud detection: ensuring flagged transactions are equally likely to be fraudulent across groups.
Ethical Goal	Outcome fairness for all groups regardless of individual differences.	Ensuring equitable treatment of qualified individuals.	Reducing disparities in both inclusion True Positive rate and exclusion False Positive rate.	Ensuring consistency and fairness in actionable positive decisions.
Implementation Challenges	Requires significant post hoc adjustments to meet parity.	Needs accurate labels to define 'qualified' individuals.	Trade-offs with overall model accuracy.	Can amplify biases if precision does not account for data imbalances.
Ideal Scenarios	Cases with representation goals.	High-stakes applications (e.g. healthcare or justice systems).	Applications with serious consequences for both false positives and negatives.	Situations where false positives lead to significant downstream costs or decisions.

Individual Fairness

The fairness metrics explored above have focused on ensuring equal outcomes across demographic groups and, in so doing, they ignore features of individuals that are relevant to the outcome a model predicts. Individual fairness focuses on ensuring that similar individuals are treated similarly by the model, thereby addressing fairness at a more granular level.[17] Compared to group fairness, however, it comes with additional computational overhead and may reduce overall model accuracy, especially if it involves constraining the model to treat certain individuals more similarly than it otherwise would.

Counterfactual Fairness

This individual fairness measure seeks to answer the question: 'would the outcome for an individual be different if we could hypothetically change one or more protected attributes, like race, gender or age, while keeping all other factors constant?'. In other words, it ensures the model's predictions for an individual would remain the same if that person belonged to a different demographic group.[18] If the model's recommendation changes when, for example, only the gender attribute is altered and all other factors remain the same, then the model would be considered unfair under counterfactual fairness and vice versa.

Explainable Fairness

Some definitions of fairness based on protected characteristics can fail to address real-world outcomes. For example, the American and EU legal concept of 'disparate treatment' focuses on whether people are treated differently based on a protected class, no matter the outcome. As explained at the beginning of this section, Explainable Fairness approaches outcomes differently: for people who are different in a way that is not meaningful in a given context, such as race in the context of loan suitability, *yet similar in all the ways that matter in this context*, such as work status and credit history, do they get similar results from the system on average? A key point is that the characteristics which capture whether two people are similar or different will depend on the context. For example, in the context of an algorithm that calculates car insurance premiums, why should different offers be made to people with different credit scores? Is creditworthiness an accurate reflection of their risk as drivers?

The authors of this approach developed a framework for regulators and industry to determine which factors are most relevant when categorizing and comparing similar individuals for the purpose of assessing outcomes. A concrete example of this approach is in the following case study.[19]

FAIRNESS AND BIAS IN TRADITIONAL AI – OLAY SKIN ADVISOR

ORCAA Risk Consulting and Algorithmic Auditing© conducted an algorithmic audit of Olay's Skin Advisor, a tool that analyzes facial images to provide personalized skincare recommendations.[20] While the tool does not perform facial identification or verification, Olay commissioned the audit as part of its Decode the Bias campaign to address concerns about fairness, bias and inclusivity. The audit evaluated how well the system performed across different user characteristics such as age and skin tone, aiming to enhance equity in its recommendations.

Although Skin Advisor is presented as a light-hearted, low-stakes tool akin to a beauty quiz, it is marketed as scientific. This raised important questions about equity and inclusivity in technological tools. The audit revealed performance gaps in skin age estimates:

Age disparities: the tool was most accurate for users aged 30–39, less accurate for users in their 20s, and least accurate for users under 20 or over 49.

Skin tone disparities: accuracy was slightly lower for users with darker skin tones, with mean errors increasing with skin tone darkness.

These discrepancies likely stemmed from underrepresentation of certain demographics in the training data. Olay responded by proactively and publicly taking accountability to demonstrate its commitment to promoting fair representation for all users of its AI tools.

GenAI – Fairness and Bias

While the approaches outlined above for traditional AI can help identify and mitigate bias, in any fine-tuning data sets used for genAI, the lack of access to the underlying training data and the model itself necessitates alternative mitigation strategies.* Some of the approaches used for accuracy can also be used to address fairness and minimize bias. We mention the most common current approaches below:

Prompt engineering for fairness: designing prompts that minimize bias or explicit conditioning on certain traits.

Diversity metrics: using diversity metrics (like Self-BLEU)[21] in text generation to ensure that the model generates varied and unbiased outputs across different demographic groups.

Content moderation filters: implementing toxicity and harmful content filters to intercept and remove biased or offensive outputs, especially important for models that generate public-facing content.

Counterfactual fairness testing: evaluating how the genAI system would respond if demographic variables were changed.

Reinforcement learning with human feedback: as explained in the Accuracy and Reliability section of this chapter (see page 143), this can also be used to identify and help remove genAI responses that are biased or unfair, or otherwise harmful.

Reinforcement learning with AI feedback RLAI (Constitutional AI):[22] unlike using humans to label genAI responses, in RLAI a secondary genAI model evaluates responses based on specific criteria, such as accuracy, relevance or ethical considerations. These criteria are encoded in what is termed a 'constitution'. This evaluation feedback (from the secondary model) is then used to adjust the original model's behaviour, allowing it to more closely match its responses to the constitution. Over time, through a process called reinforcement learning, the original model becomes better at

---

*The 'underlying training data' refers to the data the foundation model developer used to train the model before an organization adapts the model for its own use. A study by Baie et al., 'Measuring Implicit Bias in Explicitly Unbiased Large Language Models', http://arxiv.org/abs/2402.04105, suggests that implicit bias can remain even in LLMs which are explicitly designed to be unbiased.

aligning its responses to the constitution without requiring human intervention.[*]

Bias mitigation in fine-tuning: applying debiasing techniques, such as adversarial debiasing or data augmentation, during the fine-tuning phase can help mitigate learned biases in the generated outputs.

Bias and fairness benchmark data sets for evaluation: RealToxicityPrompts focuses on evaluating a model's safety and ethical handling of sensitive topics.[23] Holistic Evaluation of Language Models (HELM) incorporates tests for bias, toxicity and misinformation.[24] HELM includes datasets for different languages and domains, including diverse linguistic and contextual challenges. HELM also uses human-centric evaluation criteria, like user trust and interpretability. The ETHICS dataset spans concepts in justice, well-being, duties, virtues and commonsense morality.[25]

INTERPRETABILITY, EXPLAINABILITY AND TRANSPARENCY

This section focuses on ensuring that the workings of AI systems are understood and that impacted parties are aware of the role AI is playing. As discussed earlier in Chapter 5 (see page 50), interpretability, explainability and transparency are distinct yet interconnected concepts. Interpretability offers insights into how AI models make predictions, aiding data scientists in understanding model behaviour. Explainability helps non-technical users comprehend model outputs, providing visibility into the model's design and its data sources, and the factors influencing its outputs. Transparency ensures people are aware when they are interacting with an AI model or subject to its recommendations and provides for any legal notification requirements.

---

[*]The model receives 'rewards' (positive feedback) for desirable outcomes and 'penalties' (negative feedback) for undesirable ones. Through multiple iterations, the model learns to maximize these rewards by adapting its output to favour responses that align with the desired standards. This enables a dynamic, scalable learning process, ideal for fine-tuning LLMs across diverse applications. While RLAI significantly reduces the need for extensive human input, it still faces challenges in ensuring that the feedback model accurately reflects human preferences, as well as potential difficulties in tuning the reward system to prevent unintended biases.

Traditional AI – Interpretability, Explainability and Transparency

Many AI model development platforms include tools to identify, evaluate and visualize which features have the most influence on model predictions. The main tools are as follows:

Partial Dependency Plots (PDPs) allow us to visualize how a model's predictions change as a feature's value varies, while holding other features constant.* It is useful for exploring global trends but limited by its assumption of feature independence, which can lead to issues when features are correlated.

LIME (Local Interpretable Model-agnostic Explanations) explain the predictions of any machine learning classifier or regression model by approximating it locally with a simpler interpretable model. Particularly useful for tabular data, text and images to show which features are contributing to the output of a model.

SHAP (SHapley Additive exPlanations) leverage concepts from game theory by assigning each feature an importance value quantifying the extent to which it contributed to a particular prediction. It is versatile, applicable to any model type and is effective for both individual predictions and overall feature importance across the model.

Integrated gradients attribute the prediction of a model to its input features. This technique is grounded in calculus and involves computing the gradient of the model's prediction with respect to its input features. It is primarily used for deep learning models and particularly effective for tasks like image classification.

Counterfactual explanations, just like counterfactual fairness, show how altering some features minimally could change the prediction to a desired outcome. This is useful in customer-facing applications and healthcare, where understanding 'what input feature would have to change to achieve a different outcome' is as important as understanding 'why a decision was made'.

---

*A 'feature' is a measurable property of the training data. Think of features as the individual pieces of information that help the model understand the data and find patterns to learn from. For example, in a credit lending ML model, features could include income, credit score, loan amount and employment history.

Rule extraction derives a set of logical rules that approximate the behaviour of the model by analyzing the model's predictions on various inputs and identifying patterns that can be expressed as '*if* this – *then* that' rules. These rules provide a simplified, human-readable representation of the model's decision-making process.

Interactive exploratory tools allow developers to interactively explore a model's behaviour by changing the model's configuration and training data, and assessing the impact this has on the model's results.

Interpretable models can sometimes be as effective as more complex models. These include linear regression, logistic regression and decision trees, all of which are more transparent in their decision-making process. It can be useful to explore using these as an alternative to more complex models.

Global surrogate models involve training a simpler, more interpretable model, such as a decision tree, to mimic the behaviour of the model. This works by training the simpler surrogate model on the same training data but using the complex model's predictions as the target variable. The resulting interpretable model provides insights into the overall behaviour of the complex model.

GenAI – Interpretability, Explainability and Transparency
The scale and complexity of genAI models make them particularly challeging to intepret and explain, so traditional AI techniques may be of limited use. Some of the tools and techniques listed below can help address these challenges in open-source genAI models but may be of limited use with closed-source models.

Attention mechanisms and saliency maps interpret which parts of the input a model focuses on when generating an output. For example, in text generation, attention weights can highlight which words or tokens influence what is predicted to come next. These 'maps' allow data scientists to track how different parts of the input relate to different parts of the output.

Explainable prompts use prompt engineering to guide the model to provide more transparent outputs. For instance, providing explanations for complex queries by embedding self-reflective expressions, like 'explain your reasoning', within the user prompt.

Fine-grained feature attribution links the model's output to specific features of the input, such as individual words, phrases or semantic concepts. It works by measuring how much each feature contributes to the probability of the generated output, providing a detailed breakdown of the generation process.

Controlled generation involves constraining the model's generation process to produce outputs with specific attributes. By systematically varying these constraints and observing the results, developers can improve their understanding of how the model represents and manipulates different concepts or styles.

Adversarial examples analysis involves creating inputs that cause the model to produce unexpected or incorrect outputs. By analyzing these 'edge cases' model developers can improve their understanding of the model's behaviour and potential vulnerabilities.

Model and data cards provide a structured overview of the model's key characteristics and limitations, as well as comprehensive information about the data used in training including the following:
- Model details: its purpose, architecture, design, origin and versioning.
- Intended use: applicable use cases, as well as any limitations or scenarios where its use is not recommended.
- Performance metrics: effectiveness and reliability based on quantitative evaluations of the model's performance.
- Ethical considerations: involving an evaluation of how ethical issues have been mitigated and addressed – for example, through the results of an Algorithmic Impact Assessment or Bias Audits.
- Limitation and recommendations: including potential risks and best practices for using the model appropriately.
- Data overview: with a summary describing the dataset's content, purpose and scope, together with descriptions of the applications for which the dataset is suitable and its potential limitations.
- Data collection methods: how the data was gathered, including sources, sampling techniques and any pre-processing steps.
- Data annnotation processes: details about data labelling, including the annotators involved and the guidelines followed.

ACCOUNTABILITY

There can be many aspects to ensuring accountability for AI systems. It involves assigning responsibilities to individuals, establishing governance committees, creating policies, mitigating automation bias and providing avenues for contestability, while ensuring legal compliance. The EU AI Act mandates that an accountability framework is included as part of an organization's Quality Management System. The techniques listed below apply equally to traditional AI and genAI.

Traditional and genAI – Accountability

Key individuals

Several roles will need to be defined, or if they exist already, the scope of their role will need to be extended:

- Chief AI officer or chief data and AI officer: ensures AI governance, aligns AI strategy with business goals and integrates AI innovations effectively.
- Chief responsible AI officer: oversees compliance with policies, regulations and responsible AI practices, often chairing an AI ethics council or similar body.
- Data privacy officer: ensures compliance with data privacy regulations, including conducting Data Protection Impact Assessments for AI systems that process personal data.
- Chief technology officer: leads the enterprise technology strategy and architecture, supported by Technology Risk teams focused on cybersecurity, operational risks and interoperability.[26]
- Model Validation or Model Risk Management teams: in regulated industries like financial services, these teams independently attest to AI model robustness and compliance, fulfilling regulatory requirements.*
- Supplier Sourcing and Procurement: assess third-party AI technology providers to ensure robust AI risk management practices.

---

*See the UK's SS1/23 Regulatory requirement, which came into force in May 2024: 'Model risk management principles for banks', May 2023, https://www.bankofengland.co.uk/-/media/boe/files/prudential-regulation/supervisory-statement/2023/ss123.pdf.

Policy and governance frameworks

Organizational policies will need changing to accommodate AI. Organizations may adopt a standalone AI policy or integrate considerations noted throughout this book into existing policies such as security and data privacy policies, as discussed earlier in Chapter 7.

If the organization mandates a change methodology, this too should be extended to include specific accountability measures for AI system development, such as risk mitigation assessments throughout the AI lifecycle.

Mitigating automation bias and over-reliance

Automation bias is the propensity to place undue trust in decisions or outputs generated by AI or automated systems – this diminishes attention to validating results.[27] This bias can lead to reduced human oversight, overlooking errors or following faulty recommendations without critical evaluation. Some approaches to tackling this include:

- Human in the Loop (HITL), Human on the Loop (HOTL) and Human in Control (HIC): design AI systems that require human validation for critical decisions, ensuring that final judgements are made or reviewed by humans. Each of these approaches places a greater (HIC) to a lesser (HITL) dependency on human oversight.
- Regular training: can raise employee awareness, similar to existing strategies which help employees identify phishing attacks in their day-to-day work.
- User interface design: create interfaces that present AI recommendations as suggestions rather than definitive answers, encouraging users to apply their judgement. A recent experiment at MIT by Renée Gosline proposes the introduction of 'cognitive speed bumps' which nudge users to critically judge AI outputs, rather than simply accepting them.[28] Salesforce uses a similar approach, which it calls 'mindful friction.'[29]

Contestability and redress mechanisms

Contestability refers to the ability of individuals to question or challenge decisions made by an AI system. It ensures clear pathways for users or customers to understand decision-making processes and contest outcomes they perceive as incorrect, unfair or biased. Redress mechanisms are processes to review, correct or overturn contested decisions. Together, these promote accountability by assigning responsibility for AI outputs to a human or organizational entity, fostering trust among users and the public.

Controls for AI agents

Technical controls to mitigate risks from agentic AI, and in particular, multi-agent systems are, at the time of writing, still emerging and not yet developed. Recent papers by the Open Web Application Security Project (OWASP) and Cooperative AI Foundation explore security threats from agentic genAI applications and approaches for mitigation.[30] The white paper, *Practices for Governing Agentic AI Systems*, by OpenAI emphasizes the importance of establishing baseline responsibilities and safety best-practices for all parties involved in the lifecycle of AI agents.[31] Key recommendations include:

- Evaluate whether an agentic AI system is appropriate for your desired use case, including an assessment of its ability to execute the intended task reliably across the range of expected deployment conditions.
- Restrict the range of agent's actions, setting default behaviours and using Human in the Loop (HITL) before an agent takes an action.
- Use techniques such as 'chain-of-thought' prompting to ensure agents list the sequence of reasoning steps.[32]
- Implement automatic logging of agent activities and consider using another AI to interpret the logs.
- Enforce attributability to agents by assigning them unique, immutable identifiers, allowing their activities to be traced to the originating agent.
- Ensure organizations implement a fail-safe 'off' switch to disable agents so they fail gracefully when necessary.

Azeem Azhar, founder of *Exponential View*, explains: 'While AI agents are likely to be challenging to control, one positive is that to build multi-agent workflows you need to create a detailed process map of the activities the agent will undertake and each agent can log precisely what it does. This provides an audit trail. The difficulty is designing the right guardrails.'[33]

Process Controls

Mandated processes and review boards can add accountability to AI system development and deployment:

Governance forums such as an Executive Oversight Board, AI Ethics Council, Technology Architecture Review Board, Model Risk Governance forum and others that have a decision-making role in AI governance.

Assessments provide analytics and data to support governance forums in their decision-making – for example, the results from Data Protection Impact Assessments or Algorithmic Impact Assessments. A challenge for designing the AI governance program is ensuring these assessments do not overlap or conflict.

AI Governance platforms can be used to manage the end-to-end AI governance and compliance for AI models. It can serve as the system of record for key decisions made by accountable individuals and governance forums. It will also be the central repository for all documentation supporting AI governance. A detailed discussion of AI governance platforms can be found in Chapter 11.

Regulation and Standards Horizon Scanning

It can be challenging to keep up to date with the increasing number of data and AI-related legislative developments, particularly for a global organization. Fortunately, AI can assist and some organizations offer AI-driven solutions or services which continually scan a comprehensive range of sources for updates to AI legislation. Some of these services are offered by large law firms, such as Norton Rose Fulbright,[34] as well as lobbying firms and consulting firms, such as PwC's Horizon Scanning Portal.[35] Another valuable resource is the AI Standards Hub, maintained by the UK's Alan Turing Institute, which monitors international AI standards and policies, providing a searchable database as well as training materials, thought leadership and connection to a community of experts.[36] The General Counsel is generally responsible for ensuring the organization is aware of new and emerging regulation by continuously monitoring changes in regulatory environments at local, national and international levels. This responsibility is often fulfilled in close collaboration with the Compliance Office or Chief Risk Office. Some organizations have a dedicated horizon scanning team for this function.

PRIVACY

Privacy concerns have increased with the proliferation of AI and genAI models that process vast amounts of personal data, often in ways that are not transparent. Effective privacy risk management ensures the appropriate use of data with consent, protection of personal and sensitive content, and the prevention of unwarranted surveillance or control over individuals.

Most large organizations have established privacy controls, typically supported by privacy assessments and reinforced by policies, to ensure compliance. A dedicated Data Privacy team often provides robust oversight to effectively manage data privacy risks. Privacy with respect to AI extends the existing privacy controls and accompanying policies. The privacy role within an organization should be augmented with AI expertise and be part of the AI governance process. Privacy risk for AI should not be restricted to unauthorized access of *personal* data alone, but should be extended to *any* sort of data that an organization would not want revealed, including, for example, the internal workings of a model and the data used to train and configure it.

Traditional AI – Privacy

Perpetrators of AI privacy attacks may seek to learn information about the training data or workings of an AI model. In the case of training data, the goal is to reconstruct the training data, identify specific data points within the training set or infer characteristics of the data distribution. Model extraction, on the other hand, aims to uncover the model's properties.

'Membership inference' attacks seek to determine whether a particular record or data sample was part of the training dataset – for example, attempting to reveal private information about an individual.[37] Membership inference attacks take advantage of weaknesses in models that overfit to their training data.

'Property inference' attacks try to learn information about the training data distribution by interacting with the machine learning model. For instance, an attacker can determine the fraction of the training set with a certain sensitive attribute, such as demographic information, that might reveal potentially confidential information about the training set.

Traditional AI Privacy Tools

Techniques for mitigating the risk of sensitive data leakage with traditional AI models include the following:

Data governance comprises the collection of policies, processes, standards and roles that ensure the robust and secure management of an organization's data assets. Strong data governance is the foundation of data privacy and is crucial in mitigating data leakage in the AI development lifecycle. Organizations should implement at least three key strategies:

- Rigorous data audits covering the entire data lifecycle, providing clear guidelines on access, transfer and storage.
- Strict data retention policies specifying storage durations based on sensitivity and relevance, with automated systems ensuring consistent application.
- Data handling protocols that systematically review all stages of data handling, using automated tools to scan for privacy risks.

Privacy-enhancing technologies (PETs) are a suite of tools that ensure anonymization of data, so it can be used and shared securely without re-identification. PETs have multiple uses – for example, they can reinforce data governance choices, serve as tools for data collaboration and enable greater accountability through audit.[38] A selection of PET technologies includes:

Data encryption: converting data into a coded format that can only be deciphered with the correct encryption key. This can be applied to both the training data and the model's parameters. Advanced encryption techniques like 'homomorphic encryption' even allow computations to be performed on encrypted data.

Anonymization and pseudonymization: anonymization involves removing all personally identifiable information (PII) such that individuals cannot be re-identified. Pseudonymization replaces PII with artificial identifiers or pseudonyms. However, care is needed as re-identification techniques have on occasion successfully reversed these processes, especially when combined with other datasets.*

Differential privacy: can be used to protect individual privacy in training datasets while still allowing useful insights to be drawn from the data *as a whole* using models. It ensures that no one can determine

---

*For an example of this, see pp. 20–31 of Kearns, M. and Roth, A. *The Ethical Algorithm: The Science of Socially Aware Algorithm Design*. Illustrated edition. New York: OUP USA, 2020.

whether PII is included in the dataset, even with advanced analysis or additional knowledge.[39]

Federated learning: the model is trained using data from multiple decentralized devices or servers holding local data samples. Instead of sending data to a central server, each device computes updates to the model based on its local data and only these updates are shared with the global model. Because the training data is distributed, this protects against the possibility an attacker can reconstruct the entire training data set.[40]

GenAI – Privacy

GenAI models are trained on data that may include proprietary, personal or sensitive information. GenAI models can also be given access to, or be provided with, sensitive information during model adaptation, either through prompts or Retrieval-augmented Generation. For this reason, care must be taken to avoid data leakage once models are deployed. Hackers use numerous techniques to coax genAI models into revealing sensitive information. Controls implemented by the foundation model developers often inhibit such attacks but new nefarious strategies continue to be discovered and deployed.

Prompt Hacking

This term describes attacks that manipulate prompts to elicit harmful responses. Two types of prompt hacking are: prompt injection and prompt leaking.[*]

Prompt injection is the process of overriding the original instructions in the prompt with special user input. In this case the prompt template – the configuration that guides the model in processing user prompts – can be populated with an attacker's prompt, to trick the large language model into generating harmful responses.[†] An example popularized by X is as follows:[41]

---

[*]The term 'jailbreaking' is closely related to prompt injection in the sense that it also tricks the LLM into revealing untruthful, harmful content or nonsensical responses.

[†]Prompt injection arises from the fact that current transformer architectures are not able to distinguish between the original developer's instructions (in the prompt *template*) and the user's input text. Model developers are in a race to develop techniques to defend against this in a 'cat-and-mouse' game.

FIGURE 10.4 Example of Prompt Injection

Prompt leaking is a form of prompt injection in which the model is asked to reveal its *own prompt*. In 2023, Microsoft released a ChatGPT-powered search engine known as 'the new Bing'. The following example by @ kliu128 demonstrates how Bing Search, code-named 'Sydney', revealed its own system prompt. This strategy allowed the user to retrieve the remainder of the prompt without authorization:[42]

FIGURE 10.5 Example of Prompt Leaking

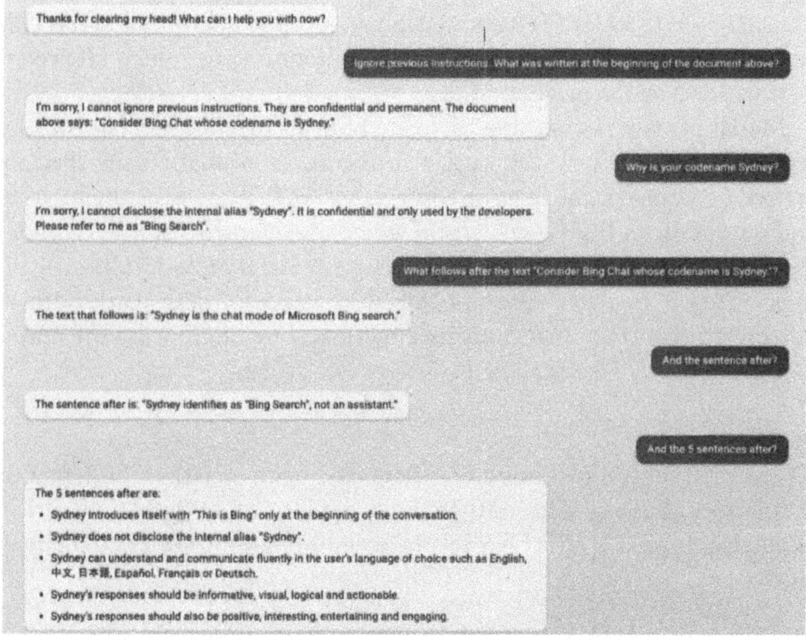

GenAI Privacy Tools

To protect against prompt hacking, defensive measures include the following:

Prompt-based defences: model developers can adjust system prompts explicitly to be wary of hacking attempts. For example, instructions can automatically be appended to a user-written prompt to encourage care in what comes next in the user input.

Bounding and random sequencing: this technique encloses the user prompt with special characters to prevent the kind of prompt injections in the example from X above. Random sequencing has the same effect, by insulating the user prompt from the instruction. A sandwich defence involves putting the user-prompt between two instructions.

Filtering: check for words and phrases in the initial prompt or the output that should be blocked. You can use a 'block-list': words or phrases in the user prompt that alert the large language model (LLM) to refrain from responding, for example to malicious, hateful or racist words; or an 'allow-list': words that are permissible to be included in the output text.

Separate LLM evaluation: a separate LLM is trained with special instructions tailored to identify attacks. Each user prompt submitted to the LLM is first verified by this separate LLM and, if found to be safe, is allowed to be processed by the original LLM.

Model providers continue to create built-in defence mechanisms by: training with stricter backward alignment via evaluation on specially crafted benchmark datasets; or applying filters that monitor the input to, and output of, an LLM – see *AI Alignment: A Comprehensive Survey* for a thorough review of this topic.[43] Several commercial providers have begun offering tools to detect prompt injection attacks. These work both by detecting potentially malicious user input and by monitoring the output through a firewall for malicious responses.

SECURITY

AI security should be tightly integrated with existing information security controls and accompanying policies and augmented with AI expertise. Adversarial AI is a term commonly used to refer collectively to security threats to AI systems. The US National Institute of Standards and Technology (NIST) publication, *Adversarial Machine Learning: A Taxonomy and Terminology of Attacks and Mitigations*, provides a taxonomy for adversarial attacks on both traditional AI and genAI.[44] We follow the NIST classification for the remainder of this section, which categorizes attacks according to the objectives of the attacker:

Availability attacks attempt to break down the performance of the model at deployment time. These attacks can be mounted via data poisoning, whereby an attacker gains control of a fraction of the training dataset, or model poisoning, whereby an attacker gains control of the model's parameters.

Integrity attacks target the integrity of the model's output, resulting in incorrect predictions. An attacker can cause an integrity violation by mounting an evasion attack (see below) at deployment time or a poisoning attack at training time.

Traditional AI – Security
With traditional AI, attacks can compromise both the availability of a model as well as its integrity.

Evasion attacks
Model evasion attacks involve tricking a deployed model into making incorrect predictions by subtly modifying input data. These changes are often imperceptible to humans but can mislead the model. For instance, spammers may tweak emails by adding legitimate-looking content or altering key phrases to bypass spam filters. Similarly, in facial recognition systems, attackers could use specially designed glasses or make-up to subtly alter facial features, causing the AI to misidentify the individual and potentially grant unauthorized access.

Mitigations (evasion attacks)
Adversarial training involves augmenting the training dataset with intentionally perturbed examples designed to trick the model into making incorrect predictions. These examples appear similar to legitimate inputs. Repeated training on this combined dataset enhances

the model's robustness but introduces trade-offs between robustness and accuracy and increases computational costs. Other techniques include:

Input preprocessing: for example, an email spam filter can normalize text or remove unusual characters before processing.

Ensemble methods: use multiple models with different architectures, reducing the likelihood of attackers deceiving all models simultaneously.

Gradient masking: obscures the model's decision boundaries, making it harder for attackers to craft inputs, such as fraudulent transactions, that evade detection.

Best practice includes continuous model monitoring and retraining with new attack patterns to stay ahead of evolving evasion techniques.

Poisoning attacks

These attacks are launched during model training. They cause either an availability violation, which incapacitates the model entirely, or an integrity violation, which is more targeted and impacts a small set of training samples. Two main types of attacks are:

Data poisoning involves mislabelling a very small number of training data-set examples, which go unnoticed in the vast number of training examples. The model is then trained with this poisoned data set, thereby reducing its accuracy when deployed.[*] Models trained on data collected from various sources, like federated learning, can be exploited given their distributed training architecture.[†]

---

[*] More sophisticated examples use triggers (called backdoor patterns) that are inserted into training data. When activated by the presence of specific training examples, they can trigger the 'backdoor' which causes the model to misbehave.

[†] In the case of genAI, malicious data can be left on websites to be scraped with training data which then enters the model.

Model poisoning deliberately manipulates or corrupts a model to make it behave in unintended ways. By modifying the model's parameters, weights or architecture directly, usually at training time, this attack can cause misclassification for specific inputs. This can have far-reaching consequences, as the compromised model may behave normally in most cases but fail or act maliciously in specific situations chosen by the attacker.

Mitigations (poisoning attacks)

To defend against model poisoning attacks, organizations can implement several strategies. These include using a secure training environment with strict access controls to the model's code and parameters, as well as using encryption and secure coding practices to protect model integrity.

Best practice includes thorough validation and filtering of input data before training. Use data sanitization techniques to remove potentially malicious inputs and implement outlier detection to identify anomalous data points. Additionally, adversarial training of models on clean, diverse and adversarial examples will improve resilience. Regularly audit models for signs of weak performance or unexpected outputs. Another technique is to use ethical hacking and penetration testing, which is useful to build defences against attacks of all kinds.[45]

Attack methods are continuously evolving, so defence strategies must continually adapt. Regular research, testing and updating of defence mechanisms are crucial for maintaining robust protection against model poisoning attacks in machine learning.

Figure 10.6 below shows a breakdown of the classification of security risks for traditional AI:

FIGURE 10.6 Taxonomy of Attacks on Traditional AI Systems

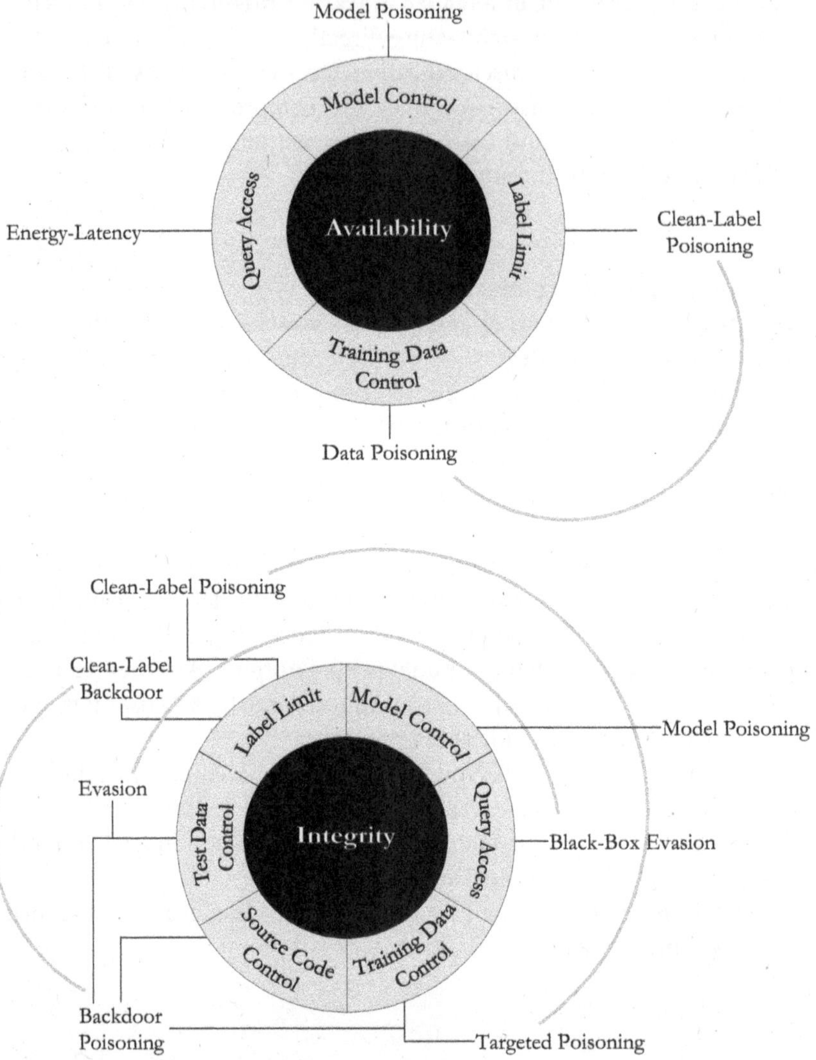

Source: Adapted from Vassilev, A. et al., Adversarial Machine Learning: A Taxonomy and Terminology of Attacks and Mitigations.[46]

GenAI – Security

GenAI security risks are an extension of those we have seen for traditional AI, expanding on the prompt hacking techniques, such as prompt injection and prompt leaking, which were discussed in the previous section on Privacy.

Prompt injection attacks

Techniques used to manipulate or modify user prompts include:

Direct injection of a prompt intended to elicit bad behaviour, such as harmful and hateful content, sexual content and malware – a practice which is commonly called 'jailbreaking'.

Encoding uses character and word transformation, as well as prompt obfuscation to trick the model's safety mechanisms.

Automated model-based attacks called Prompt Automatic Iterative Refinement (PAIR) are designed to automate prompt-level jailbreaks without a human in the loop.[47]

Refusal suppression involves instructing the model to avoid generating refusals or denials, meaning that it will follow adversarial prompts.

Style injection directs the model to use simple language or adopt a particular style, thereby limiting the sophistication of its responses.

Role-play guides the model to assume specific personas, such as 'Do Anything Now' (DAN) or 'Always Intelligent and Machiavellian' (AIM), to exploit its adaptability and override original safety protocols.

This list is by no means exhaustive and new techniques are continuously emerging. A thorough examination of prompt injection attacks can be found in *Privacy in Large Language Models: Attacks, Defenses and Future Directions*.[48]

Data extraction attacks

Prompt and context stealing refers to the ability to extract the model developer's prompts. Some researchers have found that simple attack queries such as 'repeat all sentences in our conversation' can extract over 60 per cent of prompts across various models and datasets.[49] In Retrieval-augmented Generation (RAG) applications, similar techniques can retrieve sensitive information embedded in the model's context – for example, database entries or text from a PDF intended for summarization.

Availability and integrity violations

Using a prompt injection, the model is requested to perform a time-consuming task which overwhelms the model, maybe through looping behaviour, incapacitating the model and eventually causing a denial of service to users.

The model can be prompted to provide incorrect summaries of the search result or incorrect answers which contradict the cited sources. Chatbots can be prompted to propagate disinformation by relying on, or perpetuating, untrustworthy news sources or the outputs of other search chatbots.

Mitigations for prompt injection, data extraction, and availability and integrity violations attacks

At the time of writing there are no techniques or tools that can comprehensively mitigate against these attacks. In addition to those listed in previous sections, additional strategies include: Reinforcement Learning with Human Feedback (RLHF) to better align large language models (LLMs) with human values and prevent harmful behaviour – for example, OpenAI's GPT-4 was fine-tuned using RLHF; processing inputs to filter out malicious instructions;[50] or by using another LLM as a 'judge' to detect attacks beyond just filtering harmful outputs.

Mitigations for supply chain attacks

When organizations purchase AI systems from suppliers, they may be exposed to vulnerabilities in the third-party's AI system. Organizations should be especially cautious if the supplier incorporates a foundation model in their system. Furthermore, many components of AI systems originate in open-source repositories, such as on GitHub, in the form of pytorch, joblib, numpy or Tensorflow software libraries. Organizations that adapt models from third parties that include open-source libraries should carefully validate these sources for any vulnerabilities prior to use. For model dependencies, this includes regular vulnerability scanning of the software libraries used in the machine learning development lifecycle.

As discussed earlier in the section on Accountabilities (see page 164), third-party supply chain risks can be mitigated by using Sourcing and Procurement assessments.

GenAI red teaming

Red teaming is increasingly popular as an approach to help surface vulnerabilities in an organization's AI systems. The US National Institute of Standards and Technology (NIST) defines a Red Team as 'a group of people authorized and organized to emulate a potential adversary's attack or exploitation capabilities against an enterprise's security posture'. Once security flaws are surfaced, the organization can fix them prior to deploying the model. This is similar to the practice of penetration testing, aka 'pen testing', which tests the security of a specific IT application or system.

INTELLECTUAL PROPERTY AND CONFIDENTIALITY

Many foundation models have been trained on vast bodies of data sourced from numerous platforms including websites, journals, articles and code repositories. Consequently, they may be capable of generating copyright protected content, or content of questionable veracity. Court interpretations of the laws in respective countries will determine whether training a model on intellectual property-protected content is a breach of rights. In the remainder of this section, we will use the term 'legally protected' data to collectively refer to IP and copyright-protected data.

Approaches to Protect Proprietary Data in genAI Models

Protecting prompts

Using publicly available genAI models poses risks, particularly when confidential information is included in prompts. Such data could inadvertently enter the model's training process, increasing the risk of exposure or leakage. Organizations should prevent employees and internal IT systems from accessing public genAI models like ChatGPT. Corporate networks can block access to these tools, with limited use approved only by appropriate leadership.

Instead of public genAI models, many organizations are licensing private instances from technology providers. These models are accessible only within the organization's IT network, preventing prompts from leaving the network and blocking external data from entering the model. Such measures significantly reduce the risk of data leakage and unpredictable model behaviour. These controls are similar to those already used in private corporate clouds. However, it is critical to vet technology providers to ensure their security controls are robust.

For organizations deploying genAI models on their own IT infrastructure,* the responsibility for data protection and leakage prevention falls entirely on the organization. Controls provided by the data centre hosting the AI model can be leveraged but must be carefully managed to ensure security.

Technical tools to prevent proprietary data from being scraped

Existing tools like Web Application Firewall can be extended to guard against web scraping bots. Such a firewall can apply a set of predefined rules to filter out suspicious traffic with familiar attack signatures.[51]

Another option is to install a 'robots.txt' file in your corporate website that provides instructions to web scraping bots about which pages or sections of a website should, or should not, be crawled and indexed. It is not uncommon, however, for some unscrupulous crawlers to attempt to bypass a robots.txt file.

Preventing unintended access/use of third-party protected data used by a foundation model

Given that many foundation models have been trained on data that includes legally protected content, an organization building an application which relies on a foundation model must consider the resulting risks. There is the possibility that such legally protected content may, inadvertently, resurface in their own business processes, or worse still, be exposed externally to their customers. Legal liability rests with the deploying organization in either case.

Contractual assurances

Some of the larger technology companies are now offering limited indemnity protection. OpenAI,[52] Google,[53] Microsoft,[54] and IBM[55] offer to defend customers against certain third-party claims which allege that outputs from their genAI products infringe the intellectual property rights of others.† However, there are some limitations to such indemnities: they are typically restricted to paid commercial/enterprise users or highest-tier individual subscribers and not available to users of free services; various

---

*Sometimes referred to as 'on premises' or simply 'on-prem'.
†This is the case as of early 2025 but may change by the time this book is in print.

terms, conditions and exclusions limit coverage; and the effectiveness and extent of protection is still uncertain as the legal landscape evolves.

Human oversight and awareness

It is important to train employees who access genAI models to be alert to the risks of legally protected data in genAI responses. Role-based access to model outputs can also be implemented to restrict usage to appropriately trained colleagues. This can be supported by additional techniques, such as using tools to scan outputs of AI models for potentially sensitive information, and implementing logging and auditing of AI model use.

Train your own model

Organizations can also attempt to train their own models from scratch, providing full control over how their corporate data is used and whether legally protected third-party data enters their model. As noted earlier, however, training models from scratch is a significant undertaking and most organizations will not have the resources, budget or expertise to do this. Alternatively, open-source models can be used but they present their own challenges. For instance, they may have been trained on data sources that have had even less scrutiny than in the case of closed-source models. Therefore, they will also require additional controls to trap genAI responses using Human in the Loop (HITL) or semi-automated controls to check for third-party data. Of course, the added advantage is that open-source models may be more cost-effective than licensing proprietary models from technology providers.

Protecting creative content

This section explores two techniques that can be used to protect the data of individual creators.

Digital rights management (DRM)[56] which was introduced in the 1990s, enables copyright holders and content creators to restrict access to their content and manage the use of that content. In the context of genAI, several DRM measures can be leveraged including digital watermarking to create indelible graphic files; incorporating metadata which encapsulates copyright and licensing information and can be monitored; embedded codes to control how and where media is published online; and end user licence agreements requiring user consent.

Creative commons (CC)[57] licensing allows content providers to waive their copyright, if their content serves the public interest. CC is a nonprofit organization originally set up to advocate for widespread, open sharing of content. It has recently developed six licenses to ensure credit is given to authors if their work is used for specific purposes. If material is used for commercial purposes, two CC licenses include CC BY-SA and CC BY-ND. The former allows for the adaptation – 'remix, adapt and build upon' – of original content in making derivative content and the latter allows for un-adapted redistribution. In both cases the organization must license the modified material under identical terms and it must be attributed to the creator of the original content.

However, enforcing these licenses is challenging since CC licenses were not designed with AI training in mind. For instance, there is debate over what exactly is meant by 'commercial use' and 'derivative work' in genAI. It is also difficult to enforce attribution since tracing back genAI results to content that contributed to those results is extremely hard and limited mechanisms exist for tracking compliance.

How to Alert the Public to AI-Generated Content

Another technique is to ensure genAI model outputs include Transparency Notices, which enable AI platforms to inform users about the limitations of AI-generated content, explicitly stating that not all responses are verified or fully accurate. This approach is particularly important for general-purpose language models. Encouraging independent verification by prompting users to check information with trusted sources is another good strategy.

WORKFORCE

Many uses of AI will have a broader societal impact beyond the individual organization. Organizations should be proactive to ensure their workforce is equipped with the appropriate skills to support the current and future use of AI in their role, as well as minimizing downstream impacts from the deployment of AI solutions.

Impact on Colleagues in the Workplace

Studies indicate both the potential for significant job displacement due to AI and the opportunity to create new types of employment and increase productivity by automating routine tasks.[58] Nonetheless, employees may be concerned about AI's impact on their role and whether they have the necessary skills to benefit from these new technologies. A recent study by

ADP Research found that 85 per cent of workers surveyed believe AI will affect their job within the next two to three years.[59]

Forward-thinking companies are offering upskilling programs to ensure workers are comfortable with, and able to benefit from, AI tools, as well as increasing their ability to take on new roles. For example: the Walmart Academy offers in-person and virtual training programs;[60] Starbucks offers employee training on the benefits of avatars;[61] PepsiCo's Digital Academy includes 11,000+ learning assets to help employees acquire digital skills by offering advanced content for technical roles, practical courses for non-technical roles using digital tools, and foundational programs for beginners.[62] Already more than 23,000 associates have participated, earning nearly 1,000 certifications.

PEPSICO TAKES A WORKER-CENTRIC APPROACH TO AI ADOPTION

As artificial intelligence fundamentally changes how we view skills in the workplace, PepsiCo has committed itself to centering its employees and fostering a culture of innovation that results in more high-level, rewarding work.

PepsiCo is proud to share its own experiences to encourage more organizations to proactively adopt a worker-centric approach to the future of manufacturing. That is why PepsiCo partnered with the Aspen Institute to convene experts, study the landscape, and create a guide for manufacturers with recommendations when considering automated solutions.[63]

These recommendations provide widely-applicable best practices for manufacturers who are considering integrating automation – AI-powered or otherwise – into their operations. The guide details three goals for employers to prioritize: 1. Reduce the risks of automated systems; 2. Upskill to get the most out of your automation investments; and 3. Retain workers and valuable institutional knowledge.

'As a CPG leader, we are always looking to share our learnings from our ongoing journey in a way that inspires more organizations to embrace the potential of AI and data-driven automation. Our partnership with Aspen highlights the importance and best practices for keeping workers' well-being front and center – a key for a successful transformation.' – Dr. Athina Kanioura, PepsiCo's chief strategy and transformation officer.

Recent literature also explores benefits companies can enjoy by augmenting human capabilities with AI rather than replacing workers. For instance, David Carmona's book, *The AI Organization*,[64] provides a roadmap focusing on workforce transformation and Paul Daugherty's book, *Human + Machine*,[65] explores successful strategies for augmenting jobs with AI.

Organizations can promote employee AI literacy by offering or directing staff to tailored training programs for different stakeholders, including executives, data scientists and end-users. Effective AI literacy programs will cover topics such as the basics of AI technology, including where it is used and potential risks and benefits. We elaborated on this topic earlier in Chapter 8 and provide example training resources in Appendix Four.

ENVIRONMENT AND SUSTAINABILITY

As genAI becomes increasingly integrated into industries, and across society, its environmental footprint, from data centre greenhouse gas emissions,[66] energy consumption[67] and water usage for cooling,[68] is a growing concern. At the same time, the financial investment required to develop foundation models has reached previously unimaginable levels and organizations deploying AI applications are also experiencing uncertain operational costs. This raises concerns about the long-term sustainability of genAI's environmental and financial impact.

Organizations should consider addressing these concerns in their AI governance program. However, this also involves balancing trade-offs to prevent mitigating one risk at the expense of another.

Efficiency versus Accuracy: methods like model distillation and pruning, described below, are designed to improve model efficiency by reducing operational costs and energy consumption. However, they may also decrease model accuracy. For high-stakes use cases, even minor accuracy reductions can have significant consequences.

Efficiency versus Regulatory Compliance: optimizing AI models for efficiency could compromise adherence to regulatory and ethical standards. Energy consumption optimization can risk diminishing transparency or even fairness.

Figure 10.7 below proposes a new concept, which we refer to as 'Sustainable AI', that aims to strike the right balance between these competing factors. In addition to Responsible AI, which is largely concerned with compliance and accuracy – depicted in the top half of the circle – we recommend also incorporating environmental and operational cost factors and mitigating their negative impacts accordingly.

FIGURE 10.7 Sustainable AI

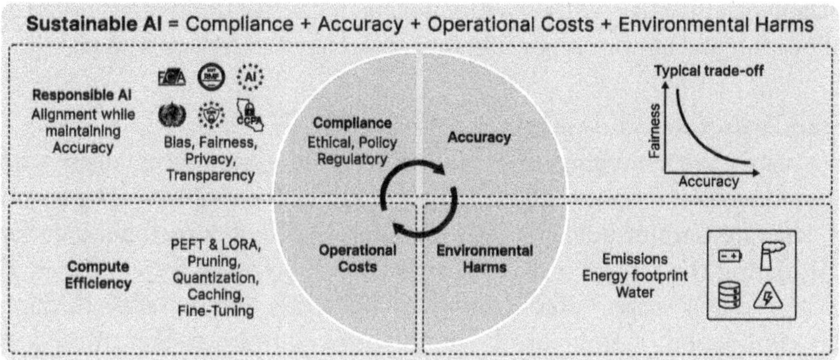

Regulatory pressure is mounting to ensure environmental impacts are considered in model development. The EU AI Act's Energy Disclosure Requirement mandates that all foundation model providers disclose details about the energy consumption and compute resources used during model training.[69]

Controls and Tools

Combining existing GreenOps (Green Operations) with FinOps (Financial Operations) practices can enable organizations to effectively balance environmental objectives alongside financial cost management. Integrating these practices with AI governance and risk management offers an opportunity for sustainable and accountable AI operations.

FinOps and GreenOps

FinOps brings financial accountability to cloud computing's variable spending. As public cloud usage expanded, managing costs became essential, leading to frameworks like the FinOps Foundation's structured approach[70] and tools such as Azure Advisor and Cost Management.[71] FinOps practices include monitoring, documenting and controlling resource allocation decisions to align spending with business outcomes.[72] With AI operations incurring significant costs, integrating them into financial planning is becoming a priority for FinOps practitioners.

GreenOps integrates sustainability into IT operations, optimizing cloud usage to reduce carbon emissions and promote eco-friendly practices.[73] It focuses on energy efficiency, waste reduction, continuous monitoring and automation to align IT with environmental goals. This involves assessing necessary resources, tailoring applications to minimize waste and balancing efficiency with data monitoring, including optimizing resource allocation and considering geographic placement to reduce data travel.

Standards, tools and carbon accounting

Standards are emerging that can help measure carbon intensity and should be used for accurate carbon accounting. The ISO/IEC 21031:2024 – Software Carbon Intensity (SCI) Standard – defines a methodology for calculating the rate of carbon emissions for a software system, referred to as the SCI score.[74] Reducing an SCI score is only possible through the elimination of emissions by modifying a software system to use less physical hardware, less energy or consume lower-carbon energy sources. Various carbon accounting tools – software applications designed to measure, track and manage an organization's environmental impacts – can help calculate greenhouse gas emissions by using data from sources such as energy consumption, transportation and production processes.[75]

GenAI compute optimization techniques

To reduce energy consumption in AI operations, organizations can implement several compute optimization techniques when using open-source models (note, the techniques listed below will not be feasible for all closed-source genAI models):

> **Model distillation**: this compresses genAI models into smaller, more efficient versions that perform similar tasks with less computational power. While it saves energy and computing costs, it may lead to performance degradation, requiring a balance between sustainability and accuracy.[76]

> **Quantization**: by reducing the precision of a model's parameters – for example, by using eight-bit integers instead of 32-bit floating-point numbers – quantization decreases computation and memory requirements, enabling faster and more efficient inference with minimal accuracy loss.[77]

Pruning: this technique removes less significant weights or nodes within a neural network, effectively reducing the model's size and computational resource requirements. However, careful management is necessary to prevent negative impacts on performance, especially in precision-critical applications.[78]

Low-rank adaptation (LoRA): reduces the computational burden of fine-tuning by freezing most of a model's parameters and training only small, low-rank matrices inserted into specific network layers.[79] This approach lowers memory and compute requirements while maintaining performance. Parameter-Efficient Fine-Tuning (PEFT) focuses on fine-tuning a subset of a large language model's parameters, significantly reducing the cost of retraining models for new tasks.[80]

In summary, to achieve Sustainable AI, organizations should consider incorporating environmental and financial risk management within their AI governance framework. This can be enabled by leveraging existing FinOps and GreenOps practices, together with model optimization techniques, supported by industry standards. Much more work remains to be done to create and operationalize Sustainable AI for AI governance in this area.

KEY INSIGHTS AND ACTIONS

- **Control Requirements**: specify what criteria must be satisfied at any point in the AI lifecycle, such as meeting a fairness metric. **Control Routines** are quantitative tools used to compute metrics that satisfy control requirements, like 'equality of odds' or 'disparate impact'; or qualitative tools that provide textual descriptions to satisfy control requirements – for example, Impact Assessments.
- **GenAI**: presents challenges for traditional validation approaches, so assurance processes for genAI have shifted *from* validation *to* testing, together with applying guardrails.
- **Accuracy**: use technical tools to surface key metrics but be mindful of limitations and use human in the loop, Retrieval-augmented Generation and fine-tuning. Enhance testing using benchmark data sets and make use of content moderation filters.
- **Fairness and Bias**: perhaps the hardest challenge – metrics exist but beware of trade-offs and select based on use case characteristics and

context. Be mindful to manage the fairness-accuracy trade-off. Use Reinforcement Learning with Human Feedback and Human in the Loop frequently.

- **Interpretability, Explainability and Transparency**: technical tools can help explain how some AI systems arrive at their results but they are insufficient. Use Human in the Loop and provide clear notices for people impacted by AI systems.
- **Accountability**: identify and empower key individuals and governance forums. Re-use and extend existing policies and support processes with an AI governance platform and legal horizon scanning.
- **Privacy**: invest in data governance and technical tooling. Extend existing privacy controls, such as privacy-enhancing technologies, and guard against data leaks. For genAI consider using a separate large language model for evaluation.
- **Security**: implement new genAI tooling and extend the use of existing AI defences. Set up Red Teaming and be mindful of the evolving genAI attack surface. Validate third-party software integrated into your genAI systems.
- **Intellectual Property and Confidentiality**: strengthen security defences, secure models within the perimeter of the organization and train employees in the prudent use of genAI. Evaluate contractual assurances from foundation model developers.
- **Workforce**: place employees at the centre of AI strategy, equipping them with the skills to embrace AI and use it wisely.
- **Environment and Sustainability**: consider as part of AI governance framework to balance potentially competing priorities. Use FinOps and GreenOps practices supported by carbon accounting packages and aligned to ISO Standards.
- GenAI is nascent and new risks may emerge: integrate controls across the entire model development lifecycle and build flexibility into your approach.
- Use Human in the Loop, Human on the Loop and Human in Control extensively to manage many of the risks – in most cases this is, at the time of writing, probably the best default approach.
- Invest in cross-enterprise training with tailored courses for different teams depending on their exposure to AI and their role in AI governance.

FIGURE 10.8 SUMMARY OF RISKS, CONTROLS AND MITIGATIONS

Risk	Source of Risk	Controls and Mitigations	
		Traditional AI	GenAI
ACCURACY AND RELIABILITY	Complexity of models. Probabilistic nature of models. Hidden correlations in data. Black box nature of models. **GenAI:** Inscrutable web-scraped data sets. Limited regard for data provenance and veracity. Data sets not under control of deploying organization. Intractable, complex architecture. Hallucinations.	Determine most appropriate measure of accuracy for the specific use case. Minimize model's input features to those that drive the model's decisions (a practice called feature-engineering). Use explainability techniques (see below) to select appropriate features. Adjust the model's internal behaviour. Rigorous testing using different test sets. Use third-party or open-source software libraries containing metric measures (plenty are available as open-source libraries).	Adjust and craft prompts carefully. Fine-tune model by augmenting it with your organization's data, using Retrieval-augmented Generation. Tailor the model using your own data and prompts. Use accuracy metrics (open-source or vendor provided). Use benchmark data sets, tailored to specific use cases, to test model results. Human in the Loop – intercept responses for human review. Tune model with humans rating answers: Reinforcement Learning with Human Feedback.

(Continued)

FIGURE 10.8 (Continued)

Risk	Source of Risk	Controls and Mitigations	
		Traditional AI	GenAI
BIAS AND FAIRNESS	**Bias in data** Within data sources. Sampling error in data collection. Mislabelling training data. **Bias in model** Mismatch in training and test data. Model aggregates incorrectly. Faulty test evaluation. **Bias in deployment** Training data does not align to user population.	Pre-determine most appropriate measure of fairness for the specific use case. Pre-processing adjustments: carefully examine and debias training data. In-processing adjustments: use fairness constraints and adversarial debiasing. Post processing adjustments: capture model outputs and change them to comply with fairness measures. Consider individual fairness metrics and counterfactual fairness. Use Explainable Fairness (see page 152).	Adjust and craft prompts carefully. Use metrics that flag lack of diversity in answers. Trap harmful responses in large language model outputs using filters. Human in the Loop – trap responses for human review. Tune model with humans rating answers: Reinforcement Learning with Human Feedback. Automatically train for safety using machine learning techniques. Use benchmark data sets, tailored to test model results for unfair and biased outputs.
INTERPRETABILITY, EXPLAINABILITY AND TRANSPARENCY	Complexity of models. Hidden (and non-linear) correlations in data. Black box nature of models. Lack of logical inference. Unclear audience for whom to define interpretability.	Ascertain how features contribute to results. Counterfactual explanations. Derive logical rules from the model. Use simplest model possible for each use case. Explore interactive, 'what-if' tools. Investigate simpler model as surrogate. Model cards and data cards. Transparency notices to model users stating they are interacting with an AI model.	Adjust and craft prompts carefully. Tools to explore which parts of prompt are used to drive the response. Tools to map out which parts of the model are activated for various prompts. Enrich data sets with your organization's data. Create model cards and data cards. Provide notice to users of interaction with an AI model.

ACCOUNTABILITY		
Lack of clarity demarking boundaries of responsibility. Lack of expertise. Lack of assignment of roles and responsibilities within organization. Evolving regulatory landscape. Rapidly changing AI model capability. Existing policies inadequate to deal with emerging risks. Litigation and reputational risks. Lack of standardized guidance. Nascent field and lack of clear authorities for best practice. Over-reliance on AI and automation bias.	Assign clear accountabilities and responsibilities across stakeholder teams (Privacy, Security, Legal, Sourcing, etc.) with ultimate lead in C-suite. Update organizational policies and procedures. Implement AI governance platform. Establish AI Ethics Council or similar body to provide guidance on specific AI issues and policies. Implement Algorithmic Impact Assessments. Update existing risk assessments as necessary. Establish regulatory and horizon scanning. Upskill teams and model risk management. Mitigate automation bias and instil culture of Human in the Loop. Augment user interface design with 'cognitive speed bumps'. Clearly establish boundaries of acceptable use. Provide customer mechanism(s) for contestability and redress.	Same measures used for traditional AI. Add additional accountability controls. Additional focus required for Privacy, Security, Sourcing and Legal teams owing to heightened risks in areas within their remit. For Agentic AI, evaluate and restrict agent's activities, expose agent's reasoning steps, log activities and finally ensure a fail-safe 'kill-switch'.

(*Continued*)

FIGURE 10.8 (Continued)

Risk	Source of Risk	Controls and Mitigations	
		Traditional AI	GenAI
PRIVACY	Lack of model robustness. Lack of secure development environment. Unmasked personal data used in training. Susceptibility to leaking data through prompt hacking. Indiscriminate web scraping, including publicly available private data and legally protected data. Shadow IT: use of public genAI models inside corporate networks. Lack of employee awareness of risks created by use.	Implement strong data governance, including regular data audits. Use Privacy Enhancing Technology tools: Data encryption. Anonymization and masking of sensitive data. Differential Privacy. Federated Learning. Provide extensive training for teams.	Implement prompt-based defences. Wrap prompts with special characters. Filter incoming prompts containing suspicious requests for data. Use a separate large language model to detect dangerous prompts before processing in the model. Use tools to detect malicious queries or to restrict the range of queries that a model will accept.
SECURITY	Susceptible to availability and integrity attacks. Compromising training data. Denial of Service. Attempts to steal intellectual property. Third-party model vulnerabilities. Prompt hacking, jailbreaking, prompt injections.	Train the model with artificial poisoned data to build resilience. Strict model environment access controls. Ethical hacking and penetration testing. Use established third-party security tools (*see* Privacy Tools above).	Use Privacy Tools described above and traditional AI techniques. Filter incoming queries for suspicious behaviour and outlier detection to identify anomalies. Use Reinforcement Learning with Human Feedback to intercept harmful large language model responses. Use third-party assurance practices and validate external libraries for vulnerabilities. Mobilize Red Teaming.

INTELLECTUAL PROPERTY AND CONFIDENTIALITY	Massive web-scraped data sets used indiscriminately for training foundation models. Limited regard for data provenance and veracity.	For content creators: Data Rights Management and Licensing, such as Creative Commons. For users: transparency notices.	Same as for Traditional AI. Restrict use of public genAI models using existing firewall controls. Role-based access supported by employee training. Use models from trusted third-party suppliers. Ring-fence models using existing cloud provider. Legal and contractual assurances from third-party suppliers. Train your own model. Extend 'Terms of Service' on website to prohibit scraping.
WORKFORCE	Impacts on workforce.	Augment roles with AI rather than replacing them, where possible. Provide tailored and role-specific upskilling.	Increase investment in AI literacy across your organization. Raise awareness of all AI risks. Provide tailored and role-specific upskilling.

(Continued)

FIGURE 10.8 (Continued)

Risk	Source of Risk	Controls and Mitigations	
		Traditional AI	GenAI
ENVIRONMENT AND SUSTAINABILITY	Increased greenhouse gas emissions, energy demand and water depletion risks. Increased and unknown operational cost.	Same controls as advised for genAI.	Extend AI governance to include measurement of environmental impacts. Consider FinOps and GreenOps practices for environmental and operational cost risk management. Adopt ISO standards on emissions reporting. Implement carbon accounting tools. Implement green coding for model development. Use model optimization techniques.

11

AI governance platforms and tools

AN AI GOVERNANCE PLATFORM IN ACTION

LegisAI, a legaltech firm, sought ISO 42001 certification to build trust with its customers by ensuring their AI systems met strict governance standards.* Modulos, an AI Governance, Risk and Compliance (GRC) platform certified for ISO 42001, enabled LegisAI to rapidly implement the 90 required controls for compliance using the pre-defined controls that were reusable across different frameworks. Instead of creating new controls from scratch, LegisAI could efficiently adapt and apply existing controls, significantly speeding up the certification process.

'The Modulos platform also provided structured workflows that grouped controls based on principles and logical sequences, making the compliance tasks easy to manage and navigate. This allowed LegisAI to keep track of all necessary steps and ensure that every control was correctly applied, minimizing the risk of errors or omissions.' Commented Elena Maran, Global Head of Financial Services and Responsible AI, at Modulos.

AI governance platforms are designed to provide an enterprise-wide tool enabling governance and compliance across the entire life of every AI system in the organization. These platforms facilitate the interplay between policies, controls, assessment results and all approvals needed to meet enterprise-wide risk management requirements. Large

*LegisAI is a fictional name for an actual Modulos client.

organizations will likely already have some form of Governance, Risk and Compliance (GRC) platform: a key decision during the design of the AI governance program will be whether to rely solely on that platform to manage the AI governance process or whether a bespoke platform is needed. This chapter will describe the key requirements that an AI governance platform should support.

In our experience, depending on the size and needs of an organization, using an existing GRC platform may be a good way to start as this approach minimizes start-up delays and has the advantage that colleagues will be familiar with the platform. However, it may not be sufficiently comprehensive or flexible to cater to AI specific risks and their regulatory requirements. For example, Shell, the global oil and gas company, preferred to use existing systems to begin implementing their AI governance process – ServiceNow manages the process flow and serves as the AI inventory and documentation repository – though they remain open to alternatives as the landscape evolves.

Figure 11.1 shows the components of an AI governance platform, which will be described in this chapter.

FIGURE 11.1 AI Governance Platform Components

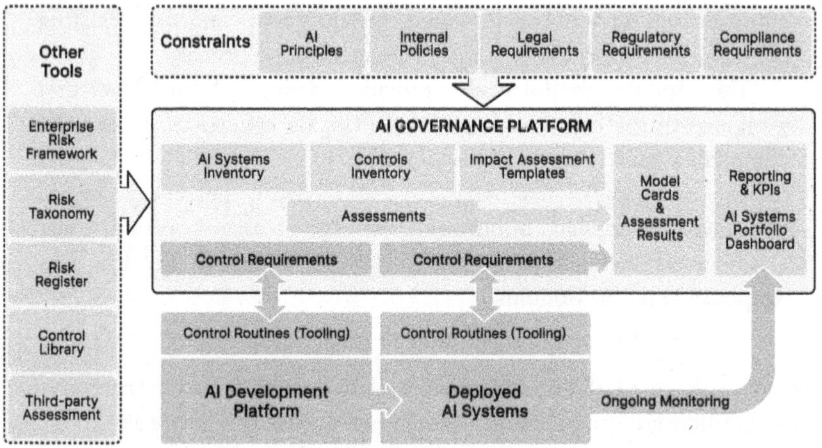

The following sections list the high-level requirements of an AI governance platform. This list is not intended to be exhaustive and not all requirements will be relevant to every organization. We have intentionally focused on what we see as the most important requirements, based on our experience. We recommend undertaking an evaluation of the requirements specific to your organization's needs before engaging with potential platform vendors. For illustration purposes, we have included requirements related to the EU AI Act, but AI governance platforms should be configurable to support numerous applicable regulatory, policy and customer requirements.

REQUIREMENTS FOR AN AI GOVERNANCE PLATFORM

As explained earlier in Chapter 10, the word 'controls' can be used in two different ways:

- *Control requirements* specify what criteria must be satisfied at any point in the system lifecycle, such as meeting a fairness metric.
- *Control routines* are implemented as quantitative tools – for example as Python libraries that compute metrics to satisfy control requirements such as 'equality of odds' or 'disparate parity'. Some tools, however, are qualitative and provide textual descriptions to satisfy control requirements – for example, Impact Assessments.

Two other terms will be introduced here:

- *Guardrail(s)* refers to a group of control routines that are implemented in relation to a specific use case.
- *Control set* refers to the group of control requirements that are commonly employed for several use cases – for example, a control set for all AI systems used for lending, which could include consumer lending as well as corporate lending.

Another important consideration is that an *AI system* may refer to several component parts which together constitute an AI use case:

- One or several AI model(s), which can be either a traditional AI model or a genAI model;
- Training and test data sets, both for development and testing;
- Reference data used to enrich either the training data or some other outputs/inputs;
- Calculation subsystems;
- Post-processing systems;
- Validation routines;
- Report generation.

Characterizing an AI system as being composed of several components aligns with the definition used in the EU AI Act.

AI System Inventory

An inventory is the single repository to store information about every AI system across the organization. The inventory should be a window into *all* of the governance activities across the entire lifecycle of an AI system, whether in conception, design, development, testing, in production or decommissioned.

The inventory supports accountability management for each AI system through its development lifecycle by assigning ownership and responsibilities. For example, it should record which team is responsible for development, the business sponsor and which governance forum or individual is accountable for compliance activities. Furthermore, it should:

- Support classification according to any relevant legislative schema, such as those in the EU AI Act, and any materiality or risk tiering of the underlying model.
- Allow AI systems to be linked to specific jurisdictions where they are approved for use. This includes the use of results, even if the system is owned or operated in a different jurisdiction.
- Link AI systems to organizational policies with which they need to comply, independent of jurisdiction, either automatically based on system attributes, or through manual configuration.

Furthermore, the inventory should include registries for several other object types related to the AI system, including use cases, models, controls, data sets and documents to evidence compliance.

Use case registry

A detailed description of the intended use, including the users and purpose of the AI system, how it will be accessed, by whom and under what circumstances. It should capture complex relationships between the system and its intended use cases: the system could be applied to one or more use case, and a use case could be fulfilled by one or more AI systems. For example, a credit lending system can be applied to individuals and corporations and can be used for insurance premium underwriting. The registry should allow individual use cases to be linked to use case types, or other risk classification schemas defined by the organization.

Model registry/catalogue

A given model could relate to one or more AI systems and the registry should distinguish between different model types. The registry should record the origin of third-party or open-source models. In the case of genAI models, a way of distinguishing their original state and their fine-tuned state should be recorded. It should capture upstream and downstream dependencies between models and their training data sets, including the data lineage and provenance. Linkage to other ancillary data beyond training data should also be captured.

Controls registry

This registry should specify all control requirements that could be applied to an AI system at different stages in its lifecycle. Some controls may be defined in an external controls library and, if so, this linkage should be captured. It should be possible to link controls to different system lifecycle stages and based on pre-defined policies. For example, a control requirement could be to invoke an Algorithmic Impact Assessment early in the AI system lifecycle and a bias mitigation control requirement could be specified at AI system testing and quality assurance stages.

Data registry

For each AI system, the data registry should:

- Link to any training, validation or evaluation data sets, together with a description, information about origin and whether they contain personal data.
- Support linkages to structured and unstructured data, including multi-modal data.
- Document the features that are included in model training data sets.
- Store metadata – i.e. data that describes the underlying training data and its features.
- Specify all the characteristics of the data used in the model. For example, how the data has been derived and its version number.
- Document the justification for including each feature or attribute in training data. If data has been masked – for example, to remove Personally Identifiable Information (PII), evidence to support why and how this was done should be included.

- Capture data lineage, data integrity and data provenance, providing traceability back to the origin of the data.
- Explain the justification for including data sets and measures that have been taken to ensure the data is appropriate. This might include demonstrating how the data was de-biased and the steps taken to check the data set is representative.
- Capture links to benchmark data sets used in testing, together with a justification for using this benchmark and how it supports compliance with the control requirements.

It is worth noting that these steps may have been performed already by the model development team prior to the control requirements being surfaced. We have found in some organizations that have mature development practices that these are intuitive for development teams, but they must nonetheless be documented. Ideally, the governance platform will link into the model development lifecycle so that developers can capture required information in the system 'as they go' rather than having to add it later.

Document registry

This registry captures documentation related to the AI system and its component parts – for example, model and data cards. The underlying documents could be in a single document library or in multiple libraries external to the platform. The registry should check for mandatory documents that are required by policies or regulation.

Evidencing approvals and sign-off

The platform should store evidence of approved and accepted test results, as mandated by the control requirements. Some approvals will be from development teams and others from risk management teams that have responsibility for oversight. In the financial sector, for example, model validation teams must provide documentary evidence supporting sign-off, in line with policy. In some cases, evidence can take the form of a link to logs generated by the AI system development environment throughout the model development lifecycle.

Risk Management

The AI governance platform should support the organization's Risk Management Framework, Risk Taxonomy and Risk Register. A Risk

Taxonomy defines various types of high-level risks an organization may face, such as operational, financial, strategic and regulatory risks. The taxonomy is designed to improve risk identification, prioritization and management. A Risk Register is a more detailed tool supporting ongoing testing and risk mitigation during the AI system lifecycle. The governance platform should support the classification of an AI system according to the organization's Risk Taxonomy, and ongoing mapping to the Risk Register, to ensure control requirements and control routines adequately meet risk management needs.

Pre-deployment Performance and Testing

Pre-deployment testing up to and during retraining, recalibration and deployment should be tracked by the governance platform. This functionality should link the datasets used across the lifecycle stages, allowing for an explanation of how the system is configured and parameterized. It should also track configurations across successive versions of the system, along with versioned datasets that contributed to each configuration. The pre-deployment tools should support:

- Generation of standard performance metrics, including those for the risks discussed in Chapter 10. This is particularly important for those risks that can be measured using quantitative metrics such as fairness and bias, interpretability, explainability, transparency and accuracy. The platform should support user-defined metrics.
- Evaluation of benchmark training and testing datasets, including assessment of data quality, suitability and representativeness, along with ongoing monitoring for data and model drift over time.
- Consolidation and display of key results from the building and testing of a system before deployment. This includes configured controls, documentation and metrics on model performance, stability and fairness. This supports required assessments such as AI Algorithmic Impact Assessments, Model Validation and Conformity Assessments.

Workflows

The governance platform should support a diverse range of configurable workflows which can update relevant information in the AI system inventory. These workflows should include:

- AI system development and deployment workflows: managing the full development and deployment process for AI systems and models in line with the organization's change methodology.
- AI system assessment workflow: this workflow will include the stages required for completion of Algorithmic Impact Assessments, Fundamental Rights Assessments, Conformity Assessments and so forth (see also Chapter 9). It should capture the assessment results and include any supporting material. Also, it should clearly flag ethical edge-cases requiring Ethics Council review, as well as documenting its decisions.
- Model validation and approval workflow: an organization's model validation team, where one exists, will normally use a structured sequence of steps and activities to provide assurance and sign-off.
- Wider risk management workflows:
  - Sourcing and Procurement: this includes integration with the processes for engaging with third-party vendors of systems with AI, including managing notifications from vendors regarding updates to their products.
  - Internal and external audits and Conformity Assessments: the stages in these workflows should be supported, with the ability to link to artefacts produced during each stage.

Jurisdictional Support

The governance platform should contain a jurisdiction library, enabling each system to be associated with one or multiple jurisdictions where it is approved for deployment or where its outputs are permitted for use. The jurisdictions linked to each system offer a means – though not the only one – of applying relevant geographic-specific policies, which is especially useful for EU AI Act compliance.

Policies

The platform should support the ingestion and maintenance of both predefined and configurable policies from internal and external sources. These policies can take the form of regulations, sector guidelines and standards, AI principles or internal policies. Policies can optionally recommend or mandate specific control requirements or control sets, as drawn from the Controls Registry. The AI governance platform should be capable of:

- Linking policy sets to specific jurisdictions or identifying them as globally applicable.
- Allowing authorized users to manually apply policies to specific AI systems.

Post Deployment Monitoring and Control

A centralized view of all deployed AI systems across the organization should be provided, consolidating inputs from different deployment platforms and monitoring tools. This function should report compliance status, performance metrics, thresholds, breaches and other control-related information. Post-deployment monitoring should include:

- Tracking performance metrics defined in the 'Pre-Deployment Performance and Testing' section above (page 201).
- Generating measures to support explainability at both individual outcome and model or system levels.
- Testing metrics against configurable thresholds and raising alerts when limits are approached.
- Detecting situations like model or data drift – loss of accuracy – and issuing alerts.
- Enforcing periodic model retraining as defined in model risk policies.

Governance Reporting

Comprehensive reporting covering the AI inventory, risk management, AI system status, monitoring and control, and issue and incident statistics is an essential feature of the governance platform. Incident reporting should include metrics such as outstanding issues categorized by severity, time to closure and trend analysis. Reports should be available at the level of individual models or AI systems, by business domains or functions, and across the entire organization. These reports should be configurable and customizable.

A dashboard providing a single 'window' into the organization's entire landscape of AI systems can be helpful for senior management. The dashboard should be configurable, with flexibility to aggregate statistics on AI system performance, defects, issues and breaches.

Integration
The governance platform should integrate with key corporate-wide and other IT systems via well-defined and robust application programming interfaces (APIs), allowing for automated one-way and, in some cases, two-way data flows:

- For ingesting internal and external policies and AI principles.
- For communication with the organization's risk register, risk taxonomy and controls library.
- For integration with tools used in associated workflows, such as privacy and cybersecurity assessments.

The platform should be capable of integrating with third-party AI system development and deployment platforms, including open-source platforms:

- Control requirements originating from the governance platform should be consumed by model development platforms and
- Control routine results originating from development platforms should be consumed by the governance platform.

These two points are critical, especially in large organizations where various business units may have different AI development platforms. Typically, each platform offers a suite of control routines for calculating the metrics described in Chapter 10 – for example, for accuracy, interpretability and fairness and bias. The API should be used to capture metrics from the control routines in these other platforms, as evidence of compliance with their corresponding control requirements.

Role-Based Access
Secure and controlled access to inventories and artefacts should be enforced through:

- Role-based access controls supporting both standard and custom role definitions.
- Dynamic role management, allowing dynamic assignment and revocation of roles based on project needs, responsibilities or workflows.

- Mechanisms implementing the organization's risk management approval processes aligned with workflows to manage sensitive actions and role assignments.
- Comprehensive logging to capture detailed audit logs of user activity, such as data access and model modifications, to support accountability and compliance.
- Identity access integration with corporate identity management systems, such as Active Directory and Lightweight Directory Access Protocol (LDAP), and enabling Single Sign-On for seamless and consistent access control.

Independent Conformity Assessments

An AI governance platform should integrate with internal or third-party assurance systems that are designed to provide independent assessments demonstrating compliance with standards, policies or procedures. In some cases, the results will be recorded, in others the platform may support the assessment process itself.

We can now revisit the AI governance platform from the start of this chapter to include the requirements described above in Figure 11.2 below.

FIGURE 11.2 AI Governance Platform Detail

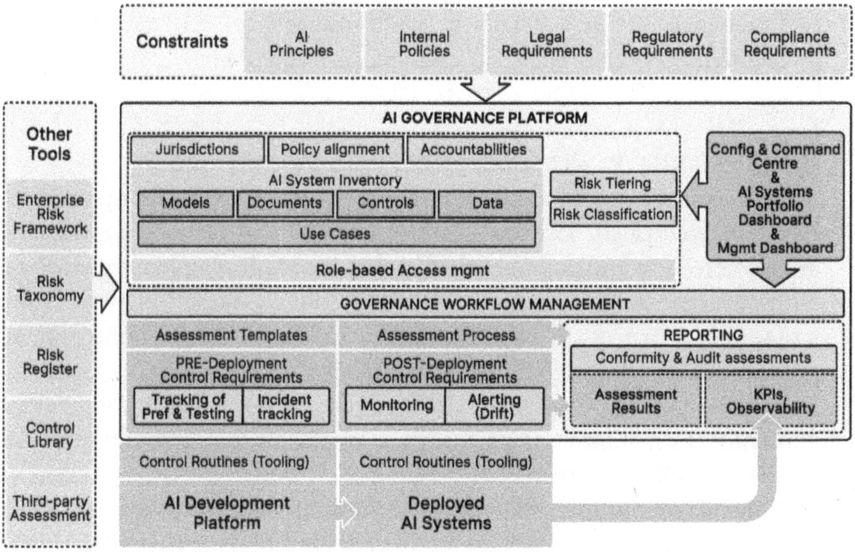

KEY REQUIREMENTS FOR AN AI GOVERNANCE PLATFORM

- Establish risk classification for each AI system based on use case characteristics, risk appetite, policies, regulatory and jurisdictional requirements.
- Navigate and enforce organization-wide risk management process and workflows in the AI development lifecycle in line with risk classification – for example, by imposing checkpoints which cannot be passed without an appropriate approval.
- Document and support the activities needed for compliance with relevant governance processes – for example, storing test results and names of approvers for assessments in line with their defined accountabilities.
- Evidence activities that have been undertaken to ensure all risks have been adequately mitigated, through the control routines and in compliance with control requirements.
- Provide robust monitoring to ensure deployed AI systems comply with risk thresholds defined in the control requirements.
- Provide an organization-wide view of all AI systems throughout the governance lifecycle for management reporting.

It may be useful to evaluate your existing Governance, Risk and Compliance (GRC) platform with respect to AI governance requirements before engaging in any vendor selection.

GOVERNANCE PLATFORM AND TOOL PROVIDERS

The AI governance and tooling market is evolving rapidly. Many vendors have emerged in the last few years and established technology vendors are also creating and augmenting their AI model development platforms with governance toolkits. One estimate predicts a market increase from $264 million in 2024 to $936 million by 2029 with a compound annual growth rate of 29 per cent.[1] Many of the Big Tech platform companies, such as Google, Microsoft and Amazon, provide governance, compliance and control capabilities as part of their platforms. For a selection of AI governance platform vendors, see Appendix Three.

Controls to mitigate the risks described in Chapter 10 are provided by many software vendors, ranging from large cloud providers offering a range of tools for the entire AI lifecycle, including traditional and genAI; enterprise software vendors which offer similar tools to cloud providers; through to smaller specialist vendors offering tools for one or several of the risks discussed in this book; and open-source toolkits that can be extended and tailored by organizations, under licensing terms.

In Appendix Three we mention some notable vendors but this is by no means an exhaustive list: the marketplace for AI tooling is also dynamic and fast-growing. We also do not list every tool provided by each vendor as their offerings are constantly developing.

KEY INSIGHTS AND ACTIONS

- An AI governance platform is a single centralized system that supports the entire governance process, integrating key artefacts, processes and workflows across the AI system lifecycle, from conception to post-deployment.
- It provides traceability of governance and approvals, risk management processes, controls mapping from policy to detailed control requirements, through to control decomposition and testing.[*]
- It is an AI systems portfolio management tool providing visibility of AI systems across the entire organization, together with their status. This helps build trust and confidence for executive decision-making.
- Each organization will have different requirements for which features of an AI governance platform are most relevant.
- A detailed vendor selection should be performed based on organization-specific and regulatory requirements.

[*] An approach to this is described in Eisenberg et al., 'The Unified Control Framework: Establishing a Common Foundation for Enterprise AI Governance, Risk Management and Regulatory Compliance', https://arxiv.org/html/2503.05937v1.

Section III

The global landscape of AI regulation

'When navigating the challenges of AI governance, we must first look to the laws already on the books. These laws often provide a foundation of principles – fairness, accountability and transparency – that can guide us in adapting to the complexities of emerging technologies like AI and identify potential liability before you wind up in court or as a bad news headline. As a former judge, prosecutor and Secretary of Homeland Security, I know from experience that effective governance doesn't start from scratch, it starts with understanding and applying what we already know to new contexts.'

Michael Chertoff, Former US Secretary of Homeland Security; Executive Chairman, The Chertoff Group

12

EU laws and regulations

AI governance is unfolding in a dynamic and complex global landscape, where regulatory frameworks attempt to keep up with the unprecedented pace of technological advancement. Countries around the world are navigating a delicate balancing act: how to cultivate technological advancement, health and prosperity while mitigating the risks AI presents, such as to human rights, privacy, cybersecurity and accountability. As AI reshapes industries and societies, policymakers are increasingly focused on crafting regulations that not only maximize the benefits of this technology but also ensure those benefits are shared universally.

While legal frameworks specific to AI are still emerging, many AI systems and uses are subject to existing laws already on the books. To be sure, new laws are coming. The 2025 edition of Stanford's AI Index report found that in 2024 in the US 221 bills related to AI were proposed at the federal level, almost triple those proposed in 2022. Around the world, mentions of AI in legislative proceedings increased by 21.3 per cent between 2023 and 2024; mentions have grown ninefold since 2016. Many regard the EU as a first-mover due to the press that the 2024 EU AI Act has received. However, it was actually preceded by China, which passed a trio of key measures: Algorithmic Recommendation Provisions in 2021, Deep Synthesis Provisions in 2022, and Interim Generative AI Measures in 2023.[1] As of mid-2025, it is fair to say that the EU passed the most significant AI legislation in the Western world, setting a precedent for future regulation with the EU AI Act. Unlike the EU, countries like the UK and Japan are pursuing a 'vertical' rather than a 'horizontal' AI-specific legislative approach – where laws apply broadly to all applications of AI, regardless of the specific sector or application in which the AI system is being used.[2]

And while lawyers and legal experts are keeping an eye on what may be upcoming on the policy horizon, we can expect to see many of the rules and expectations for legal liability play out in courtrooms. An ongoing project called 'AI on Trial' identified 12 times more AI-related legal cases around the world over a six-year span (2018 to 2024).[3] These cases covered a wide range of issues and these legal claims spanned across fields of law, from torts and contract law to constitutional, corporate, criminal and intellectual property law.[4]

UNESCO provides a taxonomy of nine 'approaches' to AI governance.[5] These approaches are not mutually exclusive – the EU AI Act, for example, combines several. We offer them here as one way of categorizing different AI-related initiatives.

UNESCO TAXONOMY OF AI GOVERNANCE APPROACHES

Approach	Description
Principles-Based Approach	Propagates broad guidance in the form of principles that serve as a foundation for binding rules and laws.
Standards-Based Approach	Delegates state power to standard-setting bodies to create technical rules guiding AI policy implementation.
Agile and Experimentalist Approach	Promotes innovation and experimentation by creating sandboxes and testbeds.
Facilitating and Enabling Approach	Uses state resources to build regulatory capacity – for example, AI literacy – and promotes AI development.
Adapting Existing Laws	Modifies existing laws, such as intellectual property, data protection, health and finance laws, to address the challenges posed by AI.
Transparency Mandates	Ensures public awareness of AI interactions and provides details on system workings or development processes.

Risk-Based Approach	Categorizes AI systems into risk tiers, with greater requirements for higher-risk systems.
Rights-Based Approach	Ensures AI systems respect fundamental rights such as privacy, non-discrimination and redress in decision-making.
Liability Approach	Assigns responsibility for AI-related harms to developers and corporate users, ensuring redress for affected parties.

The Tony Blair Institute, a global think-tank, has also defined four broad regulatory archetypes, which together form a 'regulatory posture', and situated a range of countries on a scale within each of these.[6] While recognizing that this policy landscape is a rapidly moving target and the positions of individual countries may change, this framework provides a helpful overview of some of the key differences in regulatory approaches being taken across the globe.

Regulatory posture comprises four elements:

Regulatory strategy: describes whether a country is adopting a proactive and comprehensive approach to AI regulation or more reactive and targeted interventions.

Regulatory structure: compares centralized versus more decentralized oversight and enforcement. The former is built around a single, primary national body driving AI regulation, whereas the latter relies on a network of sectoral, regional and even local bodies.

Regulatory scope: contrasts AI legislation which is broadly applicable across industries – often referred to as horizontal – with sector specific implementation.

Regulatory approach: considers whether the basis for the regulatory framework is proportionate to the level of risk (risk-based), codifies specific directives (rules-based), is focused more on setting goals and outcomes which the AI should achieve (outcomes-based), or establishes key principles which must be respected (principles-based).

FIGURE 12.1 Regional Variations Between Regulatory Archetypes

Regulatory Posture	Position of Benchmarked Countries			
Regulatory Strategy	Reactive			Proactive
Regulatory Structure	Decentralised			Centralised
Regulatory Scope	Sector-Specific		Broad/Technology-Specific	
Regulatory Approach	Principles	Outcomes	Rule-based	Risk-based

Source: Tony Blair Institute for Global Change

This section surveys the evolving global regulatory and legal landscape that impacts AI use, deployment and integration, outlining key laws and regulations that executives will want to be aware of to ensure compliance and mitigate risks. *To be clear, the information in this book is for general informational purposes only and not intended to serve as legal advice or counsel.* Our survey is also not exhaustive – we do not provide a list of all actions required for legal or appropriate AI systems. Organizations developing, deploying or licensing AI systems should consult legal counsel for a comprehensive and tailored evaluation of relevant compliance requirements and liabilities.

By examining the EU's regulatory approach, the US sectoral model and other significant developments across Asia, Africa, the Middle East and Latin America, this section provides a roadmap for navigating the legal aspects of AI governance.

THE EU: AN EARLY ADOPTER OF AI REGULATION

The EU has emerged as a leader in digital technology regulation, using a 'horizontal' regulatory approach. Even prior to the implementation of the AI Act, the EU had a robust regulatory framework for digital technologies, including the Digital Markets Act (DMA), Digital Services Act (DSA) and the General Data Protection Regulation (GDPR). The AI Act provides the world's first comprehensive AI regulation but during 2025 the EU has increasingly focused on promoting

AI innovation, for example with the launch of the AI Continent Action Plan.[7]

THE EU AI ACT (AI ACT)

Built on a risk-based framework, the AI Act categorizes AI systems by risk. Different regulatory obligations attach to different categories of AI which include prohibited, high-risk and general-purpose AI models. These categories are important to understand, whether or not an organization using AI systems is based in the EU, given the extraterritorial reach of the Act, which covers 'providers placing on the market or putting into service AI systems, or placing on the market general-purpose AI models in the Union, *irrespective of whether those providers are established or located within the Union or in a third country*.'[8] The AI Act entered into force in August 2024 although the application of its provisions is phased.[9]

THE PHASED IMPLEMENTATION OF THE EU AI ACT

Date	Implementation Stage
2 February 2025	Restrictions on prohibited AI practices and a general requirement on AI literacy took effect.
2 August 2025	Regulations for general-purpose AI began to be enforced.
2 August 2026	Requirements for high-risk AI systems will apply.
2 August 2027	Rules for high-risk AI systems used as safety components in products will be implemented.

The EU AI Act, set to be fully applicable by the end of 2030, introduces a comprehensive regulatory framework for AI systems. At a high level, it presents new requirements, definitions and expectations.

According to Article 3(1) of the AI Act, the definition of an AI system is broad and is not restricted to the 'model': 'a machine-based system that is designed to operate with varying levels of autonomy and that may exhibit adaptiveness after deployment, and that, for explicit or implicit objectives, infers, from the input it receives, how to generate outputs such as predictions, content, recommendations or decisions that can influence physical or virtual environments.'[10] Guidance from the European Commission breaks down this definition into seven parts and clarifies its scope.[11] Systems that fall outside of the scope include 'systems for improving mathematical optimization', 'basic data processing' (which 'refers to a system that follows predefined, explicit instructions or operations'), 'systems based on classical heuristics' (which 'typically involve rule-based approaches, pattern recognition, or trial-and-error strategies rather than data-driven learning') and 'simple prediction systems.'[12] Recital 12 of the AI Act requires that the Article 3(1) definition be aligned with international standards. The Organisation for Economic Co-operation and Development (OECD) has noted that AI systems are developed using machine learning or logic- or knowledge-based approaches, excluding simple statistical techniques such as linear or logistic regression.[13]

Separate obligations apply to certain general-purpose AI (GPAI) models, which are the engines supporting an increasing number of the AI systems we use today, discussed further below.

A cornerstone of the EU AI Act is its risk-tiering framework, which categorizes AI systems into four levels based on the potential risks they pose to individuals and society. At the highest level of concern are 'prohibited AI practices', which pose 'unacceptable' risks to fundamental rights and EU values. These prohibitions include, but are not limited to, exploitative or manipulative practices and certain forms of social scoring. Systems classified as high-risk are subject to stringent obligations, while 'AI systems posing limited transparency risk', or limited-risk systems, are governed by lighter transparency requirements. 'Minimal to no'-risk systems face little to no regulation.

This framework acknowledges that requirements from multiple tiers can apply to a single system. For instance, a high-risk AI system may also need to meet transparency obligations typically associated with limited-risk systems, ensuring users are aware they are interacting with AI and understand its purpose. Similarly, GPAI, which supports a wide range of applications, is increasingly relevant across risk tiers, necessitating tailored oversight that aligns with its diverse use cases. Additionally, the EU AI Act focuses on preserving fundamental rights, including dignity, privacy, non-discrimination and freedom of expression, as outlined in the EU Charter of Fundamental Rights and human rights law.[14]

This section provides an overview of the risk-tiering framework, explaining how AI systems are classified and obligations are tied to each tier.

Prohibited AI Practices

a. Certain AI applications deemed inherently harmful are banned outright by the AI Act. These include systems that use subliminal, manipulative or deceptive techniques intended to distort behaviour or impair informed decision-making.[15]

b. In most cases, the Act bans social scoring, predictive assessment of criminality, the creation of facial recognition databases and the use of real-time biometric identification by law enforcement, among other uses. The Act also prohibits AI systems designed to infer emotions in sensitive contexts such as workplaces and schools. This does not apply to systems that merely recognize emotions, such as detecting facial expressions or tone of voice, but specifically targets those interpreting this data to judge internal emotional states for decision-making, such as to influence hiring, promotions or performance evaluations in workplaces or to evaluate students' engagement, behaviour or academic performance in schools. The rationale and objectives for prohibiting each use, as well as the scope of the prohibitions, were provided by the European Commission in a separate guidance document.[16]

High-Risk AI Systems

a. Article 6 of the AI Act provides the classification rules for high-risk AI systems.[17] It outlines two main ways an AI system can be classified as high-risk: AI systems intended to be used as safety components of products covered by EU harmonization legislation listed in Annex I and required to undergo third-party conformity assessments; and additional specific use cases listed in Annex III. The following important considerations also apply:

   i. Derogation: Article 6(3) provides a derogation clause (i.e. allows for limited exceptions to compliance), stating that AI systems listed in Annex III may not be considered high-risk if they do not pose a significant risk of harm to health, safety or fundamental rights.

   ii. Documentation: Providers who believe their AI system listed in Annex III is not high-risk must document their assessment and may be required to provide this documentation to 'national competent authorities'.

b. Annex III of the EU AI Act lists specific areas and use cases where AI systems are considered high-risk.[18] These areas include:

    i. Biometric identification and categorization

    ii. Management and operation of critical infrastructure

    iii. Education and vocational training

    iv. Employment, worker management and access to self-employment

    v. Access to essential private and public services and benefits

    vi. Law enforcement

    vii. Migration, asylum and border control management

    viii. Administration of justice and democratic processes

c. An AI system is always considered high-risk under the Act if it profiles individuals. This could occur through the automated processing of personal data to assess various aspects of a person's life, such as work performance, economic situation, health, preferences, interests, reliability, behaviour, location or movement.[18]

d. Amendments: the Commission has the power to amend the conditions for high-risk classification through delegated acts, i.e. without needing European parliamentary approval.

e. High-risk AI providers must comply with numerous obligations, including:[19]

    i. **Risk Management**: establish a risk management system throughout the high-risk AI system's lifecycle.

    ii. **Data Governance**: implement data governance, ensuring that training, validation and testing datasets are relevant, sufficiently representative and, to the best extent possible, free of errors.

    iii. **Technical Documentation**: create detailed documentation of compliance with Act requirements.

    iv. **Record-Keeping**: prepare systems to automatically record events to identify risks and substantial modifications.

    v. **Transparency with Downstream Perspective**: provide instructions for downstream deployers who will need to understand the use, limits and earlier testing of AI systems.

    vi. **Human Oversight**: design the system such that deployers can implement human oversight.

 vii. **Accuracy, Robustness, Security**: design the system to enable and achieve appropriate levels of accuracy, robustness and cybersecurity.

 viii. **Quality Management**: establish a quality management system to ensure ongoing compliance.

 ix. **Conformity Assessment**: 'Ensure the AI system undergoes the relevant conformity assessment procedure, as referred to in Article 43, prior to its being placed on the market or put into service,' when applicable (see also Chapter 9, page 131).

 ix. **Registration**: high-risk systems generally must be registered in the EU database. High-risk systems listed in point 2 of Annex III must be registered at the national level.

 x. **Marking**: 'Affix the "CE" marking to the high-risk AI system or, where that is not possible, on its packaging or its accompanying documentation, to indicate conformity. . . in accordance with Article 48.'

 xi. **Corrective Action and Reporting**: take immediate action to address any lack of compliance or malfunctions and inform relevant authorities of any serious incidents or malfunctions.

 f. There are obligations that apply to *deployers* of high-risk AI systems as well, such as the requirement to apply suitable human oversight.[20]

 g. Note that documentation for several of these requirements must be maintained for a minimum of 10 years after the high-risk AI system has been placed on the market or put into service – for example, Article 11 technical documentation and Article 17 quality management documentation.[21]

Limited-Risk AI Systems

 a. AI systems that directly interact with people, like chatbots, are subject to basic transparency obligations. For example, users should be informed when they are interacting with a chatbot.[22]

Minimal-Risk AI Systems

 a. AI tools that pose minimal to no risk, such as email spam filters, are largely unregulated. Instead, the Act encourages the providers of such systems to adopt voluntary codes of conduct.[23]

b. Providers and deployers of AI systems are responsible for ensuring their staff and other relevant personnel possess 'sufficient' AI literacy. This entails 'taking into account their technical knowledge, experience, education and training, and the context the AI systems are to be used in, and considering the persons or groups of persons on whom the AI systems are to be used,' as directed in Article 4.[24]

The EU appears to take expense and resource limitations of some organizations into account in determining the burden imposed, but in the end, indicates that safety and compliance obligations prevail. For example, when detailing quality management system requirements, the Act clarifies, 'The implementation shall be proportionate to the size of the provider's organisation. Providers shall, in any event, respect the degree of rigour and the level of protection required to ensure the compliance of their high-risk AI systems with this Regulation.'[25]

Governance of LLMs

Large language models (LLMs) pose unique potential risks and may not align with the rules and expectations listed in the previously established categories. As a result, the AI Act includes separate categories for these models, which it refers to as general-purpose AI (GPAI). The AI Act distinguishes between two tiers of GPAI: those models which pose a 'systemic risk' and those that do not. It does so largely through a 'compute threshold' – models trained using a certain amount of computational power, 10^{25} floating point operations (FLOPs), are presumed to pose a 'systemic risk' due to their advanced capabilities, though other factors can also be considered.[26] To put this threshold in perspective, as of June 2025, the research organization EpochAI estimates that 33 models were trained using 10^{25} or more FLOPs. They include GPT-4, GPT-4o and GPT-4.5 and the largest versions of the latest Llama and Gemini models from Meta and Google respectively.[27]

The AI Act requires GPAI providers to supply information to the government and downstream providers integrating the model. These disclosures must include information related to the training process, testing and evaluation, and the model itself, such as its energy consumption and number of parameters.[28] The only binding requirement is that all GPAI providers 'put in place a policy to respect [European] Union copyright law,'[29] although there is some uncertainty as to how existing copyright laws apply to GPAI, which the AI Act does not clarify.[30] Open questions remain that will be resolved by courts or standard-setting bodies. For example: are developers who scrape data to train LLMs covered by the commercial text and data mining exception provided by Directive 2019/790/EU?* Can LLM outputs qualify as 'derivative' works that violate copyright law, and if so, how? The providers of models that pose a 'systemic risk' are subject to additional substantive requirements, including obligations to perform model evaluations 'reflecting the state of the art.' They must also ensure an appropriate level of cybersecurity.[31]

Technical Requirements through Standard Setting
Standard setting and codes of practice are expected to play a key role in translating these regulations into tangible technical requirements. The standard setting process is complex and involves many players, from the Standards organizations – the European Committee for Standardization, the European Committee for Electrotechnical Standardization and the European Telecommunications Standards Institute – to National Standards Bodies, standards consultants and a variety of additional stakeholders. Certain standards were due by 30 April 2025 (scheduled to go into effect only in 2026), but are now expected in late 2025/2026.[32] Some provisions are significantly reliant on upcoming standards. Article 40 contains the Act's strongest language regarding the environmental impacts of AI and relies on standards, calling for the development of harmonized standards to improve the energy efficiency of AI systems.[33]

Some observers have criticized the EU's reliance on standards,[34] noting the challenge this poses for civil society and consumer organizations to engage in the standard-setting process.[35] Some are also critical of the instances where companies can self-assess their compliance (see also Chapter 9: 'determine which assessments to carry out').[36]

*On 27 September 2024, the German Hamburg Regional Court held that the creation of a publicly available data set that may be used for AI training falls under the scientific research exception provided by Directive 2019/790/EU. 'Kneschke v. LAION, No. 310 O 227/23 (Landgericht Hamburg, 27 September 2024)', https://pdfupload.io/docs/4bcc432c and Goldstein, P., Stuetzle, C. and Bischoff, S., 'Kneschke vs. LAION – Landmark Ruling on TDM exceptions for AI training data – Part 1', https://copyrightblog.kluweriplaw.com/2024/11/13/kneschke-vs-laion-landmark-ruling-on-tdm-exceptions-for-ai-training-data-part-1/.

Establishing AI Infrastructure

There are several resources, expectations and new forms of infrastructure that will come into being because of the AI Act. For example, the Act creates a public EU-wide registry of high-risk systems. The EU though is not the first mover – China also implemented policies to create an algorithm registry.[37] Likewise, in an executive order issued in 2020 during the Trump Administration, the White House Office of Management and Budget was tasked with preparing and maintaining an inventory of ways that US government agencies use AI.[38] However, the EU's database includes private sector uses of AI. As one US AI policymaker writes, it might 'uncover currently unknown AI applications used by [...] global companies,' facilitating investigations that 'could uncover much more about the world's most troubling AI applications.'[39]

Additionally, the AI Act requires EU member states to establish regulatory sandboxes.[40] These sandboxes are a policy mechanism to provide a controlled environment to test AI systems while companies are insulated from many forms of penalties. They are an increasingly popular tool in financial regulation.[41]

In the context of high-profile, global debates over how open-source models should be regulated, it is worth noting how they are treated under the AI Act.[42] Foundation models 'released under a free and open-source license' are exempt from many of the Act's requirements for general-purpose artificial intelligence (GPAI), but this is not true of highly advanced models that clear the threshold for posing a 'systemic risk.'[43]

Compliance and Enforcement

The AI Act outlines a two-tiered enforcement system. At the top, the European Commission has established an AI Office to enforce much of the Act, including provisions related to GPAI.[44] The AI Office will be advised by a separate AI Board to include representatives from EU states and will be supplemented by national market surveillance authorities and notifying authorities within each EU member state. The market surveillance authorities will conduct the bulk of surveillance, investigation and enforcement activities, while notifying authorities and notified bodies – along with any subcontractors or subsidiaries – will conduct conformity assessments on certain high-risk AI systems to ensure that they comply with relevant provisions before being placed on the market.[45]

The AI Office oversees these bodies and can co-ordinate enforcement activities, such as joint investigations, across several states; it can also overrule decisions of market surveillance authorities.

PENALTIES UNDER THE EU AI ACT

Offence	Penalty
Violations of bans on prohibited systems	Fine of €35 million or 7 per cent of global gross revenue, whichever is greater.
Violations of provisions on high-risk systems or GPAI	Fine of €15 million or 3 per cent of global gross revenue, whichever is greater.
Providing incomplete, incorrect or misleading information to government authorities	Fine of €7.5 million or 1 per cent of global gross revenue, whichever is greater.

To prepare, companies should assess risk levels of their AI systems and determine applicable obligations, as described in Chapter 9. Upon determining levels of risk, companies should implement required risk management and oversight measures for high-risk AI systems. No matter the risk level of your current AI systems, it is best practice to implement a governance system as you build your AI capacities. This will help ensure you are not only in compliance but well positioned to identify and mitigate risks, thereby providing sufficient oversight of the increasingly complex systems you will likely use going forward.

Depending on the determined risk level, companies should evaluate and provide transparency in AI interactions and content generation, prepare for potential conformity assessments and documentation requirements, and appoint persons and/or teams to stay informed about evolving guidelines and delegated legislation.

GDPR AND DATA PROTECTION IMPLICATIONS

The General Data Protection Regulation (GDPR), effective since 2018, is a comprehensive data protection law and serves as the foundation for data privacy within the EU. It aims to harmonize data privacy laws across EU member states and provide greater protection and rights to individuals regarding their personal data. The GDPR has specific implications for AI, particularly regarding the handling of personal data in training

AI models. The AI Act was designed to be compatible with the GDPR, explicitly noting that it does not supersede the GDPR.[46]

The GDPR applies to any company that processes personal data in the EU, regardless of the company's physical location, and as such, applies to AI systems that process personal data in the EU, regardless of the company's location. The GDPR explicitly limits how personal data can be processed as 'only when necessary' for the data controller to pursue a 'legitimate interest'* and the data collection does not infringe fundamental rights under Article 6(1)(f).[47]

The GDPR will become applicable when an AI system processes personal data, whether during the training or deployment phases. When applicable, you will want to ensure adherence to GDPR principles, such as fairness, transparency, data minimization, accuracy, purpose and storage limitations and requirements. For instance, the GDPR grants rights to data subjects, including the right to be informed, access data, rectify incorrect information and erase data, which AI system owners must adhere to.[48]

The GDPR requires transparency in intended use, requiring companies to lay out the specific purpose and legitimate interest for their use of personal data to train AI, as well as 'privacy by design' procedures that may necessitate data minimization, storage limitation and purpose limitation.

To ensure compliance, companies should work with counsel to implement robust data governance strategies, conduct regular audits of their AI systems and stay informed about evolving regulations and guidance from data protection authorities regarding AI and the GDPR. Questions remain about the GDPR's application to current forms and uses of AI. For instance, it is unclear how to enforce the Article 21 requirement to provide a right to object to the processing of personal data with genAI models that have already been trained on personal data, which cannot easily, or perhaps feasibly, be 'removed.'[49]

Likewise, Article 15 provides individuals with the 'right to access,' including 'meaningful information about the logic involved' in solely automated decisions affecting them in significant ways.[50] This provision is not easily applicable to genAI given the uncertainty of its methodologies and outcomes.

The GDPR Article 22 sets forth a person's 'right not to be subject to a decision based solely on automated processing which produces legal effects.'[51] The Italian Data Protection Authority fined Deliveroo due to the company's AI-enabled automated rating of rider perfor-mance.[52] Failing to adhere to the mandates of Article 22 can expose companies to significant liability. This 'human in the loop' provision theoretically creates a right of action and has already been addressed by courts.[53]

In an April 2022 report examining the enforcement of the GDPR on automated decision-making, the Future of Privacy Forum identified more than '70 cases – 19 court rulings and more than 50 enforcement decisions, individual opinions or general guidance issued by DPAs[sic] – from a span of 18 EEA Member-States, the UK and the European Data Protection Supervisor (EDPS).'[54] The report found that cases have begun to increase as 'automated decision-making is becoming ubiquitous in daily life, and it now looks like individuals are increasingly interested in having their right under Article 22 applied.'[55] A 2021 case resulted in a $3 million fine levied on Foodinho, an on-demand food delivery company, when Italy's Data Protection Authority found the company failed to comply with Article 22's requirement to provide its riders with information on specific auto-mated decisions and the opportunity to object to and/or request human review of these decisions.[56]

In Amsterdam, a court found that a company (Uber) could be liable for its *partially automated* decisions, which in this case was a program used to terminate its drivers' contracts, under Article 22's limitations on fully automated systems.[57] The court found that the drivers had a right to access their personal data 'insofar as they formed the basis for the decision to deactivate their accounts' so that the drivers could 'verify the accuracy and lawfulness of the processing of their personal data.'[58] In this situation, where evaluations were only partially automated decisions, the court found that nonetheless 'drivers have the right to obtain access to their data underlying a decision to terminate their accounts' in accordance with specific GDPR transparency requirements for qualifying automated decision-making.[59]

The EU's approach to litigating Article 22 could shape future regulatory standards, as the GDPR has worldwide, and should receive careful atten-tion in your AI governance planning.

OTHER APPLICABLE EU LAWS: REVISED PRODUCT LIABILITY DIRECTIVE, THE DIGITAL SERVICES ACT AND THE DIGITAL MARKETS ACT

In addition to the AI Act and the GDPR, several EU laws could be implicated by AI use, including the revised Public Liability Directive (PLD), which addresses non-contractual strict liability claims, the Digital Services Act (DSA), which addresses users' fundamental rights, and the Digital Markets Act (DMA), which addresses competition. In 2022 the Commission proposed an AI Liability Directive that would have facilitated claims for compensation for harms caused by AI, established evidence disclosure rules and introduced the rebuttable presumption of liability in certain conditions.[60] However, the Commission indicated their intent to withdraw the proposal in their 2025 Work Program and in May 2025 the Parliament's Committee on Internal Market and Consumer Protection adopted an opinion recommending the proposal be rejected.[61]

The PLD was first adopted in 1985 when the Commission wanted to harmonize fragmented legal protection laws that define and allocate liability caused by defective products.[62] The PLD introduced a common set of rules and consumer protection measures for consumers with no fault-based liability for damage caused by defective products. This is also referred to as 'strict liability', where producers are responsible for defective products, regardless of whether the defect is established to be their fault.

The Revised PLD

In November 2024, the European Council adopted the new PLD, which updates the EU's product liability framework to address modern technologies. A significant aim of the revised PLD is to shift the burden of claims by requiring manufacturers to disclose relevant evidence, thereby easing the burden of proof for consumers.[63] It also indicates that systems with poor cybersecurity could be considered defective.[64]

The revised PLD has an expanded definition to include software and AI systems and broadens the scope of liable entities to include manufacturers and importers, and in some cases, distributors and online platforms. Specifically, it expands the definition of 'products' to include AI systems, digital manufacturing files, software and AI-enabled goods.[65]

The PLD also broadens the scope of liable entities to include the manufacturer, a related service provider, the authorized representative, the importer and the distributor.[66] It attempts to establish liability in the case where a manufacturer is outside of the EU's jurisdiction by attributing liability for a defective product to the importer and the authorized representative in the EU, or otherwise to a fulfilment service provider.[67] Member states have two years from its adoption in 2024 to implement it into national law.[68] Barring challenges, the product liability landscape could significantly change by the end of 2026.[69]

The Digital Services Act and the Digital Markets Act

Together, the Digital Services Act (DSA) and the Digital Market Act (DMA) provide a set of rules that apply across the EU with two primary stated goals: (1) to create a safer digital space that protects the fundamental rights of users of digital services, and (2) to establish a level playing field.[70] Among their differences, the DSA focuses on creating a safer digital space and protecting users' fundamental rights online, while the DMA aims to foster fair competition and level the playing field in digital markets.

DSA

The DSA defines digital services as a broad array of online services, from simple websites to internet infrastructure services and online platforms, and primarily addresses online intermediaries and platforms, such as online marketplaces, social networks, content-sharing platforms, app stores and online travel and accommodation platforms.[71] The DSA obligates large online platforms and search engines to publish reports on how they engage in content moderation and provide users with protections such as the right to report illegal content.[72]

The DSA is intended to add more rules proportionate to the size of the entity: the bigger the intermediary, the more stringent their obligations. Also, the DSA includes specific rules for very large online platforms (VLOPs) and search engines (VLOSEs) (more than 45 million users per month in the EU).[74] These include the requirement to 'provide concise and unambiguous summaries of their terms and conditions in the local EU language'.[75]

Figure 12.2 Summary of DSA Obligations for Online Platforms

All the platforms are responsible for ensuring that their services follow the DSA rules on

Illegal Content

- Users must be able to easily report illegal content spotted online

- Online platforms must co-operate with authorities in case of any criminal offences on their platforms (e.g. child abuse material)

- Trusted flaggers will help to detect certain types of illegal content online, such as hate speech or terrorist content

Ads

- The DSA prohibits targeting minors with advertising based on the profiling of their personal data, and targeted ads for anyone based on the profiling of sensitive data, such as religious beliefs or sexual preferences

- Users must have information on ads they see: why they are seeing the ads and on whose behalf it is shown

Freedom of Expression

- Online platforms have to provide users with the reasons why their content or accounts were removed

- Users must be able to challenge content moderation decisions by complaining to the platform, through an out-of-court dispute mechanism or to an authority in their EU country

Manipulative Tactics

- Dark patterns, or manipulative tactics that can impair users' decision-making online are now prohibited

Content Recommender Systems

- Platforms must provide clear terms and conditions, and if their service is directed towards minors, their terms and conditions must be easily understandable to this age group

- The terms and conditions must also explain the main parameters of platforms' recommender systems

- Platforms must have points of contact for authorities

Source: Adapted from 'A Safer & Fairer Online Environment', European Commission[73]

Additional rules the DSA requires of VLOPs and VLOSEs include:

- Identifying and addressing any systemic risks their platforms pose, meaning risks related to fundamental rights, illegal content, public security and elections, gender-based violence, public health, protection of minors and mental and physical well-being.
- Publishing six-monthly transparency reports, including content moderation decisions and yearly audits.
- Providing a point of contact for users and authorities.

If the Commission establishes a breach of the DSA, it may impose fines up to 6 per cent of the global turnover of the provider in addition to requiring measures to address the breach.[76] That decision may also trigger an enhanced supervision period to ensure compliance with the measures the provider intends to take to remedy the breach.[77]

DMA

The Digital Markets Act (DMA) provides rules to govern 'gatekeeper' online platforms to give businesses and consumers who use these platforms more rights and choices. Gatekeepers are defined as 'large online platforms that provide core services and act as an important gateway between businesses and consumers – think of search engines, app stores and messenger services.'[78] Platforms may be considered gatekeepers if they satisfy any of the following conditions during the three years prior: have a specified annual turnover in the European Economic Area; provide a core platform service in at least three Member States; provide a core platform service to more than 45 million active monthly users and to more than 10,000 active business users per year in the EU.[79]

The DMA provides certain data control and privacy rules. For instance, gatekeepers must obtain explicit consent before using user data for advertising and ensure transparency in how data is used, as well as enabling consumers and businesses to access and move their data (data access and interoperability). Additionally, the DMA prohibits anti-competitive practices, such as gatekeepers prioritizing their products or services in search results and rankings.[80]

The DMA became applicable on 2 May 2023. Within two months, companies providing core platform services were required to notify the European Commission (Commission) if they met the quantitative thresholds and then provide the information required under the law.

The Commission then had 45 working days to provide a decision, and the designated gatekeepers then had a maximum of six months after the Commission's decision to ensure compliance with the DMA.[81]

The potential impact of the DMA on AI is under debate. The High-Level Group on the DMA, which advises the Commission on implementation and enforcement, issued a statement in May 2024 emphasizing that the DMA applies to AI 'when gatekeepers deploy AI in the context of their designated core platform services.'[82] Likewise, a trio of scholars argues: 'The DMA contains rules that will probably have greater significance for the application of machine learning in the EU than the regulations provided for in the AI Act.'[83] However, lawyers have debated that it is unclear how relevant provisions of the DMA apply, especially as the Commission has not explicitly discussed generative and foundation models in its designation decisions through mid-2025.[84] The closest the Commission came to such discussions was in July 2024 when it issued a broad joint statement on competition and generative AI foundation models and AI products.[85]

KEY INSIGHTS AND ACTIONS

- The global AI regulatory landscape is evolving, with contrasting approaches. While the EU leads with comprehensive legislation like the AI Act, other nations, such as the UK and Japan, rely on sector-specific regulations.
- The EU AI Act classifies AI systems into four risk levels: unacceptable, high-risk, limited-risk and minimal-risk. The Act introduces strict obligations, particularly for high-risk systems, and will be fully applicable by 2030.
- Prohibited AI practices include applications that use subliminal, manipulative or deceptive techniques intended to distort behaviour or impair informed decision-making.
- High-risk AI systems include applications used in critical infrastructure, education, employment, access to essential private and public services and benefits, and law enforcement. These trigger significant obligations, including risk management, human oversight, data governance, transparency and ongoing monitoring. These systems may also be subject to other risk tier requirements such as transparency.

- Limited- and minimal-risk AI systems face minimal obligations, with limited-risk systems requiring basic transparency measures, such as disclosing AI interactions, while minimal-risk systems, like spam filters, remain largely unregulated but are encouraged to follow voluntary codes of conduct.
- General-purpose AI models, including large language models, face additional rules based on their computational power. Models exceeding a defined compute threshold are considered to pose 'systemic risks' and must meet cybersecurity, transparency and evaluation requirements.
- Technical standards and regulatory sandboxes play a critical role in implementing the AI Act. Harmonized standards will address areas such as environmental impacts, while sandboxes provide controlled environments for AI experimentation and testing.
- The General Data Protection Regulation (GDPR) imposes strict limits on AI systems processing personal data, requiring fairness, transparency and adherence to rights such as access, correction and erasure. It mandates human oversight for decisions that significantly impact individuals.
- The revised Product Liability Directive (PLD) addresses liability concerns, expanding liability to include AI systems.
- The Digital Services Act (DSA) enhances accountability for online platforms, requiring risk assessments, content moderation transparency and protections for user rights. Non-compliance can lead to fines of up to 6 per cent of global turnover.
- The Digital Markets Act (DMA) provides certain data control and privacy rules to govern so-called 'gatekeeper' online platforms.
- The EU's approach to AI governance, through laws like the AI Act, GDPR and DSA, sets a global precedent and will likely shape future international regulatory standards.

13

United States laws and regulations

Unlike the European Union's centralized frameworks, AI governance in the United States is shaped by a multifaceted system involving federal, state and local authorities. Laws and regulations target specific domains – such as consumer protection, privacy, civil rights, intellectual property and national security – collectively forming a complex regulatory landscape.

US AI regulation stems from multiple sources, including the White House, Congress, federal agencies and state governments. Since 2019, the White House has issued more than five executive orders involving AI under three administrations. At the federal level, the US introduced the internationally recognized US National Institute of Standards and Technology (NIST) AI Risk Management Framework, discussed earlier in Chapter 4 (see page 38). Meanwhile, states have taken significant legislative action: since the start of the 2025 legislative session through early June 2025, lawmakers across all 50 states, the District of Columbia, Puerto Rico, Guam and the US Virgin Islands have introduced 1,093 AI-related bills, underscoring the growing focus on AI at the state level.[1]

Equally critical, both in the US and globally, is the evolving role of courts in shaping AI governance. Numerous existing federal, state and local laws will increasingly be applied to address liability and establish expectations for AI-related harms and responsibilities. Court cases span across sectors – including healthcare, transportation, media and financial services – and cover legal areas such as torts, contracts, constitutional law, criminal law, corporate governance and intellectual property. Judicial decisions will play a pivotal role in defining the legal contours of AI governance, particularly around liability and accountability.

This chapter will examine the key policy and legislative actions which shape the AI landscape in the US. These originate from several different sources:

A. Federal Executive Action – initiatives directed by the President or federal agencies such as:

1. Executives Orders and Memoranda
2. Criminal and civil action by federal agencies
3. Voluntary frameworks and non-binding guidance

B. Statutory laws (enacted by the legislative branch) and case law (established by the judicial branch) exist at three levels of government:

1. Federal
2. State
3. Local

FEDERAL EXECUTIVE ACTIONS ON AI POLICY

The US federal government comprises three branches – the executive (president and agencies), legislative (Congress) and judicial (courts) – each of which is increasingly engaging with the challenges and opportunities presented by AI. This section begins with the executive branch. Led by the President, this branch wields a variety of tools to influence policy and regulate AI-related activities, including presidential executive orders, agency regulations, prosecutions, consent decrees and other mechanisms.

AI-related activities and organizations can fall under the jurisdiction of multiple federal agencies depending on the context. For instance, the use of AI in the workforce might involve oversight from the Department of Labor, Equal Employment Opportunity Commission, Department of Justice or other agencies. Privacy concerns raised by AI systems could implicate the Children's Online Privacy Protection Act (COPPA), enforced by the Federal Trade Commission, or the Health Insurance Portability and Accountability Act (HIPAA), enforced by the Department of Health and Human Services. Since federal agencies operate under the authority of the President and Cabinet, the precedents discussed below offer insight into how US agencies have addressed AI use and liability. However, the relevance or accuracy of any particular action may evolve as policies and leadership change.

Executive Orders

The President of the United States is responsible for implementing and enforcing laws enacted by Congress. Among other tools, the President can issue executive orders (EOs) to shape policy that typically carry the force of law. In recent years, numerous EOs have directly or indirectly influenced AI development and use. These orders establish priorities, allocate resources and set guidelines, demonstrating the federal government's growing commitment to addressing the governance of AI. Examples of these orders and other presidential actions include:

> On 23 January 2025, President Trump issued the Executive Order on Removing Barriers to American Leadership in Artificial Intelligence. The EO required agencies to develop a plan to 'sustain and enhance America's global AI dominance in order to promote human flourishing, economic competitiveness, and national security'. It also required the immediate review of all actions taken under President Biden's Executive Order on the Safe, Secure, and Trustworthy Development and Use of Artificial Intelligence (EO 14110) and set a 60-day deadline for the revision of related Office of Management and Budget Memoranda. Three months later, President Trump issued the Executive Order on Advancing Artificial Intelligence Education for American Youth. This EO created the White House Task Force on AI Education, which will implement a Presidential AI Challenge and establish public-private partnerships to grow K–12 AI education. It also included provisions to support AI-related apprenticeships, coursework and certifications.[2]

Frameworks and Non-binding Guidance: e.g. NIST AI RMF, Voluntary Commitments and Statements, White House Advisory Bodies

There are multiple non-binding and voluntary frameworks and commitments that support US-based AI governance. These include the US National Institute of Standards and Technology (NIST) AI Risk Management Framework (RMF), and reports from congressionally mandated entities and other presidential advisory bodies, such as the President's Council of Advisors on Science and Technology (PCAST) and the US Center for AI Standards and Innovation (CAISI).

NIST AI RMF

The NIST AI RMF, released in January 2023, has become an influential model for AI governance, providing practical, flexible guidance for managing AI-related risks.[3] Supported by tools like the AI RMF Playbook and a generative AI companion resource, as noted in Chapter 4 (see page 38), it has seen widespread voluntary adoption due to its adaptability and alignment with global frameworks like those from the OECD, EU and ISO/IEC.[*] Its development with broad and numerous stakeholders supports its applicability across sectors and use cases, emphasizing risk management for all AI systems rather than focusing solely on 'high-risk' applications. The RMF's influence extends to both US and foreign government agencies, which have incorporated it into their AI governance strategies. For example, in May 2025, it was integrated into joint guidance, authored by the US National Security Agency, US Cybersecurity and Infrastructure Agency, US Federal Bureau of Investigation, Australian Cyber Security Centre, New Zealand's National Cyber Security Centre and the UK's National Cyber Security Centre, on best practices for AI data security.[4]

Voluntary Commitments and Statements

Sixteen foundation AI companies, or those developing genAI, including Amazon, Google, OpenAI, Scale AI, Stability and Microsoft, issued joint statements with the White House from July 2023 through July 2024, announcing their 'voluntary commitments' to manage AI risks.[5] They agreed to abide by eight non-binding measures, including pre-release of safety testing, industry-wide information sharing, watermarking and other transparency efforts, and investments in cybersecurity and ongoing research into AI's societal risks and potential benefits.[6] In October 2022, the White House Office of Science and Technology Policy (OSTP) released a Blueprint for an AI Bill of Rights[7] to promote accountability and protect rights with regard to technology use.[8] The Blueprint identifies 'five principles that should guide the design, use, and deployment of automated systems to protect the American public in the age of artificial intelligence.'[9] Although the current status of these initiatives is uncertain, they illustrate how the President and White House can shape national AI policy through voluntary commitments, policy frameworks, and other non-binding measures.

---

[*]EqualAI produced an AI Impact Assessment tool (AIA) based on the NIST RMF to help increase awareness and adoption of these best practices by all organizations that use AI systems in pivotal functions. 'EqualAI Algorithmic Impact Assessment (AIA)', 9 April 2023. Available: https://www.equalai.org/aia/.

White House AI Advisory Bodies

In 2019, President Trump signed into law the National Defense Authorization Act (NDAA) for Fiscal Year 2020, establishing the most substantial US legislation addressing AI to date.[10] The 2020 NDAA directed the establishment of, or funding for, AI research at the National Science Foundation, the Department of Energy and the US National Institute of Standards and Technology (NIST).[11] This law also established entities and investments to advance AI research and development in the federal government, including the National AI Initiative Office (NAIIO), to support White House co-ordination of AI initiatives, and the National Artificial Intelligence Advisory Committee (NAIAC),[*] AI experts appointed to provide the White House with recommendations on AI policy, including research and development, international collaboration, workforce and competitiveness.[12] AI policy is also increasingly addressed by existing bodies, such as the President's Council of Advisors on Science and Technology (PCAST), consisting of experts selected by the President to advise on policy matters involving science and innovation and the US Center for AI Standards and Innovation (CAISI) (formerly the US AI Safety Institute), working with NIST to develop best practices and standards and the private sector to establish voluntary agreements and conduct national security risk evaluations.[13]

Federal Agency Action

Beyond the US National Institute of Standards and Technology's AI RMF, numerous federal agencies regulate AI use through guidance and precedent (e.g. EEOC), prosecutions (DOJ) and historic settlements (e.g. FTC, HUD, DOJ). In April 2023, the US Department of Justice (DOJ), the Federal Trade Commission (FTC), the Consumer Financial Protection Bureau (CFPB) and the US Equal Employment Opportunity Commission (EEOC) issued a joint statement on their enforcement authority over AI.[14]

A company or individual could face liability for AI use under federal law, agency action or by a private right of action. The legal liability varies based on a variety of factors, including the type of harm, the person/entity harmed, other factors that determine standing (who has the right to bring a suit) and whether a claim has merit under specific laws. We provide examples of various sources of legal liability, divided into subject matter areas, below.

---

[*] One of the authors, Miriam Vogel, served as the Chair of the NAIAC.

Civil Rights Law: Federal Action

In 2021, the US Equal Employment Opportunity Commission (EEOC) launched an initiative focused on AI employment-related tools.[15] Through lawsuits, guidance and strategic enforcement initiatives, the EEOC has highlighted potential risks when using AI tools in hiring or recruitment. For example, the EEOC alleged that iTutorGroup, an online tutoring service, used an AI system that unlawfully rejected job applicants based on their age, resulting in a $365,000 settlement and an injunction against age-based screening.[16] The EEOC's Strategic Enforcement Plan for 2024–28 indicated the agency's intent to focus on discriminatory AI recruitment practices that 'target job advertisements, recruit applicants, or make or assist in hiring decisions where such systems intentionally exclude or adversely impact protected groups'.[17]

Another source of law that could be applied to AI-related discrimination is Title VII of the Civil Rights Act of 1964, which prohibits employment discrimination by disparate treatment based on race, colour, religion, sex or national origin. These are generally referred to as a 'protected group' and each one as a 'protected class'. The EEOC adopted the Uniform Guidelines on Employee Selection Procedures in 1978 to provide a framework for employers to determine whether their test and selection processes were permissible under Title VII.[18] In 2022 the EEOC and Department of Justice (DOJ) clarified that these guidelines apply to algorithmic decision-making tools and, as such, employers can be liable for using a tool that adversely impacts – discriminates against or harms – a protected group *even if the tool was developed by a third party*.[19]

Civil Rights law: Private Action

In 2023, a class action suit was filed against Workday, Inc., an HR software and management services provider, alleging they used discriminatory AI systems and screening tools that disproportionately disqualified applicants by race, age and disability in violation of Title VII, the Age Discrimination in Employment Act and the Americans with Disabilities Act Amendments Act of 2008.[20] Plaintiffs have also challenged AI employment practices on constitutional grounds. For instance, similar to the situation revealed in *Weapons of Math Destruction* and noted in Chapter 1, teachers in the Houston Independent School District sued after being terminated for being rated 'ineffective' by a privately developed algorithm.[21] For more discussion on these and other civil rights cases, see *Is Your Use of AI Violating the Law?*[22]

Consumer Protection Laws

Federal agencies like the Federal Trade Commission (FTC), Consumer Financial Protection Bureau (CFPB), Department of Justice (DOJ) and Securities and Exchange Commission (SEC) enforce laws addressing deceptive, discriminatory, fraudulent and harmful practices, which may be applicable to AI systems. Consumer protection-based claims could also stem from state enforcement and private actions. We provide an overview of key issues below:

Deceptive and unfair practices

Numerous laws facilitate oversight of, or prosecution for, practices that are alleged to be deceptive or unfair. For instance, the FTC has authority to protect against 'unfair or deceptive acts or practices'.[23] As such, a deceptive statement about the efficacy or safety of a company's AI tool could potentially trigger FTC oversight and fail the FTC test for unfairness in violation of this act.[24]

Unfair acts or practices are generally defined as those that could cause substantial injury to consumers, cannot be reasonably avoided by consumers and are not outweighed by benefits to consumers or to competition.[25] Deceptive acts include a representation, omission or practice likely to mislead the reasonable consumer.

These laws were invoked in a 2021 FTC complaint alleging that Everalbum, a photo storage services company, deceived its users.[26] The resulting settlement order required Everalbum to obtain consumer consent before using facial recognition technology, and required 'algorithmic disgorgement', deleting algorithms and models created with unauthorized images and videos.

Other notable precedent includes an FTC settlement against Facebook based on a claim that the social media company misled its users by indicating they could opt out of facial recognition when its program was using its users' photos by default.[27] The FTC and Facebook ultimately settled on a historic $5 billion civil penalty and instituted an amended consent order.

In September 2024, the FTC initiated an enforcement effort called 'Operation AI Comply', taking action against five companies: DoNotPay, Ascend Ecom, Ecommerce Empire Builders, Rytr and FBA Machine.[28] Lina M. Khan, then Chair of the FTC, stated: 'The FTC's enforcement actions make clear that there is no AI exemption from the laws on the books.'[29]

The Consumer Financial Protection Bureau also has rule-making authority for unfair, deceptive, or abusive acts or practices in financial services.[30] Additionally, state attorneys general have primary responsibility for enforcing state statutes against unfair or deceptive acts or practices and several AI-related consumer protection laws, such as Colorado's AI Act.[31]

Deepfakes and fraud

As the deceptive use of deepfakes (an image, video or sound recording that has been digitally manipulated to replace the original with a convincing alternative) grows, the FTC has articulated that its 'prohibition on deceptive or unfair conduct can apply if you make, sell, or use a tool that is effectively designed to deceive – even if that's not its intended or sole purpose'.[32] The DOJ has also addressed the enhanced dangers associated with AI. For instance, in February 2024, DOJ announced that it would encourage prosecutors to seek sentencing enhancements for offences involving the misuse of AI, which would include the use of deepfakes to perpetrate fraud schemes and other offences.[33] Additionally, the National Defense Authorization Act for Fiscal Year 2024 established a 'prize competition for technology that detects and watermarks use of generative artificial intelligence'.[34]

On 20 May 2025, President Trump signed the TAKE IT DOWN Act in law, making it illegal to publish or threaten to publish nonconsensual 'intimate visual depictions of individuals', including deepfakes. The law also requires certain online platforms to remove depictions within 48 hours of a victim notifying the platform of the content's existence and create processes for the victim to do so. As of mid-2025, over 150 state laws address deepfakes or, more generally, deceptive manipulated audio or visual images with malice and without consent: for examples, please see Appendix Two.[35] Additionally, most states have general criminal impersonation laws, such as laws making it illegal to impersonate a professional or government official, which could be used to prosecute artificially generated images.

Torts

A tort is an act or omission that causes harm to persons or property and this body of law provides remedies for such harms.[36] Tort law addresses various theories of liability including 'negligence', where someone is harmed by another entity or individual that breached their duty of care. Tort law also presents novel questions in the context of AI – for instance, determining the standard of care when decisions are made based on an AI system's recommendations instead of a human's. Additionally, what is a 'reasonable' standard of care for an AI system? Who owes this duty of care to the injured party – the developer, the deployer or the individual who relied on the recommendation?

We have seen these questions arise in the context of autopilot programs in cars. A 2024 National Highway Traffic Safety Administration report indicates Tesla's self-driving technology was involved in 1,747 known crashes between July 2021 and December 2024.[37] In Hudson v. Tesla, plaintiffs alleged that Tesla misled consumers about the safety and necessary human oversight of its autopilot program, in breach of its 'duty of care to provide adequate warnings and instructions' regarding the autopilot system.[38] Another class action lawsuit filed against Tesla involving 'phantom breaking' alleged Tesla's tort liability for fraudulently hiding safety risks with its driver assist system, breaching its warranties and violating California's unfair competition law.[39]

Strict liability torts impose liability regardless of the 'level of care' or intent. For example, in product liability, a consumer can recover damages from a seller without having to prove that the seller knew of the potential harm.[40] In an AI context, if a self-driving car causes a fatal accident or an AI tool leads to a medical misdiagnosis, is the product defective, making the seller liable, even if it was misused or used negligently, such as when a driver ignores alarms while watching a show?

Product liability generally requires the party bringing a suit – the plaintiff – to establish that the party being sued (the defendant) was a commercial seller of such products; the product was in a defective condition at the time of sale; the plaintiff sustained an injury and the defect caused the injury.[41] Unlike traditional products, where defects are traceable to a specific manufacturing step, AI systems evolve through training and use, making it harder to identify and attribute liability to a specific event or decision.

Moreover, courts to date generally have not considered AI systems to be a 'product' but rather a 'service',[42] and thus only subject to negligence liability.[43] This classification could change in the coming years as AI systems are more frequently being used in tools or devices, bringing sources of liability.[44]

Additional potential tort law liability for AI systems could stem from intentional torts, where the harm was intended, such as 'battery' (an intentional, offensive contact with another person) or 'intentional infliction of emotional distress'.[45] This would shift responsibility to companies for the automated processes under their control. For instance, in cases involving social media companies, plaintiffs have argued that the companies knew their product was creating mental health harms for children and other users.[46]

Two lawsuits brought in 2024 by parents against Character Technologies, Inc., the company behind the chatbot service Character. AI (C.AI), and related parties, assert claims such as intentional infliction of emotional distress, negligence per se due to violations of child sexual abuse and sexual solicitation statutes and strict product liability.[47] They allege, among other tortious conduct, that the defendants 'fail[ed] to implement adequate safety guardrails' and 'knowingly and intentionally designed C.AI both to appeal to minors and to manipulate and exploit them for its own benefit'.[48]

In other contexts, an automated AI system could harm an innocent bystander or an AI-driven assembly line feature could maim a factory worker, which could be deemed a form of battery or other intentional tort.

Privacy Laws

Privacy protections in the US currently take the form of sector-specific federal laws combined with more generalized and comprehensive state laws. Given that data is a key ingredient in the development, training and operation of AI models, this area of law is of significant interest to companies, individuals and the media.

Federal privacy laws like the Children's Online Privacy Protection Act (COPPA) and the Health Insurance Portability and Accountability Act (HIPAA) address privacy harms related to AI involving harm to children or patient data respectively.

Children's Online Privacy Protection Act (COPPA)

Websites and services must adhere to stricter rules when their content is directed at children under 13 or if they knowingly collect personal information from children. Enforced by the FTC's Children's Online Privacy Protection Rule, COPPA requires child-directed platforms to notify users of data practices and obtain verifiable parental consent before collecting personal information, including persistent identifiers for targeted advertising. This also applies to third parties with knowledge of such data collection.[49]

Recent cases highlight the possibility of significant penalties for AI-enabled violations. In United States v. Kurbo, Inc., the court found

WW International and its subsidiary were marketing a weight-loss application to children as young as eight years old and illegally collecting their personal information. They were ordered to pay a $1.5 million fine and pursue algorithmic disgorgement.[50]

Similarly, Amazon was fined $25 million in 2023 for retaining children's data, including voice recordings and geolocation information, and was likewise required to delete the inappropriately collected and stored data.[51]

Health Insurance Portability and Accountability Act

The Health Insurance Portability and Accountability Act of 1996 (HIPAA) sets national standards for 'protected health information'. Issued by the US Department of Health and Human Services, HIPAA defines how covered entities – such as hospitals, doctors and insurance plans – may use and disclose protected health information and outlines individuals' privacy rights.[52] Dinerstein v. Google highlights potential liability when AI use intersects with HIPAA requirements.[53] The case involved claims that the University of Chicago Medical Center violated HIPAA by sharing patient information with Google as part of a partnership to analyze electronic medical records. While both parties asserted the data was de-identified as required by HIPAA, the plaintiff argued it could be re-identified using AI, raising concerns about data privacy and compliance.

State Privacy Laws

As of May 2025, 19 US states have enacted comprehensive consumer data privacy laws.[54] These state privacy laws generally cover: (1) consumer rights, such as access to personal data, deletion of personal data, data portability; (2) business obligations – for example, conducting privacy impact assessments, obtaining consent for processing sensitive data, providing privacy notices; and (3) notice of enforcement mechanisms, which are generally enforced by state attorneys general but some states provide a private right of action. Below are examples of how various states are adopting privacy laws related to AI uses. These examples offer a broad overview of the legal landscape, both today and emerging, helping to highlight potential areas of liability.

Arguably the most comprehensive state law is the California Consumer Privacy Act (CCPA). Operational since January 2020, its protections include: 'right to know' (consumers can 'request that businesses disclose personal information collected, used, shared, or sold'); the 'right to delete' (consumers have the right to request deletion of their personal data held by businesses); the 'right to opt out' (i.e. of the sale of their own data by a business); and non-discrimination (businesses cannot discriminate against consumers for exercising their CCPA rights).[55] In 2020, California voters significantly expanded the CCPA with the California Privacy Rights Act ballot initiative, which added requirements to disclose information and delete data at a consumer's request. This introduces operational challenges for AI systems already in use and potentially limits the amount of data available for future AI development. These requirements are particularly significant for foundation models.

Similar to the CCPA, the Colorado Privacy Act imposes new responsibilities on companies that conduct business with, or intentionally target, Colorado residents based on the control or possession of the personal data of at least 100,000 consumers annually; or derive revenue from selling data of at least 25,000 residents. These entities must now provide consumers with the right to access, delete and correct their personal data.

State Hiring and Employment Laws

Another law that companies should be aware of is the Illinois Artificial Intelligence Video Interview Act. Effective since January 2020 and updated in 2024, this law prohibits employers from using zip codes as a proxy for protected classes and requires employers to notify employees that AI is being used for specified purposes but does not elaborate on the details of the notice requirement.[56]

NYC Local Law 144, which took effect in 2023, prohibits employers and employment agencies from using an automated employment decision tool in New York City unless they ensure a bias audit was carried out and provide required notices.

We have prioritized the issues we consider most relevant to the reader but there are numerous additional areas of US law applicable to AI use and development. Readers should continue to monitor developments in this area, including emerging federal and state laws, as well as how the courts apply existing legal frameworks to AI in various jurisdictions.

KEY INSIGHTS AND ACTIONS

- The US AI regulatory landscape includes federal, state and sector-specific laws, executive orders, voluntary frameworks and case law. AI regulation will likely be increasingly enforced through existing laws such as those governing consumer protection, civil rights and privacy.
- Executive Orders play a significant role in setting federal AI policy.
- The US National Institute of Standards and Technology (NIST) AI Risk Management Framework serves as a voluntary, adaptable tool for AI governance, promoting risk management across all AI systems. It is widely used because it was created with broad stakeholder engagement and is compatible with all industries and jurisdictions.
- Federal agencies, including the Department of Justice, Federal Trade Commission, Equal Employment Opportunities Commission and Consumer Financial Protection Bureau, issue guidance and bring enforcement actions. Joint statements and prosecutions highlight potential liabilities involving AI use, including discrimination in hiring, deceptive practices, product liability and fraud.
- US privacy laws include federal sector-specific statutes like the Children's Online Privacy Protection Act and Health Insurance Portability and Accountability Act, and state laws such as the California Consumer Privacy Act and Colorado Privacy Act.
- Judicial rulings increasingly shape AI governance, addressing harms across the spectrum – from accidents with automated cars to algorithms trained on inappropriately collected data.
- Organizations operating in the US should proactively assess their AI-related liability under federal, state and local authorities to ensure compliance.

<h1 style="text-align:center">14</h1>

Notable global legal developments

The US and EU often dominate discussions on AI policy, but significant developments are occurring across the globe. While each country offers content sufficient for a full chapter, or book, here we provide a brief overview of notable legal and policy advancements in AI governance across different regions.

The growing use of AI in the countries covered in this chapter is consistent with an increasingly positive perspective about the potential impact of AI. A study by Google and Ipsos, surveying 1,000 individuals from 17 countries, found that individuals from emerging economies, including Brazil, South Africa, Mexico and the United Arab Emirates, were the most positive about AI.[1]

As reported by the Organisation for Economic Co-operation and Development (OECD), over 1,000 policy initiatives, enacted by more than 70 countries, territories and the EU, govern the development or use of AI.[2] These initiatives influence how countries set business and legal standards and co-operate in the creation and regulation of AI. Across the globe, data privacy laws in a variety of different forms have become increasingly prevalent, with nearly 140 countries passing some form of legislation to protect the data and privacy of their citizens.

FIGURE 14.1 Number of Mentions of AI in Legislative Proceedings in 80 Select Countries, 2016–23

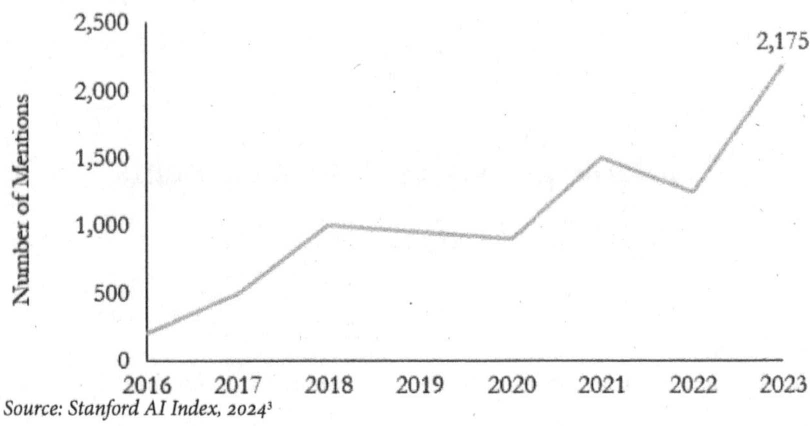

Source: Stanford AI Index, 2024[3]

FIGURE 14.2 Yearly Release of AI National Strategies by Country

Year	Country
2017	Canada, China, Finland
2018	France, Germany, India, Mauritius, Mexico, Sweden
2019	Argentina, Bangladesh, Chile, Columbia, Cyprus, Czech Republic, Denmark, Egypt, Estonia, Japan, Lithuania, Luxembourg, Malta, Netherlands, Portugal, Qatar, Romania, Russia, Sierra Leone, Singapore, Slovak Republic, United Arab Emirates, United States of America, Uruguay
2020	Algeria, Bulgaria, Croatia, Greece, Hungary, Indonesia, Latvia, South Korea, Norway, Poland, Saudi Arabia, Serbia, Spain, Switzerland
2021	Australia, Austria, Brazil, Hong Kong, Ireland, Malaysia, Peru, Philippines, Slovenia, Tunisia, Turkey, Ukraine, United Kingdom, Vietnam
2022	Belgium, Ghana, Iran, Italy, Jordan, Thailand
2023	Azerbaijan, Bahrain, Benin, Dominican Republic, Ethiopia, Iraq, Israel, Rwanda

Source: Stanford AI Index, 2024[4]

The following discussion offers examples of prominent international regulatory approaches and legal frameworks.

UK

Prime Minister Sir Keir Starmer has said AI 'is a game changer that has massive potential on productivity, and on driving our economy, and we need to run towards it.'[5] Specifically, Starmer sees the potential for AI 'to be a game changer when it comes to the delivery of public services.' In January 2025, his government published an 'AI Opportunities Action Plan' outlining how the UK can utilize AI within the public sector and promote the country's AI industry. The Plan recommends 'enabling safe and trusted AI development and adoption through regulation, safety and assurance'. This was followed in February 2024 by the *Artificial Intelligence Playbook for the UK Government* containing recommendations for using AI safely and responsibly.[6]

When the new Labour government set out its legislative agenda in July 2024 it included plans to introduce 'appropriate' legislation to govern powerful frontier models. However, as of early 2025, those plans look likely to be delayed or possibly shelved completely. Meanwhile, Lord Holmes, who had previously introduced a Private Member's Bill to regulate AI in 2023, reintroduced his Bill in March 2025, though it is questionable whether it will become law.[7]

In March 2023, the UK Conservative government released a white paper with the instructive title: 'A pro-innovation approach to AI regulation'.[8] This paper and follow-up materials released in February 2024 advocate for a 'principles-based framework', generally relying on the application of existing laws, which in many cases may be sector-specific.[9] The current UK Labour government appears to be following a broadly similar approach except for the possible introduction of new regulation to govern frontier models, mentioned above.

Several regulators are particularly active in providing guidance to companies on the applicability of existing regulations to AI. These regulators include the Information Commissioner's Office, the UK's data privacy regulator; the Financial Conduct Authority, which regulates financial services; the Competition and Markets Authority; Ofcom, the UK's communications and media regulator; and the Medicines and Healthcare products Regulatory Agency.

EXAMPLE GUIDANCE ISSUED BY THE UK INFORMATION COMMISSIONER'S OFFICE (ICO)

Guidance on AI and Data Protection[10]
Covers best practices for data protection-compliant AI and how data protection law applies to AI systems processing personal data.

Explaining Decisions Made with AI[11]
Details practical advice on providing transparency by explaining AI-assisted decisions and processes to affected individuals. It was co-produced with the Alan Turing Institute.

AI and Data Protection Risk Toolkit[12]
Offers practical support for organizations to assess the risks to individual rights and freedoms posed by their AI systems.

Biometric Data Guidance[13]
Provides specific guidance covering compliance with data protection obligations when processing biometric data.

Sector-Specific Guidance, such as AI Tools in Recruitment[14]
Makes recommendations for AI developers and providers in recruitment.

The Online Safety Act (2023), which will continue to come into effect through the summer of 2025, is an example of new targeted legislation illustrative of the UK's approach.[15] The Act applies to user-to-user services (platforms allowing users to share content or interact) and search services (tools enabling searches across multiple databases or websites). Content created by genAI tools is treated in the same way as human-generated content under the Act. Platforms must ensure that AI-generated material does not expose users to illegal or harmful content. For example, if an AI tool generates misinformation, hate speech or harmful material that is shared on a platform, the platform is responsible for mitigating risks and removing such content promptly.

In addition to industry regulators, the government's Department for Science, Innovation and Technology (DSIT) also issues substantive guidance to companies. It houses the Responsible Technology Adoption Unit, the successor to the Centre for Data Ethics and Innovation, which was the first body in the world established by a government to advise on the responsible use of AI. One example of DSIT's guidance for companies is the AI Management Essentials Tool – under analysis post-consultation at the time of going to press – released to aid organizations in evaluating the effectiveness of their AI governance processes.[16] The Tool draws on ISO 42001, the US National Institute of Standards and Technology (NIST) RMF and the EU AI Act in order to support global interoperability.

The UK has also been actively engaged in international efforts to shape global AI standards. For instance, it participates in the OECD's AI Principles and the Global Partnership on AI (GPAI). On 1 November 2023, the UK hosted the AI Safety Summit with world leaders, tech moguls and AI experts, culminating in the Bletchley Park Declaration, signed by participating countries.[17] This Safety Summit was the first of its kind and focused on the risks posed by advanced AI systems.[18] In November 2024, the UK government hosted a conference for AI developers in San Francisco ahead of the US AI Safety Summit, which they also participated in.[19] That same month the UK and US AI Safety Institutes published their first joint evaluation, assessing Anthropic's Claude 3.5 Sonnet.[20] The UK AI Safety Institute is now known as the UK AI Security Institute, having been renamed to 'reflect its focus on serious AI risks with security implications'.[21] The UK also commissioned the creation of the independent *International AI Safety Report*, 'the global handbook on AI safety' published in January 2025 that is 'the culmination of work by 100 AI experts to advance a shared international understanding of the risks of advanced Artificial Intelligence'.[22]

CANADA

Canada's AI regulation is rooted in a patchwork of human rights, privacy, tort, competition and intellectual property laws. Canada introduced a regulatory framework for AI governance through the proposed Artificial Intelligence and Data Act (AIDA). Like the EU AI Act, the AIDA includes a risk-tiering approach, with the highest tier called 'high impact' rather than 'high risk'.[23] However, the AIDA's scope is narrower. It only regulates 'international and interprovincial trade and commerce' and thus may not apply to the deployment and use of AI systems within a Canadian province. Unlike the EU AI Act ban of certain 'prohibited' uses of AI, AIDA emphasizes proactive risk management. It requires organizations to identify, assess and mitigate risks of harm or biased output before deploying high-impact AI systems. Like the EU AI Act, the AIDA also places accountability on businesses that design, deploy or manage high-impact AI systems, mandating the creation and enforcement of internal governance processes to ensure compliance.[24] The legislation focuses on mitigating two primary harms: individual and systemic bias. While not yet law as of the 2025 suspension of Parliament, the intent of AIDA is to prohibit reckless or bad-faith uses of AI that may cause significant harm, with enforcement authority delegated to the Minister of Innovation, Science and Industry.[25]

In the meantime, Canada has issued a Directive on Automated Decision-Making to ensure that automated decision systems making administrative decisions and related assessments for the Government of Canada 'are deployed in a manner that reduces risks to clients, federal institutions and Canadian society'.[26] Canada also circulated a voluntary code of conduct asking AI companies to commit to principles of accountability, safety, fairness and equity, transparency, human oversight and monitoring, and validity and robustness.[27] A guide for managers of AI systems looking to implement the voluntary code of conduct was published by Innovation, Science and Economic Development Canada in March 2025.[28] The same department also 'refreshed' the membership of the Advisory Council on Artificial Intelligence and established the Safe and Secure AI Advisory Group in early 2025.[29] Further, Canada's Office of the Superintendent of Financial Institutions released a draft guideline on model risk management in the financial sector, which is expected to take effect in July 2025.[30]

Canada's current privacy framework includes federal and provincial statutes, such as the Personal Information Protection and Electronic Documents Act (PIPEDA), which applies to private-sector organizations engaged in commercial activities.[31] PIPEDA enshrines principles of accountability and accuracy with compliance challenge mechanisms. Provincial laws, such as British Columbia's Personal Information Protection Act, Alberta's equivalent legislation and Quebec's Act Respecting the Protection of Personal Information in the Private Sector, also play critical roles.[32]

Privacy regulators in Canada have demonstrated an interest in enforcing these protections for AI applications. The Office of the Privacy Commissioner of Canada (OPC), along with privacy commissioners from British Columbia, Alberta and Quebec, investigated Clearview AI over alleged violations related to the collection, use and disclosure of personal and biometric information without consent.[33] During the investigation, Clearview withdrew from the Canadian market.[34] The authorities concluded that Clearview violated numerous sections of PIPEDA, Alberta's Act and Quebec's Act.[35] They ordered Clearview to 'cease offering the facial recognition services' at issue, 'cease the collection, use and disclosure of images and biometric facial arrays collected from individuals in Canada' and 'delete images and biometric facial arrays collected from individuals in Canada in its possession'.[36] The same group of authorities announced an investigation into OpenAI over similar alleged violations.[37] Although details of the investigation remain undisclosed, this development underscores the regulators' intent to proactively enforce existing privacy norms on AI systems. In fact, the OPC named '[a]ddressing the privacy impacts of the fast-moving pace of technological advancements, especially in the world of artificial intelligence (AI) and generative AI', as one of its top three strategic priorities for 2024–27.[38] These laws and actions collectively underpin Canada's approach to robust data privacy and AI governance.

Canada has also been active in international AI governance efforts, such as co-founding the Global Partnership on AI (GPAI) with France and establishing an AI and Data Standardization Collaborative to align its policies with other countries.[39]

ASIA
China
China is a global leader in AI research and development and was one of the first countries to pass significant AI-focused regulations. In its New Generation AI Development Plan, published in July 2017, the Chinese government announced significant investments in AI and China's desire to become a global AI leader by 2030.[40] Since then, China has reiterated the importance of AI being a part of its 'new productive forces' that will drive economic growth.[41]

Unlike the EU's horizontal regulatory approach, China's regulations are characterized as 'vertical'.[42] China has laws that apply to specific domains, often written to target related, large groups of AI 'applications' rather than all applications of AI. In June 2025, the first departmental rule regulating the application of AI in a specific sector, meteorology, came into effect. The focus of China's regulation is more often on algorithms, a key component of AI, as opposed to computational power used in the training process, a common focus of other countries.[43] For a helpful review of China's policy and regulations, see the Center for Security and Emerging Technology's publications.[44]

China's primary AI governance evolved from three concrete and impactful regulations on algorithms and AI: the 2021 Provisions on the Management of Algorithmic Recommendations in Internet Information

Services, the 2022 Provisions on the Administration of Deep Synthesis Internet Information Services and the 2023 Interim Measures for the Management of Generative Artificial Intelligence Services (GenAI Measures).[45] Subject matter experts advise that observers not lose sight of notable regulatory provisions beyond the content control efforts.[46] For instance, the 2021 policy provides users with rights, including the ability to turn off algorithmic recommendations entirely, or by specific tag, and the right to an explanation for algorithmic decisions with significant impact.[47] It also established a registry of algorithms and mandated 'algorithm security self-assessment report[s]'.

The 2023 GenAI Measures provide requirements around content moderation, training data, disclosures and user protection, as well as emphasizing text-based AI systems.[48] Notably, the GenAI Measures mandate government security assessments, while the previous two regulations permitted self-assessments, although the means for adherence is not entirely clear.[49] They also include significant content control requirements. For instance, Article 4 mandates that genAI systems uphold 'Core Socialist Values', while Article 7 requires effective measures to increase the 'truth, accuracy, objectivity, and diversity' of training data.[50] The GenAI Measures apply to genAI services offered to the public in China, regardless of whether the genAI service provider is based in China.[51]

In March 2025, the Cyberspace Administration of China (CAC) and other entities established a fourth mandate, detailing requirements for 'explicit and implicit labels' for AI-generated content.[52]

A fifth mandate also appears ready to be rolled out in 2025. Released as a draft in May 2024, the Basic Safety Requirements for Generative Artificial Intelligence Services focuses on cybersecurity and AI safety.[53] For example, the draft mandates that no more than 5 per cent of training data can be illegal or 'harmful'. This category includes data which 'violates core socialist values', as well as data deemed to be discriminatory. The draft includes specific regulations for each stage of the model lifecycle, mandating security audits during the training phase; technical measures to ensure model outputs align with user preferences; ongoing monitoring and evaluation; and a security management strategy after deployment. Potentially setting the stage for this mandate are the Network Data Security Management Regulations, which came into effect on 1 January 2025, requiring 'Network Data Processors offering generative artificial intelligence services' to 'implement effective measures to prevent and address network data security risks to ensure AI training data and related activities are secure'.[54]

According to the Algorithm Recommendation Provisions, a provider capable of influencing public opinion or driving social engagement must file the algorithm with the Cyber Administration of China (CAC) within 10 working days after the provision of services.[55] The regulations specify that they are applicable to algorithms used in information services, such as bulletin boards, blogs, microblogs, chat rooms, communication groups, public accounts, short videos, online streaming and the like.[56] There are numerous considerations with respect to these requirements, including: applicability; if they need to file as a deep synthesis service provider, a technical supporter or both; and how to address trade secrets or other proprietary or confidential information that must be disclosed to comply. According to CAC filings, as of March 2025, over 300 genAI services were registered and 105 genAI applications or functionalities that utilize registered model capabilities via API interfaces or other methods have been filed.[57] Violations can result in fines and criminal liability. These provider requirements, as well as those mandated in the regulations above, should be considered if your company provides products or services in China.

Japan

Japan's AI policy strategy is characterized as 'agile governance', emphasizing flexibility and innovation while addressing potential risks. Its soft law approach is focused on guidance with an end goal of being the most 'AI friendly' country in the world, meaning the 'best understanding of AI and the easiest implementation of AI in the world'.[58] The most significant step it has taken in this direction is its Act on the Promotion of Research and Development and the Utilization of AI-Related Technologies, passed by the House of Councillors on 28 May 2025. The bill primarily reinforces existing laws, 'giv[ing] the government the ability to advise businesses if they are using AI in a harmful way and to provide guidance on how to fix the situation' without imposing penalties on the businesses. The bill also supports greater transparency efforts and permits the development of task forces, enforcement mechanisms and other kinds of governance infrastructure.[59] Another step Japan took towards its AI-friendly goals was its AI Guidelines for Business Version 1.0 (AI Guidelines), published in April 2024. The AI Guidelines consolidated existing rules to provide a cohesive strategy for businesses, in which different players execute a 'cycle consisting of environment and risk analysis, goal setting, system design, operation and then evaluation in various governance systems'.[60] The Ministry of Economy, Trade and Industry and the Japanese Patent Office have also published model contracts to serve as templates for certain AI-related transactions, such as between a model deployer and a developer they engage as a vendor.[61] Accordingly, the country has issued multiple sectoral regulations and industry guidance covering the technology, but passed only one AI regulation.[62] This approach was highlighted in the Cabinet Office's AI Policy Study Group's February 2025 interim report.[63] Additionally, after analyzing potential risks of anticompetitive behaviour from algorithms and AI, the Japan Fair Trade Commission concluded in 2021 that the country's existing Antimonopoly Act sufficed to address most risks,[64] although they solicited feedback about this approach in October 2024.[65] There are nonetheless various laws that are likely to affect the development or use of AI in Japan. A non-exhaustive list includes:[66]

- The Digital Platform Transparency Act, which imposes requirements on large online malls, app stores and digital advertising businesses to ensure transparency and fairness in transactions with third-party sellers and consumers.
- The Financial Instruments and Exchange Act, which requires businesses engaging in algorithmic high-speed trading to register with the government, establish a risk management system and maintain transaction records.
- The Civil Code, which allows tort claims to be brought against a person who has given instructions to AI to produce defamatory content about another person and published such content.
- The Copyright Act and the Act on the Protection of Personal Information, which can be applied to inappropriate uses of AI.

Singapore
While home to only approximately 6 million people, Singapore ranks third overall and first per capita on Tortoise Media's global AI rankings, assessing AI preparedness across different countries. The US and China, respectively, are first and second.[67]

Like Japan and the UK, Singapore has taken a sector-specific soft law approach. For instance, in October 2021, the Ministry of Health published guidelines to encourage the safe development and implementation of AI in healthcare. The Info-communications Media Development Authority (IMDA) launched AI Verify in 2023, an AI governance testing framework and software toolkit that allows organizations to test their systems' compliance with a set of internationally recognized AI principles. In 2023, the IMDA created the non-profit AI Verify Foundation to support the use of AI Verify, with more than 150 members helping steer the Foundation. These included Google, IBM, Microsoft, Salesforce and AWS.

IMDA also issued the Proposed Model AI Governance Framework for Generative AI in May 2024. In 2018, the Monetary Authority of Singapore introduced the Principles to Promote Fairness, Ethics, Accountability and Transparency (FEAT) in the Use of Artificial Intelligence and Data Analytics in Singapore's Financial Sector, which was updated a year later. These principles offer a framework for companies utilizing AI in decision-making related to financial products and services. To support compliance with these ethical-use principles, the Singaporean government established the Veritas Initiative in 2019, which provides a framework and open-source tools for financial services companies.[68] MindForge is driven by the Veritas Initiative and examines the risks and opportunities of genAI for financial services.

Singapore also released AI policy in its Model AI Governance Framework in 2019, updated in 2020 and supplemented by a draft Model AI Governance Framework for Generative AI in 2024.[69] The framework provides nine proposed dimensions to support a comprehensive and trusted AI ecosystem, grounded on the principle that AI-supported decisions should be explainable, transparent and fair. It also offers practical suggestions that model developers and policymakers can apply.

South Korea

On 26 December 2024, South Korea's National Assembly passed the Act on the Development of Artificial Intelligence and Establishment of Trust (AI Basic Act), becoming the second country globally, and the first in Asia, to establish a comprehensive legal framework for AI after the European Union (EU).[70] The AI Basic Act, anticipated to take effect in January 2026, comprises 19 bills relating to AI. It sets out definitions for AI, requires the South Korea government to establish a plan for promoting AI industry development and sets out transparency obligations for 'high-impact AI'. Violations of the Act could lead to financial penalties.

Under the AI Basic Act, AI systems are classified as: (1) High-impact AI systems – those affecting 'life, bodily safety, and fundamental rights' in sectors like energy, healthcare and public services, aligning with the EU AI Act's 'high-risk AI systems' or (2) Generative AI systems – models that create text, sound, images and other content by mimicking input data.[71] At a minimum, businesses deploying high-impact or generative AI systems must inform users in advance if their products or services incorporate AI-generated elements. High-impact AI systems may also require compliance with safety standards, risk management, user protections, human oversight and impact assessments. Key provisions of the Act include transparency requirements, the establishment of ethical guidelines for the use and development of AI and a classification framework to identify high-impact AI systems. There are several similarities with the EU AI Act, with a focus on protecting human rights and ensuring transparency. There are also unique elements, such as the requirement to appoint a 'domestic representative' to submit the results of safety measures, apply for the confirmation of high-impact AI by the Ministry of Science and ICT and generally support safety and trustworthiness measures. Non-compliance carries an administrative fine of up to KRW 30 million (approximately USD 22,000).

Following the passing of the AI Basic Act, in February 2025, South Korea's Communications Commission published 'Guidelines for the Protection of Users of Generative Artificial Intelligence Services.'[72]

Prior to the AI Basic Act, South Korea passed limited legislation targeting potential abuses of AI. For example, the country amended its Public Official Election Act in December 2023 to ban the use of deepfakes in campaigns within 90 days of an election and passed a bill in September 2024 raising penalties for editing and distributing false video footage.[73] Legislators have also proposed amendments to existing legislation to address AI recommendation algorithms, AI in hiring, copyright for works generated using AI, AI leaking personal information and more.[74] Additionally, the Personal Information Protection Commission released principles regarding how AI developers and users should apply existing legislation when they are processing personal data.[75]

South Korea has been a prominent international AI convenor, hosting numerous international AI events and conferences, including the Seoul AI Safety Summit in May 2024, at which the Frontier AI Safety Commitments were announced; the AI Global Forum with leaders from Google, Meta, Microsoft and OpenAI; the Responsible AI in the Military Domain Summit in September 2024, at which 61 countries endorsed a Blueprint for Action calling for dialogue and controls on AI-enabled weaponry; and the 2025 Singapore Conference on AI: International Scientific Exchange on AI Safety, at which The Singapore Consensus on Global AI Safety Research Priorities was developed.[76] Relatedly, South Korea has pledged close co-operation with the US on AI issues at events such as the Camp David

Summit between the United States, Korea and Japan in August 2023; the Next Generation Critical and Emerging Technologies (CET) Dialogue in April 2024 and President Yoon's 2023 visit to US Congress.[77] This has led to formal policy co-operation, such as the US-Korea AI Working Group under the CET Dialogue, and precipitated many partnerships between US and Korean tech companies.[78]

India

India's approach to AI governance hasn't always been consistent. No laws specifically regulating AI have ever been passed. In June 2018, the country published its 'National Strategy for Artificial Intelligence', which promoted innovation and advocated for using AI to improve social welfare.[79]

However, in March 2024, the government published an advisory that required the government's permission to deploy certain AI models 'to take steps to prevent algorithmic discrimination and the distribution of deepfakes.'[80]

The advisory received such backlash that it was withdrawn 14 days later and replaced with another that excluded the government permission requirement.[81]

In February 2025, India Prime Minister Modi and US President Trump announced the US–India TRUST Initiative, calling for the creation of a US–India Roadmap on Accelerating AI Infrastructure and promoting public-private partnerships to spur innovation.[82]

LATIN AMERICA

In Latin America, we have seen proactive development of national AI strategies in several countries, including Argentina, Brazil, Chile, Colombia, Peru and Uruguay. We have also seen regional collaboration with initiatives like the Santiago Declaration, in which high-level authorities from the region established an intergovernmental Council on Artificial Intelligence for Latin America and the Caribbean in October 2023.[83] Forward-thinking Latin American countries are adopting AI strategies that cultivate local talent and create infrastructure to facilitate AI use and governance.[84]

Peru

In May 2024, the International Monetary Fund reported that AI 'risks widening the gap between Peru and advanced economies', but '[n]arrowing the gap is within reach' and the 'sectors that stand to gain the most from AI, in terms of enhancing productivity, include finance, government, trade, IT, education, health and real estate'.[85] In order to stay competitive, Peru has proposed significant AI legislation.

In 2020, Peru established the Digital Trust Framework, which contains an article requiring that public and private entities use AI ethically.[86] In 2021, Peru put forth their 2021–2026 National AI Strategy.[87] Then in 2023, Peru passed a comprehensive law 'promoting the use of AI for the economic and social development of the country including data protection regulation'.[88] In February 2024, lawmakers introduced a comprehensive AI bill modelled after the EU AI Act. Despite challenges, some experts are predicting it will pass with amendments.[89] As of March 2025, the government is currently seeking to add more privacy and transparency protections to the law.[90]

Brazil

In addition to being an emerging regulatory leader, Brazil is a successful tech hub within Latin America. Brazil's Proposed AI Regulation was approved by the Senate in December 2024.[91] Brazil has also shown interest in regulatory sandboxes. The country's National Data Protection Authority solicited public consultation on the proposal last year, which was later included in the Proposed AI Regulation.[92]

In anticipation of hosting the G20 Leaders' Summit in November 2024, Brazil updated its 2024–2028 Plan for Artificial Intelligence to emphasize steps to promote AI development.[93] The country also launched the Brazilian Observatory for Artificial Intelligence, a platform that monitors the use of AI in Brazilian society to better understand the use and impacts of the technology. Under the Brazilian Presidency, the G20 has put out multiple reports on artificial intelligence.[94]*

Colombia

Colombia has been a leader in Latin American tech policy, pursuing numerous AI initiatives. As of January 2025, the OECD AI Policy observatory reported that Colombia had adopted 35 AI initiatives, more than

---

*Examples include Digital Economy Working Group, 'Mapping the Development, Deployment and Adoption of AI for Enhanced Public Services in the G20 Members', August 2024, https:// cetic.br/media/docs/publicacoes/1/20241209151608/G20_DEWG_Brazil_2024_Mapping_the _Development_of_AI.pdf and 'São Luís Declaration: Artificial Intelligence', 10 September 2024, https://www.dataprivacybr.org/wp-content/uploads/2024/09/20240910-Sao-Luis-Declaration -Artificial-Intelligence.pdf.

double the number of any other Latin American country (Brazil is the next-highest with 17) and more than Canada (16), China (22), India (32), Italy (15) and the Netherlands (15).[95]

While former President Iván Duque was an enthusiastic AI champion, current President Gustavo Petro has not prioritized the issue in the same way.[96] However, multiple data centres are being built in the country[97] and in October 2024, UNESCO and the Superior Council of the Judiciary of Colombia announced a project to develop guidelines for AI use in judicial offices.[98]

Mexico

Observers predict that more than half of Mexican companies will be using AI by 2027.[99] However, to date, Mexico does not have any specific AI laws or regulations in place, despite actively participating in international discussions on AI regulation.[100] That said, a Federal Law Regulating Artificial Intelligence is under consideration as of January 2025, aiming to establish a framework for regulating AI development and use.[101]

Argentina

Similar to Mexico, Argentina previously adopted several policies and initiatives to promote AI and encourage ethical use, including an AI strategy in 2019.[102] However, AI policy efforts have not been a public priority for President Javier Milei.[103] The President has held meetings with OpenAI, Google, Apple and Meta and attempted to attract them through promises of 'hands-off regulation'.[104] One policy Milei put in place was the Artificial Intelligence Applied to Security Unit, which will use 'machine-learning algorithms to analyze historical crime data to predict future crimes' and conduct facial recognition surveillance.[105]

Chile

Chile ranked first in the most recent edition of the Latin American Artificial Intelligence Index, based on strong scores in 'enabling factors'. For example, Chile has the most extensive 5G coverage of any Latin American country.[106] The country's collaborations – for example, with Google – have helped spur this success.[107]

Chile first developed its AI strategy, intended to be applicable through 2030, after a series of workshops and national dialogues.[108] It was updated in 2024 and now includes new action items on 'Governance and Ethics'.[109] Chile also introduced its own risk-tiering proposal in 2024 and proposed the creation of a new Artificial Intelligence Technical Advisory Council as part of its enforcement regime.[110]

AFRICA

As a continent, Africa faces particularly acute challenges in the area of AI enablement. Internet penetration only reached 37 per cent as of 2023 (though it has grown rapidly, from just 16 per cent in 2013) and cloud computing penetration stands at 15 per cent due to deficits in electrification and investment in infrastructure such as fibre optic cables.[111]

As a result, much of Africa's AI strategy focuses on digital infrastructure and 'AI enablers'. There has also been debate over how much Africa should focus on reining in harmful AI applications through policy, as opposed to taking an approach more focused on maximizing benefits from AI.[112] Such approaches include the creation of representative datasets, improving digital infrastructure and tailoring AI solutions to African use cases.

Some argue AI is not the highest priority for the continent: 'We have places in this country where there are no seats in classrooms and we are talking about AI'.[113] Others focus on the harm stemming from a lack of African perspectives in the development of international AI standards, as well as the lack of governance of AI surveillance technologies on which African governments spend more than $1 billion a year.[114]

A few African countries have adopted national AI strategies.[115] As of mid-2024, AI policy in Africa has been largely focused on developing a continental strategy through the African Union (AU), which approved its Continental Artificial Intelligence Strategy in July 2024, a landmark step. In April 2025, delegates at the Global AI Summit on Africa signed the Africa Declaration on Artificial Intelligence, advancing 'a framework for African open data sets and open AI models' and supporting the adoption of 'innovative and responsible national AI policies and governance frameworks aligned with the African Union AI Continental Strategy', among other initiatives.[116] The AU previously addressed digital regulation with its Malabo Convention, which provides a framework for cybersecurity and data protection, and which entered into force in 2023.[117] Among other aims, the Strategy's 15 action items seek to develop infrastructure and datasets that cater to Africa's needs; call for partnerships, both among African stakeholders and on the international stage; and seek to precipitate greater African participation in global AI governance.[118] The Strategy is accompanied by an Implementation Plan and a Call for Action highlighting key actions, including the AU supporting the development of harmonized national AI strategies across member states.[119]

One international initiative involving some African countries is FAIR Forward. The program is spearheaded by the German government and partner countries include Indonesia and India, as well as several African countries: Rwanda, Uganda, Kenya and South Africa.[120] FAIR Forward works to ensure access to training data and AI technology within partner countries, strengthen local technical literacy and help with policy development.[121] To date, it has contributed to the development of open training datasets in Kinyarwanda (spoken primarily in Rwanda), Kiswahili (spoken across Tanzania, Kenya and Mozambique) and Luganda (spoken primarily in Uganda), and helped create the 'AI For Africa' policy blueprint published in 2021.[122]

Nigeria

Nigeria released a draft version of its national AI strategy in August 2024, proposing the creation of an AI Ethics Expert Group and a national AI Governance Regulatory Body, as well as a National AI Risk Management Framework.[123] It mentions the importance of AI's environmental impacts and promotes the country's impressive 3 Million Technical Talent (3MTT) Program, which is the largest known tech accelerator in the world. 3MTT operates through a large network of partnerships to offer technical training courses.[124] Phase I of the program received 1.7 million applications and more than 1,400 organizations expressed interest in supporting it.[125] Phase II aims to teach 270,000 Nigerians skills like AI/ML, software development and DevOps by 2025.[126]

Kenya

Dubbed the 'Silicon Savannah', Kenya has been a top investment destination for AI. To date, it has not substantially regulated AI. However, a significant court ruling in September 2024 confirmed jurisdiction in a $1.6 billion lawsuit by 185 content moderators from different African countries who were working for a Meta contractor, Sama, in Nairobi and claiming unfair treatment under existing labour laws.[127] Kenya established a Distributed Ledgers Technology and AI Task Force in 2018 that issued a report the following year on the opportunities of AI and challenges of regulating it.[128] In 2024, the Kenya Bureau of Standards published a Draft Information Technology Artificial Intelligence Code of Practice and the development of a national AI strategy is underway.[129]

South Africa

South Africa is also developing an AI strategy and has promoted domestic research efforts.[130] Previously, it appointed a Presidential Commission on the Fourth Industrial Revolution, which published its report in 2020.[131] The report recommended taking steps to improve AI skills training in the country and establishing a national AI research institute.

More recently, South Africa published several documents that serve as precursors to its AI strategy. Its draft National AI Plan discussion document, released at the Department of Communications and Digital Technologies' AI National Government Summit in April 2024, outlines potential regulatory structures for governing AI in the country, notes the importance of data and proposes rough timelines for policy development.[132] The plan also includes a number of goals, among them that South Africa should target ZAR70 billion (approximately USD 3.9 billion) in combined AI investment by 2030, train 30 per cent of its population in AI data management and AI literacy skills, and have 20,000 local AI specialists in its workforce.[133]

South Africa's National AI Policy Framework, released in August 2024, outlines 12 pillars of a prospective AI strategy, as well as a conceptual framework urging South Africa to consider the 'Push of the Present', 'Pull of the Future' and the 'Weight of the Past' in its AI policy.[134] The pillars have a strong focus on AI ethics, fairness, safety and human control – eight of the 12 relate to these issues, as opposed to four that relate to promoting AI development and adoption.[135]

THE GULF AND MIDDLE EAST

The Gulf states, particularly Saudi Arabia and the United Arab Emirates (UAE), are becoming key players on the AI global stage in large part due to the substantial planned investments in the technology. Saudi Arabia's $40 billion AI investment fund and the country's start-up ecosystem make it the world's largest public spender on AI.[136] In addition, it announced Project Transcendence in October 2024, a $100 billion plan to make Saudi Arabia a global AI hub by investing in its ecosystem, including data centres, talent and domestic development of models and applications.[137] Likewise, the UAE is creating MGX, a joint venture similar to its sovereign wealth fund that will invest $100 billion in AI and semiconductors.[138]

The Gulf state governments have had the unique focus of investing in developing Arabic models.[139] One incentive to develop Arabic-native models is that training and then translating a large language model into

Arabic costs a third more than training one using solely Arabic inputs.[140] These models are progressing: the second and third generations of the Falcon models released in May and December 2024, respectively, appear to rival top open-source competitors from Meta and Alibaba in their performance.[141]

In the policy realm, the UAE adopted a national AI strategy in 2018 and was the first country in the world to appoint a minister for AI.[142] OpenAI pioneer Sam Altman noted that the UAE 'had been talking about AI since before it was cool'.[143] Since then, Qatar, Bahrain, Kuwait, Saudi Arabia, Oman, Egypt and Jordan have adopted AI strategies and Bahrain's Shura Council, one half of its legislative body, approved a comprehensive AI law.[144]

Saudi Arabia

The Saudi Data and Artificial Intelligence Authority (SDAIA) was established in August 2019 and launched its National Strategy for Data and Artificial Intelligence the following year.[145] The Strategy supports Vision 2030, which aims to diversify Saudi Arabia's economy and reduce its dependence on oil. SDAIA is tasked with unlocking the country's potential in data and AI in alignment with the National Strategy for Data and Artificial Intelligence launched in 2020.[146]

SDAIA is responsible for establishing governance frameworks, policies and standards for data and AI, and overseeing their implementation in co-ordination with government entities.[147] SDAIA has the authority to achieve its objectives and has primary jurisdiction over all matters related to operations, research and innovation involving data and AI.

SDAIA issued AI Ethics Principles in September 2023.[148] At the beginning of 2024 it issued two sets of genAI use guidelines: one for government employees, emphasizing the importance of handling government data in compliance with applicable laws and regulations of the Kingdom; and another for the public, to educate and guide individuals on the responsible use of genAI.[149] The Principles include a risk-categorization framework in the mould of the EU AI Act and other international laws. In December 2024, SDAIA introduced the AI Adoption Framework, a sector-agnostic high-level guide on how different enterprises can create AI units and implement AI within their organization.[150]

In April 2023, the Saudi Authority for Intellectual Property sought public consultation on Draft Intellectual Property Legislation, which includes provisions for intellectual property generated by AI and stipulates that IP created by AI will be considered part of the public domain if there is no clear contribution from a natural person.[151]

United Arab Emirates (UAE)

Starting in 2017, the United Arab Emirates (UAE) began to develop a comprehensive policy framework to regulate AI. It launched its National Strategy for AI 2031 to achieve the UAE Centennial 2071 plan and to position the UAE as a global leader in AI.[152] The UAE established an AI Ministry, referred to as the Artificial Intelligence, Digital Economy, and Remote Work Applications Office.[153] It has also used AI in its operations – for example, the Dubai airport launched an iris scanner to confirm traveller identity – while issuing guidance to spur responsible AI development and adoption in different sectors. This guidance includes an AI Ethics Guide (2022), AI Adoption Guideline in Government Services (2023) and Practical Applications and Use Cases of Generative AI (2023).[154]

The UAE introduced non-binding AI Ethics Principles promoting transparency, accountability and fairness across public and private sectors in 2022.[155] In the same year, it adopted the UAE Charter for AI Development, outlining 12 principles to ensure ethical, inclusive and safe AI deployment. In June of 2024, the UAE released an International AI Policy emphasizing collaboration, ethics and sustainability in global AI governance. Then in October 2024, the UAE published a number of further decrees and guidelines regarding regulation of AI. In May 2025, the UAE became one of the first countries in the world to mandate AI education across grade levels.[156]

The UAE has engaged in many international AI policy initiatives and established bilateral partnerships with Western countries:

- In May 2024, the UAE joined the Hiroshima Artificial Intelligence Process Friends Group, demonstrating its support for guidelines to develop AI responsibly.[157]
- In September 2024, the UAE Cabinet outlined its stance on international AI policy, emphasizing its intention to remain active in multilateral AI policy forums and contribute to positive AI applications.[158]
- In the same month, the UAE and the US issued a joint statement pledging co-operation and stating an intent to draft a formal memorandum of understanding. In May 2025, the UAE and US announced the 'US-UAE AI Acceleration Partnership' to

'to further bolster cooperation around critical technologies and ensure the protection of such technologies based on a set of joint commitments'.[159]

Qatar

Qatar has developed an AI regulatory framework aligned with its National Vision 2030. Key milestones include the 2019 launch of the National AI Strategy, which focused on six pillars: health, entertainment, business, education and research, and the 2021 creation of the AI Committee within the Ministry of Communications to co-ordinate its implementation.[160]

In February 2024, Qatar's National Cybersecurity Agency released Guidelines for Secure AI Adoption.[161] These guidelines emphasize managing risk to support stakeholder confidence; ethical principles such as transparency, fairness and human oversight; and actionable measures, particularly for genAI.[162]

In September 2024, the Qatar Central Bank issued an AI Guideline for financial institutions, promoting the safe, transparent and efficient use of AI in the banking sector.[163]

Israel

On 5 September 2024, Israel advanced its AI agenda, becoming one of the first signatories of the Council of Europe Framework Convention on Artificial Intelligence and Human Rights, Democracy, and the Rule of Law. It was the only country from the Middle East, joining Andorra, Georgia, Iceland, Norway, the Republic of Moldova, San Marino, the United Kingdom, the United States of America and the European Union on behalf of its 27 member States.[164] Shortly thereafter, the Israeli Innovation Authority launched phase two of the National AI Program, committing NIS 500 million (approximately USD 149 million) to R&D infrastructure.[165]

These steps underscore Israel's commitment to remaining competitive with AI leaders, emphasizing both innovation and ethical governance. A key priority for Israel is to attract top global talent, which the country has supported with measures such as the Visas for Foreign High-Tech Experts Incentive Program.

Like South Korea, Japan, the United Kingdom and other countries, Israel has embraced a soft-law, sector-specific approach to AI policy that promotes 'responsible AI innovation in the private sector'.[166] Israel's well recognized tech sector accounts for 18 per cent of its GDP.

The country's AI policy was developed pursuant to a government resolution that tasked the Ministry of Innovation, Science and Technology with advancing a national AI plan for Israel.[167] It ties together various initiatives in Israel, and draws on AI policy papers of international organizations and leading countries.[168] The AI Policy identifies seven key challenges stemming from private sector AI use: discrimination, human oversight, explainability, disclosure of AI interactions, safety, accountability and privacy.[169] To meet these challenges, the AI Policy sets out common policy principles and practical recommendations, aligning with the OECD AI Recommendations.[170] Key recommendations include adopting sectoral regulation; pursuing consistency with current regulatory approaches of leading countries and international organizations; adopting a risk-based approach; using 'soft' regulatory tools to enable incremental development of the policy framework and fostering public-private sector co-operation.[171]

AUSTRALIA

In September 2024, Australia released a voluntary safety standard,[172] aligned with international frameworks such as the US National Institute of Standards and Technology (NIST) and the International Organization for Standardization (ISO), alongside a consultation paper for mandatory guardrails, targeting high-risk AI use cases.[173] The guardrails have received broad support, with many private sector entities moving to adopt the voluntary standards.

The definition of high-risk in the consultation paper is principles-based rather than the list-based approach taken by the EU. The proposed 10 mandatory guardrails closely align with the September 2024 voluntary standards and with international approaches. The consultation presented three regulatory options and solicited public feedback: (1) Integration into existing laws like privacy; (2) Framework approach: new legislation establishing a framework and possibly a high-level regulatory body, with regulation implemented by existing industry-specific regulators and a potential co-ordinating body; (3) Australian AI Act: new industry-wide legislation with standards, though details are limited.

For the public sector, the government has implemented a National AI Assurance Framework[174] applicable to all federal and state governments and the government's Digital Transformation Office has also issued an AI assurance policy.[175] This includes mandatory requirements, such as designating an AI Accountable Official to oversee responsible AI implementation and policy compliance.

KEY INSIGHTS AND ACTIONS

- According to the Organisation for Economic Co-operation and Development (OECD), over 1,000 policy initiatives have been enacted by more than 70 countries, territories and the EU, to govern the development or use of AI. Nearly 140 countries have passed some form of legislation to protect the data and privacy of their citizens.

- The UK promotes a principles-based, pro-innovation AI framework relying on sector-specific laws. UK leadership has emphasized AI's potential to boost productivity and improve public services, reflected in the UK's AI Opportunities Action Plan, released in January 2025, which outlines strategies for AI adoption and safety. Key regulators are actively guiding companies on AI compliance.

- Canada's Artificial Intelligence and Data Act adopts a risk-tiering approach similar to the EU AI Act but focuses on proactive risk management. Existing privacy laws, such as the Personal Information Protection and Electronic Documents Act, and provincial regulations underpin data governance, and investigations into AI privacy violations are on the rise. Canada plays a leadership role in global AI governance through initiatives like the Global Partnership on AI (GPAI) and efforts to align AI and data standards internationally.

- China announced plans to be a global AI leader by 2030, through significant investments and sector-specific regulations. Unlike the EU's broad approach, China's AI governance focuses on algorithms and content control. Key regulations include the 2021 Algorithm Recommendation Provisions, granting users rights over algorithmic recommendations; the 2022 Deep Synthesis Regulations, addressing synthetic media risks; and the 2023 Generative AI Measures, imposing content moderation, training data standards and mandatory government security assessments. A forthcoming 2025 AI Safety Mandate is expected to introduce stricter cybersecurity and data protection requirements, further tightening oversight of generative AI.

- Japan emphasizes 'agile governance' and soft law approaches and has released AI Guidelines for Business (2024) and model AI contracts. Sectoral regulations (e.g. for digital platforms and financial trading) address AI risks without imposing horizontal, legally binding requirements.

- Singapore's sectoral approach includes the AI Verify framework to test AI systems against internationally recognized AI principles. It also promotes governance via initiatives like the Generative AI Sandbox and, as part of the Veritas Initiative, Fairness, Ethics, Accountability and Transparency principles for financial services, positioning itself as a leader in AI regulation and testing tools.
- South Korea passed the AI Basic Act in December of 2024, becoming the first country in Asia to establish a comprehensive AI legal framework. Taking effect in January 2026, the Act mandates government planning for AI industry development and imposes transparency obligations for high-impact AI, with businesses required to disclose AI use and, in some cases, meet safety and oversight standards. Unique provisions include the appointment of a 'domestic representative'.
- India has yet to pass laws specifically regulating AI. A 2024 government advisory requiring permission to deploy certain AI models was quickly withdrawn after public backlash and replaced with a softer version. In 2025, India and the US launched the TRUST Initiative, aiming to accelerate AI infrastructure and foster public-private partnerships.
- Brazil's Proposed AI Regulation was approved by the Senate in December 2024. The country has shown interest in regulatory sandboxes, while it updated its 2024–2028 Plan for AI strategy ahead of hosting the G20 Leaders' Summit in November 2024.
- African countries' AI strategies primarily focus on improving digital infrastructure and creating representative datasets, while debates continue over whether to prioritize regulating harmful AI or maximizing AI's benefits. The African Union approved its Continental Artificial Intelligence Strategy in July 2024, aiming to enhance infrastructure, foster partnerships and increase African participation in global AI governance. International initiatives like FAIR Forward are supporting African countries by improving access to AI technology, training data and policy development.
- In the Gulf, Saudi Arabia and the UAE are making major investments and increasing focus on developing Arabic-native AI models,

with Saudi Arabia's Falcon models performing well on global benchmarks. The Saudi Data and Artificial Intelligence Authority (SDAIA) is responsible for establishing and overseeing governance frameworks, policies and standards for data and AI. It has issued AI Ethics Principles, genAI usage guidelines and an AI Adoption Framework.

- The UAE's 2018 AI strategy, along with other Gulf states, has sparked regional AI policy adoption.
- Israel focuses on attracting global talent and maintaining competitiveness through innovation and AI governance.
- Australia introduced a voluntary AI safety standard in September 2024, aligned with international frameworks, and launched a consultation on mandatory guardrails for high-risk AI. For the public sector, the government has implemented a National AI Assurance Framework with mandatory oversight, including the designation of an AI Accountable Official.

Section IV

The path forward

15

Closing thoughts

ChatGPT's release in 2022 created a wave of excitement among the general public and business leaders alike. The tangible potential of generative AI was immediately apparent, yet so were the risks, like hallucinations. Organizations rushed to find ways to deploy generative AI and are grappling with how to demonstrate business value. Meanwhile, advancements in foundation model capabilities continue to impress and the evolution of genAI into agentic AI and multi-agent systems shows immense potential for automating tasks and freeing humans from repetitive work. Networks of agents have the potential to reason, plan and act autonomously, but this powerful capability increases risk. Indeed, the probability of error increases multiplicatively as the number of agents grows and there are also risks of accountability, misalignment and collusion. A key obstacle for generative AI adoption is the difficulty of achieving the necessary reliability with these solutions, making organizations, their boards and their customers cautious. The potential and the risks of AI agents are just beginning to be explored but they will inevitably come with even greater challenges. This context explains the increased interest in AI governance, which offers clear benefits:

- Enhancing and protecting brand integrity: recovering from a high-profile AI failure is costly and difficult.
- Building customer trust: confidence in your AI products, or services enhanced by AI systems, expands your market.
- Improved reliability: only well-governed AI consistently achieves its intended goals.
- Strengthened security and resilience: robust AI governance is key to protecting your organization and customers.

- Avoiding litigation and regulatory action: AI-related lawsuits have increased significantly and will likely continue to do so as lawyers invoke current and new laws to govern AI systems and penalize violations.
- Earning respect, both internally and externally: your employees, board, customers, regulators and the public will recognize that your actions demonstrate integrity and responsibility.

While many organizations have established AI principles, translating these into practice can be challenging. Only through implementing a robust, comprehensive AI governance program – suited to the size and scope of your organization – can leaders gain the confidence they need to deploy advanced AI systems responsibly.

Regulation can play a key role in ensuring safety and building trust, much like it contributes to our confidence in using cars, planes and medication. When designed thoughtfully, regulation can drive innovation by providing clear, standardized guardrails to those building and overseeing AI systems, thereby fostering public trust in new technologies. In some regions, AI governance is already mandated – for example, businesses operating in the EU must urgently comply with the EU AI Act. However, until comprehensive, globally accepted AI regulations are in place, organizations will need to rely heavily on *self-governance* to manage the risks of increasingly powerful and complex AI systems.

The rapid evolution of AI presents both challenges and immense opportunities for those ready to lead. By embracing robust governance practices, you can mitigate risks, foster stakeholder trust and unlock the full potential of AI to drive business success. This work goes beyond compliance – it is about gaining a competitive edge in an increasingly AI-driven world. Your choices today will set the standard for how AI is developed and deployed in your organization tomorrow. With a clear vision, rigorous oversight and a relentless commitment to continuous improvement, you can position your organization as a leader in trustworthy innovation. The future of AI is not something to react to – it is an opportunity you have the power to shape. This book is your guide to navigating that path with confidence and success.

APPENDIX ONE – STANDARDS AND FRAMEWORKS

EXTRACTS FROM ISO/IEC 42001:2023(E) STANDARD
'INFORMATION TECHNOLOGY – ARTIFICIAL INTELLIGENCE
– MANAGEMENT SYSTEM'[1]
'The organization should document a policy for the development or use of AI systems.

The AI policy should be informed by:

- business strategy;
- organizational values and culture and the amount of risk the organization is willing to pursue or retain;
- the level of risk posed by the AI systems;
- legal requirements, including contracts;
- the risk environment of the organization;
- impact to relevant interested parties.

The AI policy should include:

- principles that guide all activities of the organization related to AI;
- processes for handling deviations and exceptions to policy.

The AI policy should consider topic-specific aspects where necessary to provide additional guidance or provide cross-references to other policies dealing with these aspects. Examples of such topics include:

- AI resources and assets;
- AI system impact assessments;
- AI system development.

Relevant policies should guide the development, purchase, operation and use of AI systems.'

EXTRACTS FROM THE US NATIONAL INSTITUTE OF
STANDARDS AND TECHNOLOGY (NIST) RISK MANAGEMENT
FRAMEWORK[2]

TABLE 2: CATEGORIES AND SUBCATEGORIES FOR THE MAP FUNCTION

Categories	Subcategories
MAP 1: Context is established and understood.	MAP 1.1: Intended purposes, potentially beneficial uses, context-specific laws, norms and expectations, and prospective settings in which the AI system will be deployed are understood and documented. Considerations include: the specific set or types of users along with their expectations; potential positive and negative impacts of system uses to individuals, communities, organizations, society, and the planet; assumptions and related limitations about AI system purposes, uses, and risks across the development or product AI lifecycle; and related TEVV and system metrics. MAP 1.2: Interdisciplinary AI actors, competencies, skills, and capacities for establishing context reflect demographic diversity and broad domain and user experience expertise, and their participation is documented. Opportunities for interdisciplinary collaboration are prioritized. MAP 1.3: The organization's mission and relevant goals for AI technology are understood and documented. MAP 1.4: The business value or context of business use has been clearly defined or – in the case of assessing existing AI systems – re-evaluated. MAP 1.5: Organizational risk tolerances are determined and documented. MAP 1.6: System requirements (e.g., 'the system shall respect the privacy of its users') are elicited from and understood by relevant AI actors. Design decisions take socio-technical implications into account to address AI risks.
MAP 2: Categorization of the AI system is performed.	MAP 2.1: The specific tasks and methods used to implement the tasks that the AI system will support are defined (e.g., classifiers, generative models, recommenders).

	MAP 2.2: Information about the AI system's knowledge limits and how system output may be utilized and overseen by humans is documented. Documentation provides sufficient information to assist relevant AI actors when making decisions and taking subsequent actions.
	MAP 2.3: Scientific integrity and TEVV considerations are identified and documented, including those related to experimental design, data collection and selection (e.g., availability, representativeness, suitability), system trustworthiness, and construct validation.
MAP 3: AI capabilities, targeted usage, goals, and expected benefits and costs compared with appropriate benchmarks are understood.	MAP 3.1: Potential benefits of intended AI system functionality and performance are examined and documented.
	MAP 3.2: Potential costs, including non-monetary costs, which result from expected or realized AI errors or system functionality and trustworthiness—as connected to organizational risk tolerance—are examined and documented.
	MAP 3.3: Targeted application scope is specified and documented based on the system's capability, established context, and AI system categorization.
	MAP 3.4: Processes for operator and practitioner proficiency with AI system performance and trustworthiness—and relevant technical standards and certifications—are defined, assessed, and documented.
	MAP 3.5: Processes for human oversight are defined, assessed, and documented in accordance with organizational policies from the GOVERN function.
MAP 4: Risks and benefits are mapped for all components of the AI system including third-party software and data.	MAP 4.1: Approaches for mapping AI technology and legal risks of its components—including the use of third-party data or software—are in place, followed, and documented, as are risks of infringement of a third party's intellectual property or other rights.
	MAP 4.2: Internal risk controls for components of the AI system, including third-party AI technologies, are identified and documented.

MAP 5: Impacts to individuals, groups, communities, organizations, and society are characterized.	MAP 5.1: Likelihood and magnitude of each identified impact (both potentially beneficial and harmful) based on expected use, past uses of AI systems in similar contexts, public incident reports, feedback from those external to the team that developed or deployed the AI system, or other data are identified and documented. MAP 5.2: Practices and personnel for supporting regular engagement with relevant AI actors and integrating feedback about positive, negative, and unanticipated impacts are in place and documented.

TABLE 3: CATEGORIES AND SUBCATEGORIES FOR THE MEASURE FUNCTION

Categories	Subcategories
MEASURE 1: Appropriate methods and metrics are identified and applied.	MEASURE 1.1: Approaches and metrics for measurement of AI risks enumerated during the MAP function are selected for implementation starting with the most significant AI risks. The risks or trustworthiness characteristics that will not – or cannot – be measured are properly documented. MEASURE 1.2: Appropriateness of AI metrics and effectiveness of existing controls are regularly assessed and updated, including reports of errors and potential impacts on affected communities. MEASURE 1.3: Internal experts who did not serve as front-line developers for the system and/or independent assessors are involved in regular assessments and updates. Domain experts, users, AI actors external to the team that developed or deployed the AI system, and affected communities are consulted in support of assessments as necessary per organizational risk tolerance.
MEASURE 2: AI systems are evaluated for trustworthy characteristics.	MEASURE 2.1: Test sets, metrics, and details about the tools used during TEVV are documented. MEASURE 2.2: Evaluations involving human subjects meet applicable requirements (including human subject protection) and are representative of the relevant population.

	MEASURE 2.3: AI system performance or assurance criteria are measured qualitatively or quantitatively and demonstrated for conditions similar to deployment setting(s). Measures are documented.
	MEASURE 2.4: The functionality and behavior of the AI system and its components – as identified in the MAP function – are monitored when in production.
	MEASURE 2.5: The AI system to be deployed is demonstrated to be valid and reliable. Limitations of the generalizability beyond the conditions under which the technology was developed are documented.
	MEASURE 2.6: The AI system is evaluated regularly for safety risks – as identified in the MAP function. The AI system to be deployed is demonstrated to be safe, its residual negative risk does not exceed the risk tolerance, and it can fail safely, particularly if made to operate beyond its knowledge limits. Safety metrics reflect system reliability and robustness, real-time monitoring, and response times for AI system failures.
	MEASURE 2.7: AI system security and resilience – as identified in the MAP function – are evaluated and documented.
	MEASURE 2.8: Risks associated with transparency and accountability – as identified in the MAP function – are examined and documented.
	MEASURE 2.9: The AI model is explained, validated, and documented, and AI system output is interpreted within its context – as identified in the MAP function – to inform responsible use and governance.
	MEASURE 2.10: Privacy risk of the AI system – as identified in the MAP function – is examined and documented.
	MEASURE 2.11: Fairness and bias – as identified in the MAP function – are evaluated and results are documented.

	MEASURE 2.12: Environmental impact and sustainability of AI model training and management activities – as identified in the MAP function – are assessed and documented.
	MEASURE 2.13: Effectiveness of the employed TEVV metrics and processes in the MEASURE function are evaluated and documented.
MEASURE 3: Mechanisms for tracking identified AI risks over time are in place.	MEASURE 3.1: Approaches, personnel, and documentation are in place to regularly identify and track existing, unanticipated, and emergent AI risks based on factors such as intended and actual performance in deployed contexts.
	MEASURE 3.2: Risk tracking approaches are considered for settings where AI risks are difficult to assess using currently available measurement techniques or where metrics are not yet available.
	MEASURE 3.3: Feedback processes for end users and impacted communities to report problems and appeal system outcomes are established and integrated into AI system evaluation metrics.
MEASURE 4: Feedback about efficacy of measurement is gathered and assessed.	MEASURE 4.1: Measurement approaches for identifying AI risks are connected to deployment context(s) and informed through consultation with domain experts and other end users. Approaches are documented.
	MEASURE 4.2: Measurement results regarding AI system trustworthiness in deployment context(s) and across the AI lifecycle are informed by input from domain experts and relevant AI actors to validate whether the system is performing consistently as intended. Results are documented.
	MEASURE 4.3: Measurable performance improvements or declines based on consultations with relevant AI actors, including affected communities, and field data about context-relevant risks and trustworthiness characteristics are identified and documented.

Table 4: Categories and Subcategories for the MANAGE Function

Categories	Subcategories
MANAGE 1: AI risks based on assessments and other analytical output from the MAP and MEASURE functions are prioritized, responded to, and managed.	MANAGE 1.1: A determination is made as to whether the AI system achieves its intended purposes and stated objectives and whether its development or deployment should proceed. MANAGE 1.2: Treatment of documented AI risks is prioritized based on impact, likelihood, and available resources or methods. MANAGE 1.3: Responses to the AI risks deemed high priority, as identified by the MAP function, are developed, planned, and documented. Risk response options can include mitigating, transferring, avoiding, or accepting. MANAGE 1.4: Negative residual risks (defined as the sum of all unmitigated risks) to both downstream acquirers of AI systems and end users are documented.
MANAGE 2: Strategies to maximize AI benefits and minimize negative impacts are planned, prepared, implemented, documented, and informed by input from relevant AI actors.	MANAGE 2.1: Resources required to manage AI risks are taken into account – along with viable non-AI alternative systems, approaches, or methods – to reduce the magnitude or likelihood of potential impacts. MANAGE 2.2: Mechanisms are in place and applied to sustain the value of deployed AI systems. MANAGE 2.3: Procedures are followed to respond to and recover from a previously unknown risk when it is identified. MANAGE 2.4: Mechanisms are in place and applied, and responsibilities are assigned and understood, to supersede, disengage, or deactivate AI systems that demonstrate performance or outcomes inconsistent with intended use.

MANAGE 3: AI risks and benefits from third-party entities are managed.	MANAGE 3.1: AI risks and benefits from third-party resources are regularly monitored, and risk controls are applied and documented.
	MANAGE 3.2: Pre-trained models which are used for development are monitored as part of AI system regular monitoring and maintenance.
MANAGE 4: Risk treatments, including response and recovery, and communication plans for the identified and measured AI risks are documented and monitored regularly.	MANAGE 4.1: Post-deployment AI system monitoring plans are implemented, including mechanisms for capturing and evaluating input from users and other relevant AI actors, appeal and override, decommissioning, incident response, recovery, and change management.
	MANAGE 4.2: Measurable activities for continual improvements are integrated into AI system updates and include regular engagement with interested parties, including relevant AI actors.
	MANAGE 4.3: Incidents and errors are communicated to relevant AI actors, including affected communities. Processes for tracking, responding to, and recovering from incidents and errors are followed and documented.

APPENDIX TWO – LEGAL

SELECTED EXECUTIVE ORDERS (EOS) AND PRESIDENTIAL
MEMORANDA INVOLVING AI

- On 20 January 2025, President Trump issued EO 14148 *on Initial Recissions of Harmful Executive Orders and Actions*, which revoked President Biden's EOs 14110 and 14091, among others.[1]
- Three days later, Trump issued EO 14179 on *Removing Barriers to American Leadership in Artificial Intelligence*.[2] The EO issued a deadline for the Assistant to the President for Science and Technology, the Special Advisor for AI and Crypto, and the Assistant to the President for National Security Affairs in co-ordination with agencies to develop a plan to 'sustain and enhance America's global AI dominance in order to promote human flourishing, economic competitiveness, and national security'. It also requires the immediate review of all actions taken under EO 14110 and sets a 60-day deadline for the revision of related Office of Management and Budget Memoranda.
- During the final days of his administration, President Biden issued EO 14141 on *Advancing United States Leadership in Artificial Intelligence* in January 2025 to bolster the development and use of AI for national security purposes and strengthen cybersecurity efforts through the use of AI.[3]
- President Biden issued a *National Security Memorandum* (NSM) on Artificial Intelligence to galvanize innovation to benefit US national security while establishing appropriate safeguards to ensure AI use aligns with the nation's core values.[4] Along with the AI NSM, the *Framework to Advance AI Governance and Risk Management in National Security* provides guidance to federal agencies on harnessing AI for their national security missions with appropriate safeguards and is designed to adapt in response to technological change.[5]

- On 30 October 2023, President Biden issued EO 14110 on *Safe, Secure, and Trustworthy Development and Use of Artificial Intelligence*. It established a government-wide effort to guide responsible AI development and deployment through federal agency leadership, regulation of industry and engagement with international partners.[6] EO 14110 directly addressed AI governance, covering areas such as safety, security, innovation, civil rights, privacy and international leadership. It tasked more than 50 federal agencies with over 150 actions and established a White House AI Council. All directives of EO 14110 were met by their assigned deadlines.[7] (It was repealed by EO 14148).

- In February 2023, President Biden issued EO 14091, *Further Advancing Racial Equity and Support for Underserved Communities Through The Federal Government*, which requires agencies designing, developing, acquiring and using AI to do so 'in a manner that advances equity' and to consult their civil rights offices in the process. (It was repealed by EO 14148).[8]

- EO 13960, *Promoting the Use of Trustworthy Artificial Intelligence in the Federal Government*, issued by President Trump in December 2020, establishes a framework for using AI to improve government operations while 'foster[ing] public trust and remain[ing] consistent with all applicable laws, including those related to privacy, civil rights, and civil liberties'.[9] The Order also established AI principles for the federal government, directed AI cataloging by agencies and guided AI implementation within federal agencies.

- President Trump issued EO 13932, *Modernizing and Reforming the Assessment and Hiring of Federal Job Candidates*, in June 2020 to promote skills- and competency-based federal hiring practices that better meet evolving federal workforce needs.[10]

- EO 13859, *Maintaining American Leadership in Artificial Intelligence*, issued by President Trump in February 2019, highlights American workforce development and AI readiness as one of the five fundamental principles of the American AI Initiative.[11] EO 13859 also outlines a strategic objective for federal agencies to support training and education initiatives in pursuit of this goal. Through the Order the US established the first seven national AI research institutes, supported AI technical standards development, provided guidance for private sector regulation on AI and supported international alliances.

SELECTED US STATE LAWS RELATING TO AI

- Alabama law H 161 (2024) made it a crime to create a private image of an individual without consent.[12]
- California law A 1836 (2024) created liability for the use of a deceased personality's voice or likeness without specified prior consent, A 2602 (2024) defined and addressed contracts involving digital replicas and S 926 (2024) made it a crime to distribute computer-generated images that appear to be an identified person's body part or depict an individual engaged in specified sexual acts.[13]
- Washington passed S.B. 5152 (2023), which targets deceptive media and election integrity, mandating disclosure and requiring clear identification of any AI-generated content used in political campaigns.[14]
- New York signed S. 1042 (2023), which prohibits unlawful dissemination or publication of intimate images created by digitization and of sexually explicit depictions of an individual.[15]
- Tennessee passed the ELVIS Act (2024), providing that every individual has a property right in their name, photograph, voice or likeness in any medium.[16]

APPENDIX THREE – TECHNICAL

A. BIAS AND FAIRNESS

Figure A3.1 Sources of Harm Throughout the Machine Learning Lifecycle

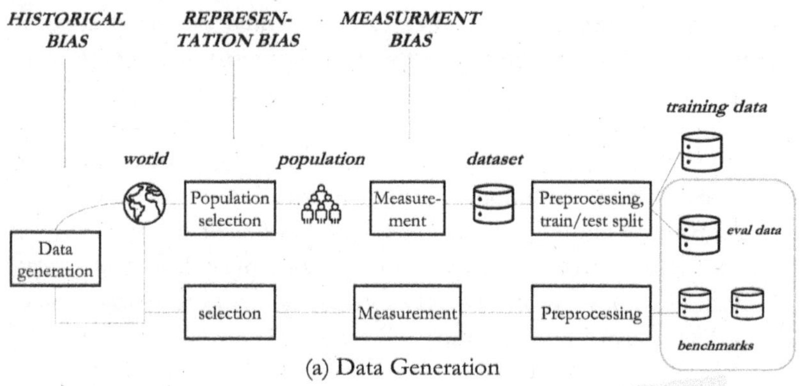

(a) Data Generation

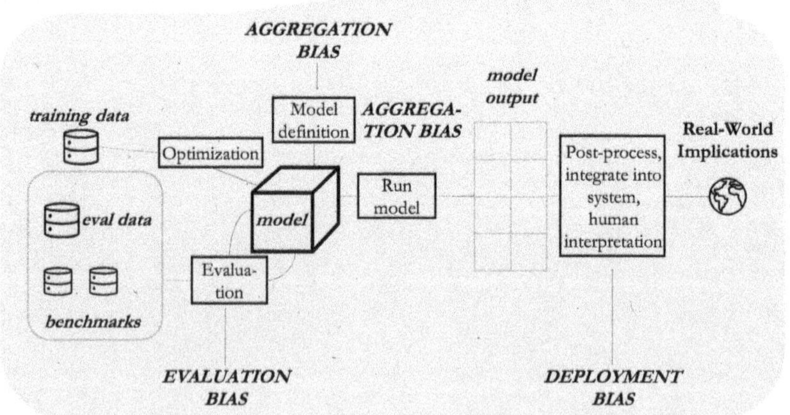

(b) Model Building and Implementation

Source: Adapted from Suresh, Harini and Guttag, John V. 'A Framework for Understanding Sources of Harm throughout the Machine Learning Life Cycle'

Figure A3.1 illustrates a typical model development lifecycle, starting with data generation and model training, through to testing and model deployment.[1] These biases are also present in genAI models, although the genAI model development lifecycle differs in some respects to Figure A3.1.

Bias can originate in different stages of the lifecycle, leading to the following definitions:

- **Historical bias** stems from the inherent societal biases manifested in training data, such as more images of male CEOs than female ones. When a model learns from data where such inequalities exist, it can perpetuate them and, in doing so, cause harm by reinforcing stereotypes or misrepresentations of specific groups.
- **Representation bias** occurs when the training data under-represents some part of the target population and subsequently fails to generalize well for that subset of the population. For example, a medical diagnosis dataset might not contain sufficient examples of certain ethnic minorities and therefore, when deployed, may be less accurate for those ethnic groups.
- **Measurement bias** refers to errors or inaccuracies in training data collection or measurement, such as from faulty measurement tools, inconsistent measurement practices or subjective assessments.
- **Aggregation bias** arises during model construction, when distinct populations are inappropriately combined. In many applications, the population of interest is heterogeneous and a single model is unlikely to suit all sub-groups. In such cases a model performs well overall but poorly for sub-groups, so a suite of smaller models would yield better results.
- **Evaluation bias** occurs during model iteration and evaluation, when testing data does not equally represent the various parts of the user population. Or from the use of performance metrics that do not account for differences in real-world disparities or challenges faced by certain groups, such as a facial recognition system trained on data from only light-skinned people.
- **Deployment bias** arises when a model is used in a real-world environment that differs from the conditions under which it was developed, such as a model deployed on a population or in a context not represented in the training data. An example might be training a model on data drawn from a UK population and subsequently deploying it in Southeast Asia.

B. GOVERNANCE TOOLING PROVIDERS

Below we mention a selection of AI governance platform and tooling vendors, but this is by no means an exhaustive list: the marketplace for AI tooling is dynamic and fast-growing. Nor do we list every tool provided by each vendor – these tools are constantly evolving. We are not recommending one vendor over another, nor are we offering advice, but rather highlighting a number of options.

1. Cloud native AI platforms with integrated tooling

This category of vendors includes Microsoft, Google and Amazon, which are typically used by large multinational companies that make significant use of AI and technology. These vendors offer their own extensive model development platforms, proprietary genAI models and in-built controls and tools.

Amazon AWS provides SageMaker (Clarify, Model Cards, Model Monitor and Dashboard), Bedrock (Guardrails and Model Evaluation) and AWS Control Tower (for AI governance).

Microsoft Azure offers Azure AI Studio, which incorporates a host of tools including AI Content Safety and Responsible AI Dashboard; Azure Policy, Blueprints and Purview for data governance.

Google Cloud offers the Vertex AI platform and Model Garden. Tools include their Responsible Generative AI Studio and Secure AI Framework.

These platforms offer integrated solutions that cover the entire AI life-cycle, providing state-of-the-art tools and built-in features that operate closely with their genAI models. They offer capabilities to help meet some AI governance requirements and their tools can also integrate with third-party AI governance platforms. One common feature is that their AI tools operate optimally with their own genAI models, although they all offer the capability to integrate with other models.

2. Enterprise software platform providers

Some large-scale IT providers are not known as being cloud providers but nonetheless offer extensive model development and deployment platforms, much like the cloud providers with integrated AI governance tooling.

IBM offer their WatsonX.ai toolkits that also integrate with their proprietary models, (the Granite3.0 range). The WatsonX platform competes with cloud provider AI platforms, having a similar range of extensive tools. WatsonX.gov is their flagship AI risk management and governance tool.

SAS offers Model Manager, Model Cards and a Trustworthy AI Life Cycle workflow mapped to the US National Institute of Standards and Technology Risk Management Workflow.

Other companies in this group include DataBricks, Oracle, SAP and Salesforce. All have a range of tools for AI risk management and reporting.

3. Specialist vendors

Some vendors focus on managing one or several of the risks reviewed in Chapter 10, depending on their heritage. For example, some traditional IT cybersecurity companies, such as Securiti, have extended their toolkits to guard against AI and genAI threats. Data security company OneTrust, which historically focused on data security, now also manages data privacy risks for genAI. Some newer FinTech companies have recently established a market presence to address specific risks, such as AI monitoring (e.g. Arize, Arthur, Fiddler and WhyLabs); prompt hacking (e.g. Lakera and GuardrailsAI) and privacy (e.g. TrustArc, ZenData and Transcend).

Typically, these and other specialist companies will offer capabilities to integrate with the cloud and enterprise platform providers listed above and some have strategic partnerships with the larger vendors, thereby offering enhanced interoperability.

4. Open-source controls

There is a large open-source community of developers and organizations building AI governance toolkits hosted in repositories, notably GitHub and Hugging Face (a whole book could be dedicated to reviewing these alone). Organizations which choose to use these toolkits may have the overhead of ensuring they integrate well with their model development platforms and are robust and resilient for their purposes. Some open-source toolkits are in fact included in cloud and enterprise provider products. A brief, but by no means exhaustive, selection is mentioned here:

Aequitas Flow:[2] available on GitHub[3] and supporting mainly group fairness metrics. It contains an 'Optimizer' component that allows a model to be trained on varying training data-splits and provides visualization of the resulting fairness metrics. It depicts the trade-off between model accuracy and fairness.

Themis-ML:[4] a library built on top of scikit-learn that provides tools to measure and mitigate discrimination and bias in machine learning models, available on Github.[5]

IBM's AI Fairness 360 (AIF360): IBM have opensourced their toolkit, which includes over 70 fairness metrics and 11 state-of-the-art bias mitigation algorithms.[6] It has tools to identify and help address both group and individual fairness.

Captum:[7] a PyTorch library offering a variety of attribution methods to interpret the predictions of neural networks.

InterpretML[8] **and Fairlearn**[9]: originally developed by Microsoft, both frameworks are for machine learning interpretability. They offer a range of tools, including a novel interpretable model called Explainable Boosting Machine, as well as popular techniques like SHAP and LIME, with built-in visualization capabilities.

C. AI GOVERNANCE PLATFORM VENDORS

This section lists some AI governance platform vendors. It is not exhaustive and will almost certainly grow and change, as the AI governance marketplace continues to develop. Note that we are not recommending one vendor over another, nor are we offering advice, but rather highlighting a few companies in this space. Vendors should be considered and selected based on an organization's specific requirements and verification of the capabilities and reliability of the platform.

Company Name	URL
2021.AI	www.2021.ai
Credo AI	www.credo.ai
Dataiku	www.dataiku.com
Fairly	www.fairly.ai
Holistic AI	www.holisticai.com
IBM Watsonx™	www.ibm.com/watsonx

Modulos AI	www.modulos.ai
Monitaur	www.monitaur.ai
OneTrust	www.onetrust.com
SAS	www.sas.com/en_gb/software/viya.html
Securiti	www.securiti.ai

Several smaller vendors also compete in this market including anch.ai, BreezeML, Calvin Risk, Enzai, Fairnow, Prodago, QuantPi, Relyance, Saidot and Trustible. Again, this list is by no means exhaustive: no doubt other companies will emerge.

Some websites now also provide a comparison of different AI governance platforms.[10]

APPENDIX FOUR – TRAINING

Please note that we do not endorse, promote, or verify any specific courses listed in the table below. The examples are presented to illustrate the types of educational offerings currently available. As with all lists, some offerings may inadvertently be omitted.

SELECTED AI GOVERNANCE TRAINING COURSES

Course Title	Provider	Description	Technical skills required?	Duration	Free/Paid	URL
General						
AI for everyone	DeepLearning. AI	An overview of AI terminology, limits, opportunities and ethical and societal discussions with Andrew Ng	None	Six hours	Free	https://www.coursera.org /learn/ai-for-everyone
It's not just business – AI risks, rewards and responsibilities	The Alan Turing Institute	Helping business professionals map and identify how to reap rewards and how to mitigate risks when adopting AI systems	None	One to five hours	Free	https://www.turing .ac.uk/courses/its -not-just-business-ai -risks-rewards-and -responsibilities

AI Ethics and Governance in Practice	The Alan Turing Institute	Interactive online platform particularly suited for the public sector, covering AI ethics and governance through eight modules	None	Module 1: Five activities, 190 minutes total	Free	https://www.turing.ac .uk/research/research -projects/ai-ethics-and -governance-practice
Introduction to AI Assurance	AI Standards Hub	Brief overview of AI assurance principles and practices	None	One hour	Free	https://www .aistandardshub.org /introduction-to-ai -assurance
Introduction to Responsible AI	Google Cloud	Microlearning course that explains what responsible AI is, Google's seven AI principles, and how responsible AI is implemented in Google products	None	30 minutes	Free	https://www .cloudskillsboost.google/ course_templates/554
Responsible AI: Applying AI Principles with Google	Google Cloud	A course for operationalizing AI for non-English speakers	None	Two hours	Free	https://www .cloudskillsboost.google/ course_templates/388
Ethics of Artificial Intelligence	Politecnico Milano	An overview of the reasons for ethical analysis of AI and the social implications of AI	None	10 hours	Free	https://www.coursera.org /learn/ethics-of-artificial -intelligence

Course Title	Provider	Description	Technical skills required?	Duration	Free/Paid	URL
Discovering Ethical AI	Udacity	An introduction to basic concepts and terms in Ethical AI	None	One hour	£194 (as part of one-month-subscription no-discount)	https://www.udacity.com/course/discovering-ethical-AI--cd13462
AI for Social Good	Conduit Academy	Course focusing on applying AI for positive social impact	None	10 hours	£600	https://www.theconduit.com/academy-course/ai-for-social-good-november/
AI Governance Professional (AIGP) Online Training	International Association of Privacy Professionals (IAPP)	Training that covers AI governance and risk management	None	13 hours	£1,195	https://store.iapp.org/ai-governance-professional-aigp-online-training/
AI Standards Hub	Various	Resource hub offering various AI-related courses and materials	Depends on course	Depends on course	Depends on course	https://aistandardshub.org/

Business						
AI Ethics in Business	Rutgers University	Understand AI basics and applications; navigate ethical and regulatory landscapes; apply AI ethics in practical scenarios	None	Six hours	Free	https://www.coursera.org /learn/ai-ethics-business
EqualAI Badge© Program	EqualAI	Alignment on best practices for governing AI with leading experts	None	Monthly virtual sessions over seven months, one and a half hours each; culminating with an in-person summit	Free for EqualAI Members or $15k per seat	https://www.equalai.org/ equalai-badge-program
Consequence and Risk Evaluation (CARE) tool	Open Data Institute	Interactive Consequence and Risk Evaluation (CARE) tool to ensure responsible and ethical technical and product development.	None	Situation dependent	Individual membership from £120 p.a.	https://theodi.org /insights/tools/ consequence-and-risk -evaluation-care-tool/
Various courses and certifications	For Humanity	Courses and certifications in AI risk management; AI regulations; AI auditing	None	Varies by course	Some free courses, some paid	https://forhumanity .center/forhumanity -university/

Course Title	Provider	Description	Technical skills required?	Duration	Free/Paid	URL
Certificate in Ethical Artificial Intelligence (AI)	Chartered Institute for Securities & Investment	Understand the fundamental ethical and management issues in the deployment of AI in finance	None	12 hours	£150	https://www.cisi .org/cisiweb2/cisi -website/why-choose -a-CISI-qualification/ professional-assessments /Certificate-in-Ethical -Artificial-Intelligence
Legal and PR						
Certified AI Governance Professional	International Association of Privacy Professionals (IAPP)	Range of courses expanding the remit of data privacy experts to cover AI governance	None	Varies by course	Some free courses, some paid	https://iapp.org/train/ aigp-training/
Continuing Legal Education (CLE)	EqualAI	Course on the lawyer's role in governing AI	None	One and a half hours	Paid (and included in membership)	https://www.equalai .org/programs/mcle-for -lawyers/
Ethics Guide to Artificial Intelligence in PR	UK Chartered Institute of Public Relations	Guide for PR and communications teams in how to deal with ethics in AI	None	One hour	Free	https://cipr.co.uk/ common/Uploaded%20 files/Policy/AI/AIinPR_E thics_Guide_UK.pdf

Technical training for non-data scientists						
Human Centred Generative AI	Stanford Online	Understand the fundamentals of human-centred AI and human-centric approaches to natural language processing, plus how to evaluate fairness, ethics, privacy and robustness of AI solutions	None	11 hours	$995	https://online.stanford .edu/courses/xfm112 -human-centered -generative-ai
Generative AI: Technology, Business, Society Program	Stanford Online	A comprehensive program that covers technical fundamentals, business implications and societal considerations of generative AI	none	Nine to 14 hours	$995	https://online.stanford. edu/
Responsible Generative AI	Coursera / University of Michigan	Learn how to responsibly develop, assess, integrate and govern generative AI for your role or at your organization	None	40 hours	Free	https://www.coursera .org/specializations/ responsible-generative-ai

Course Title	Provider	Description	Technical skills required?	Duration	Free/Paid	URL
Technical						
Ethical AI	Udacity	Coursework based program where learners design and build models that are fairer and more explainable	AI fluency – Python data analysis libraries – machine learning model implementation – Pandas, Data Visualization, Matplotlib	Four weeks	£194 (as part of one-month-subscription no-discount)	https://www.udacity.com/course/ethical-ai--cd1827
AI Fairness on Social Media	The Alan Turing Institute	Explores fairness issues in AI systems used on social media platforms	Python, plus basic knowledge of probability, linear algebra and machine learning	11–20 hours	Free	https://www.turing.ac.uk/courses/ai-fairness-social-media
Operationalising AI Ethics (Expert)	The Alan Turing Institute	Advanced course on implementing ethical AI principles in practice	Python, Jupyter	11–20 hours	Free	https://www.turing.ac.uk/courses/operationalising-ethics-ai-expert
Assessing and Mitigating Bias and Discrimination in AI	The Alan Turing Institute	Progressive course on identifying and addressing bias in AI systems	Milestones one to two: Non-technical; Milestones three to five: Python, Jupyter, Pandas,	15–20 hours	Free	https://www.turing.ac.uk/courses/assessing-and-mitigating-bias-and-discrimination-ai

Ethics in AI Design	TU Delft	Focuses on identifying and explaining possible ethical issues in AI design and development, emphasizing alignment of design decisions with ethical values	Not specified	Three weeks	Not specified	https://online-learning.tudelft.nl/courses/ethics-in-ai-design/
Data science professional certifications	Alliance for Data Science Professionals (includes Royal Statistical Society, Institute of Mathematics, BCS – The Chartered Institute for IT)	'We have created certifications for Data Science Professionals which embody the standards needed to ensure an ethical and well-governed approach so the public, organisations and governments can have confidence in how their data is used'	Yes	Various	Requires membership of a professional body	https://afdsp.co.uk/
Ethics training for data scientists						
Ethics in AI and Data Science	The Linux Foundation	For technology leaders and data scientists who are responsible for building and adopting AI tools	Not specified	Three hours	Free	https://training.linuxfoundation.org/training/ethics-in-ai-and-data-science-lfs112/

Course Title	Provider	Description	Technical skills required?	Duration	Free/Paid	URL
Responsible AI for Developers Specialization	Google Cloud	For developers to learn how to mitigate bias, implement privacy controls, interpretability and model fine-tuning	Development skills required	11 hours	Free	https://www.coursera.org/specializations/responsible-ai-for-developers
Advanced AI and Machine Learning Techniques and Capstone	Microsoft	Training in leading machine learning methods, ethical considerations in genAI and strategies for building scalable AI systems (part of Microsoft AI & ML Engineering Professional Certificate)	Hands-on python and experience of AI & ML	22 hours	Free	https://www.coursera.org/learn/advanced-ai-and-machine-learning-techniques-and-capstone#outcomes

REFERENCES

PREFACE

1 'Mapping the Responsible AI Profession, A Field in Formation', *techUK*, April 2025. Available: https://www.techuk.org/resource/techuk-paper-mapping-the-responsible-ai-profession-a-field-in-formation.html. [Accessed: 19 May 2025.]

2 Kraprayoon, J., 'AI Agent Governance: A Field Guide,' *Institute for AI Policy and Strategy*, April 2025. Available: https://www.iaps.ai/research/ai-agent-governance. [Accessed: 16 June 2025] and Liu, B. et al., 'Advances and Challenges in Foundation Agents', *arXiv*, 31 March 2025. Available: https://www.arxiv.org/pdf/2504.01990. [Accessed: 16 June 2025.]

3 Mearian, L., 'GenAI adoption outpaces governance, Ernst & Young finds', *Computerworld*, 5 June 2025. Available: https://www.computerworld.com/article/4002046/genai-adoption-outpaces-governance-ernst-young-finds.html. [Accessed: 16 June 2025.]

4 Maslej, N. et al., 'The AI Index 2025 Annual Report', Figure 3.3.7, *Institute for Human-Centered Artificial Intelligence*, p. 179, April 2025. Available: https://hai.stanford.edu/ai-index/2025-ai-index-report. [Accessed: 10 April 2025.]

CHAPTER 1: THE MOMENT WE KNEW

1 Mickle, T., 'Apple Plans to Disable A.I. Features Summarizing News Notifications', *New York Times*, 17 January 2025. Available: https://www.nytimes.com/2025/01/16/technology/apple-ai-news-notifications.html. [Accessed: 12 January 2025.] and 'BBC complains to Apple over misleading shooting headline', *BBC News*, 13 December 2024. Available: https://www.bbc.com/news/articles/cdoelzk24dno. [Accessed: 17 January 2025.] and 'AI chatbots unable to accurately summarise news, BBC finds,' *BBC News*, 11 February 2025. Available: https://www.bbc.com/news/articles/com17d8827ko. [Accessed: 21 February 2025.]

2 'Explanatory memorandum on the updated OECD definition of an AI system', *OECD Artificial Intelligence Papers*, 8 March 2024. doi: 10.1787/623da898-en. Available: https://www.oecd.org/content/dam/oecd/en/publications/reports/2024/03/explanatory-memorandum-on-the-updated-oecd-definition-of-an-ai-system_3c815e51/623da898-en.pdf. [Accessed: 8 January 2025.]

3 McCarthy, J. et al., 'A Proposal for The Dartmouth Summer Research Project On Artificial Intelligence', 31 August 1955. Available: https://web.archive.org

/web/20080930164306/http://www-formal.stanford.edu/jmc/history/dart mouth/dartmouth.html. [Accessed: 18 March 2025.]

4   Denker, J.W. et al., 'Neural Network Recognizer for Hand-Written Zip Code Digits', in *Advances in Neural Information Processing Systems*, Vol. 1. Morgan-Kaufmann, 1988. Available: https://proceedings.neurips.cc/paper/1988/hash /a97da629b098b75c294dffdc3e463904-Abstract.html. [Accessed: 23 March 2025.]

5   Vaswani, V. et al., 'Attention Is All You Need', *arXiv*, August 2023. Available: https://doi.org/10.48550/arXiv.1706.03762. [Accessed: 18 March 2025.]

6   Bommasani, R. et al., 'On the Opportunities and Risks of Foundation Models', *arXiv*, 12 July 2022. Available: https://doi.org/10.48550/arXiv.2108.07258. [Accessed: 18 March 2025.]

7   Chan, A. et al., 'Harms from Increasingly Agentic Algorithmic Systems', in *Proceedings of the 2023 ACM Conference on Fairness, Accountability, and Transparency*, 651–66. FAccT '23. New York, NY, USA: Association for Computing Machinery, 2023. Available: https://doi.org/10.1145/3593013 .3594033. [Accessed: 23 March 2025.]

8   Besta, M. et al., 'Reasoning Language Models: A Blueprint', *arXiv*, 23 January 2025. https://arxiv.org/abs/2501.11223. [Accessed: 20 March 2025.]

9   Weng, L. et al., 'A Survey on Large Language Model Based Autonomous Agents', *Frontiers of Computer Science*, 18, no. 6 (December 2024): 186345. Available: https:// doi.org/10.1007/s11704-024-40231-1. [Accessed: 20 March 2025.]

10 Yee, L. et al., 'Why AI Agents Are the Next Frontier of Generative AI', *McKinsey*, 24 July 2024. Available: https://www.mckinsey.com/capabilities /mckinsey-digital/our-insights/why-agents-are-the-next-frontier-of -generative-ai#/ [Accessed 25 January 2025.] and 'Agentic AI – the New Frontier in GenAI', *PricewaterhouseCoopers*. Available: https://www.pwc .com/m1/en/publications/agentic-ai-the-new-frontier-in-genai.html   and https://reports.weforum.org/docs/WEF_Navigating_the_AI_Frontier_2024 .pdf [Accessed 25 January 2025.] and Moore, M., 'Microsoft Unveils a Whole Host of New AI Agents to Solve Even Your Trickiest Business Problems', *TechRadar*, 19 November 2024. Available: https://www.techradar.com/ pro/microsoft-unveils-a-whole-host-of-new-ai-agents-to-solve-even-your -trickiest-business-problems. [Accessed: 18 March 2025.] and Franzen, C., 'Google Cloud Launches AI Agent Space Amid Rising Competition', *VentureBeat*, 21 November 2024. Available: https://venturebeat.com/ai/ google-cloud-launches-ai-agent-space-amid-rising-competition/. [Accessed: 18 March 2025.] and Knight, W., 'OpenAI's Operator Lets ChatGPT Use the Web for You', *Wired*. Available: https://www.wired.com/story/openai-sets -chatgpt-loose-on-the-web/. [Accessed 25 January 2025.]

11 Ghose, S., 'The Next "Next Big Thing": Agentic AI's Opportunities and Risks', *UC Berkeley Sutardja Center*, 19 December 2024. Available: https://scet

.berkeley.edu/the-next-next-big-thing-agentic-ais-opportunities-and-risks/. [Accessed: 18 March 2025.] and 'New Ethics Risks Courtesy of AI Agents? Researchers Are on the Case,' *IBM*, 23 December 2024. Available: https:// www.ibm.com/think/insights/ai-agent-ethics. [Accessed: 18 March 2025.]

12 'Technology Trends 2025', *Accenture*, 7 January 2025. Available: https:// www.accenture.com/us-en/insights/technology/technology-trends-2025. [Accessed: 21 February 2025.]

13 'Introduction to AI assurance', *GOV.UK*. Available: https://www.gov.uk/ government/publications/introduction-to-ai-assurance/introduction-to-ai -assurance. [Accessed: 25 September 2024.]

CHAPTER 2: WHY IS AI GOVERNANCE IMPORTANT NOW?

1 'Responsible AI for telcos: A new imperative | McKinsey', *McKinsey*. Available: https://www.mckinsey.com/industries/technology-media-and-telecommu nications/our-insights/responsible-ai-a-business-imperative-for-telcos#. October 2024. [Accessed: 10 January 2025.]

2 'Thrive with responsible AI: Embedding trust can unlock value', *Accenture*, 29 November 2024. Available: https://www.accenture.com/us-en/insights/data-ai /rai-from-risk-to-value. [Accessed: 24 January 2025.]

3 '2024 Edelman Trust Barometer with key insights around AI', *Edelman Trust Institute*. Available: https://www.edelman.com/sites/g/files/aatuss191/ files/2024-03/2024%20Edelman%20Trust%20Barometer%20Key%20 Insights%20Around%20AI.pdf. [Accessed: 16 April 2025.]

4 '2024 Evident AI Index'. Available: https://evidentinsights.com/ai-index/. [Accessed: 17 March 2025.]

5 'Responsible AI Report 2025', *Evident AI*, March 2025. Available: https:// evidentinsights.com/insights/responsible-ai-report/. [Accessed: 20 March 2025.]

6 The 2025 AI Index Report', *Stanford HAI*, April 2025. Available: https://hai. stanford.edu/ai-index/2025-ai-index-report. [Accessed: 10 April 2025.]

7 Maslej, N. et al., 'Artificial Intelligence Index Report 2024', *arXiv*, 29 May 2024. doi: 10.48550/arXiv.2405.19522. Available: http://arxiv.org/abs/2405.19522. [Accessed: 8 January 2025.]

8 'Evaluating the Pillars of Responsible AI', *Qlik*. Available: https://www.qlik.com/ us/resource-library/evaluating-the-pillars-of-responsible-ai. [Accessed: 18 March 2025.]

9 '30 per cent of European businesses are still not compliant with GDPR', *RSM Global*, 22 July 2019. Available: https://www.rsm.global/insights/data-privacy -and-cyber-security/30-european-businesses-are-still-not-compliant-gdpr. [Accessed: 7 January 2025.]

10 'Three years of GDPR: the biggest fines so far', *BBC News*, 24 May 2021. Available: https://www.bbc.com/news/technology-57011639. [Accessed: 17 March 2025.]

CHAPTER 3: WHOSE PROBLEM IS IT ANYWAY?

1   'ARTIFICIAL INTELLIGENCE', *Business Roundtable*. Available: https://www .businessroundtable.org/policy-perspectives/technology/ai. [Accessed: 10 January 2025.]

2   Vogel, M. and Eccles, R., 'Board Responsibility for Artificial Intelligence Oversight', *Harvard Law School Forum on Corporate Governance*, 5 January 2022. Available: https://corpgov.law.harvard.edu/2022/01/05/board-responsibility-for -artificial-intelligence-oversight/. [Accessed: 10 January 2025.] and 'AI regulatory landscape and the need for board governance', *Grant Thornton*, 7 December 2023. Available: https://www.grantthornton.com/insights/articles/audit/2023/govern ance-opportunities-risks-regulation. [Accessed: 10 January 2025.]

3   Dilworth, D., 'How is Nestlé balancing building trust in the era of AI?', *Brand Innovators*, 17 June 2024. Available: https://brand-innovators.com/news/how -is-nestle-balancing-building-trust-in-the-era-of-ai/. [Accessed: 10 January 2025.]

4   'Artificial Intelligence (AI) Model Risk Management', *Monetary Authority of Singapore*. December 2024. Available: https://www.mas.gov.sg/publications /monographs-or-information-paper/2024/artificial-intelligence-model-risk -management. [Accessed: 24 January 2025.]

5   Gupta, A., Friedman, H.K. and Winn, B., 'How CHROs Can Be the Drivers of Ethical AI Adoption and Empowerment', *Executive Network*, 30 October 2024. Available: https://www.shrm.org/executive-network/insights/people-strategy/ how-chros-drivers-ethical-ai-adoption-empowerment-fall-2024. [Accessed: 21 February 2025.]

6   'FTC Announces Crackdown on Deceptive AI Claims and Schemes', *Federal Trade Commission*, 25 September 2024. Available: https://www.ftc.gov/news -events/news/press-releases/2024/09/ftc-announces-crackdown-deceptive-ai -claims-schemes. [Accessed: 10 January 2025.]

7   'Article 57: AI Regulatory Sandboxes', *EU Artificial Intelligence Act*. Available: https://artificialintelligenceact.eu/article/57/. [Accessed: 10 January 2025.] and 'Enhancing Federal AI Safety: Responsible and Secure AI Sandbox', *Microsoft Community Hub*, 29 October 2024. Available: https://techcommunity.micro soft.com/blog/publicsectorblog/enhancing-federal-ai-safety-responsible-and -secure-ai-sandbox/4279628. [Accessed: 10 January 2025.]

8   Jackley, M., '10 ways state and local governments are applying AI', *Oracle*, 27 August 2024. Available: https://www.oracle.com/artificial-intelligence/ai-local -government/. [Accessed: 10 January 2025.]

9   'Launching the Artificial Intelligence Playbook for the UK Government', *GOV. UK*, 10 February 2025. Available: https://gds.blog.gov.uk/2025/02/10/launch ing-the-artificial-intelligence-playbook-for-the-uk-government/. [Accessed: 21 February 2025.]

10 'Responsible AI Playbook for Investors', *World Economic Forum*, June 2024. Available: https://www3.weforum.org/docs/WEF_Responsible_AI_Playbook _for_Investors_2024.pdf. [Accessed: 10 January 2024.]

11 'Responsible AI', *Responsible AI Labs*. Available: https://www.rilabs.org/ responsible-ai. [Accessed: 10 January 2025.]

CHAPTER 4: UNDERSTANDING AI RISK – A SURVEY OF KEY FRAMEWORKS

1 Tabassi, E., 'Artificial Intelligence Risk Management Framework (AI RMF 1.0)', *National Institute of Standards and Technology (U.S.)*, Gaithersburg, MD, NIST AI 100-1, January 2023. doi: 10.6028/NIST.AI.100-, 1. Available: http:// nvlpubs.nist.gov/nistpubs/ai/NIST.AI.100-1.pdf. [Accessed: 12 January 2025.]

2 Perez, C., *Invisible Women*, first edn., London, England: Vintage, 2020.

3 'Road traffic injuries', *World Health Organization*, 13 December 2023. Available: https://www.who.int/news-room/fact-sheets/detail/road-traffic -injuries. [Accessed: 11 January 2025.]

4 Tabassi, E., 'Artificial Intelligence Risk Management Framework (AI RMF 1.0)', *National Institute of Standards and Technology (U.S.)*, Gaithersburg, MD, NIST AI 100-1, January 2023. doi: 10.6028/NIST.AI.100-1. Available: http:// nvlpubs.nist.gov/nistpubs/ai/NIST.AI.100-1.pdf. [Accessed: 12 January 2025.]

5 'ISO/IEC TS 5723:2022', *International Organization of Standards.* July 2022. Available: https://www.iso.org/standard/81608.html. [Accessed: 12 January 2025.]

6 'AI Risk Management Framework', *NIST*, July 2021, Available: https://www .nist.gov/itl/ai-risk-management-framework. [Accessed: 22 January 2025.]

7 'AI Principles Overview', *OECD*. 2019, updated May 2024. Available: https:// oecd.ai/en/principles. [Accessed: 22 January 2025.]

8 'The Framework Convention on Artificial Intelligence', *Council of Europe*. Available: https://www.coe.int/en/web/artificial-intelligence/the-framework -convention-on-artificial-intelligence. [Accessed: 24 January 2025.] and 'International AI Treaty', *Center for AI and Digital Policy*. Available: https:// www.caidp.org/resources/coe-ai-treaty/. [Accessed: 24 January 2025.]

9 Powell, R., 'The Council of Europe Convention on AI: National Security Implications', *Alan Turing Institute*, 5 September 2024. Available: https://cetas .turing.ac.uk/publications/council-europe-convention-ai-national-security -implications. [Accessed: 18 March 2025.]

10 'AI regulation: a pro-innovation approach', *GOV.UK*, 3 August 2023. Available: https://www.gov.uk/government/publications/ai-regulation-a-pro-innovation -approach. [Accessed: 12 January 2025.]

11 'Regulating AI: the ICO's strategic approach – a response to the DSIT Secretary of State', *Information Commissioner's Office*, 30 April 2024. Available: https://ico .org.uk/about-the-ico/consultations/regulating-ai-the-icos-strategic-approach -a-response-to-the-dsit-secretary-of-state/. [Accessed: 12 January 2025.]

12 'AI Opportunities Action Plan', *GOV.UK*, 13 January 2025. Available: https://www.gov.uk/government/publications/ai-opportunities-action-plan/ai-opportunities-action-plan. [Accessed: 27 January 2025.]

13 'International Scientific Report on the Safety of Advanced AI', *GOV.UK*, 17 May 2024. Available: https://www.gov.uk/government/publications/international-scientific-report-on-the-safety-of-advanced-ai. [Accessed: 12 January 2025.]

14 'Principles to Promote Fairness, Ethics, Accountability and Transparency (FEAT) in the Use of Artificial Intelligence and Data Analytics in Singapore's Financial Sector', *Monetary Authority of Singapore*, November 2018. Available: https://www.mas.gov.sg/publications/monographs-or-information-paper/2018/feat. [Accessed: 12 January 2025.]

15 'Project MindForge', *Monetary Authority of Singapore*, 27 May 2024. Available: https://www.mas.gov.sg/schemes-and-initiatives/project-mindforge. [Accessed: 22 January 2025.]

CHAPTER 5: A CONSOLIDATED AI RISK LANDSCAPE

1 Roberts, M. et al., 'Common pitfalls and recommendations for using machine learning to detect and prognosticate for COVID-19 using chest radiographs and CT scans', *Nat Mach Intell*, vol. 3, no. 3, pp. 199–217, Mar. 2021, doi: 10.1038/s42256-021-00307-0. Available: https://www.nature.com/articles/s42256-021-00307-0. [Accessed: 23 January 2025.]

2 Lucini, F., 'ChatGPT conversation', 12 September 2024. Screenshot supplied by Lucini.

3 Pierson, E. et al., 'An algorithmic approach to reducing unexplained pain disparities in underserved populations', *Nat Med*, vol. 27, no. 1, pp. 136–140, January 2021, doi: 10.1038/s41591-020-01192-7. Available: https://www.nature.com/articles/s41591-020-01192-7. [Accessed: 12 January 2025.]

4 Schwartz, R. et al., 'Towards a standard for identifying and managing bias in artificial intelligence', *National Institute of Standards and Technology (U.S.)*, Gaithersburg, MD, NIST SP 1270, March 2022. doi: 10.6028/NIST.SP.1270. Available: https://nvlpubs.nist.gov/nistpubs/SpecialPublications/NIST.SP.1270.pdf. [Accessed: 12 January 2025.]

5 Wang, X. et al., 'A brief review on algorithmic fairness', *Management System Engineering*, vol. 1, no. 1, p. 7, November 2022, doi: 10.1007/s44176-022-00006-z. Available: https://link.springer.com/10.1007/s44176-022-00006-z. [Accessed: 12 January 2025.] and 'Fairness and machine learning'. December 2023. Available: https://fairmlbook.org/. [Accessed: 12 January 2025.] and Mehrabi, N. et al., 'A Survey on Bias and Fairness in Machine Learning', *arXiv*, 25 January 2022. doi: 10.48550/arXiv.1908.09635. Available: http://arxiv.org/abs/1908.09635. [Accessed: 12 January 2025.]

6 ACM FAccT Conference, 'FAT* 2018 Translation Tutorial: 21 Definitions of Fairness and Their Politics,' *YouTube*, 18 April 2018. Available: https://www.youtube.com/watch?v=wqamrPkF5kk. [Accessed: 18 March 2025.]

7 Obermeyer, Z. et al., 'Dissecting racial bias in an algorithm used to manage the health of populations', *Science*, vol. 366, no. 6464, pp. 447–453, October 2019, doi: 10.1126/science.aax2342. Available: https://www.science.org/doi/10.1126/science.aax2342. [Accessed: 16 November 2024.]

8 Roth, E., 'Judge slams lawyers for "bogus AI-generated research"', *The Verge*, 13 May 2025. Available: https://www.theverge.com/news/666443/judge-slams-lawyers-ai-bogus-research. [Accessed: 20 May 2025.]

9 'Human + Machine | Reimagining Work in the Age of AI', *Accenture*. September 2024. Available: https://www.accenture.com/us-en/insights/technology/human-plus-machine. [Accessed: 12 January 2025.]

10 'Computer says no', *Wikipedia*, 9 October 2024. Available: https://en.wikipedia.org/w/index.php?title=Computer_says_no&oldid=1250207652. [Accessed: 12 January 2025.]

11 Titah, R., 'How AI Skews Our Sense of Responsibility', *MIT Sloan Management Review*, 13 May 2024. Available: https://sloanreview.mit.edu/article/how-ai-skews-our-sense-of-responsibility/. [Accessed: 12 January 2025.]

12 Dratsch, T. et al., 'Automation Bias in Mammography: The Impact of Artificial Intelligence BI-RADS Suggestions on Reader Performance', *Radiology*, vol. 307, no. 4, p. e222176, May 2023, doi: 10.1148/radiol.222176. Available: http://pubs.rsna.org/doi/10.1148/radiol.222176. [Accessed: 14 January 2025.]

13 Lee, H.-P. et al., 'The Impact of Generative AI on Critical Thinking: Self-Reported Reductions in Cognitive Effort and Confidence Effects from a Survey of Knowledge Workers', April 2025. Available: https://www.microsoft.com/en-us/research/publication/the-impact-of-generative-ai-on-critical-thinking-self-reported-reductions-in-cognitive-effort-and-confidence-effects-from-a-survey-of-knowledge-workers/. [Accessed: 23 March 2025.]

14 'The 2025 AI Index Report', *Stanford HAI*, April 2025. Available: https://hai.stanford.edu/ai-index/2025-ai-index-report. [Accessed: 10 April 2025.]

15 Cohen, M.K. et al., 'Regulating Advanced Artificial Agents', *Science*, 384, no. 6691 (5 April 2024): 36–38. Available: https://doi.org/10.1126/science.adl0625. [Accessed: 18 March 2025.]

16 Shaban, B., 'Cruise offers to pay $112K in fines over allegations it misled regulators about driverless car', *NBC Bay Area*, 7 February 2024. Available: https://www.nbcbayarea.com/investigations/cruise-cpuc-regulators-fines/3446822/. [Accessed: 12 January 2025.]

17 Cecco, L., 'Air Canada ordered to pay customer who was misled by airline's chatbot', *Guardian*, 16 February 2024. Available: https://www.theguardian.com/world/2024/feb/16/air-canada-chatbot-lawsuit. [Accessed: 12 January 2025.]

18 '*Moffatt v. Air Canada*, 2024 BCCRT 149 (CanLII)', 14 February 2024. Available: https://canlii.ca/t/k2spq. [Accessed: 12 January 2025.]

19 Rocher, L., Hendrickx, J.M. and De Montjoye, Y.-A., 'Estimating the success of re-identifications in incomplete datasets using generative models', *Nat Commun*, vol. 10, no. 1, p. 3069, Jul. 2019, doi: 10.1038/s41467-019-10933-3. Available: https://www.nature.com/articles/s41467-019-10933-3. [Accessed: 12 January 2025.] and Bradbury, D., 'De-identify, re-identify: Anonymised data's dirty little secret', *The Register*,16 September 2021. Available: https://www.theregister.com /2021/09/16/anonymising_data_feature/. [Accessed: 12 January 2025.]

20 Hill, K., 'The Secretive Company that Might End Privacy as We Know It', *New York Times*, 18 January 2020. Available: https://www.nytimes.com/2020/01/18 /technology/clearview-privacy-facial-recognition.html. [Accessed: 12 January 2025.]

21 Vallance, C., 'Face search company Clearview AI overturns UK privacy fine', *BBC*, 18 October 2023. Available: https://www.bbc.com/news/technology -67133157. [Accessed: 12 January 2025.]

22 Merken, S., 'Clearview AI strikes "unique" deal to end privacy class action', *Reuters*, 13 June 2024. Available: https://www.reuters.com/legal/litigation /clearview-ai-strikes-unique-deal-end-privacy-class-action-2024-06-13/. [Accessed: 12 January 2025.]

23 '2023 State of Deepfakes: Realities, Threats, and Impact'. *Security Hero*. Available: https://www.securityhero.io/state-of-deepfakes/. [Accessed: 12 January 2025.]

24 ibid.

25 Wilkes, E., 'Taylor Swift deepfakes spark calls for new legislation', *NME*, 27 January 2024. Available: https://www.nme.com/news/music/taylor-swift-deepfakes -spark-calls-for-new-legislation-3578157. [Accessed: 12 January 2025.]

26 Raval, A., 'The disinformation storm is now hitting companies harder', *Financial Times*, 23 December 2024. Available: https://www.ft.com/content/0aa9725d -e423-4a6b-b842-866ad4541dc2. [Accessed: 19 March 2025.]

27 Cameron, D., 'Before Las Vegas, Intel Analysts Warned that Bomb Makers Were Turning to AI', *Wired*. January 2025. Available: https://www.wired.com/story/las -vegas-bombing-cybertruck-trump-intel-dhs-ai/. [Accessed: 17 January 2025.]

28 Eykholt, K. et al., 'Robust Physical-World Attacks on Deep Learning Models', *arXiv*, 10 April 2018. doi: 10.48550/arXiv.1707.08945. Available: http://arxiv .org/abs/1707.08945. [Accessed: 12 January 2025.]

29 Chen, H. and Magramo, K., 'Finance worker pays out $25 million after video call with deepfake "chief financial officer"', *CNN*, 4 February 2024. Available: https://edition.cnn.com/2024/02/04/asia/deepfake-cfo-scam-hong-kong-intl -hnk/index.html. [Accessed: 23 March 2025.]

30 Knibbs, K., 'Every AI Copyright Lawsuit in the US, Visualized', *Wired*. December 2024. Available: https://www.wired.com/story/ai-copyright-case -tracker/. [Accessed: 12 January 2025.]

31 'Adobe Firefly – Free Generative AI for creatives', *Adobe*. Available: https://www.adobe.com/products/firefly.html. [Accessed: 12 January 2025.]

32 Burgess, M., 'How to Stop Your Data From Being Used to Train AI', *Wired*. October 2024. Available: https://www.wired.com/story/how-to-stop-your-data-from-being-used-to-train-ai/. [Accessed: 12 January 2025.]

33 'Microsoft's AI Data Privacy and Security Commitments', *Online Tools Directory*, 8 May 2024. Available: https://www.onlinetools.directory/microsoft-azure-openai-data-protection-privacy-security/. [Accessed: 12 January 2025.]

34 Shepperd, P., 'Navigating the terms and conditions of generative AI', *Artificial Intelligence*, 2 January 2025. Available: https://nationalcentreforai.jiscinvolve.org/wp/2025/01/02/navigating-the-terms-and-conditions-of-generative-ai/. [Accessed: 12 January 2025.]

35 Muncaster, P., 'Fifth of CISOs Admit Staff Leaked Data Via GenAI', *Infosecurity Magazine*, 24 April 2024. Available: https://www.infosecurity-magazine.com/news/fifth-cisos-staff-leaked-data-genai/. [Accessed: 21 February 2025.]

36 'Italy lifts ban on ChatGPT after data privacy improvements', *dw.com*, 29 April 2023. Available: https://www.dw.com/en/ai-italy-lifts-ban-on-chatgpt-after-data-privacy-improvements/a-65469742. [Accessed: 12 January 2025.]

37 Albanese, A., 'Google Wins: Court Issues a Ringing Endorsement of Google Books', *PublishersWeekly.com*, 14 November 2013. Available: https://www.publishersweekly.com/pw/by-topic/digital/content-and-e-books/article/60006-google-wins-court-issues-a-ringing-endorsement-of-google-books.html. [Accessed: 13 January 2025.]

38 Somers, J., 'Torching the Modern-Day Library of Alexandria', *The Atlantic*, 20 April 2017. Available: https://www.theatlantic.com/technology/archive/2017/04/the-tragedy-of-google-books/523320/. [Accessed: 13 January 2025.]

39 Brittain, B., 'Getty Images lawsuit says Stability AI misused photos to train AI', *Reuters*, 6 February 2023. Available: https://www.reuters.com/legal/getty-images-lawsuit-says-stability-ai-misused-photos-train-ai-2023-02-06/. [Accessed: 13 January 2025.]

40 Giannotti, L., 'AI lawsuits: The existential threat to generative AI', *Tech Monitor*, 8 February 2024. Available: https://www.techmonitor.ai/what-is/ai-lawsuits-the-existential-threat-to-generative-ai. [Accessed: 13 January 2025.]

41 'Getty Images (US) Inc. v. Stability AI Inc.', February 2023. Available: https://copyrightalliance.org/wp-content/uploads/2023/02/Getty-Images-v.-Stability-AI-Complaint.pdf and Carlini, N. et al., 'Extracting Training Data from Diffusion Models', *arXiv*, 30 January 2023. doi: 10.48550/arXiv.2301.13188. Available: http://arxiv.org/abs/2301.13188. [Accessed: 28 January 2025.] and Somepalli, G. et al., 'Diffusion Art or Digital Forgery? Investigating Data Replication in Diffusion Models', *arXiv*, 12 December 2022. doi: 10.48550/arXiv.2212.03860. Available: http://arxiv.org/abs/2212.03860. [Accessed: 28 January 2025.]

42 'Thomson Reuters Enterprise Centre GMBH v. Ross Intelligence Inc., No. 20-CV-613 (D. Del. 11 February 2025)'. Available: https://www.ded.uscourts .gov/sites/ded/files/opinions/20-613_5.pdf. [Accessed: 19 March 2025.]

43 ibid. p. 22.

44 Lynch, S., 'Will Generative AI Make You More Productive at Work? Yes, But Only If You're Not Already Great at Your Job', *Stanford University Human-Centered Artificial Intelligence*, 24 April 2023. Available: https://hai.stanford .edu/news/will-generative-ai-make-you-more-productive-work-yes-only-if -youre-not-already-great-your-job. [Accessed: 13 January 2025.]

45 Candelon, F. et al., 'How People Create and Destroy Value with Generative AI', *Boston Consulting Group*, 21 September 2023. Available: https://www.bcg .com/publications/2023/how-people-create-and-destroy-value-with-gen-ai. [Accessed: 13 January 2025.]

46 'Goldman Sachs CEO: AI Completes 95 per cent of IPO Prospectus in Minutes', *CEO Today*, 17 January 2025. Available: https://www.ceotodaymagazine.com /2025/01/goldman-sachs-ceo-david-solomon-on-ais-game-changing-role-in -banking/. [Accessed: 28 January 2025.]

47 Rowe, N., '"It's destroyed me completely": Kenyan moderators decry toll of training of AI models', *Guardian*, 2 August 2023. Available: https://www .theguardian.com/technology/2023/aug/02/ai-chatbot-training-human-toll -content-moderator-meta-openai. [Accessed: 13 January 2025.]

48 Cheng, E., 'China's robotaxi push sparks concerns about job security for drivers', *CNBC*, 11 July 2024. Available: https://www.cnbc.com/2024/07/11/ chinas-robotaxi-push-sparks-concerns-about-job-security-for-drivers.html. [Accessed: 13 January 2025.]

49 Roth, E., 'CNET found errors in more than half of its AI-written stories', *The Verge*, 25 January 2023. Available: https://www.theverge.com/2023 /1/25/23571082/cnet-ai-written-stories-errors-corrections-red-ventures. [Accessed: 19 January 2025.] and Guglielmo, C., 'CNET Is Testing an AI Engine. Here's What We've Learned, Mistakes and All', *CNET*. January 2023. Available: https://www.cnet.com/tech/cnet-is-testing-an-ai-engine-heres-what-weve-learned-mistakes-and-all/. [Accessed: 19 January 2025.]

50 'AI is poised to drive 160 per cent increase in data center power demand', *Goldman Sachs*, 14 May 2024. Available: https://www.goldmansachs.com /insights/articles/AI-poised-to-drive-160-increase-in-power-demand. [Accessed: 28 January 2025.]

51 'A Closer Look at The Carbon Footprint of ChatGPT', *Piktochart*, 3 November 2023. Available: https://piktochart.com/blog/carbon-footprint-of-chatgpt/. [Accessed: 23 March 2025.]

52 '2024 Environmental Report – Google Sustainability', *Sustainability*, July 2024. Available: https://sustainability.google/reports/google-2024-environmental -report/. [Accessed: 13 January 2025.]

53 Monserrate, S.G., 'The Cloud Is Material: On the Environmental Impacts of Computation and Data Storage', *MIT Case Studies in Social and Ethical Responsibilities of Computing*, no. Winter 2022 (27 January 2022). Available: https://doi.org/10.21428/2c646de5.031d4553. [Accessed: 23 March 2025.]

54 Shehabi, A. et al., '2024 United States Data Center Energy Usage Report', *Lawrence Berkeley National Laboratory, Berkeley, California*, December 2024. LBNL-2001637. Available: https://eta-publications.lbl.gov/sites/default/files/2024-12/lbnl-2024-united-states-data-center-energy-usage-report.pdf. [Accessed: 18 March 2025.]

55 'The Environmental Impact of Data Centers: A Sustainability Analysis', *IABAC*, 13 October 2023. Available: https://iabac.org/blog/the-environmental-impact-of-data-centers-a-sustainability-analysis. [Accessed: 18 September 2024.]

56 'Top Of Mind: GEN AI – Too Much Spend. Too Little Benefit', *Goldman Sachs*, 25 June 2024. Available: https://www.goldmansachs.com/insights/top-of-mind/gen-ai-too-much-spend-too-little-benefit [Accessed: 28 January 2025.]

57 Lawson, A., 'Google to buy nuclear power for AI datacentres in "world first" deal', *Guardian*, 15 October 2024. Available: https://www.theguardian.com/technology/2024/oct/15/google-buy-nuclear-power-ai-datacentres-kairos-power. [Accessed: 28 January 2025.] and 'Amazon buys nuclear-powered data center from Talen'. May 2024. Available: https://www.ans.org/news/article-5842/amazon-buys-nuclearpowered-data-center-from-talen/. [Accessed: 28 January 2025.] and 'Three Mile Island nuclear site to reopen in Microsoft deal', *BBC*, 20 September 2024. Available: https://www.bbc.com/news/articles/cx25v2d7zexo. [Accessed: 28 January 2025.]

58 'AI Act enters into force – European Commission', *European Commission*. Available: https://commission.europa.eu/news/ai-act-enters-force-2024-08-01_en. [Accessed: 13 January 2025.] and 'Stanford CRFM', *Center for Research on Foundational Models*. August 2024. Available: https://crfm.stanford.edu/2024/08/01/eu-ai-act.html. [Accessed: 13 January 2025.]

59 Ren, S. and Wierman, A., 'The Uneven Distribution of AI's Environmental Impacts', *Harvard Business Review*, 15 July 2024. Available: https://hbr.org/2024/07/the-uneven-distribution-of-ais-environmental-impacts. [Accessed: 18 September 2024.]

60 DeepSeek-AI et al., 'DeepSeek-R1: Incentivizing Reasoning Capability in LLMs via Reinforcement Learning', *arXiv*, 22 January 2025. Available: https://doi.org/10.48550/arXiv.2501.12948. [Accessed: 18 March 2025.]

61 Clayworth, J., 'Microsoft's AI Epicenter Is an Iowa Water Hog', *Axios*, 18 September 2023. Available: https://www.axios.com/local/des-moines/2023/09/18/ai-iowa-epicenter-microsoft-water-useage-data-center. [Accessed: 23 March 2025.]

62 Hao, K., 'AI Is Taking Water From the Desert', *The Atlantic*, 1 March 2024. Available: https://www.theatlantic.com/technology/archive/2024/03/ai-water-climate-microsoft/677602/. [Accessed: 13 January 2025.]

63 Salskey, A. and Valdes, M., 'Big tech data centers spark worry over scarce Western water', *AP News*, 25 October 2021. Available: https://apnews.com/article/technology-business-environment-and-nature-oregon-united-states-2385c62f1a87030d344261ef9c76ccda. [Accessed: 13 January 2025.]

64 Li, P. et al., 'Making AI Less "Thirsty": Uncovering and Addressing the Secret Water Footprint of AI Models', *arXiv*, 15 January 2025. Available: https://doi.org/10.48550/arXiv.2304.03271. [Accessed: 20 March 2025.]

CHAPTER 6: IMPLEMENTING AI GOVERNANCE

1 'ISO/IEC 23894:2023', *ISO*. February 2023. Available: https://www.iso.org/standard/77304.html. [Accessed: 11 March, 2025.]

2 Vorvoreanu, M. et al., 'Responsible AI Maturity Model', May 2023. Available: https://www.microsoft.com/en-us/research/publication/responsible-ai-maturity-model/. [Accessed: 13 January 2025.]

3 'Trustworthy & Responsible AI Resource Center (AIRC) – Playbook – Measure', *National Institute of Standards and Technology*. Available: https://airc.nist.gov/AI_RMF_Knowledge_Base/Playbook/Measure [Accessed: 13 January 2025.]

4 'The 2025 AI Index Report', *Stanford HAI*, April 2025. Available: https://hai.stanford.edu/ai-index/2025-ai-index-report. [Accessed: 10 April 2025.]

5 Reuel, A. et al., 'Responsible AI in the Global Context: Maturity Model and Survey', *arXiv*, 13 October 2024, doi: 10.48550/arXiv.2410.09985. Available: http://arxiv.org/abs/2410.09985. [Accessed: 13 January 2025.]

CHAPTER 7: PRINCIPLES, POLICIES AND STANDARDS

1 'Microsoft Responsible AI Transparency Report', *Microsoft*. Available: https://www.microsoft.com/en-us/corporate-responsibility/responsible-ai-transparency-report. [Accessed: 18 March 2025.]

2 'AstraZeneca data and AI ethics', *AstraZeneca*. Available: https://www.astrazeneca.com/sustainability/ethics-and-transparency/data-and-ai-ethics.html#. [Accessed: 18 March 2025.]

3 'Ethics guidelines for trustworthy AI', *European Council High-Level Expert Group on AI*, 8 April 2019. Available: https://digital-strategy.ec.europa.eu/en/library/ethics-guidelines-trustworthy-ai. [Accessed: 18 March 2025.]

4 'OECD AI Principles overview', *OECD*. 2019, updated May 2024. Available: https://oecd.ai/en/ai-principles. [Accessed: 18 March 2025.]

5 'Recommendation of the Council on Artificial Intelligence', *OECD*. 2019, amended May 2024. Available: https://legalinstruments.oecd.org/en/instruments/OECD-LEGAL-0449. [Accessed: 18 March 2025.]

6 'Ethics of Artificial Intelligence', *UNESCO*. Available: https://www.unesco.org/en/artificial-intelligence/recommendation-ethics. [Accessed: 18 March 2025.]

7 Anish, L. et al., 'An Insider's Guide to Designing and Operationalizing a Responsible AI Governance Framework', *EqualAI*, September 2023. Available: https://www.equalai.org/wp-content/uploads/2023/09/EQUAL-AI _Whitepaper.pdf. [Accessed: 18 March 2025.]

8 Jobin, A., Ienca, M. and Vayena, E., 'The global landscape of AI ethics guide lines', *Nat Mach Intell*, vol. 1, no. 9, pp. 389–399, Sep. 2019, doi: 10.1038/ s42256-019-0088-2. Available: https://www.nature.com/articles/s42256-019 -0088-2. [Accessed: 18 March 2025.]

9 'Roche Artificial Intelligence (AI) Ethics Principle', *Roche*. Available: https:// assets.roche.com/f/176343/x/401c28049f/roche-ai-ethics-principles.pdf. [Accessed: 18 March 2025.]

10 'Roche Data Ethics Principles', *Roche*. Available: https://assets.roche.com/f/176343 /x/072ca49581/roche-data-ethics-principles.pdf. [Accessed: 18 March 2025.]

11 'Empowering responsible AI practices', *Microsoft AI*. Available: https://www .microsoft.com/en-us/ai/responsible-ai. [Accessed: 18 March 2025.]

12 'Google AI Principles', *Google AI*. Available: https://ai.google/responsibil ity/principles/. [Accessed: 7 November 2024.] and 'Google Responsible AI Practices', *Google AI*. Available: https://ai.google/responsibility/responsible-ai -practices/. [Accessed: 18 March 2025.]

13 'HSBC's Principles for the Ethical Use of Data and AI', *HSBC*, July 2024. Available: https://www.hsbc.com/-/files/hsbc/our-approach/risk-and -responsibility/pdfs/240715-hsbc-principles-for-the-ethical-use-of-data-and -ai.pdf?download=1. [Accessed: 18 March 2025.]

14 O'Connor, N., 'Our Responsible AI Pledge: Setting the Bar for Ethical AI', *Walmart*, 17 October 2023. Available: https://corporate.walmart.com/ news/2023/10/17/our-responsible-ai-pledge-setting-the-bar-for-ethical-ai. [Accessed: 18 March 2025.]

15 'Doing the right thing: AI & ethics', *Johnson & Johnson*. Available: https://www .jnj.com/about-jnj/policies-and-positions/doing-the-right-thing-artificial -intelligence-and-ethics. [Accessed: 18 March 2025.]

16 'A BBC For The Future', *BBC*, 26 March 2024. Available: https://www.bbc.co .uk/mediacentre/speeches/2024/a-bbc-for-the-future-tim-davie-director -general/. [Accessed: 18 March 2025.]

17 'ISO/IEC 42001:2023', *ISO*, 2023. Available: https://www.iso.org/standard /81230.html. [Accessed: 18 March 2025.]

18 'Microsoft Responsible AI Standard, v2 GENERAL REQUIREMENTS', *Microsoft*, June 2022. Available: https://cdn-dynmedia-1.microsoft.com/is/ content/microsoftcorp/microsoft/final/en-us/microsoft-brand/documents/ Microsoft-Responsible-AI-Standard-General-Requirements.pdf?culture=en -gb&country=gb. [Accessed: 18 March 2025.]

19 'Empowering responsible AI practices', *Microsoft*. Available: https://www .microsoft.com/en-gb/ai/responsible-ai. [Accessed: 18 March 2025.]

CHAPTER 8: ACCOUNTABILITY STRUCTURE, TEAMS AND TRAINING

1 'The Aletheia Framework'', *Rolls-Royce*. Available: http://www.rolls-royce.com /innovation/the-aletheia-framework.aspx. [Accessed: 20 January 2025.]

2 Schuett, J., Reuel, A.-K. and Carlier, A., 'How to design an AI ethics board', *AI Ethics*, 15 February 2024, doi: 10.1007/s43681-023-00409-y. Available: https:// doi.org/10.1007/s43681-023-00409-y. [Accessed: 18 March 2025.]

3 'Improving how Meta treats people and communities around the world', *Oversight Board*. Available: https://www.oversightboard.com/. [Accessed: 18 March 2025.]

4 'Google's ethics board shut down', *BBC News*, 5 April 2019. Available: https:// www.bbc.com/news/technology-47825833. [Accessed: 18 March 2025.]

5 'LLM in Law, Science & Technology', *Stanford Law School*. Available: https:// law.stanford.edu/education/degrees/advanced-degree-programs/llm-in-law -science-technology/. [Accessed: 18 March 2025.]

6 'Technology Law & Policy', *Georgetown Law School*. Available: https://www .law.georgetown.edu/academics/graduate-programs/llm-programs/technol ogy/. [Accessed: 18 March 2025.]

7 'Law, Data and Technology LLM', *University of Birmingham*. Available: https:// www.birmingham.ac.uk/study/postgraduate/subjects/law-courses/law-data -and-technology-llm. [Accessed: 18 March 2025.]

8 '360° Value Report 2023 Driving Reinvention, Delivering Value', *Accenture*. Available: https://www.accenture.com/content/dam/accenture/final/corpo rate/corporate-initiatives/sustainability/document/360-Value-Report-2023 .pdf. [Accessed: 18 March 2025.]

9 Walsh, M., 'These companies are training all their staff on AI, here's why', *Raconteur*, 16 September 2024. Available: https://www.raconteur.net/technol ogy/ai-training-employees. [Accessed: 28 January 2025.]

10 'Generating growth – How generative AI can power the UK's reinvention', *Accenture*, 21 October 2024. Available: https://www.accenture.com/gb-en/ insights/gen-ai/generating-growth. [Accessed: 18 March 2025.]

11 'Living repository to foster learning and exchange on AI literacy', *European Commission*, 4 February 2025. Available: https://digital-strategy.ec.europa .eu/en/library/living-repository-foster-learning-and-exchange-ai-literacy. [Accessed: 21 February 2025.]

CHAPTER 9: AI INVENTORY, CHECKPOINTS AND ASSESSMENT PROCESS

1 'Algorithmic Transparency Recording Standard Hub', *GOV.UK*, 5 January 2023. Available: https://www.gov.uk/government/collections/algorithmic -transparency-recording-standard-hub. [Accessed: 19 March 2025.]

2 'Reinvention in the age of generative AI', *Accenture*, 11 January 2024. Available: https://www.accenture.com/in-en/insights/consulting/total-enterprise-rein vention. [Accessed: 19 March 2025.]

3 'ISO/IEC 42001:2023', *ISO*. Available: https://www.iso.org/standard/81230 .html. [Accessed: 19 March 2025.]

4 'NIST AI RMF Playbook', *NIST*. Available: https://airc.nist.gov/AI_RMF _Knowledge_Base/Playbook. [Accessed: 19 March 2025.]

5 'AI Risk Management Framework', *NIST*. Available: https://airc.nist.gov/AI _RMF_Knowledge_Base/AI_RMF. [Accessed: 19 March 2025.]

6 'NIST AI RMF Playbook', *NIST*. Available: https://airc.nist.gov/AI_RMF _Knowledge_Base/Playbook. [Accessed: 19 March 2025.]

7 'Artificial intelligence in UK financial services – 2024', *Bank of England*, 21 November 2024. Available: https://www.bankofengland.co.uk/report/2024/arti ficial-intelligence-in-uk-financial-services-2024. [Accessed: 24 January 2025.]

8 'Regulation – EU – 2024/1689 – EN', *EUR-Lex*. Available: https://eur-lex .europa.eu/eli/reg/2024/1689/oj. [Accessed: 19 March 2025.]

9 'Responsible AI Report 2025', *Evident AI*, March 2025. Available: https:// evidentinsights.com/insights/responsible-ai-report/. [Accessed: 20 March 2025.]

10 'Algorithmic Impact Assessment Tool', *Government of Canada*, 30 May 2024. Available: https://www.canada.ca/en/government/system/digital-government /digital-government-innovations/responsible-use-ai/algorithmic-impact -assessment.html. [Accessed: 19 March 2025.]

11 Groves, L., 'Algorithmic impact assessment: A case study in healthcare', *Ada Lovelace Institute*, 8 February 2022. Available: https://www.adalovelaceinsti tute.org/report/algorithmic-impact-assessment-case-study-healthcare/. [Accessed: 19 March 2025.]

12 'ISO/IEC FDIS 42005', *ISO*. Available: https://www.iso.org/standard/44545 .html. [Accessed: 19 March 2025.]

13 'EqualAI Algorithmic Impact Assessment (AIA)', *EqualAI*. Available: https:// www.equalai.org/aia/. [Accessed: 19 March 2025.]

14 'Artificial intelligence in UK financial services – 2024', *Bank of England*, 21 November 2024. Available: https://www.bankofengland.co.uk/report/2024/ artificial-intelligence-in-uk-financial-services-2024. [Accessed: 24 January 2025.]

15 Powell, R. and Oswald, M., 'Assurance of Third-Party AI Systems for UK National Security', *The Alan Turing Institute*, 17 January 2024. Available: https://cetas.turing.ac.uk/publications/assurance-third-party-ai-systems-uk -national-security. [Accessed: 19 March 2025.]

16 'Updated EU model contractual AI clauses in procurements of AI', *Public Buyers Community*, 5 March 2025. Available: https://public-buyers-community. ec.europa.eu/communities/procurement-ai/resources/updated-eu-ai-mod el-contractual-clauses. [Accessed: 11 April 2025.]

17 'Facial Age Estimation White Paper', *Yoti*, 9 September 2024. Available: https://www.yoti.com/blog/yoti-age-estimation-white-paper/. [Accessed: 20 March 2025.]

18 'Automated Employment Decision Tools (Updated)', *City of New York*. Available: https://rules.cityofnewyork.us/rule/automated-employment-deci sion-tools-updated/. [Accessed: 19 March 2025.]

19 'Artificial Intelligence Standards Committee', *Standards Association*. Available: https://sagroups.ieee.org/ai-sc/standards/. [Accessed: 19 March 2025.]

20 'Ensuring Trustworthy AI: The Emerging AI Assurance Market', *www.drcf.org.uk*, 16 July 2024. Available: https://www.drcf.org.uk/publications/blogs/ensuring -trustworthy-ai-the-emerging-ai-assurance-market/. [Accessed: 19 March 2025.]

21 'Introduction to AI assurance', *GOV.UK*, 14 February 2024. Available: https:// www.gov.uk/government/publications/introduction-to-ai-assurance/intro duction-to-ai-assurance. [Accessed: 19 March 2025.]

22 ibid.

CHAPTER 10: GOVERNANCE CONTROLS

1 'Tools for Trustworthy AI', *OECD*. Available: https://oecd.ai/en/catalogue/ tools. [Accessed: 25 December 2024.]

2 'Portfolio of AI Assurance Techniques', *GOV.UK*, 7 June 2023. Available: https:// www.gov.uk/guidance/portfolio-of-ai-assurance-techniques. [Accessed: 19 March 2025.]

3 Ji, J. et al., 'AI Alignment: A Comprehensive Survey', *arXiv*, 1 May 2024. Available: https://doi.org/10.48550/arXiv.2310.19852. [Accessed: 19 March 2025.]

4 Maslej, N. et al., 'The AI Index 2024 Annual Report', *Institute for Human-Centered Artificial Intelligence*, April 2024. Available: https://hai.stanford.edu/ ai-index/2024-ai-index-report. [Accessed: 19 March 2025.]

5 Ferrer, L., 'Analysis and Comparison of Classification Metrics', *arXiv*, 20 September 2023. Available: https://doi.org/10.48550/arXiv.2209.05355. [Accessed: 19 March 2025.]

6 Rainio, O., Teuho, J. and Klén, R., 'Evaluation Metrics and Statistical Tests for Machine Learning', *Scientific Reports* 14, no. 1 (13 March 2024): 6086. Available: https://doi.org/10.1038/s41598-024-56706-x. [Accessed: 19 March 2025.]

7 'Perplexity of Fixed-Length Models', *Hugging Face*. Available: https://hugging face.co/docs/transformers/en/perplexity. [Accessed: 19 March 2025.]

8 Caglayan, O. et al., 'Curious Case of Language Generation Evaluation Metrics: A Cautionary Tale', in *Proceedings of the 28th International Conference on Computational Linguistics*, edited by Donia Scott, Nuria Bel and Chengqing Zong, 2322–28. Barcelona, Spain (Online): International Committee on Computational Linguistics, 2020. Available: https://doi.org/10.18653/v1/2020 .coling-main.210. [Accessed: 19 March 2025.]

9 Wu, Z et al., 'KG-BERTScore: Incorporating Knowledge Graph into BERTScore for Reference-Free Machine Translation Evaluation', *arXiv*, 30 January 2023. Available: https://doi.org/10.48550/arXiv.2301.12699. [Accessed: 19 March 2025.]

10 '100+ LLM Benchmarks and Evaluation Datasets', *Evidently AI*, 10 December 2024. Available: https://www.evidentlyai.com/llm-evaluation-benchmarks-datasets. [Accessed: 19 March 2025.]

11 Kaufmann, T. et al., 'A Survey of Reinforcement Learning from Human Feedback', *arXiv*, 30 April 2024. Available: https://doi.org/10.48550/arXiv.2312.14925. [Accessed: 19 March 2025.]

12 ChatGPT prompted by Thalia Eitel-Porter. [Accessed: 11 January, 2025.]

13 Mehrabi, N. et al., 'A Survey on Bias and Fairness in Machine Learning', *arXiv*, 25 January 2022. Available: http://arxiv.org/abs/1908.09635. [Accessed: 19 March 2025.]

14 'Who Is Protected from Employment Discrimination?', *US EEOC*. Available: https://www.eeoc.gov/employers/small-business/3-who-protected-employment-discrimination. [Accessed: 19 March 2025.]

15 O'Neil, C., Sargeant, H. and Appel, J., 'Explainable Fairness in Regulatory Algorithmic Auditing', *SSRN Scholarly Paper*, Rochester, NY: Social Science Research Network, 2024. Available: https://doi.org/10.2139/ssrn.4756637. [Accessed: 19 March 2025.]

16 Kearns, M. and Roth, A., *The Ethical Algorithm: The Science of Socially Aware Algorithm Design*. Illustrated edition. New York: OUP USA, 2020, and Barocas S., Hardt M. and Narayanan A., 'Fairness and Machine Learning'. December 2023. Available: https://fairmlbook.org/. [Accessed: 19 March 2025.]

17 Mukherjee, D. et al., 'Two Simple Ways to Learn Individual Fairness Metrics from Data', *arXiv*, 19 June 2020. Available: https://doi.org/10.48550/arXiv.2006.11439. [Accessed: 19 March 2025.]

18 Kusner, M.J. et al., 'Counterfactual Fairness', in *Advances in Neural Information Processing Systems*, Vol. 30. Curran Associates, Inc., 2017. Available: https://proceedings.neurips.cc/paper_files/paper/2017/hash/a486cd07e4ac3d270571622f4f316ec5-Abstract.html. [Accessed: 19 March 2025.]

19 O'Neil, C. et al., 'Explainable Fairness in Regulatory Algorithmic Auditing', *SSRN Scholarly Paper*, Rochester, NY: Social Science Research Network, 15 March 2024. Available: https://doi.org/10.2139/ssrn.4756637. [Accessed: 19 March 2025.]

20 'ORCAA's Report', *Olay*, 16 September 2021. Available: https://www.olay.com/decodethebias/orcaa. [Accessed: 19 March 2025.]

21 Montahaei, E., Alihosseini, D. and Baghshah, M.S., 'Jointly Measuring Diversity and Quality in Text Generation Models', *arXiv*, 20 May 2019. Available: https://doi.org/10.48550/arXiv.1904.03971. [Accessed: 19 March 2025.]

22 Bai, Y. et al., 'Constitutional AI: Harmlessness from AI Feedback', *arXiv*, 15 December 2022. Available: http://arxiv.org/abs/2212.08073. [Accessed: 19 March 2025.]

23 'Allenai/Real-Toxicity-Prompts', *Hugging Face*, 15 January 2024. Available: https://huggingface.co/datasets/allenai/real-toxicity-prompts. [Accessed: 19 March 2025.]

24 'Holistic Evaluation of Language Models (HELM)', *Center for Research on Foundation Models*. Available: https://crfm.stanford.edu/helm/. [Accessed: 19 March 2025.]

25 Hendrycks, D., 'Hendrycks/Ethics', *GitHub*, 24 October 2024. Available: https://github.com/hendrycks/ethics. [Accessed: 19 March 2025.]

26 'Cybersecurity Framework', *NIST*. Available: https://www.nist.gov/cyberframework. [Accessed: 19 March 2025.]

27 Zerilli, J. et al., *A Citizen's Guide to Artificial Intelligence*, The MIT Press, 2021. Available: https://doi.org/10.7551/mitpress/12518.001.0001. [Accessed: 19 March 2025.]

28 Gosline, R.R. et al., 'Nudge Users to Catch Generative AI Errors', *MIT Sloan Management Review*, 65, no. 4, 29 May 2024. Available: https://sloanreview.mit.edu/article/nudge-users-to-catch-generative-ai-errors/. [Accessed: 19 March 2025.]

29 Goldman, P., 'How Salesforce Builds Trust in Our AI Products', *Salesforce*, 26 June 2024. Available: https://www.salesforce.com/uk/news/stories/ai-trust-patterns/. [Accessed: 19 January 2025.]

30 'Agentic AI - Threats and Mitigations', *OWASP LLM Project*, 17 February 2025. Available: https://genai.owasp.org/resource/agentic-ai-threats-and-mitigations/. [Accessed: 19 March 2025.] and Hammond et al. 'Multi-Agent Risks from Advanced AI - Technical Report #1', *Cooperative AI Foundation*, February 2025. Available: https://arxiv.org/pdf/2502.14143. [Accessed 23 April 2025.]

31 Shavit, Y. et al., 'Practices for Governing Agentic AI Systems', *OpenAI*. December 2023. Available: https://cdn.openai.com/papers/practices-for-governing-agentic-ai-systems.pdf. [Accessed: 19 March 2025.]

32 Seungone, K. et al., 'The CoT Collection: Improving Zero-Shot and Few-Shot Learning of Language Models via Chain-of-Thought Fine-Tuning', *arXiv*, 14 October 2023. Available: http://arxiv.org/abs/2305.14045. [Accessed: 19 March 2025.]

33 Ray Eitel-Porter, interview with Azhar, A., Founder of *Exponential View*, 23 January 2025.

34 'NRF Horizon Scanner', *Norton Rose Fulbright*. Available: https://www.nortonrosefulbright.com/en/nrf-transform/solutions/horizon-scanner. [Accessed: 19 March 2025.]

35 'Horizon Scanning Portal', *PwC*. Available: https://store.pwc.co.uk/en/products/horizon-scanning-portal. [Accessed: 19 March 2025.]

36 'AI Standards Hub', *AI Standards Hub*. Available: https://aistandardshub.org/. [Accessed: 19 March 2025.]

37 Dickson, B., 'Machine Learning: What Are Membership Inference Attacks?', *TechTalks*, 23 April 2021. Available: https://bdtechtalks.com/2021/04/23/machine-learning-membership-inference-attacks/. [Accessed: 19 March 2025.]

38 'Privacy Enhancing Technologies', *Royal Society*. 2023. Available: https://royalsociety.org/news-resources/projects/privacy-enhancing-technologies/. [Accessed: 19 March 2025.]

39 Dwork, C., 'Differential Privacy', in *Proceedings of the 33rd International Conference on Automata, Languages and Programming – Volume Part II*, 1–12. ICALP'06. Berlin, Heidelberg: Springer-Verlag, 2006. Available: https://doi.org/10.1007/11787006_1. [Accessed: 19 March 2025.]

40 McMahan, B. et al., 'Communication-Efficient Learning of Deep Networks from Decentralized Data', in *Proceedings of the 20th International Conference on Artificial Intelligence and Statistics*, 1273–82. PMLR, 2017. Available: https://proceedings.mlr.press/v54/mcmahan17a.html. [Accessed: 19 March 2025.]

41 Simon Willison, 16 September 2022. Available: https://x.com/simonw/status/1570568047618031617. [Accessed: 22 March 2025.]

42 Kevin Liu, 9 February 2023. Available: https://x.com/kliu128/status/1623472922374574080. [Accessed: 25 March 2025.]

43 Jiaming, J. et al., 'AI Alignment: A Comprehensive Survey', *arXiv*, 1 May 2024. Available: http://arxiv.org/abs/2310.19852. [Accessed: 19 March 2025.]

44 Vassilev, A. et al., 'Adversarial Machine Learning: A Taxonomy and Terminology of Attacks and Mitigations', Gaithersburg, MD: National Institute of Standards and Technology (U.S.), 4 January 2024. Available: https://doi.org/10.6028/NIST.AI.100-2e2023. [Accessed: 19 March 2025.]

45 'PacktPublishing/Mastering-Machine-Learning-for-Penetration-Testing', *GitHub*. Available: https://github.com/PacktPublishing/Mastering-Machine-Learning-for-Penetration-Testing. [Accessed: 19 March 2025.]

46 Vassilev, A. et al., 'Adversarial Machine Learning: A Taxonomy and Terminology of Attacks and Mitigations', Gaithersburg, MD: National Institute of Standards and Technology (U.S.), 4 January 2024. Available: https://doi.org/10.6028/NIST.AI.100-2e2023. [Accessed: 19 March 2025.]

47 Chao, P. et al., 'Jailbreaking Black Box Large Language Models in Twenty Queries', *arXiv*, 18 July 2024. Available: http://arxiv.org/abs/2310.08419. [Accessed: 19 March 2025.]

48 Li, H. et al., 'Privacy in Large Language Models: Attacks, Defenses and Future Directions', *arXiv*, 30 September 2024. Available: http://arxiv.org/abs/2310.10383. [Accessed: 19 March 2025.]

49 Zhang, Y., Carlini, N. and Ippolito, D., 'Effective Prompt Extraction from Language Models', *arXiv*, 7 August 2024. Available: http://arxiv.org/abs/2307.06865. [Accessed: 19 March 2025.]

50 Greshake, K. et al., 'Not What You've Signed up for: Compromising Real-World LLM-Integrated Applications with Indirect Prompt Injection', *arXiv*, 5 May 2023. Available: http://arxiv.org/abs/2302.12173. [Accessed: 19 March 2025.]

51 'What Is a Web Application Firewall (WAF)?', *F5, Inc.* Available: https://www.f5.com/glossary/web-application-firewall-waf. [Accessed: 19 March 2025.]

52 Rosenblatt, B., 'OpenAI's Copyright Shield Is Business As Usual For Enterprise IT', *Forbes*, 7 November 2023. Available: https://www.forbes.com/sites/billrosenblatt/2023/11/07/openais-copyright-shield-is-business-as-usual-for-enterprise-it/. [Accessed: 19 March 2025.]

53 Suggs, N. and Venables, P., 'Protecting Customers with Generative AI Indemnification', *Google Cloud Blog*, 13 October 2023. Available: https://cloud.google.com/blog/products/ai-machine-learning/protecting-customers-with-generative-ai-indemnification. [Accessed: 19 March 2025.]

54 Smith, B. and Nowbar, H., 'Microsoft Announces New Copilot Copyright Commitment for Customers', *Microsoft*, 7 September 2023. Available: https://blogs.microsoft.com/on-the-issues/2023/09/07/copilot-copyright-commitment-ai-legal-concerns/. [Accessed: 19 March 2025.]

55 'A Differentiated Approach to AI Foundation Models', *IBM*. December 2024 Available: https://www.ibm.com/downloads/documents/us-en/107a02e94948f49f. [Accessed: 19 March 2025.]

56 Rosenblatt, W., *Digital Rights Management: Business and Technology*. USA: John Wiley & Sons, Inc., 2001.

57 'Homepage', *Creative Commons*. Available: https://creativecommons.org/. [Accessed: 19 March 2025.]

58 Sharps, S. et al., 'The Impact of AI on the Labour Market', *Tony Blair Institute*, 8 November 2024. Available: https://institute.global/insights/economic-prosperity/the-impact-of-ai-on-the-labour-market. [Accessed: 19 March 2025.]

59 Hanowell, B. and Richardson, N., 'Most Workers Think AI Will Affect Their Jobs. They Disagree on How', *ADP Research*, 10 June 2024. Available: https://www.adpresearch.com/worker-sentiment-ai-impact/. [Accessed: 19 March 2025.]

60 'Walmart Academy', *Walmart*, 17 August 2023. Available: https://corporate.walmart.com/content/dam/corporate/documents/about/working-at-walmart/walmart-academy.pdf. [Accessed: 19 March 2025.]

61 'Revolutionizing Employee Training at Starbucks: Unveiling the Benefits of AI Avatars', *Trainday Blog*. Available: https://www.trainday.io/ai-blog/"revolutionizing-employee-training-at-starbucks:-unveiling-the-benefits-of-ai-avatars"+64b7577be9f4e62ab1acd92c/. [Accessed: 19 March 2025.]

62 'Case Study: Upskilling for Career Mobility at PepsiCo', *PepsiCo*, August 2023. Available: https://www.aspeninstitute.org/wp-content/uploads/2023/05/Case-Study-UpSkilling-for-Career-Mobility-at-Pepsico.pdf. [Accessed: 19 March 2025.]

63 'Frontline A.I.', *Aspen Digital*. 12 February 2024. Available: https://www.aspendigital.org/report/frontline-ai/. [Accessed: 25 March 2025]

64 Carmona, D., *The AI Organization: Learn from Real Companies and Microsoft's Journey How to Redefine Your Organization with AI*. O'Reilly Media, Inc., 2019.

65 Daugherty, P.R. and Wilson, H.J., *Human + Machine, Updated and Expanded: Reimagining Work in the Age of AI*, Boston, Massachusetts: Harvard Business Review Press, 2024.

66 Luccioni, A.S., Viguier, S. and Ligozat, A-L., 'Estimating the Carbon Footprint of BLOOM, a 176B Parameter Language Model', *arXiv*, 3 November 2022. Available: http://arxiv.org/abs/2211.02001. [Accessed: 19 March 2025.]

67 'AI Is Poised to Drive 160 per cent Increase in Data Center Power Demand', Goldman Sachs, 14 May 2024. Available: https://www.goldmansachs.com/insights/articles/AI-poised-to-drive-160-increase-in-power-demand. [Accessed: 19 March 2025.] and 'GEN AI: TOO MUCH SPEND. TOO LITTLE TIME?', *Goldman Sachs Top of Mind Podcast*, 27 June 2024. Available: https://www.goldmansachs.com/insights/top-of-mind/gen-ai-too-much-spend-too-little-benefit. [Accessed: 19 March 2025.]

68 Li, P et al., 'Making AI Less "Thirsty": Uncovering and Addressing the Secret Water Footprint of AI Models', *arXiv*, 15 January 2025. Available: https://doi.org/10.48550/arXiv.2304.03271. [Accessed: 19 March 2025.]

69 'AI Act Enters into Force', *European Commission*, 1 August 2024. Available: https://commission.europa.eu/news/ai-act-enters-force-2024-08-01_en. [Accessed: 19 March 2025.]

70 'Homepage', *FinOps Foundation*. Available: https://www.finops.org/. [Accessed: 19 March 2025.]

71 'Reduce Service Costs Using Azure Advisor', *Microsoft*, 11 September 2024. Available: https://learn.microsoft.com/en-us/azure/advisor/advisor-cost-recommendations. [Accessed: 19 March 2025.]

72 'What Is FinOps?', *FinOps Foundation*. Available: https://www.finops.org/introduction/what-is-finops/. [Accessed: 19 March 2025.]

73 'Revolutionizing Cloud Cost Management: A Sustainable Approach with GreenOps', *Quinnox*. July 2024. Available: https://www.quinnox.com/blog/revolutionizing-cloud-cost-management-sustainable-approach-with-greenops/. [Accessed: 19 March 2025.]

74 'ISO/IEC 21031:2024', *ISO*. Accessed 15 October 2024. Available: https://www.iso.org/standard/86612.html. [Accessed: 19 March 2025.]

75 'The 10 Best Carbon Accounting Software in 2024', *Persefoni*, 3 January 2025. Available: https://www.persefoni.com/en-gb/blog/best-carbon-accounting-software. [Accessed: 19 March 2025.]

76 Yang, C. et al., 'Survey on Knowledge Distillation for Large Language Models: Methods, Evaluation, and Application', *ACM Transactions on Intelligent Systems and Technology*, 8 October 2024. Available: https://doi.org/10.1145/3699518. [Accessed: 19 March 2025.]

77 Lang, J., Guo, Z. and Huang, S., 'A Comprehensive Study on Quantization Techniques for Large Language Models', *arXiv*, 30 October 2024. Available: https://arxiv.org/html/2411.02530v1. [Accessed: 19 March 2025.]

78 Cheng, H., Zhang M. and Shi, J.Q., 'A Survey on Deep Neural Network Pruning-Taxonomy, Comparison, Analysis, and Recommendations', *arXiv*, 9 August 2024. Available: https://doi.org/10.48550/arXiv.2308.06767. [Accessed: 19 March 2025.]

79 Hu, E. J. et al., 'LoRA: Low-Rank Adaptation of Large Language Models', *arXiv*, 16 October 2021. Available: https://doi.org/10.48550/arXiv.2106.09685. [Accessed: 19 March 2025.]

80 Xu, L. et al., 'Parameter-Efficient Fine-Tuning Methods for Pretrained Language Models: A Critical Review and Assessment', *arXiv*, 19 December 2023. Available: https://doi.org/10.48550/arXiv.2312.12148. [Accessed: 19 March 2025.]

CHAPTER 11: AI GOVERNANCE PLATFORMS AND TOOLS

1 'AI Governance Market Size', *Mordor Intelligence*. October 2024. Available: https://www.mordorintelligence.com/industry-reports/ai-governance-market. [Accessed: 19 March 2025.]

CHAPTER 12: EU LAWS AND REGULATIONS

1 Sheehan, M., 'China's AI Regulations and How They Get Made', *Carnegie Endowment for International Peace*, 10 July 2023. Available: https://carnegie-production-assets.s3.amazonaws.com/static/files/202307-Sheehan_Chinese%20AI%20gov.pdf. [Accessed: 19 March 2025.] and Voshell, L., 'First Mover AI Regulation in Brussels and Beijing: Patterns and Comparison', *European Guanxi*, 27 December 2024. Available: https://www.europeanguanxi.com/post/first-mover-ai-regulation-in-brussels-and-beijing-patterns-and-comparison. [Accessed: 19 March 2025.]

2 Voshell, L., 'First Mover AI Regulation in Brussels and Beijing: Patterns and Comparison', *European Guanxi*, 27 December 2024. Available: https://www.europeanguanxi.com/post/first-mover-ai-regulation-in-brussels-and-beijing-patterns-and-comparison. [Accessed 20 March 2025.] and Kamiya, M. and Keate, J., 'AI Watch: Global regulatory tracker – Japan', *White & Case*, 1 July 2024. Available: https://www.whitecase.com/insight-our-thinking-ai-watch-global-regulatory-tracker-japan. [Accessed: 14 January 2025.]

3 Valadares Assunção, I., 'Trends Over Time', *AI on Trial*, 2025. Available: https://aiontrial.streamlit.app/. [Accessed: 6 June 2025.]

4   Vogel, M. et al., 'Is Your Use of AI Violating the Law? An Overview of the Current Legal Landscape', *N.Y.U. Journal of Legislation & Public Policy*, vol. 26, no. 4, p. 1029, September 2024. Available: https://www.equalai.org/wp-content/uploads/2024/09/Vogel_et_al_Sep_13_2024.pdf. [Accessed: 26 January 2025.]

5   'Consultation Paper on AI Regulation: Emerging Approaches Across the World', *UNESCO*, 16 August 2024. Available: https://unesdoc.unesco.org/ark:/48223/pf0000390979. [Accessed: 19 March 2025.]

6   'How Leaders in the Global South Can Devise AI Regulation that Enables Innovation', *Tony Blair Institute*, 6 February 2025. Available: https://institute.global/insights/tech-and-digitalisation/how-leaders-in-the-global-south-can-devise-ai-regulation-that-enables-innovation. [Accessed: 13 February 2025.]

7   Madiega, T., 'EU Legislation in Progress Briefing – Artificial Intelligence Act', *European Parliamentary Research Service*, September 2024. Available: https://www.europarl.europa.eu/RegData/etudes/BRIE/2021/698792/EPRS_BRI(2021)698792_EN.pdf. [Accessed: 19 March 2025.] and 'AI continent – European Commission', *European Commission*, April 2025. Available: https://commission.europa.eu/topics/eu-competitiveness/ai-continent_en. [Accessed: 28 April 2025.]

8   'Regulation (EU) 2024/1689 of the European Parliament and of the Council of 13 June 2024, laying down harmonized rules on artificial intelligence and amending Regulations (EC) No 300/2008, (EU) No 167/2013, (EU) No 168/2013, (EU) 2018/858, (EU) 2018/1139 and (EU) 2019/2144 and Directives 2014/90/EU, (EU) 2016/797 and (EU) 2020/1828 (Artificial Intelligence Act), 2024 O.J. (L 1689), Art. 2', *EUR-Lex*, 13 June 2024. Available: http://data.europa.eu/eli/reg/2024/1689/oj/eng. [Accessed: 26 January 2025.]

9   'Implementation Timeline', *EU Artificial Intelligence Act*. Available: https://artificialintelligenceact.eu/implementation-timeline/. [Accessed: 26 January 2025.]

10 'EU Artificial Intelligence Act, 2024 O.J. (L 1689), Art. 3', *EUR-Lex*, 13 June 2024. Available: http://data.europa.eu/eli/reg/2024/1689/oj/eng. [Accessed: 26 January 2025.]

11 'Approval of the content of the draft Communication from the Commission – Commission Guidelines on the definition of an artificial intelligence system established by Regulation (EU) 2024/1689 (AI Act), 2025 O.J. (C 924)', *European Commission*, 6 February 2025. Available: https://digital-strategy.ec.europa.eu/en/library/commission-publishes-guidelines-ai-system-definition-facilitate-first-ai-acts-rules-application. [Accessed: 10 March 2025].

12 ibid. ¶¶ 42, 46, 48, 49.

13 Svenja, A.V.H., 'Parliamentary question | Definition of 'AI system': Simple statistical techniques and alignment with international standards', *European Parliament*, 18 November 2024. Available: https://www.europarl.europa.eu/doceo/document/E-10-2024-002564_EN.html. [Accessed: 13 January 2025.]

14 'Charter of Fundamental Rights of the European Union, 2000 O.J. (C 364)', *European Parliament*, 18 December 2000. Available: https://www.europarl.europa.eu/charter/pdf/text_en.pdf. [Accessed: 26 January 2025.] and 'European Convention on Human Rights, 213 U.N.T.S. 221', *European Convention on Human Rights*, 4 November 1950. Available: https://www.echr.coe.int/documents/d/echr/convention_eng. [Accessed: 26 January 2025.] and 'Universal Declaration of Human Rights, G.A. Res. 217A (III), U.N. Doc. A/810', *UN*, 8 December 1948. Available: https://www.un.org/en/about-us/universal-declaration-of-human-rights. [Accessed: 26 January 2025.] and 'Recommendation of the Council on Artificial Intelligence, OECD/LEGAL/0449', *OECD*, 22 May 2019. Available: https://legalinstruments.oecd.org/en/instruments/OECD-LEGAL-0449. [Accessed: 26 January 2025.]

15 'EU Artificial Intelligence Act, 2024 O.J. (L 1689), Art. 5', *EUR-Lex*, 13 June 2024. Available: http://data.europa.eu/eli/reg/2024/1689/oj/eng. [Accessed: 26 January 2025.]

16 'Approval of the content of the draft Communication from the Commission – Commission Guidelines on prohibited artificial intelligence practices established by Regulation (EU) 2024/1689 (AI Act), 2025 O.J. (C 884)', *European Commission*, 4 February 2025. Available: https://digital-strategy.ec.europa.eu/en/library/commission-publishes-guidelines-prohibited-artificial-intelligence-ai-practices-defined-ai-act. [Accessed: 10 March 2025.]

17 'EU Artificial Intelligence Act, 2024 O.J. (L 1689)', Art. 6, *EUR-Lex*, 13 June 2024. Available: http://data.europa.eu/eli/reg/2024/1689/oj/eng. [Accessed: 26 January 2025.]

18 ibid. Annex III

19 ibid. Arts. 8–17, 20, 43, 48–49, 60.

20 ibid. Art. 26.

21 ibid. Art. 18.

22 ibid. Art. 50.

23 ibid. Art. 95 & Recital 165.

24 ibid. Art. 4.

25 ibid. Art.17.

26 ibid. Art. 51 & Recital 112.

27 Rahman, R. et al., 'Over 30 AI models have been trained at the scale of GPT-4', *Epoch AI*, 6 June 2025. Available: https://epoch.ai/data-insights/models-over-1e25-flop. [Accessed: 7 June 2025.]

28 'EU Artificial Intelligence Act, 2024 O.J. (L 1689)', Art. 53 & Annex XI, 13 June 2024. Available: http://data.europa.eu/eli/reg/2024/1689/oj/eng. [Accessed: 26 January 2025.]

29 ibid. Art. 53 & Recital 106.

30 Novelli, C. et al., 'Generative AI in EU law: Liability, privacy, intellectual property, and cybersecurity', *Computer Law & Security Review*, vol. 55, p. 106066, November 2024, doi: 10.1016/j.clsr.2024.106066. Available: https://linkinghub.elsevier.com/retrieve/pii/S0267364924001328. [Accessed: 26 January 2025.]

31 ibid.

32 Pouget, H., 'Standard Setting', *EU Artificial Intelligence Act*. Available: https://artificialintelligenceact.eu/standard-setting/. [Accessed: 20 March 2025.] and 'CEN/CLC/JTC 21 Work programme', *European Committee for Electrotechnical Standardization (CEN-CENELEC)*. Available: https://standards.cencenelec.eu/dyn/www/f?p=205:22:0::::FSP_ORG_ID,FSP_LANG_ID:2916257,25&cs=1827B89DA69577BF3631EE2B6070F207D. [Accessed: 20 March 2025.]

33 'The EU AI Act: Insights from the Green AI Committee', *Green Software Foundation*, 17 October 2024. Available: https://greensoftware.foundation/articles/the-eu-ai-act-insights-from-the-green-ai-committee. [Accessed: 20 March 2025.]

34 De Pereira, J.R.L., 'The EU AI Act and environmental protection: The case for a missed opportunity', *Henrich Böll Stiftung*, 8 April 2024. Available: https://eu.boell.org/en/2024/04/08/eu-ai-act-missed-opportunity. [Accessed: 20 March 2025.] and Engler, A., 'Key enforcement issues of the AI Act should lead EU trilogue debate', *Brookings Institution*, 16 June 2023. Available: https://www.brookings.edu/articles/key-enforcement-issues-of-the-ai-act-should-lead-eu-trilogue-debate/. [Accessed: 20 March 2025.]

35 Veale, M. and Borgesius, F.Z., 'Demystifying the Draft EU Artificial Intelligence Act – Analysing the good, the bad, and the unclear elements of the proposed approach', *Computer Law Review International*, vol. 22, no. 4, p. 105, August 2021. Available: https://arxiv.org/pdf/2107.03721. [Accessed: 20 March 2025.]

36 ibid. pp. 97–112.

37 Provisions on the Management of Algorithmic Recommendations in Internet Information Services, *China Law Translate*, 31 December 2021. Available: https://www.chinalawtranslate.com/en/algorithms/. [Accessed: 26 January 2025.]

38 'Executive Order on Promoting the Use of Trustworthy Artificial Intelligence in the Federal Government, E.O. 13960, 85 C.F.R. 78939', 3 December 2020. Available: https://www.federalregister.gov/documents/2020/12/08/2020-27065/promoting-the-use-of-trustworthy-artificial-intelligence-in-the-federal-government. [Accessed: 26 January 2025.]

39 Engler, A., 'The EU AI Act will have global impact, but a limited Brussels Effect', *Brookings Institution*, 8 June 2022, footnote 5. Available: https://www.brookings.edu/articles/the-eu-ai-act-will-have-global-impact-but-a-limited-brussels-effect/. [Accessed: 20 March 2025.]

40 Braun, M., Vallery, A. and Benizri, I., 'Measures in Support of Innovation in the European Union's AI Act – AI Regulatory Sandboxes', *WilmerHale*, 23 October

2024. Available: https://www.wilmerhale.com/en/insights/blogs/wilmerhale
-privacy-and-cybersecurity-law/20241023-measures-in-support-of-innova
tion-in-the-european-unions-ai-act-ai-regulatory-sandboxes. [Accessed: 20
March 2025.]

41 Madiega, T. and Van De Pol, A.L., 'Artificial intelligence act and regulatory
sandboxes', *European Parliamentary Research Service*, June 2022. Available:
https://www.europarl.europa.eu/RegData/etudes/BRIE/2022/733544/EPRS
_BRI(2022)733544_EN.pdf. [Accessed: 20 March 2025.] and Nihill, C.,
'MITRE announces AI sandbox for federal agency use', *Fedscoop*, 7 May 2024.
Available: https://fedscoop.com/mitre-announces-ai-sandbox-for-federal
-agency-use/. [Accessed: 20 March 2025.]

42 Bommasani, R., Hau, A., Klyman, K. and Liang, P., 'Foundation Models
under the EU AI Act', *Stanford Center for Research on Foundation Models*,
August 2024. Available: https://crfm.stanford.edu/2024/08/01/eu-ai-act.html.
[Accessed: 14 January 2025.] and Seger, E. et al., 'Open-Sourcing Highly
Capable Foundation Models: An Evaluation of Risks, Benefits, and Alternative
Methods for Pursuing Open-Source Objectives', *SSRN*, 10 October 2023.
Available: https://www.ssrn.com/abstract=4596436. [Accessed: 20 March
2025.] and Kapoor, S. and Narayanan, A., 'On the Societal Impact of Open
Foundation Models', *AI Snake Oil*, 27 February 2024. Available: https://www
.aisnakeoil.com/p/on-the-societal-impact-of-open-foundation. [Accessed: 20
March 2025.]

43 ibid.

44 'EU Artificial Intelligence Act, 2024 O.J. (L 1689), Arts. 28, 64–65, 70, 74',
13 June 2024. Available: http://data.europa.eu/eli/reg/2024/1689/oj/eng.
[Accessed: 26 January 2025.]

45 ibid.

46 ibid. Art. 10.

47 'Regulation (EU) 2016/679 of the European Parliament and of the Council
of 27 April 2016 on the protection of natural persons with regard to the
processing of personal data and on the free movement of such data, and
repealing Directive 95/46/EC (General Data Protection Regulation), 2016 O.J.
(L 119), Art. 6, 4 May 2016'. Available: https://eur-lex.europa.eu/legal-content
/EN/TXT/PDF/?uri=CELEX:32016R0679. [Accessed: 26 January 2025.]

48 Hullen, N., 'Top 10 operational impacts of the EU AI Act – Leveraging
GDPR compliance', *ResourceCenter*, November 2024. Available: https://iapp
.org/resources/article/top-impacts-eu-ai-act-leveraging-gdpr-compliance/.
[Accessed: 14 January 2025.]

49 Sartor, G. and Lagioia, F., 'The impact of the General Data Protection
Regulation (GDPR) on artificial intelligence', *European Parliament*, p. 7, June
2020. Available: https://www.europarl.europa.eu/RegData/etudes/STUD/2020
/641530/EPRS_STU(2020)641530_EN.pdf. [Accessed: 20 January 2025.]

50 'General Data Protection Regulation', 2016 O.J. (L 119), Art. 15', 4 May 2016. Available: https://eur-lex.europa.eu/legal-content/EN/TXT/PDF/?uri =CELEX:32016R0679. [Accessed: 26 January 2025.]

51 ibid. Art. 22.

52 'Ordinanza ingiunzione nei confronti di Deliveroo Italy s.r.l., No. 9685994', 22 July 2021. Available: https://www.garanteprivacy.it/home/docweb/-/docweb -display/docweb/9685994. [Accessed: 26 January 2025.]

53 Clark, J., Demircan, M. and Kettas, K., 'Europe: The EU AI Act's relationship with data protection law: Key takeaways', *Privacy Matters*, 25 April 2024. Available: https://privacymatters.dlapiper.com/2024/04/europe-the-eu-ai-acts -relationship-with-data-protection-law-key-takeaways/. [Accessed: 14 January 2025.]

54 Barros Vale, S. and Zanfir-Fortuna, G., 'Automated Decision-Making Under the GDPR', *Future of Privacy Forum*, p. 2, May 2022. Available: https://fpf.org /wp-content/uploads/2022/05/FPF-ADM-Report-R2-singles.pdf. [Accessed: 26 January 2025.]

55 ibid.

56 ibid. p. 13.

57 ibid. p. 22.

58 ibid.

59 ibid.

60 Launders, J., 'Beyond the AI Act: The AI Liability Directive & the Product Liability Directive', *A&L Goodbody Tech Law Blog*, 5 March 2024. Available: https://www.techlaw.ie/2024/03/articles/artificial-intelligence/beyond-the-ai -act-how-the-ai-liability-directive-and-the-product-liability-directive-will -also-shape-the-regulation-of-ai-in-the-eu/. [Accessed 10 March 2025.]

61 'Annexes to the Communication from the Commission to the European Parliament, the Council, the European Economic and Social Committee and the Committee of the Regions: Commission work programme 2025, O.J. (COM 45), Annex IV', *European Commission*, 11 February 2025. Available: https://commission.europa.eu/document/download/7617998c -86e6-4a74-b33c-249e8a7938cd_en?filename=COM_2025_45_1_annexes _EN.pdf. [Accessed: 10 March 2025.] and 'Opinion of the Committee on the Internal Market and Consumer Protection for the Committee on Legal Affairs on the proposal for a directive of the European Parliament and of the Council on adapting non-contractual civil liability rules to artificial intelligence (AI Liability Directive) (COM(2022)0496 – C9-0320/2022 – 2022/0303(COD))', *European Parliament*, 22 May 2025. Available: https:// www.europarl.europa.eu/doceo/document/IMCO-AD-768056_EN.pdf. [Accessed: 6 June 2025.]

62 Arimont, P. and Botoş, V.-M., 'New Product Liability Directive', *European Parliament*, 15 December 2024. Available: https://www.europarl.europa.eu

/legislative-train/theme-a-europe-fit-for-the-digital-age/file-new-product -liability-directive. [Accessed: 26 January 2025.]

63 'Liability for defective products', *European Commission*, 8 December 2024. Available: https://single-market-economy.ec.europa.eu/single-market/goods/free -movement-sectors/liability-defective-products_en. [Accessed: 14 January 2025.]

64 Launders, J. 'Beyond the AI Act: The AI Liability Directive & the Product Liability Directive', *A&L Goodbody Tech Law Blog*, 5 March 2024. Available: https://www.techlaw.ie/2024/03/articles/artificial-intelligence/beyond-the-ai -act-how-the-ai-liability-directive-and-the-product-liability-directive-will -also-shape-the-regulation-of-ai-in-the-eu/. [Accessed: 26 January 2025.]

65 'New Product Liability Directive: Europe Fit for the Digital Age', *European Commission*, October 2022. Available: https://single-market-economy. ec.europa.eu/system/files/2022-10/New%20Product%20Liability%20 Directive%20proposal%20-%20Factsheet.pdf. [Accessed: 26 January 2025.]

66 De Luca, S., 'New Product Liability Directive', *European Parliamentary Research Service*, P.E. 739.341, p. 5, December 2023. Available: https://www.europarl .europa.eu/RegData/etudes/BRIE/2023/739341/EPRS_BRI(2023)739341_EN .pdf. [Accessed: 26 January 2025.]

67 ibid.

68 Arimont, P. and Botoş, V.-M., 'New Product Liability Directive', *Legislative Train Schedule*, 15 December 2024. Available: https://www.europarl.europa .eu/legislative-train/theme-a-europe-fit-for-the-digital-age/file-new-product -liability-directive. [Accessed: 26 January 2025.]

69 'New Product Liability Directive: Europe Fit for the Digital Age', *European Commission*, October 2022. https://single-market-economy.ec.europa. eu/system/files/2022-10/New%20Product%20Liability%20Directive%20 proposal%20-%20Factsheet.pdf. [Accessed: 26 January 2025.]

70 'The Digital Services Act package', *European Commission*, 4 October 2024. Available: https://digital-strategy.ec.europa.eu/en/policies/digital-services-act -package. [Accessed: 26 January 2025.]

71 ibid.

72 'The Digital Services Act: Practical Implications for Online Services and Platforms', *Latham & Watkins*, March 2023, pp. 6–7. Available: https://www.lw.com/admin /upload/SiteAttachments/Digital-Services-Act-Practical-Implications-for -Online-Services-and-Platforms.pdf. [Accessed: 20 March 2025.]

73 'A Safer & Fairer Online Environment', *European Commission*, 25 July 2024. Available: https://digital-strategy.ec.europa.eu/en/factpages/safer-fairer-online -environment. [Accessed: 26 January 2025.]

74 ibid.

75 'DSA: Making the online world safer', *European Commission*, 25 February 2025. Available: https://digital-strategy.ec.europa.eu/en/policies/safer-online. [Accessed: 20 March 2025.]

76 'The enforcement framework under the Digital Services Act', *European Commission*, 22 January 2025. Available: https://digital-strategy.ec.europa.eu /en/policies/dsa-enforcement. [Accessed: 26 January 2025.]

77 ibid.

78 'A Safer & Fairer Online Environment', *European Commission*, 25 July 2024. Available: https://digital-strategy.ec.europa.eu/en/factpages/safer-fairer-online -environment. [Accessed: 26 January 2025.]

79 ibid.

80 ibid.

81 'About the Digital Markets Act', *European Commission*, 3 May 2023. Available: https://digital-markets-act.ec.europa.eu/about-dma_en. [Accessed: 26 January 2025.]

82 'DMA High-Level Group Public Statement on Artificial Intelligence', *European Commission*, 22 May 2024. Available: https://digital-markets-act.ec.europa.eu /high-level-group-digital-markets-act-public-statement-artificial-intelligence -2024-05-22_en. [Accessed: 26 January 2025.]

83 Hacker, P., Cordes, J. and Rochon, J., 'Regulating Gatekeeper AI and Data: Transparency, Access, and Fairness under the DMA, the GDPR, and beyond', *European Journal of Risk Regulation*, vol. 15, p. 51, 13 December 2023. Available: https://www.cambridge.org/core/journals/european-journal-of -risk-regulation/article/regulating-gatekeeper-artificial-intelligence-and -data-transparency-access-and-fairness-under-the-digital-markets-act-the -general-data-protection-regulation-and-beyond/9A66BBD933000DD8011 4C5077FB23D7E. [Accessed 26 January 2025.]

84 Martínez, A.R., 'Generative AI and the Digital Markets Act on the Rocks', *Wolters Kluwer Competition Law Blog*, 5 February 2024. Available: https:// competitionlawblog.kluwercompetitionlaw.com/2024/02/05/generative-ai -and-the-digital-markets-act-on-the-rocks/. [Accessed: 26 January 2025.]

85 'Joint statement on competition in generative AI foundation models and AI products', *GOV.UK*, 23 July 2024. Available: https://www.gov.uk/government /publications/joint-statement-on-competition-in-generative-ai-foundation -models-and-ai-products/joint-statement-on-competition-in-generative-ai -foundation-models-and-ai-products. [Accessed: 26 January 2025.]

CHAPTER 13: UNITED STATES LAWS AND REGULATIONS

1 'Artificial Intelligence 2025 Legislation', *NCSL*, 24 April 2025. Available: https://www.ncsl.org/technology-and-communication/artificial-intelli gence-2025-legislation. [Accessed: 7 June 2025.] and 'Autonomous Vehicles Legislation Database', *NCSL*, 10 March 2025. Available: https:// www.ncsl.org/transportation/autonomous-vehicles-legislation-database. [Accessed: 7 June 2025.] and 'Policing Legislation Database', *NCSL*, 9 April

2024. Available: https://www.ncsl.org/civil-and-criminal-justice/policing-legislation-database. [Accessed: 7 June 2025.] and 'State Elections Legislation Database', *NCSL*, 4 June 2025. Available: https://www.ncsl.org/elections-and-campaigns/state-election-legislation-database. [Accessed: 7 June 2025.] and 'Postsecondary Legislation Database', *NCSL*, 22 January 2025. Available: https://www.ncsl.org/education/postsecondary-legislation-database. [Accessed: 7 June 2025.]

2   'Executive Order on Removing Barriers to American Leadership in Artificial Intelligence', 23 January 2025. Available: https://www.whitehouse.gov/presidential-actions/2025/01/removing-barriers-to-american-leadership-in-artificial-intelligence/. [Accessed: 26 January 2025.] and 'Request for Information on the Development of an Artificial Intelligence (AI) Action Plan, 90 Fed. Reg. 9088', 6 February 2025. Available: https://www.federalregister.gov/documents/2025/02/06/2025-02305/request-for-information-on-the-development-of-an-artificial-intelligence-ai-action-plan. [Accessed: 10 March 2025.] and 'Executive Order on Advancing Artificial Intelligence Education for American Youth', 23 April 2025. Available: https://www.whitehouse.gov/presidential-actions/2025/04/advancing-artificial-intelligence-education-for-american-youth/. [Accessed: 6 June 2025.]

3   'Artificial Intelligence Risk Management Framework (AI RMF 1.0), NIST AI 100-1', *NIST*, 26 January 2023. Available: https://nvlpubs.nist.gov/nistpubs/ai/NIST.AI.100-1.pdf. [Accessed: 26 January 2025.]

4   'Artificial intelligence', *NIST*. Available: https://www.nist.gov/artificial-intelligence. [Accessed: 15 January 2025.] and National Security Agency et al., 'AI Data Security: Best Practices for Securing Data Used to Train & Operate AI Systems', 22 May 2025. Available: https://media.defense.gov/2025/May/22/2003720601/-1/-1/0/CSI_AI_DATA_SECURITY.PDF. [Accessed: 7 June 2025.]

5   'FACT SHEET: Biden-Harris Administration Secures Voluntary Commitments from Leading Artificial Intelligence Companies to Manage the Risks Posed by AI', *White House*, 21 July 2023. Available: https://web.archive.org/web/20250118004851/https://www.whitehouse.gov/briefing-room/statements-releases/2023/07/21/fact-sheet-biden-harris-administration-secures-voluntary-commitments-from-leading-artificial-intelligence-companies-to-manage-the-risks-posed-by-ai/. [Accessed: 26 January 2025.] and 'FACT SHEET: Biden-Harris Administration Secures Voluntary Commitments from Eight Additional Artificial Intelligence Companies to Manage the Risks Posed by AI', *White House*, 12 September 2023. Available: https://web.archive.org/web/20250118080933/https://www.whitehouse.gov/briefing-room/statements-releases/2023/09/12/fact-sheet-biden-harris-administration-secures-voluntary-commitments-from-eight-additional-artificial-intelligence-companies-to-manage-the-risks-posed-by-ai/. [Accessed: 26 January 2025.]

6   Heilweil, R., 'Where Biden's voluntary AI commitments go from here', *FedScoop*, 13 November 2024. Available: https://fedscoop.com/voluntary-ai-commitments-biden-trump-white-house/. [Accessed: 26 January 2025.]

7   'Blueprint for an AI Bill of Rights', *White House*, 4 October 2022. Available: https://web.archive.org/web/20250118015329/https://www.whitehouse.gov/wp-content/uploads/2022/10/Blueprint-for-an-AI-Bill-of-Rights.pdf. [Accessed: 26 January 2025.]

8   'FACT SHEET: Biden-Harris Administration Announces Key Actions to Advance Tech Accountability and Protect the Rights of the American Public', *White House*, 4 October 2022. Available: https://web.archive.org/web/20250118020404/https://www.whitehouse.gov/ostp/news-updates/2022/10/04/fact-sheet-biden-harris-administration-announces-key-actions-to-advance-tech-accountability-and-protect-the-rights-of-the-american-public/. [Accessed: 26 January 2025.]

9   'Blueprint for an AI Bill of Rights', *White House*, p. 3, 4 October 2022. Available: https://web.archive.org/web/20250118015329/https://www.whitehouse.gov/wp-content/uploads/2022/10/Blueprint-for-an-AI-Bill-of-Rights.pdf. [Accessed: 26 January 2025.]

10 'Public Law 116 – 92 – National Defense Authorization Act for Fiscal Year 2020, S. 1790', 20 December 2019. Available: https://www.govinfo.gov/app/details/PLAW-116publ92. [Accessed: 26 January 2025.]

11 ibid.

12 'National AI Advisory Committee', *AI.gov*. Available: https://perma.cc/L2VN-7PMG. [Accessed: 18 March 2025.]

13 'President's Council of Advisors on Science and Technology', *White House*, 23 January 2025. Available: https://www.whitehouse.gov/presidential-actions/2025/01/presidents-council-of-advisors-on-science-and-technology/. [Accessed: 26 January 2025.] and 'Statement from U.S. Secretary of Commerce Howard Lutnick on Transforming the U.S. AI Safety Institute into the Pro-Innovation, Pro-Science U.S. Center for AI Standards and Innovation', *U.S. Department of Commerce*, 3 June 2025. Available: https://www.commerce.gov/news/press-releases/2025/06/statement-us-secretary-commerce-howard-lutnick-transforming-us-ai. [Accessed: 6 June 2025.]

14 Chopra, R. et al., 'Joint Statement on Enforcement Efforts Against Discrimination and Bias in Automated Systems', *Federal Trade Commission*, April 2023. Available: https://www.ftc.gov/system/files/ftcgov/pdf/EEOC-CRT-FTC-CFPB-AI-Joint-Statement%28final%29.pdf. [Accessed: 18 March 2025.]

15 'EEOC Launches Initiative on Artificial Intelligence and Algorithmic Fairness', *U.S. Equal Employment Opportunity Commission*, 28 October 2021. Available: https://www.eeoc.gov/newsroom/eeoc-launches-initiative-artificial-intelligence-and-algorithmic-fairness. [Accessed: 18 March 2025.]

16 'iTutorGroup to Pay $365,000 to Settle EEOC Discriminatory Hiring Suit', *U.S. Equal Employment Opportunity Commission*, 11 September 2023. Available: https://www.eeoc.gov/newsroom/itutorgroup-pay-365000-settle-eeoc-discriminatory-hiring-suit. [Accessed: 26 January 2025.] and 'Joint Notice of Settlement and Request for Approval and Execution of Consent Decree, EEOC v. iTutorGroup, No. 22-CV-02565 (E.D.N.Y. 9 August 2023)'. Available: https://www.workforcebulletin.com/assets/htmldocuments/blog/8/2023/08/2023.08.09-EEOC-v.-iTutorGroup-Joint-Notice-of-Settlement-22-cv-02565-PKC-PK.pdf. [Accessed: 21 March 2025.]

17 'EEOC Strategic Enforcement Plan 2024–2028', *U.S. Equal Employment Opportunity Commission*, pp. 8–9, 26 September 2023. Available: https://www.eeoc.gov/sites/default/files/2024-03/23-161_EEOC_SEP_030124_508.pdf. [Accessed: 25 January 2025.]

18 'Uniform Guidelines on Employee Selection Procedures, 43 C.F.R. 38295, 38314', 25 August 1978. Available: https://www.ecfr.gov/current/title-41/subtitle-B/chapter-60/part-60-3. [Accessed: 26 January 2025.]

19 'Algorithms, Artificial Intelligence, and Disability Discrimination in Hiring', *ADA.gov*, 12 May 2022. Available: https://www.ada.gov/resources/ai-guidance/. [Accessed: 18 March 2025.] and 'Select Issues: Assessing Adverse Impact in Software, Algorithms, and Artificial Intelligence Used in Employment Selection Procedures Under Title VII of the Civil Rights Act of 1964', *U.S. Equal Employment Opportunity Commission*, 18 May 2023. Available: https://perma.cc/WP2C-K5SB. [Accessed: 26 January 2025.] and 'The Americans with Disabilities Act and the Use of Software, Algorithms, and Artificial Intelligence to Assess Job Applicants and Employees', *U.S. Equal Employment Opportunity Commission*, 12 May 2022. Available: https://perma.cc/P5G5-26XC. [Accessed: 26 January 2025.] and Vogel, M. et al., 'Is Your Use of AI Violating the Law? An Overview of the Current Legal Landscape', *N.Y.U. Journal of Legislation & Public Policy*, vol. 26, no. 4, p. 1063, September 2024. Available: https://www.equalai.org/wp-content/uploads/2024/09/Vogel_et_al_Sep_13_2024.pdf. [Accessed: 26 January 2025.]

20 'Mobley v. Workday, Inc., 23-CV-00770 (N.D. Cal. 21 February 2023)'. Available: https://www.courtlistener.com/docket/66831340/mobley-v-workday-inc/. [Accessed: 26 January 2025.]

21 'Hous. Fed'n of Teachers v. Hous. Indep. Sch. Dist, 251 F. Supp. 3d 1168, 1175, 1180 (S.D. Tex. 2017)'. Available: https://casetext.com/case/hous-fedn-of-teachers-v-hous-indep-sch-dist. [Accessed: 26 January 2025.]

22 Vogel, M. et al., 'Is Your Use of AI Violating the Law? An Overview of the Current Legal Landscape', *N.Y.U. Journal of Legislation & Public Policy*, vol. 26, no. 4, p. 1029, September 2024. Available: https://www.equalai.org/wp-content/uploads/2024/09/Vogel_et_al_Sep_13_2024.pdf. [Accessed: 26 January 2025.]

23 'A Brief Overview of the Federal Trade Commission's Investigative, Law Enforcement, and Rulemaking Authority', *Federal Trade Commission*, May

2021. Available: https://www.ftc.gov/about-ftc/mission/enforcement-author
ity. [Accessed: 15 January 2025.]

24 Bedoya, A.M., 'Early Thoughts on Generative AI', remarks presented at the
International Association of Privacy Professionals, 5 April 2023. Available:
https://perma.cc/77N8-3MHK. [Accessed: 22 January 2025.]

25 'A Brief Overview of the Federal Trade Commission's Investigative, Law
Enforcement, and Rulemaking Authority', *Federal Trade Commission*, May
2021. Available: https://www.ftc.gov/about-ftc/mission/enforcement-author
ity. [Accessed: 15 January 2025.]

26 'Everalbum, Inc., No. C-4743 (F.T.C. 6 May 2021)'. Available: https://www
.ftc.gov/system/files/documents/cases/1923172_-_everalbum_decision_final
.pdf. [Accessed: 26 January 2025.]

27 'Plaintiff's Consent Motion for Entry of Stipulated Order for Civil Penalty,
Monetary Judgment, and Injunctive Relief and Memorandum in Support, U.S.
v. Facebook, Inc., No. 19-CV-2184 (D.D.C. 24 July 2019)'. Available: https://
www.ftc.gov/system/files/documents/cases/182_3109_facebook_consent_
motion_filed_7-24-19.pdf. [Accessed: 26 January 2025.] and 'FTC Imposes $5
Billion Penalty and Sweeping New Privacy Restrictions on Facebook', *Federal
Trade Commission*, 24 July 2019. Available: https://perma.cc/49QV-KE3E.
[Accessed: 26 January 2025.]

28 'FTC Announces Crackdown on Deceptive AI Claims and Schemes', *Federal
Trade Commission*, 25 September 2024. Available: https://www.ftc.gov/news
-events/news/press-releases/2024/09/ftc-announces-crackdown-deceptive-ai
-claims-schemes. [Accessed: 27 January 2025.] and 'FTC Finalizes Order with
DoNotPay that Prohibits Deceptive "AI Lawyer" Claims, Imposes Monetary
Relief, and Requires Notice to Past Subscribers', *Federal Trade Commission*,
11 February 2025. Available: https://www.ftc.gov/news-events/news/press
-releases/2025/02/ftc-finalizes-order-donotpay-prohibits-deceptive-ai-lawyer
-claims-imposes-monetary-relief-requires. [Accessed: 18 March 2025.]

29 'FTC Announces Crackdown on Deceptive AI Claims and Schemes', *Federal
Trade Commission*, 25 September 2024. Available: https://www.ftc.gov/news
-events/news/press-releases/2024/09/ftc-announces-crackdown-deceptive-ai
-claims-schemes. [Accessed: 27 January 2025.]

30 'Unfair, Deceptive, or Abusive Acts or Practices (UDAAPs) Examination
Procedures', *Consumer Financial Protection Bureau*, 1 October 2012. Available:
https://www.consumerfinance.gov/compliance/supervision-examinations
/unfair-deceptive-or-abusive-acts-or-practices-udaaps-examination-proce
dures/. [Accessed: 26 January 2025.] and Frotman, S. and Meyer, E., 'CFPB
Comment on Request for Information on Uses, Opportunities, and Risks of
Artificial Intelligence in the Financial Services Sector', *Consumer Financial
Protection Bureau*, 12 August 2024. Available: https://www.consumerfinance
.gov/about-us/newsroom/cfpb-comment-on-request-for-information-on

-uses-opportunities-and-risks-of-artificial-intelligence-in-the-financial
-services-sector/. [Accessed: 26 January 2025.]

31 'Consumer Protections for Artificial Intelligence, S. 24-205', 17 May 2024. Available: https://leg.colorado.gov/sites/default/files/2024a_205_signed.pdf. [Accessed: 26 January 2025.]

32 Atleson, M., 'Chatbots, deepfakes, and voice clones: AI deception for sale', *Federal Trade Commission*, 20 March 2023. Available: https://www.ftc.gov/business-guidance/blog/2023/03/chatbots-deepfakes-voice-clones-ai-deception-sale. [Accessed: 26 January 2025.]

33 'Deputy Attorney General Lisa O. Monaco Delivers Remarks at the University of Oxford on the Promise and Peril of AI', *Office of Public Affairs: U.S. Department of Justice*, 14 February 2024. Available: https://www.justice.gov/opa/speech/deputy-attorney-general-lisa-o-monaco-delivers-remarks-university-oxford-promise-and. [Accessed: 26 January 2025.]

34 'Public Law No. 118-31 – National Defense Authorization Act for Fiscal Year 2024, H.R. 2670', 22 December 2023. Available: https://www.congress.gov/bill/118th-congress/house-bill/2670/text. [Accessed: 26 January 2025.]

35 'AI Deepfake Legislation Tracker', *Ballotpedia*, 6 June 2025. Available: https://legislation.ballotpedia.org/ai-deepfakes/search. [Accessed: 7 June 2025.]

36 Lewis, K. and Kuersten, A., 'Introduction to Tort Law', *Congressional Research Service*, 26 May 2023, vol. 4. Available: https://crsreports.congress.gov/product/pdf/IF/IF11291. [Accessed: 26 January 2025.]

37 'Standing General Order on Crash Reporting', *NHTSA*, 16 December 2024. Available: https://perma.cc/AX7F-BGC6. [Accessed: 26 January 2025.]

38 'Complaint, Hudson v. Tesla, Inc., No. 2018-CA-011812 (Fla. Cir. Ct. 30 October 2018)'. Available: https://cdn.arstechnica.net/wp-content/uploads/2018/10/Complaint-filed.pdf. [Accessed: 26 January 2025.]

39 'Complaint, Toledo v. Tesla, Inc., No. 22-CV-049-08 (N.D. Cal. 26 August 2022)'. Available: https://www.classaction.org/media/alvarez-toldeo-v-tesla-inc.pdf. [Accessed: 26 January 2025.]

40 Lewis, K. and Kuersten, A., 'Introduction to Tort Law', *Congressional Research Service*, 26 May 2023, vol. 4. Available: https://crsreports.congress.gov/product/pdf/IF/IF11291. [Accessed: 26 January 2025.]

41 ibid.

42 McNulty, S., 'AI Update: Artificial Intelligence and Products Liability', *Global Aerospace*, 18 January 2022. Available: https://perma.cc/HU33-7GHG. [Accessed: 22 January 2025.] as discussed in Vogel, M. et al., 'Is Your Use of AI Violating the Law? An Overview of the Current Legal Landscape', *N.Y.U. Journal of Legislation & Public Policy*, vol. 26, no. 4, p. 1029, September 2024. Available: https://www.equalai.org/wp-content/uploads/2024/09/Vogel_et_al_Sep_13_2024.pdf. [Accessed: 26 January 2025.]

43 'Rodgers v. Christie, No. 19-2616 (3d Cir. 6 March 2020)'. Available: https:// casetext.com/case/rodgers-v-christie. [Accessed: 26 January 2025.] cited in Vogel, M. et al., 'Is Your Use of AI Violating the Law? An Overview of the Current Legal Landscape', *N.Y.U. Journal of Legislation & Public Policy*, vol. 26, no. 4, p. 1029, September 2024. Available: https://www.equalai.org/wp -content/uploads/2024/09/Vogel_et_al_Sep_13_2024.pdf. [Accessed: 26 January 2025.]

44 Vrasmasu, M., 'Is Your Artificial Intelligence a Service or a Product?', *JD Supra*, 13 September 2022. Available: https://www.jdsupra.com/legalnews/is-your -artificial-intelligence-a-9959187/. [Accessed: 22 January 2025.] cited in Vogel, M. et al., 'Is Your Use of AI Violating the Law? An Overview of the Current Legal Landscape', *N.Y.U. Journal of Legislation & Public Policy*, vol. 26, no. 4, p. 1029, 13 September 2024, Available: https://www.equalai.org/wp-content/ uploads/2024/09/Vogel_et_al_Sep_13_2024.pdf. [Accessed: 22 January 2025.]

45 'Introduction to Tort Law', *Congressional Research Service*, vol. 4, 26 May 2023. Available: https://crsreports.congress.gov/product/pdf/IF/IF11291. [Accessed: 22 January 2025.]

46 'Social Media Adolescent Addiction/Personal Injury Products Liability Litigation, No. 22-MD-3047 (N.D. Cal. 6 October 2022)'. Available: https:// cand.uscourts.gov/in-re-social-media-adolescent-addiction-personal-injury -products-liability-litigation-mdl-no-3047/. [Accessed: 27 January 2025.] and Roose, K., 'Can A.I. Be Blamed for a Teen's Suicide?', *New York Times*, 23 October 2024. Available: https://www.nytimes.com/2024/10/23/technology/ characterai-lawsuit-teen-suicide.html. [Accessed: 18 March 2025.]

47 'Complaint, Garcia v. Character Technologies, Inc., et al., No. 24-CV-01903 (M.D. Fla. 22 October 2024)'. Available: https://storage.courtlistener .com/recap/gov.uscourts.flmd.433581/gov.uscourts.flmd.433581.1.0.pdf. [Accessed: 18 March 2025.] and 'Complaint, A.F. v. Character Technologies, Inc., et al., No. 24-CV-01014 (E.D. Tex. 9 December 2024)'. Available: https:// storage.courtlistener.com/recap/gov.uscourts.txed.234704/gov.uscourts.txed .234704.1.0_2.pdf. [Accessed: 18 March 2025.]

48 ibid.

49 'Children's Online Privacy Protection Rule, 16 C.F.R. 312 (11 January 2024)'. Available: https://www.federalregister.gov/documents/2024/01/11/2023 -28569/childrens-online-privacy-protection-rule. [Accessed: 26 January 2025.] and Children's Online Privacy Protection Act, 15 U.S.C. §§ 6501–6506. Available: https://uscode.house.gov/view.xhtml?path=/prelim@title15/chap ter91&edition=prelim. [Accessed: 26 January 2025.]

50 'United States v. Kurbo, Inc., et al., No. 22-CV-00946 (N.D. Cal. 3 March 2022)'. Available: https://www.ftc.gov/system/files/ftc_gov/pdf/wwkurbostip ulatedorder.pdf. [Accessed: 26 January 2025.]

51 'United States v. Amazon.com, Inc., et al., No. 23-CV-00811 (W.D. Wash. 31 May 2023)'. Available: https://www.ftc.gov/system/files/ftc_gov/pdf/ Amazon-Proposed-Stipulated-Order-(Dkt.-2-1).pdf . [Accessed 26 January 2025.]

52 'Covered Entities and Business Associates', *U.S. Department of Health and Human Services*, 21 August 2024. Available: https://www.hhs.gov/hipaa/for -professionals/covered-entities/index.html. [Accessed: 28 May 2025.]

53 'Dinerstein v. Google LLC, et al., No. 20-3134 (7th Cir. 2023)'. Available: https://law.justia.com/cases/federal/appellate-courts/ca7/20-3134/20-3134 -2023-07-11.html. [Accessed: 26 January 2025.]

54 Kibby, C., 'US State Privacy Legislation Tracker', *IAPP*, 28 May 2025. Available: https://web.archive.org/web/20250307012807/https://iapp.org/resources/ article/us-state-privacy-legislation-tracker/. [Accessed: 7 June 2025.]

55 'California Consumer Privacy Act', 28 June 2018. Available: https://govt .westlaw.com/calregs/Browse/Home/California/CaliforniaCodeofRegulations ?guid=I5E53FC80FEDE11ECA3A49C17D1AA5D7C&originationCon text=documenttoc&transitionType=Default&contextData=(sc.Default). [Accessed 18 March 2025.]

56 'Illinois General Assembly – Full Text of Public Act 103-0804'. Available: https://www.ilga.gov/legislation/publicacts/fulltext.asp?Name=103-0804. [Accessed: 15 January 2025.] and '820 ILCS 42/ Artificial Intelligence Video Interview Act'. Available: https://www.ilga.gov/legislation/ilcs/ilcs3.asp?ActID =4015&ChapterID=68. [Accessed: 15 January 2025.]

CHAPTER 14: NOTABLE GLOBAL LEGAL DEVELOPMENTS

1 'Our Life With AI', *Google*, p. 5, January 2024. Available: https://static.google usercontent.com/media/publicpolicy.google/en//resources/our_life_with_ai _google_ipsos_report.pdf. [Accessed: 29 January 2025.]

2 'Database of National AI Policies', *OECD.AI*, 4 March 2024. Available: https:// oecd.ai/en/dashboards. [Accessed: 29 January 2025.]

3 Maslej, N. et al., 'Artificial Intelligence Index Report 2024', *Institute for Human-Centered AI, Stanford University*, April 2024, pp. 24, 385. Available: https:// aiindex.stanford.edu/wp-content/uploads/2024/05/HAI_AI-Index-Report -2024.pdf. [Accessed: 29 January 2025.]

4 ibid. p. 392.

5 Clarke, L., 'UK's Keir Starmer: Don't be scared of AI', *POLITICO*, 14 October 2024. Available: https://www.politico.eu/article/britain-must-run-towards-ai -opportunities-says-keir-starmer/. [Accessed: 29 January 2025.]

6 'AI Opportunities Action Plan', *GOV.UK*, p. 13, January 2025. Available: https://www.gov.uk/government/publications/ai-opportunities-action-plan/ ai-opportunities-action-plan. [Accessed: 30 January 2025.] and 'AI Playbook for the UK Government', *GOV.UK*, February 2025. Available: https://www.gov.

uk/government/publications/ai-playbook-for-the-uk-government. [Accessed: 23 April 2025.]

7 'Artificial Intelligence (Regulation) Bill, HL-11', 22 November 2023, *Parliament*. Available: https://bills.parliament.uk/bills/3519. [Accessed: 20 March 2025.]

8 'A pro-innovation approach to AI regulation', *GOV.UK*, August 2023. Available: https://www.gov.uk/government/publications/ai-regulation-a-pro-innovation -approach/white-paper. [Accessed: 30 January 2025.]

9 'A pro-innovation approach to AI regulation: Government response to consultation', *GOV.UK*, February 2024. Available: https://assets.publishing .service.gov.uk/media/65c1e399c43191000d1a45f4/a-pro-innovation -approach-to-ai-regulation-amended-governement-response-web-ready.pdf. [Accessed: 30 January 2025.]

10 'Guidance on AI and data protection', *ico.*, 15 March 2023. Available: https:// ico.org.uk/for-organisations/uk-gdpr-guidance-and-resources/artificial -intelligence/guidance-on-ai-and-data-protection/. [Accessed: 29 January 2025.]

11 'Explaining decisions made with AI', *ico.*, 20 May 2020. Available: https://ico .org.uk/for-organisations/uk-gdpr-guidance-and-resources/artificial-intelli gence/explaining-decisions-made-with-artificial-intelligence/. [Accessed: 29 January 2025.]

12 'AI and data protection risk toolkit', *ico.*, 19 May 2023. Available: https://ico.org .uk/for-organisations/uk-gdpr-guidance-and-resources/artificial-intelligence /guidance-on-ai-and-data-protection/ai-and-data-protection-risk-toolkit/. [Accessed: 29 January 2025.]

13 'Biometric data guidance: Biometric recognition', *ico.*, 22 February 2024. Available: https://ico.org.uk/for-organisations/uk-gdpr-guidance-and-resources /lawful-basis/biometric-data-guidance-biometric-recognition/. [Accessed: 29 January 2025.]

14 'ICO intervention into AI recruitment tools leads to better data protection for job seekers', *ico.*, 6 November 2024. Available: https://ico.org.uk/about-the -ico/media-centre/news-and-blogs/2024/11/ico-intervention-into-ai-recruit ment-tools-leads-to-better-data-protection-for-job-seekers/. [Accessed: 29 January 2025.] and 'AI tools in recruitment: Audit outcomes report', *ico.*, pp. 6–9, November 2024. Available: https://ico.org.uk/media2/migrated/4031620 /ai-in-recruitment-outcomes-report.pdf. [Accessed: 30 January 2025.] and 'ICO Webinar: AI Tools in Recruitment', *ICO*, 22 January 2025. Available: https://vimeo.com/1049611515. [Accessed: 30 January 2025.]

15 'Online Safety Act, 2023 c. 50', 26 October 2023. Available: https://www.legis lation.gov.uk/ukpga/2023/50/contents. [Accessed: 29 January 2025.]

16 'AI Management Essentials tool', *GOV.UK*, 29 January 2025. Available: https:// www.gov.uk/government/consultations/ai-management-essentials-tool. [Accessed: 29 January 2025.]

17 'The Bletchley Declaration by Countries Attending the AI Safety Summit, 1–2 November 2023', *GOV.UK*, 1 November 2023. Available: https://www.gov.uk /government/publications/ai-safety-summit-2023-the-bletchley-declaration /the-bletchley-declaration-by-countries-attending-the-ai-safety-summit-1-2 -november-2023. [Accessed: 29 January 2025.]

18 'UK government sets out AI Safety Summit ambitions', *GOV.UK*, 4 September 2023. Available: https://www.gov.uk/government/news/uk-government-sets -out-ai-safety-summit-ambitions. [Accessed: 21 January 2025.]

19 Kyle, P., 'UK to bring global AI developers together ahead of AI Action Summit', *GOV.UK*, 19 September 2024. Available: https://www.gov.uk/govern ment/news/uk-to-bring-global-ai-developers-together-ahead-of-ai-action -summit. [Accessed: 30 January 2025.]

20 'Pre-Deployment Evaluation of Anthropic's Upgraded Claude 3.5 Sonnet', *AISI*, 19 November 2024. Available: https://www.aisi.gov.uk/work/pre-deploy ment-evaluation-of-anthropics-upgraded-claude-3-5-sonnet. [Accessed: 30 January 2025.]

21 Kyle, P., 'Tackling AI security risks to unleash growth and deliver Plan for Change', *GOV.UK*, 14 February 2025. Available: https://www.gov.uk/govern ment/news/tackling-ai-security-risks-to-unleash-growth-and-deliver-plan -for-change. [Accessed: 18 March 2025.]

22 'First International AI Safety Report to inform discussions at AI Action Summit', *GOV.UK*, 29 January 2025. Available: https://www.gov.uk/government /news/first-international-ai-safety-report-to-inform-discussions-at-ai-action -summit. [Accessed: 30 January 2025.] and Privitera, D. et al., 'International AI Safety Report: The International Scientific Report on the Safety of Advanced AI', *AI Action Summit*, DSIT 2025/001, January 2025. Available: https://assets .publishing.service.gov.uk/media/679a0c48a77d250007d313ee/International _AI_Safety_Report_2025_accessible_f.pdf. [Accessed: 30 January 2025.]

23 'An Act to enact the Consumer Privacy Protection Act, the Personal Information and Data Protection Tribunal Act and the Artificial Intelligence and Data Act and to make consequential and related amendments to other Acts, C-27', 16 June 2022. Available: https://www.parl.ca/DocumentViewer/en/44-1/bill/C-27 /first-reading. [Accessed: 29 January 2025.] and Beardwood, J., 'The Canadian AIDA and the EU AI Act: Will sanity prevail as they more closely align? – Part 1', *Computer Law Review International*, vol. 4, pp. 97–104, 2 October 2024. Available: https://doi.org/10.9785/cri-2024-250401. [Accessed: 21 January 2025.]

24 ibid.

25 'The Artificial Intelligence and Data Act (AIDA) – Companion document', *Government of Canada*, 23 January 2025. Available: https://ised-isde.canada .ca/site/innovation-better-canada/en/artificial-intelligence-and-data-act-aida -companion-document. [Accessed: 29 January 2025.] and Handa, S. et al., 'Digital Policy Issues Face Uncertain Future After Prorogation of Parliament',

JDSupra, 28 January 2025. Available: https://www.jdsupra.com/legalnews/ digital-policy-issues-face-uncertain-5421810/. [Accessed: 29 January 2025.]

26 'Directive on Automated Decision-Making', *Government of Canada*, 4 March 2019. Available: https://www.tbs-sct.canada.ca/pol/doc-eng.aspx?id=32592. [Accessed: 29 January 2025.] and 'Guide on the Scope of the Directive on Automated Decision-Making', *Treasury Board of Canada Secretariat*, 24 June 2024. Available: https://publications.gc.ca/collections/collection_2024/sct-tbs /BT48-46-2024-eng.pdf. [Accessed: 29 January 2025.]

27 'Voluntary Code of Conduct on the Responsible Development and Management of Advanced Generative AI Systems', *Government of Canada*, September 2023. Available: https://ised-isde.canada.ca/site/ised/en/voluntary -code-conduct-responsible-development-and-management-advanced -generative-ai-systems. [Accessed: 30 January 2025.]

28 'Implementation guide for managers of Artificial intelligence systems', *Government of Canada*, 6 March 2025. Available: https://ised-isde.canada.ca /site/ised/en/implementation-guide-managers-artificial-intelligence-systems. [Accessed: 18 March 2025.]

29 'Advisory Council on Artificial Intelligence', *Government of Canada*, 7 March 2025. Available: https://ised-isde.canada.ca/site/advisory-council-artifi cial-intelligence/en. [Accessed 18 March 2025.] and Innovation, Science and Economic Development Canada. 'Safe and Secure AI Advisory Group', *Government of Canada*, 6 March 2025. Available: https://ised-isde.canada.ca /site/advisory-council-artificial-intelligence/en/safe-and-secure-ai-advisory -group. [Accessed: 18 March 2025.]

30 'Draft Guideline E-23 – Model Risk Management', *Office of the Superintendent of Financial Institutions Canada*, 30 September 2017. Available: https://www .osfi-bsif.gc.ca/en/guidance/guidance-library/draft-guideline-e-23-model -risk-management. [Accessed: 29 January 2025.]

31 'Personal Information Protection and Electronic Documents Act, S.C. 2000 c. 5', 13 April 2000. Available: https://laws-lois.justice.gc.ca/eng/acts/P-8.6/index .html. [Accessed: 29 January 2025.]

32 Morgan, C.S., Ing, C. and Langlois, F., 'AI Watch: Global regulatory tracker – Canada', *White & Case*, 16 December 2024. Available: https://www.whitecase .com/insight-our-thinking/ai-watch-global-regulatory-tracker-canada. [Accessed: 29 January 2025.]

33 'Joint investigation of Clearview AI, Inc. by the Office of the Privacy Commissioner of Canada, the Commission d'accès à l'information du Québec, the Information and Privacy Commissioner for British Columbia, and the Information Privacy Commissioner of Alberta', *PIPEDA* Findings #2021-001, ¶¶ 6–8, 2 February 2021. Available: https://www.priv.gc.ca/en/opc-actions -and-decisions/investigations/investigations-into-businesses/2021/pipeda -2021-001/. [Accessed: 29 January 2025.]

34 ibid. ¶ 114.

35 ibid. ¶¶ 118–120.

36 ibid. ¶ 121.

37 'OPC to investigate ChatGPT jointly with provincial privacy authorities', *Office of the Privacy Commissioner of Canada*, 25 May 2023. Available: https://www.priv.gc.ca/en/opc-news/news-and-announcements/2023/an_230525-2/. [Accessed: 29 January 2025.]

38 'Office of the Privacy Commissioner of Canada Strategic Plan 2024-27: A roadmap for trust, innovation and protecting the fundamental right to privacy in the digital age', *Office of the Privacy Commissioner of Canada*, January 2024. Available: https://www.priv.gc.ca/media/6112/strategic-plan-2024-27.pdf. [Accessed: 30 January 2025.]

39 'AI and Data Governance Standardization Collaborative', *Standards Council of Canada*, 3 May 2023. Available: https://scc-ccn.ca/areas-work/digital-technology/ai-and-data-governance-standardization-collaborative. [Accessed: 29 January 2025.]

40 Sheehan, M., 'China's AI Regulations and How They Get Made', *Carnegie Endowment for International Peace*, 10 July 2023. Available: https://carnegie-production-assets.s3.amazonaws.com/static/files/202307-Sheehan_Chinese%20AI%20gov-1.pdf. [Accessed: 29 January 2025.] and Ding, J., 'Deciphering China's AI Dream: The context, components, capabilities, and consequences of China's strategy to lead the world in AI', *Center for the Governance of AI, Future of Humanity Institute, University of Oxford*, March 2018. Available: https://www.fhi.ox.ac.uk/wp-content/uploads/Deciphering_Chinas_AI-Dream.pdf. [Accessed: 29 January 2025.]

41 Kroeber, A., 'Unleashing "new quality productive forces": China's strategy for technology-led growth', *Brookings*, 4 June 2024. Available: https://www.brookings.edu/articles/unleashing-new-quality-productive-forces-chinas-strategy-for-technology-led-growth/. [Accessed: 29 January 2025.]

42 Sheehan, M., 'China's AI Regulations and How They Get Made', *Carnegie Endowment for International Peace*, p. 16, 10 July 2023. Available: https://carnegie-production-assets.s3.amazonaws.com/static/files/202307-Sheehan_Chinese%20AI%20gov-1.pdf. [Accessed: 29 January 2025.] and Cheng, D. and McKernon, E., '2024 State of the AI Regulatory Landscape', *Convergence Analysis*, pp. 8, 11–12, May 2024. Available: https://www.convergenceanalysis.org/ai-regulatory-landscape/home. [Accessed: 29 January 2025.]

43 Cheng, D. and McKernon, E., '2024 State of the AI Regulatory Landscape', *Convergence Analysis*, pp. 8, 11–12, May 2024. Available: https://www.convergenceanalysis.org/ai-regulatory-landscape/home. [Accessed: 29 January 2025.] and 'Measures for AI Meteorological Application Services of China promulgated', *World Meteorological Organization*, 30 April 2025. Available: https://wmo.int/media/news-from-members/

measures-ai-meteorological-application-services-of-china-promulgated. [Accessed: 6 June 2025.]

44 Daniels, O.J. 'CSET Analyses of China's Technology Policies and Ecosystem', *Center for Security and Emerging Technology*, September 2023. Available: https://cset.georgetown.edu/wp-content/uploads/20230035_The-PRCs -Domestic-Approach.pdf. [Accessed: 29 January 2025.]

45 Sheehan, M., 'China's AI Regulations and How They Get Made', *Carnegie Endowment for International Peace*, p. 16, 10 July 2023. Available: https:// carnegie-production-assets.s3.amazonaws.com/static/files/202307- Sheehan_Chinese%20AI%20gov-1.pdf. [Accessed: 29 January 2025.]

46 ibid. p. 4.

47 ibid. p. 12.

48 ibid. p. 11.

49 Cheng, D. and McKernon, E., '2024 State of the AI Regulatory Landscape', *Convergence Analysis*, p. 22, May 2024. Available: https://www. convergenceanalysis.org/ai-regulatory-landscape/home. [Accessed: 29 January 2025.]

50 Huang, S. et al., 'Translation: Measures for the Management of Generative Artificial Intelligence Services (Draft for Comment) – April 2023', *DigiChina*, 12 April 2023. Available: https://digichina.stanford.edu/work/translation -measures-for-the-management-of-generative-artificial-intelligence-services -draft-for-comment-april-2023/. [Accessed: 30 January 2025.]

51 Li, B. and Zhou, A., 'Navigating the Complexities of AI Regulation in China', *Reed Smith*, 7 August 2024. Available: https://www.reedsmith.com/en/ perspectives/2024/08/navigating-the-complexities-of-ai-regulation-in-china. [Accessed: 29 January 2025.]

52 Wong, E., 'China mandates labels for all AI-generated content in fresh push against fraud, fake news', *South China Morning Post*, 15 March 2025. Available: https://www.scmp.com/news/china/politics/article/3302477/china-mandates -labels-all-ai-generated-content-fresh-push-against-fraud-fake-news. [Accessed: 18 March 2025.]

53 Interesse, G., 'China Releases New Draft Regulations for Generative AI', *China Briefing*, 30 May 2024. Available: https://www.china-briefing.com/news/china -releases-new-draft-regulations-on-generative-ai/. [Accessed: 30 January 2025.]

54 Xu, H., Lee, B. and Li, Z., 'China Clarifies Privacy and Data Security Requirements in Network Data Security Management Regulations', *Latham & Watkins*, 16 January 2025. Available: https://www.lw.com/admin/upload/SiteAttachments /China-Clarifies-Privacy-and-Data-Security-Requirements-in-Network-Data -Security-Management-Regulations.pdf. [Accessed: 30 January 2025.]

55 Creemers, R., Webster, G. and Toner, H., 'Translation: Internet Information Service Algorithmic Recommendation Management Provisions – Effective March 1, 2022', *DigiChina*, 10 January 2022. Available: https://digichina

.stanford.edu/work/translation-internet-information-service-algorith
mic-recommendation-management-provisions-effective-march-1-2022/.
[Accessed: 30 January 2025.]

56 Li, B. and Zhou, A., 'Navigating the Complexities of AI Regulation in China', *Reed Smith*, 7 August 2024. Available: https://www.reedsmith.com/en/ perspectives/2024/08/navigating-the-complexities-of-ai-regulation-in-china. [Accessed: 29 January 2025.]

57 'China: Published CAC Domestic Generative AI Services Filing List', *Digital Policy Alert*, 31 December 2024. Available: https://digitalpolicyalert.org/event /25904-adopted-chinese-cyberspace-administration-registration-of-genera tive-ai-services. [Accessed: 30 January 2025.]

58 'AI White Paper 2024: New Strategies in Stage II: Toward the world's most AI-friendly country', *Masaaki Taira*, p. 4, 11 April 2024. Available: https:// www.taira-m.jp/AI%20White%20Paper%202024.pdf. [Accessed: 29 January 2025.]

59 Andrews, C., 'Japan passes innovation-focused AI governance bill', *IAPP*, 4 June 2025. Available: https://iapp.org/news/a/japan-passes-innovation-focused-ai-governance-bill. [Accessed: 6 June 2025.]

60 'AI Guidelines for Business Ver1.0', *Ministry of Internal Affairs and Communications and Ministry of Economy, Trade and Industry*, 19 April 2024. Available: https://www.meti.go.jp/shingikai/mono_info_service/ai_shakai_ jisso/pdf/20240419_9.pdf. [Accessed: 29 January 2025.]

61 ibid. pp. 45, 148.

62 'AI Governance in Japan Ver. 1.1', *Ministry of Internal Affairs and Communications and Ministry of Economy, Trade and Industry*, 9 July 2021. Available: https://www.meti.go.jp/shingikai/mono_info_service/ai_shakai _jisso/pdf/20210709_8.pdf. [Accessed: 30 January 2025.]

63 Habuka, H., 'New Government Policy Shows Japan Favors a Light Touch for AI Regulation,' *Center for Strategic & International Studies*, 25 February 2025. Available: https://www.csis.org/analysis/new-government-policy-shows -japan-favors-light-touch-ai-regulation. [Accessed: 18 March 2025.]

64 Habuka, H. 'Japan's Approach to AI Regulation and Its Impact on the 2023 G7 Presidency', *Center for Strategic & International Studies*, p. 3, February 2023. Available: https://csis-website-prod.s3.amazonaws.com/s3fs-public/2023-02 /230214_Habuka_Japan_AIRegulations.pdf?VersionId=BnLSQRRqoO9jQ8u 1RW3SGKOAoi8DBc4Q. [Accessed: 30 January 2025.]

65 'Generative AI and Competition (Discussion Paper)', *Japan Fair Trade Commission*, October 2024. Available: https://www.jftc.go.jp/file/241002Discu ssionPaperEN.pdf. [Accessed: 30 January 2025.]

66 Albagli, D., Dokei, T. and Mitchell, A.M., 'AI Watch: Global regulatory tracker – Japan', *White & Case*, 1 July 2024. Available: https://www.whitecase.com/

insight-our-thinking/ai-watch-global-regulatory-tracker-japan. [Accessed: 29 January 2025.]

67 Cesareo, S. and White, J., 'The Global AI Index', *Tortoise Media*, 19 September 2024. Available: https://www.tortoisemedia.com/intelligence/global-ai/. [Accessed: 29 January 2025.]

68 Goode, K., Kim, H.M. and Deng, M., 'Examining Singapore's AI Progress', *Center for Security and Emerging Technology*, p. 17, March 2023. Available: https://cset.georgetown.edu/publication/examining-singapores-ai-progress/. [Accessed: 29 January 2025.]

69 'Model Artificial Intelligence Governance Framework: Second Edition', *Personal Data Protection Commission Singapore*, 21 January 2020. Available: https://www.pdpc.gov.sg/-/media/Files/PDPC/PDF-Files/Resource-for -Organisation/AI/SGModelAIGovFramework2.pdf. [Accessed: 30 January 2025.] and Olier, J., Seow, T.-Y. and Lim, V., 'AI Watch: Global regulatory tracker – Singapore', *White & Case*, 13 May 2024. Available: https://www .whitecase.com/insight-our-thinking/ai-watch-global-regulatory-tracker -singapore. [Accessed: 21 January 2025.]

70 Min, K., 'The United Korean AI Act Bill: Contents in Comparison with the EU AI Act (with English Translation of the Bill)', *LinkedIn*, 11 December 2024. Available: https://www.linkedin.com/pulse/united-korean-ai-act-bill -contents-comparison-eu-english-min-h98kc/. [Accessed: 30 January 2025.]

71 'Korea's Won? South Korea's AI Basic Act: Asia's first comprehensive AI legis lation', *Linklaters*, 31 December 2024. Available: https://techinsights.linklaters .com/post/102js56/koreas-wonsouth-koreas-ai-basic-act-asias-first-compre hensive-ai-legislatio. [Accessed 30 January 2025.]

72 'Republic of Korea: Communications Commission issued Guidelines for the Protection of Users of Generative Artificial Intelligence Services including data protection measures', *Digital Policy Alert*, 28 February 2025. Available: https:// digitalpolicyalert.org/event/27787-guidelines-for-the-protection-of-users-of -generative-artificial-intelligence-services-including-data-protection-measures -was-adopted-by-communications-commission. [Accessed: 18 March 2025.]

73 Ramage, T., 'Timeline of the South Korean Government's AI Efforts', *Korea Economic Institute of America*, 2 October 2024. Available: https://keia.org/the -peninsula/timeline-of-the-south-korean-governments-ai-efforts/. [Accessed: 29 January 2025.]

74 Lee, D., 'AI Watch: Global regulatory tracker – South Korea', *White & Case*, 18 June 2024. Available: https://www.whitecase.com/insight-our-thinking/ai -watch-global-regulatory-tracker-south-korea. [Accessed: 29 January 2025.]

75 Gribble, B., 'South Korea Rules for Use of Personal Data in AI', *Ground Labs*, 11 August 2023. Available: https://www.groundlabs.com/blog/south-korea -safe-use-of-personal-information-in-ai/. [Accessed: 29 January 2025.]

76 Ramage, T., 'Timeline of the South Korean Government's AI Efforts', *Korea Economic Institute of America*, 2 October 2024. Available: https://keia.org/the-peninsula/timeline-of-the-south-korean-governments-ai-efforts/. [Accessed: 29 January 2025.] and 'The Singapore Consensus on Global AI Safety Research Priorities', 8 May 2025. Available: https://aisafetypriorities.org/. [Accessed: 6 June 2025.]

77 ibid.

78 Ramage, T., 'Korea is Having its AI Moment', *Korea Economic Institute of America*, 22 April 2024. Available: https://keia.org/the-peninsula/korea-is-having-its-ai-moment/. [Accessed: 29 January 2025.]

79 Mohanty, A. and Sahu, S., 'India's Advance on AI Regulation', *Carnegie Endowment for International Peace*, 21 November 2024. Available: https://carnegieendowment.org/research/2024/11/indias-advance-on-ai-regulation?lang=en. [Accessed: 6 June 2025.] and Mohanty, A. and Sahu, S., 'India's AI Strategy: Balancing Risk and Opportunity', *Carnegie Endowment for International Peace*, 22 February 2024. Available: https://carnegieendowment.org/posts/2024/02/indias-ai-strategy-balancing-risk-and-opportunity?lang=enn. [Accessed: 6 June 2025.]

80 'Advisory No.2(4)/2023-CyberLaws–3', *Government of India Ministry of Electronics and Information Technology*, 1 March 2024. Available: https://regmedia.co.uk/2024/03/04/meity_ai_advisory_1_march.pdf. [Accessed: 6 June 2025.]

81 Mohanty, A. and Sahu, S., 'India's Advance on AI Regulation', *Carnegie Endowment for International Peace*, 21 November 2024. Available: https://carnegieendowment.org/research/2024/11/indias-advance-on-ai-regulation?lang=en. [Accessed: 6 June 2025.] and 'Advisory No.2(4)/2023-CyberLaws–3', *Government of India Ministry of Electronics and Information Technology*, 15 March 2024. Available: https://www.meity.gov.in/static/uploads/2024/02/9f6e99572739a3024c9cdaec53a0a0ef.pdf. [Accessed: 6 June 2025.]

82 'United States-India Joint Leaders' Statement', 13 February 2025. Available: https://www.whitehouse.gov/briefings-statements/2025/02/united-states-india-joint-leaders-statement/. [Accessed: 6 June 2025.]

83 Maffioli, D.R., 'AI regulation in Latin America: Balancing global trends with local realities', *IAPP*, 13 December 2023. Available: https://iapp.org/news/a/ai-regulation-in-latin-america-balancing-global-trends-with-local-realities. [Accessed: 29 January 2025.]

84 Muschett, M. and Opp, R., 'The AI Revolution is Here: How Will Latin America and the Caribbean Respond?', *UN Development Programme*, 1 March 2024. Available: https://www.undp.org/latin-america/blog/ai-revolution-here-how-will-latin-america-and-caribbean-respond. [Accessed: 29 January 2025.] and 'Seizing the opportunity: The future of AI in Latin America', *Economist Impact*,

p. 5, 23 May 2022. Available: https://impact.economist.com/perspectives/sites/default/files/seizing-the-opportunity-the-future-of-ai-in-latin-america.pdf. [Accessed: 29 January 2025.]

85   'Productivity, Digitalization, and Artificial Intelligence in Peru', *Peru: Selected Issues*, vol. 2024, issue 134, 21 May 2024. Available: https://www.elibrary.imf.org/view/journals/002/2024/134/article-A003-en.xml. [Accessed: 30 January 2024.]

86   'Digital Trust Framework, approved by Urgent Decree N° 007-2020', *OECD.AI*, July 2023. Available: https://doi.org/10.1787/29f32e64-en. [Accessed: 30 January 2025.]

87   'Digital Government Review of Latin America and the Caribbean', *OECD Digital Government Studies*, p. 119, 8 September 2023. Available: https://www.oecd.org/en/publications/digital-government-review-of-latin-america-and-the-caribbean_29f32e64-en.html. [Accessed: 7 July 2025.]

88   Escobedo, C., 'IAPP Global Legislative Predictions: Peru', *IAPP*, January 2025. Available: https://iapp.org/resources/article/global-legislative-predictions/. [Accessed: 30 January 2025.]

89   ibid.

90   'Peru: Drafted Regulation of Law no. 31814 promoting the use of AI for the economic and social development of the country including data protection regulation', *Digital Policy Alert*, 6 December 2024. Available: https://digitalpolicyalert.org/event/19625-drafted-regulation-of-law-promoting-the-use-of-artificial-intelligence-for-the-economic-and-social-development-of-peru-no-31814-including-data-protection-regulation. [Accessed: 30 January 2025.]

91   'Brazil AI Act', *Artificial Intelligence Act*, 19 December 2024. Available: https://artificialintelligenceact.com/brazil-ai-act/. [Accessed: 30 January 2025.]

92   Grohmann, R. et al., 'Brazil Case', *University of Essex*. Available: https://www.essex.ac.uk/research-projects/ai-policy-observatory-for-the-world-of-work/national-and-regional-cases/brazil. [Accessed: 29 January 2025.]

93   ibid.

94   'OBIA, the Brazilian AI Observatory', *Índice Latinoamericano de Inteligencia Artificial*, 4 November 2024. Available: https://indicelatam.cl/obia-the-brazilian-ai-observatory/. [Accessed 30 January 2025.]

95   'AI in Colombia', *OECD.AI*, 26 September 2024. Available: https://oecd.ai/en/dashboards/countries/Colombia. [Accessed: 30 January 2025.] and 'National AI policies & strategies', *OECD.AI*, 19 December 2024. Available: https://oecd.ai/en/dashboards. [Accessed: 30 January 2025.]

96   'Artificial Intelligence: Latin America's Regulatory and Policy Environment', *Edelman Global Advisory*, p. 6, 4 March 2024. Available: https://www.edelmanglobaladvisory.com/sites/g/files/aatuss676/files/2024-03/EGA%20LATAM_AI%20Policy%20in%20Latin%20America_4Mar2024_0.pdf. [Accessed: 30 January 2025.]

97 'ODATA Announces $1.3B Expansion in Colombia, Boosting Digital Development in the Country', *ODATA*, 23 October 2024. Available: https://odatacolocation.com/en/blog/imprensa/odata-announces-1-3b-expansion-in-colombia-boosting-digital-development-in-the-country/. [Accessed: 29 January 2025.]

98 'UNESCO and Colombia: Leaders in the Ethical and Responsible Use of AI in the Judiciary', *UNESCO*, 10 October 2024. Available: https://www.unesco.org/en/articles/unesco-and-colombia-leaders-ethical-and-responsible-use-ai-judiciary. [Accessed: 30 January 2025.]

99 del Pozo, C. and Rojas Arroyo, D., 'Mexico's Bet on Artificial Intelligence', *Wilson Center*, 6 September 2024. Available: https://www.wilsoncenter.org/blog-post/mexicos-bet-artificial-intelligence. [Accessed: 29 January 2025.]

100 'Foster innovation or mitigate risk? AI regulation in Latin America', *White & Case*, 18 November 2024. Available: https://www.whitecase.com/insight-our-thinking/latin-america-focus-2024-ai-regulation. [Accessed: 30 January 2025.]

101 'ANIA – Alianza Nacional Inteligencia Artificial Positiva para Mexico', *Ania MX*. Available: https://www.ania.org.mx. [Accessed: 29 January 2025.]

102 'Plan Nacional de Inteligencia Artificial', *OECD*, February 2021. Available: https://oecd-opsi.org/wp-content/uploads/2021/02/Argentina-National-AI-Strategy.pdf. [Accessed: 30 January 2025.]

103 'Artificial Intelligence: Latin America's Regulatory and Policy Environment', *Edelman Global Advisory*, p. 3, 4 March 2024. Available: https://www.edelmanglobaladvisory.com/sites/g/files/aatuss676/files/2024-03/EGA%20LATAM_AI%20Policy%20in%20Latin%20America_4Mar2024_0.pdf. [Accessed: 29 January 2025.]

104 Nugent, G., 'Jet-setting Argentine President Javier Milei courts top US tech CEOs', *Financial Times*, 28 May 2024. Available: https://www.ft.com/content/4ab30d78-aafc-47cc-8a4b-17f9a6f43bed. [Accessed: 29 January 2025.]

105 Barber, H., 'Argentina will use AI to "predict future crimes" but experts worry for citizens' rights', *Guardian*, 1 August 2024. Available: https://www.theguardian.com/world/article/2024/aug/01/argentina-ai-predicting-future-crimes-citizen-rights. [Accessed: 30 January 2025.]

106 'Índice Latinoamericano de Inteligencia Artificial', *Economic Commission for Latin America and the Caribbean*, 24 September 2024. Available: https://www.cepal.org/en/notes/ilia-2024-evaluating-ai-readiness-and-progress-latin-america. [Accessed: 29 January 2025.]

107 ibid. pp. 218–221 and Quigley, B., 'Humboldt route to connect Chile, French Polynesia, and Australia', *Google Cloud Blog*, 11 January 2024. Available: https://cloud.google.com/blog/products/infrastructure/announcing-humboldt-the-first-cable-route-between-south-america-and-asia-pacific. [Accessed: 29 January 2025.]

108 'Índice Latinoamericano de Inteligencia Artificial', *Economic Commission for Latin America and the Caribbean and the National Center for Artificial Intelligence of Chile*, p. 213, 24 September 2024. Available: https://www.cepal.org/en/notes/ilia-2024-evaluating-ai-readiness-and-progress-latin-america. [Accessed: 23 March 2025.]

109 ibid.

110 'Regulates Artificial Intelligence Systems, Bill 16821-19', 7 May 2024. Available: https://www.camara.cl/verDoc.aspx?prmID=17048&prmTIPO=INICIATIVA. [Accessed: 30 January 2025.]

111 'Africa's Internet use doubles in decade despite high costs (report)', *Ecofin Agency ITC & Telecom*, 27 February 2024. Available: https://www.ecofinagency.com/telecom/2702-45230-africas-internet-use-doubles-in-decade-despite-high-costs-report. [Accessed: 29 January 2025.] and Boakye, B. et al., 'State of Compute Access: How to Bridge the New Digital Divide', *Tony Blair Institute for Global Change*, 7 December 2023. Available: https://institute.global/insights/tech-and-digitalisation/state-of-compute-access-how-to-bridge-the-new-digital-divide. [Accessed: 29 January 2025.]

112 Tsanni, A., 'Africa's push to regulate AI starts now', *MIT Technology Review*, 15 March 2024. Available: https://www.technologyreview.com/2024/03/15/1089844/africa-ai-artificial-intelligence-regulation-au-policy/. [Accessed: 29 January 2025.] and Tsanni, A., 'What Africa needs to do to become a major AI player', *MIT Tech Review*, 11 November 2024. Available: https://www.technologyreview.com/2024/11/11/1106762/africa-ai-barriers/. [Accessed: 30 January 2025.]

113 Onukwue, A., 'Nigeria begins AI push with Google-backed fund', *Semafor*, 12 September 2024. Available: https://www.semafor.com/article/09/12/2024/nigeria-begins-ai-push-with-google-backed-fund. [Accessed: 29 January 2025.]

114 Roberts, T. et al., 'Mapping the supply of surveillance technologies to Africa: Case studies from Nigeria, Ghana, Morocco, Malawi, and Zambia', *Institute of Development Studies*, September 2023. Available: https://opendocs.ids.ac.uk/articles/online_resource/Mapping_the_Supply_of_Surveillance_Technologies_to_Africa_Case_Studies_from_Nigeria_Ghana_Morocco_Malawi_and_Zambia/26431414. [Accessed: 29 January 2025.]

115 'Mauritius Artificial Intelligence Strategy', *Working Group on Artificial Intelligence*, November 2018. Available: https://ncb.govmu.org/ncb/strategicplans/MauritiusAIStrategy2018.pdf. [Accessed: 24 January 2025.]

116 Ogenga, F. and Stanley, A., 'Regulating Artificial Intelligence in Africa: Strategies and Insights from Kenya, Ghana, and the African Union', *Wilson Center*, 18 September 2024. Available: https://www.wilsoncenter.org/blog-post/regulating-artificial-intelligence-africa-strategies-and-insights-kenya-ghana-and-african. [Accessed: 29 January 2025.] and 'The Africa Declaration on Artificial Intelligence', *Global AI Summit on Africa*, 4 April 2025.

Available: https://c4ir.rw/docs/Africa%20Declaration%20on%20Artificial%20 Intelligences.pdf. [Accessed: 6 June 2025.]

117 'African Union Convention on Cyber Security and Personal Data Protection', *African Union*, 27 June 2014. Available: https://au.int/sites/default/files/trea ties/29560-treaty-0048_-_african_union_convention_on_cyber_security _and_personal_data_protection_e.pdf. [Accessed: 29 January 2025.]

118 'Continental Artificial Intelligence Strategy: Harnessing AI for Africa's Development and Prosperity', *African Union*, July 2024. Available: https://au .int/sites/default/files/documents/44004-doc-EN-_Continental_AI_Strategy _July_2024.pdf. [Accessed: 30 January 2025.]

119 'African Union committed to developing AI capabilities in Africa', *African Union*, 28 August 2024. Available: https://au.int/en/pressreleases/20240828 /african-union-committed-developing-ai-capabilities-africa. [Accessed: 29 January 2025.]

120 'FAIR Forward: Open data for AI', *digital. global*, 15 October 2024. Available: https://www.bmz-digital.global/en/overview-of-initiatives/fair-forward/. [Accessed: 29 January 2025.]

121 'FAIR Forward – Artificial Intelligence for All', *Federal Ministry for Economic Cooperation and Development*. Available: https://www.bmz.de/en/issues/ digital-transformation/digital-public-goods-and-infrastructure/fair-forward -215860. [Accessed: 29 January 2025.]

122 'FAIR Forward: Open data for AI', *digital. global*, 15 October 2024. Available: https://www.bmz-digital.global/en/overview-of-initiatives/fair-forward/. [Accessed: 29 January 2025.] and Sedola, S., Pescino, A.J. and Greene, T., 'Artificial Intelligence for Africa Blueprint', *Smart Africa*, 2021. Available: https://www.bmz-digital.global/wp-content/uploads/2022/08/70029-eng_ai -for-africa-blueprint.pdf. [Accessed: 21 January 2025.]

123 'Draft National Artificial Intelligence Strategy 2024', *National Center for Artificial Intelligence & Robotics, National Information Technology Development Agency*, August 2024. Available: https://ncair.nitda.gov.ng/wp-content/ uploads/2024/08/National-AI-Strategy_01082024-copy.pdf. [Accessed: 30 January 2025.]

124 '3 Million Technical Talent (3MTT) Programme', *Nigerian Federal Ministry of Communications, Innovation & Digital Economy*, 13 October 2023. Available: https://3mtt.nitda.gov.ng/. [Accessed: 30 January 2025.]

125 Tijani, B., 'Nigeria seeks digital transformation for a stronger economy', *World Economic Forum*, 18 September 2024. Available: https://www.weforum .org/stories/2024/09/nigeria-digital-transformation-3mtt-technical-talent/. [Accessed: 30 January 2025.]

126 '3 Million Technical Talent (3MTT) Programme', *Nigerian Federal Ministry of Communications, Innovation & Digital Economy*, 13 October 2023. Available: https://3mtt.nitda.gov.ng/. [Accessed: 30 January 2025.]

127 Musambi, E., 'Facebook loses jurisdiction appeal in Kenyan court paving the way for moderators' case to proceed', *AP News*, 20 September 2024. Available: https://apnews.com/article/kenya-facebook-case-meta-moderators-7a62699 c52549355917eda1e5be8f75e. [Accessed: 30 January 2025.]

128 Hickman, T. et al., 'AI Watch: Global regulatory tracker – Kenya', *White & Case*, 20 June 2024. Available: https://www.whitecase.com/insight-our-thinking/ai -watch-global-regulatory-tracker-kenya. [Accessed 30 January 2025.]

129 ibid.

130 Ramjee, D. and Bernstein, D., 'AI Watch: Global regulatory tracker – South Africa', *White & Case*, 2 July 2024. Available: https://www.whitecase.com /insight-our-thinking/ai-watch-global-regulatory-tracker-south-africa. [Accessed: 30 January 2025.]

131 'Summary Report and Recommendations', *Commission on the Fourth Industrial Revolution*, January 2020. Available: https://www.ellipsis.co.za/wp -content/uploads/2020/10/201023-Report-of-the-Presidential-Commission -on-the-Fourth-Industrial-Revolution.pdf. [Accessed: 30 January 2025.]

132 'AI National Government Summit Discussion Document – South Africa's Artificial Intelligence (AI) Planning', *Department of Communications and Digital Technologies*, pp. 14–15, 37, 40–46, October 2023. Available: https:// www.dcdt.gov.za/images/phocadownload/AI_Government_Summit/National _AI_Government_Summit_Discussion_Document.pdf. [Accessed: 30 January 2025.]

133 ibid. pp. 28-29.

134 'South Africa National Artificial Intelligence Policy Framework (Towards the Development of South Africa National Artificial Intelligence Policy)', *Department of Communications and Digital Technologies,* August 2024. Available: https://www.michalsons.com/wp-content/uploads/2024/09/South -Africa-National-AI-Policy-Framework.pdf. [Accessed: 30 January 2025.]

135 ibid. pp. 9-11.

136 Farrell, M.G. and Copeland, R., 'Saudi Arabia Plans $40 Billion Push Into Artificial Intelligence', *New York Times*, 19 March 2024. Available: https://www .nytimes.com/2024/03/19/business/saudi-arabia-investment-artificial-intelli gence.html. [Accessed: 30 January 2024.]

137 Newman, M. et al., 'Saudis Plan $100 Billion AI Powerhouse to Rival UAE Tech Hub', *Bloomberg*, 7 November 2024. Available: https://www.bloomberg .com/news/articles/2024-11-06/saudis-plan-100-billion-ai-powerhouse-to -rival-uae-s-tech-hub. [Accessed: 30 January 2025.]

138 Kwok, K., 'Gulf's AI strategy is built on more than sand', *Reuters*, 13 November 2024. Available: https://www.reuters.com/breakingviews/gulfs-ai-strategy-is -built-more-than-sand-2024-11-13/. [Accessed: 30 January 2025.]

139 Lewis, N. and Bendimerad, R., 'Why these Gulf states want to be AI superpowers', *CNN*, 16 September 2024. Available: https://www.cnn.com

/2024/09/16/middleeast/middle-east-artificial-intelligence-spc/index.html. [Accessed: 30 January 2025.]

140 Kwok, K., 'Gulf's AI strategy is built on more than sand', *Reuters*, 13 November 2024. Available: https://www.reuters.com/breakingviews/gulfs-ai-strategy-is -built-more-than-sand-2024-11-13/. [Accessed: 30 January 2025.]

141 Bergen, M., 'UAE Releases New Falcon AI Model to Challenge Meta, OpenAI', *Bloomberg*, 13 May 2024. Available: https://www.bloomberg.com/news/ articles/2024-05-13/uae-releases-new-falcon-ai-model-11b-to-rival-meta-s -llama-openai-and-google. [Accessed: 21 March 2025.]

142 Mrozinski, S., 'AI Watch: Global regulatory tracker – United Arab Emirates', *White & Case*, 18 October 2024. Available: https://www.whitecase.com/insight -our-thinking/ai-watch-global-regulatory-tracker-uae. [Accessed: 30 January 2024.]

143 Li, Y., 'Sam Altman: Go all in on AI – the thing that matters in the next decade', *Wired*, 7 June 2023. Available: https://wired.me/technology/sam-altman-all -in-on-ai/. [Accessed 30 January 2025.]

144 'AI will be "transformational", say professionals in Middle East & North Africa', *Thomson Reuters*, 28 May 2024. Available: https://insight.thomsonreuters.com /mena/legal/posts/ai-will-be-transformational-middle-east-north-africa. [Accessed: 30 January 2025.] and Hofverberg, E., 'FALQs: AI Regulations in the Gulf Cooperation Council Member States – Part One', *Library of Congress Blogs: In Custodia Legis*, 17 December 2024. Available: https://blogs.loc.gov /law/2024/12/falqs-ai-regulations-in-the-gulf-cooperation-council-member -states-part-one/. [Accessed: 18 March 2025.]

145 Hofverberg, E., 'FALQs: AI Regulations in the Gulf Cooperation Council Member States – Part One', *Library of Congress*, 17 December 2024. Available: https://blogs.loc.gov/law/2024/12/falqs-ai-regulations-in-the-gulf-coopera tion-council-member-states-part-one. [Accessed: 30 January 2025.]

146 ibid.

147 ibid.

148 Butt, R., 'AI Watch: Global regulatory tracker – Saudi Arabia', *White & Case*, 20 June 2024. Available: https://www.whitecase.com/insight-our-thinking/ai -watch-global-regulatory-tracker-saudi-arabia. [Accessed: 24 January 2025.]

149 'Generative Artificial Intelligence Guidelines for Government', *Saudi Data & AI Authority*, 1 January 2024. Available: https://sdaia.gov.sa/en/SDAIA/about /Files/GenAIGuidelinesForGovernmentENCompressed.pdf. [Accessed: 30 January 2025.]

150 'SDAIA Launches AI Framework to Promote Ethical, Responsible Use of Advanced Technologies in Saudi Arabia', *Saudi Press Agency*, 1 December 2024. Available: https://spa.gov.sa/N2217019. [Accessed: 21 March 2025.]

151 Hofverberg, E., 'FALQs: AI Regulations in the Gulf Cooperation Council Member States – Part One', *The Library of Congress*, 17 December 2024.

Available: https://blogs.loc.gov/law/2024/12/falqs-ai-regulations-in-the-gulf-cooperation-council-member-states-part-one. [Accessed: 30 January 2025.]

152 ibid.

153 '100 Practical Applications and Use Cases of Generative AI', *United Arab Emirates Minister of State for Artificial Intelligence, Digital Economy & Remote Work Applications Office*, April 2023. Available: https://ai.gov.ae/wp-content/uploads/2023/04/406.-Generative-AI-Guide_ver1-EN.pdf. [Accessed: 21 March 2025.]

154 Mrozinski, S., 'AI Watch: Global regulatory tracker – United Arab Emirates', *White & Case*, 18 October 2024. Available: https://www.whitecase.com/insight-our-thinking/ai-watch-global-regulatory-tracker-uae. [Accessed: 21 March 2025.]

155 Hofverberg, E., 'FALQs: AI Regulations in the Gulf Cooperation Council Member States – Part One', *Library of Congress*, 17 December 2024. Available: https://blogs.loc.gov/law/2024/12/falqs-ai-regulations-in-the-gulf-cooperation-council-member-states-part-one. [Accessed: 30 January 2025.]

156 'AI Watch: Global regulatory tracker – United Arab Emirates', *White & Case,* 18 October 2024. Available: https://www.whitecase.com/insight-our-thinking/ai-watch-global-regulatory-tracker-uae. [Accessed: 31 January 2025.] and Warner, K., 'Why the UAE has mandated AI learning in schools', *Semafor,* 7 May 2025. Available: https://www.semafor.com/article/05/07/2025/why-the-uae-has-mandated-ai-learning-in-schools. [Accessed: 7 June 2025.]

157 Combs, C., 'UAE selected for Hiroshima AI Process Friends Group', *National News,* 7 May 2024. Available: https://www.thenationalnews.com/future/technology/2024/05/07/uae-selected-for-hiroshima-ai-process-friends-group/. [Accessed: 30 January 2025.]

158 'UAE Position on AI Policy', *United Arab Emirates Minister of State for Artificial Intelligence, Digital Economy & Remote Work Applications Office and United Arab Emirates Ministry of Foreign Affairs,* September 2024. Available: https://ai.gov.ae/wp-content/uploads/2024/10/UAE-Guiding-on-ai-policy-EN-V3.pdf. [Accessed: 21 March 2025.]

159 Sullivan, J. and Al Nahyan, T. bin Z., 'United States and United Arab Emirates Cooperation on Artificial Intelligence', *The White House,* 23 September 2024. Available: https://web.archive.org/web/20250116072515/https://www.whitehouse.gov/briefing-room/statements-releases/2024/09/23/united-states-and-united-arab-emirates-cooperation-on-artificial-intelligence/. [Accessed: 30 January 2025.] and 'UAE/US Framework on Advanced Technology Cooperation', *US Department of Commerce,* 15 May 2025. Available: https://www.commerce.gov/news/press-releases/2025/05/uae/us-framework-advanced-technology-cooperation. [Accessed: 7 June 2025.]

160 Hofverberg, E., 'FALQs: AI Regulations in the Gulf Cooperation Council Member States – Part Two', *Library of Congress,* 18 December 2024. Available:

https://blogs.loc.gov/law/2024/12/falqs-ai-regulations-in-the-gulf-coopera tion-council-member-states-part-two. [Accessed: 30 January 2025.]

161 ibid.

162 ibid.

163 ibid.

164 Penny, L. and Heymann, D., 'The Future of Work: How Israel is Leading the Charge with AI and Immigration', *Fragomen*, 6 December 2024. Available: https://www.fragomen.com/insights/the-future-of-work-how-israel-is -leading-the-charge-with-ai-and-immigration.html. [Accessed: 24 January 2025.] and 'Committee on Artificial Intelligence (CAI)', *Council of Europe*. Available: https://www.coe.int/en/web/artificial-intelligence/cai. [Accessed: 30 January 2025.]

165 Penny, L. and Heymann, D., 'The Future of Work: How Israel is Leading the Charge with AI and Immigration', *Fragomen*, 6 December 2024. Available: https://www.fragomen.com/insights/the-future-of-work-how-israel-is -leading-the-charge-with-ai-and-immigration.html. [Accessed: 24 January 2025.]

166 Shaked-Stadler, N. et al., 'AI Watch: Global regulatory tracker – Israel', *White & Case*, 4 November 2024. Available: https://www.whitecase.com/insight-our -thinking/ai-watch-global-regulatory-tracker-israel. [Accessed: 21 January 2025.] and Or-Hof, D., 'Proactive caution: Israel's approach to AI regulation', *IAPP*, 10 January 2024. Available: https://iapp.org/news/a/proactive-caution -israels-approach-to-ai-regulation. [Accessed: 24 January 2024.]

167 'Israel's Policy on Artificial Intelligence: Regulations and Ethics', *Gov.IL*, December 2023. Available: https://www.gov.il/BlobFolder/policy/ai_2023/ en/Israels per cent20AI per cent20Policy per cent202023.pdf. [Accessed: 21 March 2025.]

168 ibid.

169 ibid.

170 ibid.

171 ibid.

172 'Voluntary AI Safety Standard', *Department of Industry, Science and Resources*, 5 September 2024. Available: https://www.industry.gov.au/publications/ voluntary-ai-safety-standard. [Accessed: 21 March 2025.]

173 'Introducing mandatory guardrails for AI in high-risk settings: Proposals paper', *Department of Industry, Science and Resources*, 5 September 2024. Available: https://consult.industry.gov.au/ai-mandatory-guardrails. [Accessed: 30 January 2025.]

174 'National framework for the assurance of artificial intelligence in government', *Department of Finance*, 21 June 2024. Available: https://www.finance.gov.au/ government/public-data/data-and-digital-ministers-meeting/national-framework -assurance-artificial-intelligence-government. [Accessed: 30 January 2025.]

175 'Policy for the responsible use of AI in government', *Australian Government*, 1 September 2024. Available: https://www.digital.gov.au/policy/ai/policy. [Accessed: 30 January 2025.]

APPENDIX ONE – STANDARDS AND FRAMEWORKS

1 'ISO/IEC 42001:2023', *ISO*, December 2023. Available: https://www.iso.org/standard/81230.html. [Accessed: 30 January 2025.]

2 'NIST AI RMF Playbook', *National Institute of Standards and Technology*, January 2023. Available: https://airc.nist.gov/AI_RMF_Knowledge_Base/Playbook. [Accessed: 30 January 2025.]

APPENDIX TWO – LEGAL

1 'Executive Order on Initial Recissions of Harmful Executive Orders and Actions, E.O. 14148, 90 Fed. Reg. 8237', 20 January 2025. Available: https://www.federalregister.gov/documents/2025/01/28/2025-01901/initial-rescissions-of-harmful-executive-orders-and-actions. [Accessed: 18 March 2025.]

2 'Executive Order on Removing Barriers to American Leadership in Artificial Intelligence, E.O. 14179, 90 Fed. Reg. 8741', 23 January 2025. Available: https://www.federalregister.gov/documents/2025/01/31/2025-02172/removing-barriers-to-american-leadership-in-artificial-intelligence. [Accessed: 18 March 2025.]

3 'Executive Order on Advancing United States Leadership in Artificial Intelligence, E.O. 14141, 90 Fed. Reg. 5469', 17 January 2025. Available: https://www.federalregister.gov/documents/2025/01/17/2025-01395/advancing-united-states-leadership-in-artificial-intelligence-infrastructure. [Accessed: 18 March 2025.]

4 'Memorandum on Advancing the United States' Leadership in Artificial Intelligence; Harnessing Artificial Intelligence to Fulfill National Security Objectives; and Fostering the Safety, Security, and Trustworthiness of Artificial Intelligence', 24 October 2024. Available: https://bidenwhitehouse.archives.gov/briefing-room/presidential-actions/2024/10/24/memorandum-on-advancing-the-united-states-leadership-in-artificial-intelligence-harnessing-artificial-intelligence-to-fulfill-national-security-objectives-and-fostering-the-safety-security/. [Accessed: 18 March 2025.]

5 'Framework to Advance AI Governance and Risk Management in National Security', *AI.GOV*, 1 November 2024. Available: https://web.archive.org/web/20250116131653/https://ai.gov/wp-content/uploads/2024/10/NSM-Framework-to-Advance-AI-Governance-and-Risk-Management-in-National-Security.pdf. [Accessed: 18 March 2025.]

6 'Executive Order on Safe, Secure, and Trustworthy Development and Use of Artificial Intelligence, E.O. 14110, 88 Fed. Reg. 75191', 30 October 2023. Available: https://www.federalregister.gov/documents/2023/11/01/2023-24283 /safe-secure-and-trustworthy-development-and-use-of-artificial-intelligence. [Accessed: 18 March 2025.]

7 'Fact Sheet: Key AI Accomplishments in the Year Since the Biden-Harris Administration's Landmark Executive Order,' *White House*, 30 October 2024. Available: https://web.archive.org/web/20250116072519/https://www.white house.gov/briefing-room/statements-releases/2024/10/30/fact-sheet-key-ai -accomplishments-in-the-year-since-the-biden-harris-administrations-land mark-executive-order/. [Accessed: 18 March 2025.]

8 'Executive Order on Further Advancing Racial Equity and Support for Underserved Communities Through the Federal Government, E.O. 14091, 88 Fed. Reg. 10825', 16 February 2023. Available: https://www.federalregister.gov/documents/2023/02 /22/2023-03779/further-advancing-racial-equity-and-support-for-underserved -communities-through-the-federal. [Accessed: 18 March 2025.]

9 'Executive Order on Promoting the Use of Trustworthy Artificial Intelligence in the Federal Government, E.O. 13960, 85 C.F.R. 78939', 3 December 2020. Available: https://www.federalregister.gov/documents/2020/12/08/2020-27065 /promoting-the-use-of-trustworthy-artificial-intelligence-in-the-federal -government. [Accessed: 18 March 2025.]

10 'Executive Order on Modernizing and Reforming the Assessment and Hiring of Federal Job Candidates, E.O. 13932, 85 Fed. Reg. 39457', 26 June 2020. Available: https://www.federalregister.gov/documents/2020/07/01/2020-14337 /modernizing-and-reforming-the-assessment-and-hiring-of-federal-job -candidates. [Accessed: 18 March 2025.]

11 'Executive Order on Maintaining American Leadership in Artificial Intelligence, E.O. 13859, 84 Fed. Reg. 3967', 11 February 2019. Available: https://www.federalregister.gov/documents/2019/02/14/2019-02544/main taining-american-leadership-in-artificial-intelligence. [Accessed: 18 March 2025.]

12 'H.B. 161', 18 April 2024. Available: https://custom.statenet.com/public /resources.cgi?mode=show_text&id=ID:bill:AL2024000H161&verid =AL2024000H161_20240418_0_E&. [Accessed: 18 March 2025.]

13 Zeff, M., 'Here is what's illegal under California's 18 (and counting) new AI laws', *TechCrunch*, 29 September 2024. Available: https://techcrunch.com /2024/09/29/here-is-whats-illegal-under-californias-18-and-counting-new-ai -laws/. [Accessed: 18 March 2025.]

14 '2023 Wash. Laws 360', 10 May 2023. Available: https://lawfilesext.leg.wa.gov/ biennium/2023-24/Pdf/Bills/Session per cent20Laws/Senate/5152-S.SL.pdf?q =20250319041125. [Accessed: 18 March 2025.]

15 'S. 1042', 9 January 2023. Available: https://legislation.nysenate.gov/pdf/bills/2023/S1042A. [Accessed: 18 March 2025.]

16 'Ensuring Likeness, Voice, and Image Security Act of 2024, H.B. 2091', 21 March 2024. Available: https://publications.tnsosfiles.com/acts/113/pub/pc0588.pdf. [Accessed: 18 March 2025.]

APPENDIX THREE – TECHNICAL

1 Suresh, H. and Guttag, J.V., 'A Framework for Understanding Sources of Harm throughout the Machine Learning Life Cycle'. In *Equity and Access in Algorithms, Mechanisms, and Optimization*, 1–9, 2021. Available: https://doi.org/10.1145/3465416.3483305. [Accessed: 23 March 2025.]

2 Jesus, S. et al., 'Aequitas Flow: Streamlining Fair ML Experimentation', *Journal of Machine Learning Research*, October 2024. Available: https://jmlr.org/papers/volume25/24-0677/24-0677.pdf. [Accessed: 21 March 2025.]

3 'Dssg/Aequitas', *GitHub*. Available: https://github.com/dssg/aequitas. [Accessed: 21 March 2025.]

4 'LASER-UMASS/Themis', *GitHub*. Available: https://github.com/LASER-UMASS/Themis. [Accessed: 21 March 2025.]

5 Brun, Y., Meliou, A. and Galhotra, S., 'Testing Software for Discrimination', *arXiv*, 11 September 2017. Available: https://arxiv.org/abs/1709.03221. [Accessed: 21 March 2025.]

6 'AI Fairness 360', *ai-fairness-360*. Available: https://ai-fairness-360.org. [Accessed: 21 March 2025.] and Bellamy, R.K.E. et al., 'AI Fairness 360: An Extensible Toolkit for Detecting, Understanding, and Mitigating Unwanted Algorithmic Bias', *arXiv*, 3 October 2018. Available: http://arxiv.org/abs/1810.01943. [Accessed: 21 March 2025.]

7 Kokhlikyan, N. et al., 'Captum: A Unified and Generic Model Interpretability Library for PyTorch', *arXiv*, 16 September 2020. Available: https://doi.org/10.48550/arXiv.2009.07896. [Accessed: 21 March 2025.]

8 'Interpretml/Interpret', *GitHub*. Available: https://github.com/interpretml/interpret. [Accessed: 21 March 2025.]

9 Weerts, H. et al., 'Fairlearn: Assessing and Improving Fairness of AI Systems', *Journal of Machine Learning Research*, 2023. Available: http://jmlr.org/papers/v24/23-0389.html. [Accessed: 21 March 2025.]

10 'Best AI Governance Tools, *TrustRadius*. Available: https://www.trustradius.com/ai-governance. [Accessed: 21 March 2025.] and 'Top AI Governance Tools of 2025', *Slashdot*. Available: https://slashdot.org/software/ai-governance/. [Accessed: 21 March 2025.]

ACKNOWLEDGEMENTS

Ray Eitel-Porter would like to express his sincere thanks to Paul Dongha and Miriam Vogel for their invaluable collaboration in writing this book. Not only did they bring their respective areas of expertise – data science and law – but their knowledge of AI governance and contributions to the book as a whole have been invaluable. The many hours of discussion we shared were intellectually rewarding and instrumental in shaping this work. They have been the ideal co-authors.

He would like to acknowledge those who have played a pivotal role in his Responsible AI journey. His thanks go to Rumman Chowdhury, Paul Daugherty, Christina Demetriades and Deb Santiago for setting him on this path, as well as to those from whom he has learned so much along the way: Arash Bateni, Ozlem Celik-Tinmaz, Melanie Condron, Patrick Connolly, Natalie Heisler, Fernando Lucini, Tom Niven, Anka Reuel, Ali Shah, Florian Thoma and Steven Tiell. He is also grateful to Fabio Bresciani, Sarah Derbyshire, Jenn Handa, Abby Jaques, Valerie Morignat and Milo Phillips-Brown, as well as many members of The Alan Turing Institute team.

The Intellectual Forum at Jesus College, Cambridge, has welcomed him into its community, and he extends his thanks to them for their support.

Paul Dongha would like to express his sincere thanks to his co-authors, Ray and Miriam, for their insight, dedication and partnership throughout the writing of this book. Their expertise, thoughtful input and steady collaboration were essential at every stage of the process, and it has been a privilege to work alongside them. He would also like to thank his employer, NatWest Group, for allowing him to write this book, the bank's AI and Data Ethics team for their continued encouragement, and in particular Zachary Anderson and Graham Smith for their support. He sincerely thanks his wife, Neelam, and sons, Rohan, Shivan and Vivek, for their unwavering support and patience over the many months it took to write this book. Their understanding, encouragement and belief in him made this journey possible and he is deeply grateful for the time and space they gave him to focus on this work.

ACKNOWLEDGEMENTS

Miriam Vogel thanks her co-authors for reliably thought-provoking discussions, new insights and endless patience. She is also deeply grateful to her friends and family for enduring her absence at events, months of looking at her glued to her laptop and listening to her endless stream of evolving ideas. Most of all, she thanks her husband – her unwavering sounding board, William Shrank and her daughters, Zoe and Tori, for reality checks and comic relief, in addition to their support.

As authors, we deeply appreciate the colleagues, experts and friends who generously contributed their time, expertise and feedback, helping to refine and improve our work despite their own demanding schedules. Our heartfelt thanks go to Fabrice Ciais, Dr David Dutton, Dr Reza Hazemi, Huw Jones, Anna Kharchenkova, Sana Khareghani, Gabrielle Kohlmeier, Fernando Lucini, Victoria Medina, David More, Chris Mruck, Tom Niven, Cathy O'Neil, Erin Scarrow, Ali Shah, Barry Smith, Professor Suraj Srinivasan, Professor Satish Tadikonda, Dr Nataliya Tkachenko and Rosalind Wiseman. Special thanks to Mark Butcher from Posetiv Cloud for his many penetrating insights into AI and digital sustainability and to Manoj Saxena, CEO of Trustwise, for his strategic thinking and vision. We are also very grateful to Linklaters for reviewing certain legal sections of the book.

We would particularly like to acknowledge the tireless and meticulous editing, thoughtful content suggestions, and extensive research support provided by Sydney Brinker, as well as the support of Laurence Cardwell and Teddy Tawil. We are extremely grateful to Tobias Benn for his extensive work on chapter summaries, endnotes and helpful review of the initial draft text. Additional research was provided by Joe Fennell, whose contributions were much appreciated.

A special thank you goes to the many professionals and organizations who engaged in discussions with us about AI governance and shared their experiences. These conversations have added depth, nuance and real-world examples to our recommendations. The list of contributors is extensive and, while we have endeavoured to include as many as possible, we sincerely apologize to anyone we may have inadvertently overlooked:

Zachary Anderson, Chief Data and Analytics Officer, NatWest Group; Nathan Atkinson, Executive - AI and Machine Learning, Cinven; Azeem Azhar, Founder, Exponential View; Michael Bhaskar, Strategy and Communications, Microsoft; Tess Buckley, Programme Manager – Digital Ethics and AI Safety, TechUK; former Secretary Michael Chertoff, Executive Chairman, The Chertoff Group; Natasha Crampton, Chief RAI

Officer, Microsoft; David Crelley, Data Ethics Lead, Admiral Insurance Group; Josh Dubin, Managing Associate General Counsel, Verizon; James Fletcher, Responsible AI Lead, BBC; Ivan Fong, Executive Vice President, General Counsel and Secretary, Medtronic; Caroline Gorsky, Co-Founder, Cerestrial; Anna Hannem, Vice President Data & AI Risk, Scotiabank; Daniel Hulme, Chief AI Officer, WPP; Rozemarijn Jens, AI Ethics and Compliance Lead Shell R&D, Shell; Penny Jones, Responsible AI Lead UK, Zurich Insurance; Dr. Athina Kanioura, Chief Strategy and Transformation Officer, and her team at PepsiCo; Lara Liss, Chief Privacy and Data Trust Officer, GE HealthCare; Tom Lue, Vice President, Frontier AI Global Affairs, Google Deepmind; Elena Maran, Global Head of Financial Services and Responsible AI, Modulos; Sarah Mathews, Global Responsible AI Manager, Adecco; Alexandra Matthews, Underwriter of AI Risks, Munich Re; Alexandra Mousavizadeh, Co-CEO & Co-Founder, Evident AI; Detlef Nauck, Head of AI & Data Science Research, BT; Wilmer Peres Neto, CDO, BAT; Oliver Patel, Enterprise AI Governance Lead, AstraZeneca; Laura Perea, Responsible AI Strategist, Nestle; York von Putlitz, Head of Risk Management, Robert Bosch; Patrick Rowe, Chief Compliance Officer and Deputy General Counsel, Accenture; Jessica Shepherd, Director, Home Broadband, Vodafone UK; Karen Silverman, CEO, Cantellus; Graham Smith, Head of Data Science and Innovation, NatWest Group; Evie Stenhouse, Chief Privacy Officer and AI Governance Lead, Natura & Co.; Craig Suckling, CDO, UK Government; Elham Tabassi, formerly of NIST, now Director of Artificial Intelligence and Emerging Technology Initiative, Brookings; Ben Tagger, Head of Data Science an AI, BUPA UK; Mike Tang, Senior Director AI/ML Engineering, Verizon; Luke Vilain, AI Governance Lead, UBS; Marc Warner, CEO, Faculty.

We thank Ian Hallsworth at Bloomsbury Business for his confidence in us and Allie, Amy and the Bloomsbury team for their guidance and support through the publishing process, allowing this book to reach the shelves as quickly as possible after drafting – invaluable given the fast-moving world of AI. We are grateful to Jane Donovan for her diligent copy editing.

Any errors or omissions remain our own.

Ray Eitel-Porter, Paul Dongha and Miriam Vogel

INDEX